ORGANIZATIONS

A QUANTUM VIEW

Danny Miller

McGill University

École des Hautes Études Commerciales, Montreal

Peter H. Friesen

McGill University

in collaboration with

Henry Mintzberg

McGill University

Prentice-Hall, Inc., Englewood Cliffs, New Jersey 07632

1984

Library of Congress Cataloging in Publication Data

MILLER, DANNY
    Organizations: a quantum view.

    Bibliography: p.
    Includes index.
    1. Organization.   2. Organizational change.
I. Friesen, Peter H.   II. Mintzberg, Henry.   III. Title.
HD31.M4375 1984   658.4′06   83-15993
ISBN   0-13-641985-2

Editorial/production supervision and
    interior design: Eve Mossman
Cover design: Edsal Enterprises
Manufacturing buyer: Ed O'Dougherty

Printed in the United States of America

10 9 8 7 6 5 4 3 2 1

ISBN 0-13-641985-2

Prentice-Hall International, Inc., *London*
Prentice-Hall of Australia Pty. Limited, *Sydney*
Editora Prentice-Hall do Brasil, Ltda., *Rio de Janeiro*
Prentice-Hall Canada Inc., *Toronto*
Prentice-Hall of India Private Limited, *New Delhi*
Prentice-Hall of Japan, Inc., *Tokyo*
Prentice-Hall of Southeast Asia Pte. Ltd., *Singapore*
Whitehall Books Limited, *Wellington, New Zealand*

Dedication

To Our Parents and Grandparents

Contents

*All chapters are by Danny Miller and Peter H. Friesen unless otherwise indicated.

Preface

It has become more and more apparent that a unifying thread runs through much of our research. Our work of the last few years centers around three related themes. The first is that organizational data display a type of patterning or structure that has been largely ignored by other researchers. Specifically, structural, environmental, and strategic variables seem to cluster tightly to produce common "gestalts," "quantum states," or "configurations" which reflect integral interdependencies among their elements. Perhaps more important, a small number of configurations may be used to characterize a large fraction of organizations, and this gives the configurations considerable predictive power.

The second theme of our work is that different configurations will show rather different relationships among their variables. It is, therefore, important to distinguish among configuratons before making any predictions about the relationships among variables of strategy, structure, and environment. Several longstanding conflicts in the literature show promise of being resolved when we control for the type of configuration.

The final theme in our research concerns organizational change. It seems that organizational histories manifest two principal types of periods. The most common are those in which a particular configuration or orientation is maintained. These are punctuated by brief intervals of broad and concerted "quantum" change which can move organizations to a new configuration. The way organizations evolve over time, thus, seems to support the notion of configurations.

In our original work we did not stress the interrelatedness of the three themes: the fact that configurations have important implications for predicting organizational relationships and suggest a particular view of change. Although this book is by no means a full-blown theoretical synthesis of our work, it does make a preliminary effort to show the interrelationships between configurations, their predictive utility, and organizational change. But the focus is more empirical than conceptual, and the emphasis is upon making sense of our findings, in large part through *ex post facto* explanation. The book is, therefore, as much retrospective as it is speculative, its primary aim being to pull together the fragments of our past research to support a consistent view of organizations and of organizational analysis.

A word about the authorship of the various chapters seems in order. Danny Miller contributed to all but Chapter 3; Peter Friesen to all but Chapters 1, 3, 7 and 8; and Henry Mintzberg exclusively to Chapters 1 and 3.

Our three themes of configuration, prediction, and change are pursued in Parts II, III and IV of the book, respectively. Part I presents arguments to support the case for configuration and proposes a set of related methodological recommendations. Many chapters draw upon our previously published studies. Chapter 1 is a revised and expanded version of Miller and Mintzberg's paper, "The Case for Configuration," which appeared in G. Morgan, ed., *Beyond Method: Strategies for Social Research* (Beverly Hills, Calif.: Sage Publications, 1983). Chapter 2 builds upon two of Miller's papers, "The Use of Multivariate 'Q-Techniques' in the Study of Organizations," *Academy of Management Review*, 1978, 515–31; and "Toward a New Contingency Approach: The Search for Organizational Gestalts," *Journal of Management Studies*, 1981, 18, 1–27; as well as Miller and Friesen's "The Longitudinal Analysis of Organizations," *Management Science*, 1982, 28, 1013–34. Chapter 3 is drawn from Mintzberg's "Configurations of Organizational Structure," in H. Meltzer, ed., *Making Organizations Humane and Productive* (New York: Wiley, 1981), and his "Structure in 5's: A Synthesis of the Research on Organization Design," *Management Science*, 1980, 26, 322–41. Chapter 4 is partly based on Miller's doctoral dissertation, "Strategy-Making in Context: Ten Empirical Archetypes" (McGill University, 1976); and on two articles by Miller and Friesen, "Archetypes of Strategy-Formulation," *Management Science*, 1978, 24, 921–33, and "Strategy Making in Context," *Journal of Management Studies*, 1977, 14, 253–80. Chapter 5 draws upon Miller and Friesen's "Archetypes of Organizational Transition," *Administrative Science Quarterly*, 1980, 25, 268–99. Chapter 6 is a modified version of Miller and Friesen's "Innovation in Conservative and Entrepreneurial Firms," *Strategic Management Journal*, 1982, 3, 1–27. Chapter 7 is taken from Miller's "The Correlates of Entrepreneurship in Three Types of Firms," *Management Science*, 1983, 29, 770–791. Chapter 8 is based upon Miller's "Evolution and Revolution: A

Quantum View of Structural Change in Organizations," *Journal of Management Studies*, 1982, 19, 131–51. Finally, Chapters 9 and 10 are drawn in part from Miller and Friesen's "Structural Change and Performance: Quantum vs. Piecemeal-Incremental Approaches," *Academy of Management Journal*, 1982, 25, 867–92; and "Momentum and Revolution in Organizational Adaptation," *Academy of Management Journal*, 1980, 23, 591–614. We are grateful to the publishers for permission to use portions of these works.

We would like to express our gratitude to family, friends, and colleagues who helped directly and indirectly in the preparation of this work. The senior author is indebted to Jean-Marie Toulouse at H.E.C. for financial support and critical comments; to past teachers Henry Tutsch, Thomas Kubicek, Manfred Kets de Vries, Pradip Khandwalla, and Martin Evans for their intellectual guidance; and most of all to Peter Friesen and Henry Mintzberg for being mentors, collaborators, and true friends. The authors are grateful to Cheryl Kelahear, Margaret Lewis, and Sandra Guadagnino for their fine secretarial work. All royalties from this book are to be donated to the Montreal Neurological Institute to fund research on multiple sclerosis.

D.M., Montreal

Part I

THE APPROACH
OF CONFIGURATION

This book presents aspects of what we call a quantum view of organizations. Organizations are treated as complex entities whose elements of structure, strategy, and environment have a natural tendency to coalesce into quantum states or "configurations." These configurations are composed of tightly interdependent and mutually supportive elements such that the importance of each element can best be understood by making reference to the whole configuration. Organizational structures, production systems, information-processing procedures, strategies, and environments all tend to influence each other. Our thesis is that they do so in a manner that gives rise to a small number of extremely common and sometimes discretely different configurations. Some of these have been isolated in the typologies and taxonomies presented in this book. Configurations may represent common organizational structures, common scenarios of strategy making in context, and even common developmental or transitional sequences.

What is crucial is that a relatively small number of these configurations or types are believed to encompass quite a large fraction of the population of organizations. It is precisely this quality that gives the configurations their pedagogical and predictive utility. By discovering and studying the nature, behavior, and performance consequences of the most common configurations, we can ultimately bring to bear a great deal of descriptive and prescriptive knowledge concerning many organizations.

To borrow very liberally from the vernacular of the physicist, we may say that just as each atom can exist only in certain quantum states, so too do organizations exhibit common states or configurations. Although the atom is strictly prohibited from being between states, things are not quite so restricted in the world of organizations. There are certainly no laws preventing organizations from being outside the common states. Nevertheless, we shall argue that organizations will gravitate overwhelmingly to particular quantum states that we call configurations,[1] and that these will tend to surface in carefully formulated conceptual typologies and empirical taxonomies.

The roots and genesis of the tendency toward common configurations or quantum states are still uncertain. Our conviction that the quantum view is useful stems much more from the empirical work to be presented than from any really forceful theoretical imperatives. We shall, however, argue that the quantum view is reasonable; that it is in part a product of selective environmental forces that allow only the most functional forms to survive; that it relies on the well-known internal interdependencies among structural and strategic variables; that it is very consistent with managerial psychology and politics; and that it is supported by the economics of organizational change.

It is necessary to draw a crucial distinction between the quantum view and the traditional contingency view. Although both seek out and rely on the interdependencies among many organizational variables, the traditional approach, we feel, oversimplifies things by assuming that the same relationships exist among variables in different types of organizations. We shall show that this is seldom the case; that common configurations differ not only in their individual attributes but in the relationships among variables. For example, we will see that the correlates and determinants of strategy, entrepreneurship, and innovation differ greatly among different types of firms—that is, among different configurations. The isolation and examination of common configurations therefore help us to discover useful distinctions before making predictions. They enable us to avoid the errors of those who search for one single relationship among variables in heterogeneous samples of organizations.

Inherent in the notion of common configurations and quantum states is the concept of quantum change. To say that organizations are usually to be found in common states is to imply that as they change, they, a little like our atom, concertedly move from one common state or configuration to another. These changes can sometimes be very extensive. The importance of the link between quantum states and quantum change—that is, between configuration and quantum change—can best be seen by imagining what

---

[1]We shall sometimes be able to use the terms *configuration* and *quantum state* interchangeably. In our empirical research, reported in Chapters 4 and 5, however, we have grouped collections of similar quantum states into single configurations (see Appendix 4-1). In other words, quantum states were very narrowly defined, whereas empirically derived configurations possessed some latitude for internal diversity.

would happen if organizations changed in piecemeal fashion, one element at a time. If so, they would collectively exhibit far too much variety to allow the emergence of very common configurations; all organizations would be in slightly different states of mutation. Piecemeal change, in other words, is inconsistent with the notion of configurations. Only quantum change that keeps the organization in the common "permitted" configurations allows us to *find* such configurations.

Needless to say, the world of organizations is not as simple as this sketch of the quantum view suggests. All organizations are in some ways unique. Many will not fit any common configurations, and even those that do will be similar in select and important ways rather than identical. Also, the likelihood of finding configurations will be a function of the variables or phenomena studied, the taxonomic methods that are attempted, and even the scope of the samples gathered. Obviously, configurations will surface only if there exist strong interdependencies among the variables selected for analysis. Some organizational phenomena will configure neatly, others will not. In addition, samples must be broad and heterogeneous enough to allow different configurations to emerge. Finally, the nature or constitution of configurations will vary a great deal. How we characterize and investigate configurations will differ according to the phenomena under study. Because we are at an early stage of research, trial-and-error efforts will be required to find the kind of patterning in the data that leads to the most meaningful, most predictively useful, and most parsimonious taxonomies of configurations.

A more technical and accurate summary of the thesis of this book concerns the arrangement of multivariate data on organizations in n-dimensional space. Say we have characterized approximately 100 organizations along 20 or 30 dimensions of environment, structure, and strategy. We believe that complex nonlinear relationships among the variables will often cause the 100 data points collectively to make up a surface of a dimension much smaller than 20 or 30 (perhaps 5 to 10, depending, of course, on the selection of variables and the diversity of the sample). Because many of the relationships will be nonlinear, we might find a geometric representation of the data surface to look something like a five dimensional "snake," or "horseshoe." All of our empirical analyses support this finding and each of our three themes follow from it. First, the small dimensionality of the data surface relative to the total space causes there to be few common configurations. Second, its curvilinearity causes the relationships among the variables to vary from one part of the surface or configuration to another. Third, the small dimension of the surface compared to the number of variables indicates that variables must change in concert. That is, change must be of a multifaceted, quantum variety. The multifaceted nature of change can make it costly and therefore rare. Thus it is very much more likely that when change eventually comes, it will have to be revolutionary. The utility of devising parsimonious and predictive taxonomies, the need to control for the type of configurations in making predictions, and our quantum view of change all are supported by the curvilinear clustering of data in n-dimensional space. This form of clustering underlies almost all of our empirical findings. The reader is asked to keep this geometrical representation in mind throughout the book. It is the surest way to avoid being misled by our occasional oversimplifications, speculations, and shifts in emphasis.

Some Prefatory Comments on the Nature of Configurations

The concept of configuration is at best an elusive one. Although there are certain aspects common to all configurations, as we conceive them, there is also a good deal of variability in the potential ways of characterizing them. It is therefore appropriate that we provide some rough guidelines for what we mean by configurations.

Configurations are multidimensional.   When we speak of configurations, we are concerned with complex clusters of elements or variables. Configurations should comprise a large number of significant characteristics. These may collectively describe the structure and technology of an organization, its strategy, structure, and environment, or its transitional strategies. By configurations we do not mean narrow dimensions that comprise variables that are very similar or highly correlated across a broad variety of firms. Rather, we are speaking of different constellations of conceptually distinct variables or elements that commonly cluster together to characterize many aspects of organizational states and processes. The clusters should each give a fairly detailed and multidimensional portrait of some crucial aspects of their subject. For example, Mintzberg's machine bureaucracies and adhocracies of Chapter 3 fit easily into our concept of configuration because of the broad and detailed characterization he gives to each of these types and the important distinctions he makes between them.

Configurations may be derived empirically or conceptually.   Conceptual configurations are defined on the basis of a theoretical framework or a synthesis of the literature. These will be discussed by Henry Mintzberg in Chapter 3. Empirical configurations are the product of statistical analyses of multivariate data on large samples of organizations. They are the topic of Chapters 4 and 5. Conceptual configurations are defined in advance, while empirical configurations emerge from the quantitative analysis of data—from the building of taxonomies.

There are two main types of configurations—elemental and relational. In this book we shall be dealing with two essential types of configurations. The first comprise consistent—that is, thematically related—constellations of *elements*. One such configuration might be Burns and Stalker's (1961, p. 121) organic form with its expertise-based, situational authority, its open and frequent lateral communications among managers, its emphasis on advice rather than instructions to effect coordination, and its continual redefinition of tasks to adapt the organization to new challenges. These elements or qualities are said to be quite complementary and therefore occur together very commonly. Burns and Stalker's (1961, p. 120) mechanistic form may be another elemental configuration. It is very different from their organic form, given its emphasis upon task specialization, authority based on hierarchy, formal rules, and vertical communication.

A second variety of configuration is defined not in terms of elements per se, but rather by the nature of the alignment among them. We call these *relational* configurations. We can distinguish relational configurations from elemental ones using the well-known model of Lawrence and Lorsch (1967). These authors have argued that organizations must be structured to match the levels of environmental uncertainty, structural differentiation, and structural integration. They claim that unpredictable and dynamic environments require that the departments of organizations considerably differentiate their goals, time horizons, and interpersonal orientations. For example, firms in these environments might have to have futuristic, organic, and innovative research and development departments, and mechanistic, efficiency-oriented production departments. Effectiveness requires that the high levels of differentiation must in turn be met by high levels of integration in the form of extensive interdepartmental task forces and standing committees, integrative personnel, and other coordinative devices. These reduce conflict between the very different departments.

There are two types of configurations suggested by this point of view. The first are elemental configurations of effective organizations that might include the following:

Configuration 1	Configuration 2	Configuration 3
High uncertainty	Medium uncertainty	Low uncertainty
High differentiation	Medium differentiation	Low differentiation
High integration	Medium integration	Low integration

The number of such configurations will depend upon how finely one wishes to discriminate among them. They may fall along a continuum of scores ranging from very high to very low along all three classes of elements.

Perhaps a more parsimonious approach would be to say that the elements are really variables—they are characteristics that vary in their intensity from "high" to "low." One might then say that there is only *one* basic *relational* configuration among the variables, characterized by a strong positive correlation among all variables that keeps them all aligned. As one variable increases or decreases, if the others do the same, the configuration is said not to change. This may sometimes be a more convenient, although more abstract way of defining configurations.

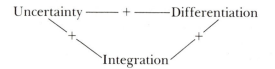

Another, possibly ineffective, relational configuration may show uncertainty and differentiation positively related, whereas differentiation and integration bear an inverse relationship:

Although we shall in this volume focus mostly on elemental configurations, we believe that relational configurations are also worth exploring. Indeed, some of the data presented in Chapters 6, 7, 9, and 10 strongly suggest their importance.

Each configuration should characterize numerous aspects of many organizations.   If we need a new configuration to account for every organization, we might as well look at things on a case-by-case basis. If all organizations fall into one configuration, we are at too high a level of generality to say anything interesting. But if a *common* configuration gives a rich account of some important relationships, processes, or states of a significant group of organizations, we have generated the basis for revealing insights. It is also important that typical organizations that are members of a configuration be significantly *like* one another, and meaningfully *different* from the typical members of other configurations along criteria of interest.

Configurations should have predictive importance.   Classifying an organization into a configuration should have predictive implications. Classification along some elements must yield significant and reliable differences among elements that were *not* used to make the classification. This could occur, for example, when we classify firms on the basis of their technology and then can infer many things about their structure. Alternatively, in the case of relational configurations, the relationships among at least some variables of interest should vary consistently among some configurations or sets of configurations. For example, the relationship between size and centralization of authority might be positive in some subsets of configurations and negative in others. If configurations have both these types of predictiveness, they become especially rewarding, revealing crucial distinctions among organizational regularities.

Establishing the boundaries of configurations may be a problem. Conceptually derived configurations generally stipulate clear boundaries. Their memberships are decided according to whether or not organizations satisfy pre-established criteria. Unfortunately, things are not always so clear with empirically derived configurations. These are defined statistically around the densest clusters of data. Where these clusters are few, dense, and distinctive, their numerical boundaries, which may take the form of score ranges along key variables, are easy to identify. They will include large homogeneous groups of organizations. But where the clusters run into one another, there are no obvious "natural" boundaries. Clusters might then have to be split at arbitrary points into regions representing configurations, each of which would be described according to its most typical member.

There is no one best set of variables (or elements) that should be used to describe all sets of configurations. Our intent is not to argue for any particular *types* of configurations. Many kinds probably exist and will be useful to investigate. The work of Hall (1972) suggests that a thorough characterization of organizational configurations would include variables describing their technology, environment, type of personnel, structure, process, and organizational output. But clearly, the variables that we choose to describe configurations must vary according to the research problems and the predictive tasks at hand. Researchers studying organizational adaptation might wish to focus on environmental, structural, and decision-making variables along with indicators of organizational effectiveness. Policy researchers might wish to look at an assortment of strategic variables as well as those describing the competitive environment of the firm. Systems theorists would be interested in a rich characterization of the inputs and outputs of the firm as well as its crucial transformation processes. Students of organizational change may even construct configurations out of variables reflecting changes in various properties of the organization (see Chapter 5). The possibilities are endless. It would therefore be counterproductive to suggest that any one set of variables be studied, since this would have to depend on the scope of the research. The prime consideration is that variables interrelate to produce predictive configurations.

Configurations may describe departments, divisions, organizations, or even networks of organizations.   Although we focus in this book on configurations describing entire organizations, there is no reason why all researchers should limit themselves to this level of analysis. In fact, it might be impossible to develop meaningful configurations that pertain to entire organizations that are extremely diverse and internally heterogeneous. It may then be very rewarding to investigate common divisional or departmental configurations. This is especially true if arguments can be made for complementarities among the elements describing these divisions and for differences in the nature of these complementarities across different types of divisions. Also, although we shall deal with configurations pertaining to business firms, there is no reason why others should not try to apply this approach to different kinds of organizations.

Outline of the Book

All our chapters will present conceptual arguments and empirical evidence in support of the quantum view. They should be taken as fragments that tentatively prop up its different aspects. Even though our findings are consistent with the quantum view, like all empirical data they are subject to a variety of interpretations. This book is therefore to be taken only as a starting point, as an incentive and an invitation for researchers and managers alike to look for a different pattern of reality in organizations—to search for common configurations around which to build descriptive insights and prescriptions, and to discover the natural order that exists within the context of organizational variety.

The book is divided into four main parts, each consisting of several chapters. Part I outlines the quantum view. It proposes an approach for discovering and using configurations, one we call the approach of synthesis. Conceptual arguments are presented for the existence of common configurations and the prevalence of quantum change. Part I also encourages the development of broadly based, highly multifaceted taxonomies of configurations as a useful means of discovering and explaining the variety and complexity of organizations. Whereas Part I argues for the feasibility and necessity of the quantum approach, Part II demonstrates the results of the approach as manifested by one conceptual typology and two empirically based taxonomies. These respectively illustrate very common ways in which organizations are structured, formulate strategies, and change. It is shown that a fairly small fraction of possible states seem to describe a large fraction of organizations. Part III then presents two empirical studies that illustrate the necessity of making distinctions between configurations in studying the relationships among organizational variables. Relationships among strategic, structural, environmental, and information-processing variables are shown to differ according to the configuration in question. In other words, while Part II demonstrates the feasibility and parsimony of the search for configurations or quantum states, Part III demonstrates its utility as a preliminary step in predicting the relationships among many organizational variables.

Part IV goes on to derive a model of organizational change based upon the presumption that a small fraction of possible states are permitted. It is argued that quantum change—that is, multifaceted and concerted change—will often be necessary to move firms decisively from one permitted quantum state to another that is in many ways different. The two empirical studies presented seem to strongly bear out these predictions, adding further support to the quantum view.

1

The Case
for Configuration

INTRODUCTION

According to the framework of Thomas S. Kuhn (1970), the field of organizational theory seems to be reaching a crisis point, a state in which a central research approach is proving to be manifestly inadequate. The situation is somewhat like that which faced Copernicus as a result of the legacy of the Ptolemaic system of astronomy. For centuries, astronomers kept trying to patch up Ptolemy's system:

> Given a particular discrepancy, astronomers were invariably able to eliminate it by making some particular adjustment in Ptolemy's system of compounded circles. But as time went on, a man looking at the net result of the normal research effort of many astronomers could observe that astronomy's complexity was increasing far more rapidly than its accuracy and that a discrepancy corrected in one place was likely to show up in another (p. 68).

A similar trend is becoming apparent in the research on organizations. There is too much emphasis given to making minor modifications to atomistic hypotheses, a process that has often been prompted by conflicting findings concerning the simple relationships among small sets of variables. The myriad conflicts in the field seem to be pointing to the need for more

Chapter 1 is authored by Danny Miller and Henry Mintzberg, and is adapted from their paper "The Case for Configuration," in *Beyond Method: Strategies for Social Research,* ed. Gareth Morgan (Beverly Hills, Cal.: Sage Publications, 1983) pp. 57–73.

than minor adjustments. A radically different approach to discovering predictive regularities in organizational data and a new view of organizations seem to be required.

The traditional approach to research has given rise to numerous debates in the literature. Are bureaucracies centralized? Does the proportion of administrative personnel increase with organizational size? Is size or technical system the key determinant of structure? None of these issues ever seems to get resolved. Research on each has prompted efforts at replication and re-replication, and endless battles ensue about conflicting findings.

What is discouraging is the manner in which these issues are researched. Simple correlational methods gradually give way to more sophisticated statistical analyses, bivariate studies develop into sharply circumscribed multivariate studies, new samples are selected, and different means of operationalizing the variables are used. Seldom is there an attempt to substantially broaden the research and view relationships within a richer interpretive context, one that incorporates many potentially relevant variables, including, perhaps, those of strategic choice and time. Rare also are efforts to look for more than one relationship among the same variables, to isolate *several* common patterns or configurations that may exist in different organizational contexts.

Were one to study the structure and efficacy of martial strategies of the eighteenth century, for example, it would be inadvisable to look only at the relationship between the magnitude of cavalry and artillery forces across a large sample of situations. Battles are too complex and varied to be understood within so narrow a perspective. The relationship between the number of cavalry and artillery would probably vary in its degree, direction, and ultimate significance according to the context of the battle: the time of year and climate, the landscape, the training of the generals and officers, troop morale, logistics, the nature of armaments, and so on. It is by looking for the most common configurations among these many variables and attributes, preferably as they evolve over time, and by seeking to distinguish one type of battle situation from another, that we would probably gain the greatest insights into the question. We shall attempt to show that the same line of reasoning holds for the study of organizations and organizational adaptation.

It is generally accepted that we best understand our world by first doing analysis and then synthesis. We divide things up into components, and then put them back together again into some form of intelligible composite. The contention in this book is that the methods traditionally favored in the study of organizations, and perhaps the social sciences in general, encourage analysis in the absence of synthesis. Specifically, they tend to focus on simple relationships among few variables in search of direct causation. We wish to advocate an approach here that favors synthesis, developing or isolating composites that take the form of what we have called "gestalts," "archetypes," and "configurations." These can be defined as commonly occurring clusters of attributes or relationships—in the case of our own research, common states and processes of the organization as well as characteristics of its situation—that are internally cohesive, such that the presence of some attributes suggest the reliable occurrence of others.

The objective of this approach of synthesis is to discover richly described, revealing configurations that are sufficiently *common* to capture an important organizational entity or occurrence, whether that be an integral network of attributes of structure; of structure, strategy, and environment; or even of the elements of transition between these networks. Ultimately the aim is to generate typologies or taxonomies—sets of different configurations that collectively exhaust a large fraction of the target population of organizations or situations under consideration. It is, of course, desirable to find a small number of common configurations that encompass a large proportion of the population. This allows many organizations to be classified using only a few distinguishing attributes, and then permits the prediction of many other organizational features or relationships simply by making reference to the configuration. Were there to be a vast proliferation of rare configurations, these would compose a taxonomy too cumbersome to make predictions, or to build theory. The major portion of this book will be devoted to demonstrating that reality is sufficiently structured to contain a relatively manageable number of common configurations and, therefore, that predictively useful taxonomies can in fact be generated.

We open the chapter with a brief review of two well-known debates in the literature of organization theory, first discussed from the perspective of analysis, and then from that of configuration, or synthesis, as it has emerged in our own research. This is followed by a discussion of a number of arguments to support our contention that organizations are more clearly and accurately described in terms of configuration. We close the chapter with a summary of the evidence for the existence and predictive utility of configurations, which serves as an outline for the next three parts of the book.

CONFUSION IN ANALYSIS

In 1957, C. Northcote Parkinson, with his tongue firmly planted in his cheek, proposed his "first law": "Work expands so as to fill the time available for its completion" (1957:33). Since then, sociologists have been struggling over their interpretation of this statement—that the proportion of administrators in an organization increases as it grows. Their approach was simple: to run statistical analyses of data on organization size and A/P ratio (administrative to production personnel).[1]

But there were problems from the outset. Two of the initial studies (Terrien and Mills, 1955; Anderson and Warkov, 1961) produced diametrically opposed results. When Rushing (1967–68) reviewed twelve studies a number of years later, he found two that showed A/P increasing with organization size, six that showed it decreasing, and four that showed no significant change. The debate continued, with more results but no resolution. Pondy (1969) found the A/P ratio to range from 9 percent in the logging industry to 131 percent in drugs, throwing into doubt the utility of generalizing across industries. Nevertheless, two years later, Blau and Schoenherr (1971) published a book entitled *The Structure of Organizations,* based on a study of employment security agencies, which concluded that "organizations exhibit an economy of scale in management overhead" (p. 309) that proceeds at a decelerating rate no matter what their size. Finally, Child (1973) went to great efforts to break down the component parts of A and P, and to include a variety of possible intervening variables (such as spatial dispersion of plant facilities and technological complexity). He concluded that no conclusions could be drawn about A/P in general, the A being composed of too many diverse groups.

The history of the bureaucratization–centralization debate is even more curious. The question was whether bureaucracies that operated with many formal and standardized procedures centralized power for decision making at the top of the firm. Pugh et al. (1968) found no strong relationship between these two factors, but Child (1973), using the same instrument but excluding non-autonomous organizations, found a negative relationship, especially in manufacturing firms. Some researchers supported this conclusion (for example, Blau and Schoenherr, 1971; Inkson et al., 1970), while others did not (for example, Holdaway et al., 1975; Manns, 1976). Donaldson (1975) went back to the Pugh et al. data, removed the non-autonomous organizations, and found that it made no difference. He concluded that "the resolution of the puzzle needs to be looked for elsewhere" (pp. 455–56). Child (1975) replied that elsewhere might be in the kind of organization, manufacturing firms being perhaps more efficient because of competition, and therefore more careful to decentralize when they bureaucratize. In response, Aldrich (1975) re-ran Donaldson's analysis of the Aston data without the government organizations, but that did not help: "In particular, 'formalization,' one of the original puzzles in Child's [data] emerges as even more of a mystery" (p. 459). Aldrich encouraged "all hands to get back to the data and look this question over a little

---

[1]The review of the two debates that follows is drawn from Mintzberg (1979: 235–40, and 195–97).

more carefully" (p. 459). So Greenwood and Hinings (1976) did just that, and concluded that perhaps the data were not so good after all, that the measures all these researchers used for centralization could not be combined into a single factor—in effect, that centralization "is a more complex concept" than previously thought (p. 155).

Let us try another tack. Imagine that the structural parameters of organizations cluster into the five configurations discussed by Mintzberg in Chapter 3 and summarized in Table 3-3. In the *simple structure,* the chief executive officer retains personal control of all major decisions, so that few other managers or staff specialists are required. Here we find a low A/P, and a nonbureaucratic and highly centralized form. In contrast, the *machine bureaucracy,* which is dominated by rules and regulations and has a fully developed line hierarchy and staff contingent, exhibits a rather high A/P. It is also very bureaucratic and rather centralized, although less so than the simple structure. Senior management retains the power to coordinate the decisions of the different functional units, but the analysts draw off some of that power by virtue of their role in designing the standards. In a third configuration, the *professional bureaucracy,* a good deal of the power is held by operating professionals who serve their clients individually through rather standardized programs. The structure is quite decentralized, yet bureaucratic, in that it has a high degree of standardization in its operating procedures. Also, there is a fairly high A/P ratio, but one that is very differently constituted from that of the machine bureaucracy. Here, there are fewer line managers to supervise and staff analysts to formalize the work, but far more support staffers to back up the expensive professionals. In a fourth configuration, the *divisionalized form,* the organization splits itself into semiautonomous units, monitored from a headquarters by performance control systems. As Mintzberg argues in Chapter 3, these systems drive the divisions toward machine bureaucratic structure—in other words, toward bureaucratization coupled with centralization—at least at the divisional level. As a result, the A/P also emerges as fairly high within the divisions, while companywide A/P is bolstered by the added administrative personnel at the headquarters.

Finally, in a configuration called *adhocracy,* line managers, staff specialists, and often operating personnel as well combine in fluid project teams to innovate. Here the degree of bureaucratization tends to be low, the degree of decentralization high, and A/P probably the highest of all. This is because (1) extensive use is made of small project teams, requiring a great many "managers," (2) staff specialists abound in the organization, and (3) the operations are frequently automated, thereby reducing drastically the requirement for production personnel.

Now, assuming this is how the world really works—that at least a good proportion of organizations tended to adopt these or some other configurations of their structural parameters—what would happen if different kinds of organizations were mixed in research samples and then relationships gauged among *A/P*, bureaucratization, and centralization? We believe that we already have the answer in the research cited earlier.

Some Criticisms of the Analytic Approach

The approach to research that we are calling analytic exhibits, in its purest form, six basic attributes. These are listed below with a number of criticisms, most of which have been discussed at length in the literature but merit brief review here as a set.

1. *The focus is on bivariate or sharply circumscribed multivariate analysis.* The problem with bivariate relationships is that critical intervening variables tend to damage their explanatory power. For example, bureaucracies may be centralized when their operating work is unskilled, decentralized when it is skilled. Likewise, measures of *A/P* could be influenced by the presence or absence of skilled experts in the operations, the need for such experts to work in teams or alone, the diversity of the organization's markets and so its tendency whether or not to divisionalize, and so on. Specification error, the use of inappropriate or insufficient predictor variables, may be an easy criticism to make, and it has been made often, but that perhaps reflects a fundamental weakness in the analytic approach to research.

2. *Relationships are generally assumed to be linear and causation unidirectional.* Discontinuities—changes in kind rather than degree—upset the assumption of linearity, and sometimes even change the direction of causality.[2] Starbuck (1965) has made a convincing case for metamorphosis in organizations; Klatsky (1970) in fact uses metamorphosis to try to explain the size–*A/P* relationship, arguing that the curve is U-shaped. As an organization outgrows a simple structure and emerges as a bureaucracy, or later divisionalizes, the relationship between size and *A/P* could change dramatically, perhaps even the direction of causation. Where growth may previously have demanded a greater proportion of administrative personnel, at some point, perhaps, the presence of a larger contingent of administrative personnel may encourage even more rapid growth. There is, in fact, a suggestion of this in some studies of the divisionalized structure (see

---

[2]The problems of nonlinearity have typically been treated in most of the literature by the use of moderated regression analysis or saturated regression models containing exhaustive interaction terms. But these techniques must be limited to situations in which a relatively small number of variables can substantially explain the phenomenon under study, and where there are good theoretical reasons for anticipating particular relationships and *specific* moderating influences. But how often do these conditions occur in research on organizations? Given the many attributes of organizations and their complex and as yet hardly understood interactions, which variables are to be selected as the key moderators? In what fashion are they to be described as moderating between dependent and independent variables (i.e., what is the nature of the interaction)? Indeed, how can one always distinguish between dependent and independent variables in the first place?

Fouraker and Stopford, 1968; Rumelt, 1974, 76–77). The research reported in Chapters 6 and 7 found that many correlational relationships among variables of innovation, strategy making, structure, and environment differed in both direction and significance from one type of firm or configuration to another.

Criticisms 1 and 2 relate closely to the use of partist and holist approaches for the selection of variables and the treatment of samples. Extreme partism in the selection of variables can result in specification error, while holism in the treatment of samples can result in unwarranted samplewide generalizations that might be avoided by segmenting the samples into more "homogeneous" parts. It is interesting to consider the interaction among partist and holist tendencies in the treatment of variables and samples. The first quadrant of Table 1-1 shows a research approach that selects many variables that richly and broadly describe a research question so that specification error is avoided. Unfortunately, the sample is not split, so that if relationships among the variables vary from one subsample to another, this will not be discovered and explanatory power will be reduced. That is, contingencies are oversimplified, since relationships are expected to remain constant throughout the sample. The second quadrant shows a partist approach with specification error in the selection of variables, coupled with a samplewide analysis that does not distinguish among different subsamples. This approach is the worst possible, since there are two potentially serious errors. The third quadrant shows an improvement, since there is an attempt to distinguish among different types of firms or contexts, but specification error remains a problem. The fourth quadrant illustrates the approach that avoids both errors and is most likely to give rich, multivariate descriptions of organizations and their processes and to allow for complex contingencies. Unfortunately, most research conforms to one of the first three quadrants.

3. *Research samples tend to be either very narrow or very broad,* from employment security agencies (Blau and Schoenherr, 1971) or stockbrokerage offices (Pennings, 1975) to a sample "as different as a large tire manufacturing firm and the public baths in Birmingham" (Holdaway et al., 1975: 30, in reference to Pugh et al., 1968). Such samples are encouraged by the

TABLE 1-1: Partism and Holism in Sample Analysis and Selection of Variables

		VARIABLE SELECTION	
		HOLISM: MANY VARIABLES	PARTISM: FEW VARIABLES
SAMPLE ANALYSIS	HOLISM: SAMPLEWIDE ANALYSIS	1. Broad and rich characterizations, unwarranted generalizations	2. Specification error & unwarranted generalization
	PARTISM: SEGMENTED SAMPLE	4. Rich description & complex contingencies	3. Piecemeal but more accurate findings

absence of a typology of configurations (or the unwillingness to use existing ones), leaving the researchers with no logical way to select their samples. Hence they tend either to narrow down to one very specific kind of organization, or else to include many different organizations indiscriminately. The narrow sample can lead to false generalizations, as seems the case in the Blau and Schoenherr conclusion about the relationship between size and *A/P*, and the broad one, by including what amounts to a conflicting array of relationships, can prove impossible to interpret. This seems to have been the case with many of the Pugh et al. and related findings, the example of bureaucratization and centralization having been cited earlier. As McKelvey has noted:

> The present tendency is to define populations broadly, presumably in the belief that the results will be generalizable to a broader and possibly more meaningful population. [A very diverse] sample is akin to a biologist's wanting to make broad statements about heartbeat rates based on a sample of one elephant, one tiger, one rabbit and an alligator (1978: 1437–38).

McKelvey argues for "more narrowly defined, more adequately described, and more universally recognized organizational populations" so as to improve "the definitiveness of the findings, the levels of variance explained, and the applicability of the results to the population" (p. 1438).

4. *Measures are generally cross-sectional in nature—that is, taken at only one point in time.* Unfortunately, time leads and lags abound in organizations. To take one important example, because structural change normally lags situational change (Chandler, 1962; Stopford and Wells, 1972; Rumelt, 1974), it is somewhat a matter of luck whether a cross-sectional study captures the structure that reflects today's situation, which it typically measures, or yesterday's, which it typically does not. Organizational relationships are sufficiently complex to warrant a careful exploration of their genesis and repercussions. This cannot be done without longitudinal analysis. The longitudinal study reported in Chapter 5 shows how some of the conflicts concerning the causal influences between strategy and structure begin to vanish when we study organizations as they evolve over time.

5. *Variables tend to be rather abstract, far removed from organizational occurrences, and the measures of them tend to be general, A/P being the most obvious example.* But the nuances and complexities present in organizations often destroy the explanatory power of such variables and measures. The *A* of *A/P* can, for example, include everyone from a mailroom clerk and a cost estimator through a production scheduler, laboratory scientist, and personnel manager, to a legal advisor and the chairman of the board. And how should one categorize the chef in the corporate cafeteria—*A* or *P*? As noted, Child (1973) found that different factors were required to explain the rate of growth of different administrative groups. And much of the centralization–bureaucratization debate has focused on the weaknesses of the measures of decentralization (e.g., Jennergren, 1974; Perrow, 1974). How can such a variable be operationalized as a composite measure anyway, when technically it must encompass all the decision processes that take place in every part of the organization?

6. *The research typically proceeds from a distance, usually through question-naires.* The detachment of the researcher from the context of the research precludes the collection and examination of anecdotal data. Typically, researchers end up with a set of general measures of a few rather abstract variables. How are they supposed to probe into causation and interpret their findings? Even if the findings do have some deep meaning, will the researchers be able to find it? Thus, the students of decentralization and of A/P have tied themselves up in knots just trying to figure out what the data they have collected really mean. They and many of their colleagues who have favored the analytic approach seem to have lacked some kind of hook—some rich example, some specific scenario—on which to hang their results in order to explain them. The overall result is that data abound, while insightful theory is sparse.

To conclude, had we to name one key weakness in the analytical approach to research, and probably in the social sciences in general, it would be that researchers have been bent upon testing for simple, circumscribed relationships instead of searching for or constructing a multiplicity of rich, revealing patterns.

THE PERSPECTIVE OF SYNTHESIS

Corresponding to these attributes of the approach we call purely analytic are a set of attributes that favor synthesis as the objective of research. In its purest form, the approach of synthesis may combine all five of the attributes discussed below, although the first two are the most critical.

1. *A large number of qualities—ideally, of state, process, and situation—are studied simultaneously in order to yield a detailed, holistic, integrated image of reality.* We concur with McKelvey (1975) and Pinder and Moore (1979), who argue for studies that employ as inclusive a set of organizational attributes as possible. Thus, studies of the organization need not be restricted to attributes of its structure, but can also consider those of its environment, its technical system, its age and size, its power relationships, its leaders, its strategy, its strategy-making procedures, its flows of information and patterns of communication, its performance, and so on.

2. *Data analysis and theory building are geared to finding common natural clusters among the attributes studied, which necessitates careful sample definition.* The objective of the research is to derive theoretical typologies or empirical multivariate taxonomies that discriminate among different configurations of the attributes—in our case, different types of organizations—each configuration revealing its own relationships among the attributes. To achieve this objective, samples have to be carefully defined. Narrow samples can be useful to uncover individual configurations intuitively, and to describe them in depth, but someone must then be prepared to build typologies or taxonomies across different studies. Alternatively, we can proceed through the use of broad and representative stratified random samples (McKelvey,

1975), coupled with the use of systematic statistical techniques for generating taxonomies and testing their predictive utility (Miller, 1978, 1981). These can enable us to make precise comparisons across different kinds of organizations. Since multivariate relationships can vary from one configuration to another, we must first try to find these configurations in the form of dense homogeneous clusters of attributes and interrelationships that together form a predictive taxonomy. A relatively small number of categories must encompass a large proportion of the population, and the configurations must be sufficiently restrictive (that is, tightly defined) to afford accurate and meaningful descriptions of their members. A taxonomy will be of value only if it is likely to classify a randomly selected organization from the population using a small number of variables, and to predict accurately many of its other attributes or relationships simply by making reference to class membership. Some methods of discovering such taxonomies will be discussed in Chapter 2.

3. *Causation is viewed in the broadest possible terms.* The search is not simply for unidirectional causation between pairs of variables or even necessarily for multiple forms of causation. The approach of synthesis is really the search for *networks* of causation. Each configuration has to be considered as a system in which each attribute can influence many of the others by being an indispensible part of an integrated whole. There are no purely dependent or independent variables in a system; over time, many things depend on many other things. An attribute that drives others at one point will itself be driven by some of those others later; and commonly, attributes drive each other concurrently.

For example, based on research findings, contingency theory postulates that growth in organizations has the effect of bureaucratizing structure (Samuel and Mannheim, 1970; Pugh et al., 1968; Udy, 1965), and that dynamic environments evoke organic structures (Burns and Stalker, 1961; Duncan, 1973; Burns, 1967; Harvey, 1968; Lawrence and Lorsch, 1967). But might it not be equally true that bureaucracies have a propensity to grow ever larger, and that organizations with organic structures seek out dynamic environments, where they can outmaneuver the bureaucracies. Similarly, bureaucracies seek out stable environments, or try to stabilize the ones they find themselves in, to facilitate the application of their standardized procedures. In other words, large size and stable environment are all wrapped up in the system or configuration we have called machine bureaucracy, and so too is the mass-production system of technology (Woodward, 1965). From the analytic perspective, debate has raged over whether it is the organization's size or its technical system that best explains its structure. From the perspective of synthesis, the search is not for any single "imperative," but rather for the variety of causal networks that occur in different contexts.

4. *Time and process are taken into account whenever possible.* The approach of synthesis favors longitudinal research where possible, in which processes are studied alongside states. Results from such studies enable the researcher to flesh out his results, helping him to explain leads and lags, and, in general, providing depth to his understanding of why organizations

behave as they do. Much of this book presents longitudinal research—mostly to support the existence of common configurations. An important collateral benefit of such research is that it allows insights into the causal texture of relationships and the extent to which they can vary over time in the same organization.

5. *Despite efforts to measure and quantify, anecdotal data are gathered to help explain the more systematic findings.* Abstract results come to life when put in the context of even one rich, detailed illustration. We fully realize that the preference for the analytic approach reflects economic and logistic practicalities no less than methodological beliefs. In more pointed terms, indirect cross-sectional research is very convenient in a world of "publish or perish." But research from the perspective of synthesis can be convenient too, since there are ways to develop significant conclusions in reasonable time frames. For example, published book histories and strings of articles on single organizations have been found to serve as reliable longitudinal data bases, rich in detail and anecdote (these constitute parts of the data base for the research reported in Chapters 4, 5, and 10). By using such sources to short-cut the collection of data and making sure to check carefully for accuracy, it is possible to build up reasonably large and reliable samples rather quickly.

Of course, as we have already noted, the approach of synthesis can be useful only if configurations do in fact reflect reality—that is, only if there occur common, internally homogeneous clusterings of attributes or relationships, a relatively small number of which can account for a large fraction of the population of organizations. Otherwise, far too many types would be needed to explain that population, and the approach of synthesis would become hopelessly inadequate. The next section of the chapter presents theoretical arguments and outlines the empirical evidence that will be supplied in the course of the book to support the existence of such configurations.

Some Reasons for Configuration

Why should common configurations exist? We propose three main arguments, woven into the following paragraphs, to account for the emergence of organizational configurations.

According to Charles Darwin:

> . . . species at any one period are not indefinitely variable, and are not linked together by a multitude of intermediate gradations, partly because the process of natural selection will always be very slow and will act, at any one time, only on a very few forms; and partly because the very process of natural selection almost implies the continual supplanting and extinction of preceding and intermediate gradations (1968: 231).

Hannan and Freeman (1977) have argued that formal organizations may be subject to selection processes similar to those of the biological species.

Both survive only if they evolve in ways adapted to their environments. Our first argument, then, is that *Darwinian forces may encourage only relatively few organizational forms to survive in the same setting,* their variety and number circumscribed by the dictates of population ecology.[3] The Darwinian argument is, of course, very tentative as applied to organizations, and we hesitate to make too much of it. It does seem, however, that a type of organizational Darwinism could very well limit the number of viable forms by selecting out those that are relatively weak and those that fail to achieve internal complementarities. The rate of bankruptcies and the relatively young median age of most organizations may indicate that many forms perish before they have a chance to become numerous (Aldrich, 1979). But how orderly and common are the forms that remain, and which forms survive?

Increasingly, researchers and practitioners alike are coming to see the world in "systems" terms. Everything seems to depend on everything else. It used to be fashionable in science and everyday affairs to isolate variables, to catch what has been called "the economist's plague"—holding all other things constant. The trouble is that other things do not remain constant. Things move together because of their interdependencies. And that may be a force for the emergence of configurations in organizations. Our second argument then is that *the organization may be driven toward configuration in order to achieve consistency in its internal characteristics, synergy (or mutual complementarity) in its processes, and fit with its situation.* Rather than trying to do everything well, the effective organization may instead concentrate its efforts on a theme, and seek to bring all its elements into line with this. Configuration, in essence, means harmony.

Consider the configuration we have called machine bureaucracy, characterized by the following attributes of structure (discussed in Chapter 3). The organization has highly specialized, routine operating tasks, very formalized procedures, and large units in its operations. The basis for grouping tasks throughout the structure is by function, and coordination is effected by rules and hierarchy. Power for decision making is quite centralized, and there exists an elaborate administrative structure with a clear hierarchy of line authority. Finally, a large contingent of staff analysts is responsible for work flow and production efficiency. Organizations that use this kind of structure tend to emphasize standardization throughout. Rules and regulations permeate their activities and, indeed, reflect an obsession with control; formal communication is favored at all levels; and decision making tends to follow the formal chain of authority. Only at the very top of the hierarchy are the different functional responsibilities

---

[3]That the number of biological species is very large does not refute the argument. Throughout, we have referred to a "relatively" small number of configurations. The number of biological species is small relative to the number of living organisms; we can hardly expect the same proportion of configurations relative to the number of human social organizations, but, under the conditions we shall discuss in Chapter 2, we can expect relatively few.

brought together; therefore, only at that level can the major decisions be made. Hence, the structure is a rather centralized one. The one center of power besides the senior management is the cadre of staff analysts on whom the organization depends for the design of its formalized systems. Such organizations are typically associated with environments that are both simple and stable. The work of complex environments cannot be rationalized into simple operating tasks, and that of dynamic environments cannot be predicted, made repetitive, and thereby standardized. These are typically mature organizations, large enough to have the scale of operations needed for repetition and standardization, and old enough to have been able to settle upon the standards they wish to use. The products or services are usually provided on a repetitive, highly standardized basis, and in mass quantities. External control is sometimes a condition, since that tends to drive an organization toward centralization and bureaucratization. These organizations, in other words, operate as machines, non-adaptive instruments designed to provide standardized outputs at the lowest possible cost.

As can be seen, these attributes are complementary and mutually reinforcing. Many are interdependent, such that a change in one would require a shift in many others. Indeed, one has difficulty determining priority or primacy among them. The stable environment enables the operating procedures to repeat and be formalized, but the existence of formalized procedures causes the organization to search out stable environments. Large size encourages standardization—since procedures tend to repeat, and also because controls must be in large part impersonal. But standardization also encourages growth—to gain economies of scale by increasing the throughput. Likewise, large size encourages the organization to seek out a stable environment, where its inflexibility is less of a weakness, but stability also encourages growth to large size, to take advantage of its opportunities. In other words, each attribute makes sense only in terms of the whole—and together they form a cohesive system. The machine bureaucracy is far from a perfect system; it often abuses its workers, and it suffers serious problems of adaptation. But it (and society) puts up with these as the costs of concentrating its efforts in order to achieve consistency, synergy, and fit. Better to do what it does well—in this case, massproduce cheaply—than to flounder trying to be all things to all people.

We do not wish to argue that all configurations are successful or even functional. The pursuit of internal harmony and consistency often requires conformity, discouraging diversity of opinion and dissent and prompting excesses. For example, the innovative organization may become reckless, squandering its resources in the pursuit of extravagant novelties. Conservative bureaucracies might, in contrast, move toward complete stagnation. So internal harmony and consistency can be a two-edged sword.

Note our departure in this second point from traditional Darwinian theory, giving rise to the two separate arguments for the emergence of configuration. Our first point argues that it is the environment that causes adaptation *in the long run* by allowing only a limited number of synergistic and compatible organizational forms to survive. Our second point, not inconsistent with the first but departing from the analogy with the biological species, argues that organizations seek to adapt *themselves* to the dictates of consistency, synergy, and fit. They are able to act "morphogenically." Unlike the biological species, which have to wait generations to adapt, organizations have the capacity to adapt themselves within their own lifetimes (Simon, 1969)—for example, by effecting transitions from less to more viable configurations.

And this brings us to our third argument. Were it common for organizations to make such transitions in piecemeal and disjointed fashion, the case for configuration could be weakened. A large number of organizations constantly undergoing piecemeal changes would cause a random cross-section of them to display a great deal of variety. In other words, clustering would break down, and so would our case for configuration. *But the economics of adaptation, as well as some recent empirical evidence, argue for a dramatic quantum approach to organizational change—long periods of the maintenance of a given configuration, punctuated by brief periods of multifaceted and concerted transition to a new one.*

Contingency theory has found that organizations must change their internal attributes—structures, strategies, and processes—to cope with changes in their environments. The question becomes, however, what form does that internal change take? Essentially, the organization has two broad choices. It can try to keep up with changes in its environment by changing itself in piecemeal and perhaps incremental fashion. By so doing, the organization maintains environmental fit, but possibly at the expense of internal consistency. Alternatively, the organization can delay transition until absolutely necessary, thereby better maintaining internal consistency, but at the price of gradually worsening environmental fit. Either choice can damage configuration. But the latter far less than the former, since the interrelationships among the state characteristics and processes—the ways in which the organization functions every day—remain intact.

There are a number of reasons why organizations often opt for the maintenance of internal consistency as long as possible, rather than for continually adapting to the environment. For one thing, environmental change can sometimes prove to be temporary or anomalous. It is sensible then to delay reaction to it, to wait at least until the signals are clear. For another, internal change tends to be costly, involving shifts in established patterns of behavior. It will therefore tend to be resisted, or at least delayed so that many changes can be made at the same time. This is apt to be especially true when a tight integration of structural and process attributes has been achieved. Any change may cause *dis*integration, resulting in discrepancies and disharmonies in the inner workings of the organization

(Miller, 1982). Finally, internal change, especially in the face of moderate success, is also resisted for cognitive, political, and ideological reasons. Human cognition is less sensitive to gradual changes in the environment than to pointed discontinuities (Turner, 1976). Adaptation is thus avoided until a major threat is perceived. Also, those in the organization who developed the existing structures and processes—often, the most powerful managers—become enamored of them, blind to their weaknesses, and politically dependent on them. Leaving this point aside, the managers of successful organizations, never sure which of the attributes of their structures and processes lie at the root of that success, will tend to avoid tampering with any one element of their "tried and true" configuration. And when an organization has long been successful, the force of internal ideology tends to impute a mythical quality to its structure and processes, evoking an attitude of conformity that can block not just change but even the perception of the need for it (Starbuck, Greve, and Hedberg, 1978).

Thus, there are a number of reasons why organizations delay adaptation to environmental change, and especially why they try to retain internal configuration as long as possible. But change must, of course, eventually come. As the environment continues to alter and the fit with it worsens, steps must be taken to initiate substantial changes in internal structure and processes. But to evoke such changes in the face of all the forces discussed above would seem to call for virtual revolution. Thus, when such changes do come, they may tend to be pervasive and dramatic, costly and disruptive. The organization is driven to change many of its attributes concurrently, not only to get all of the disruption over with at one time, but, more important, to ensure its attributes are in complementary alignment.[4] In other words, the organization tries to move to a new configuration. And it is driven to execute that move rapidly, to avoid spending too much time in a state of transition. In that state of flux, configuration in the usual sense of the word is absent: The structure and processes lack internal consistency, and the organization is no longer suited to its old environment while not yet adapted to its new one. As the most common pattern of significant adaptation, therefore, we would expect organizations to undergo lengthy periods of the maintenance of a given configuration whenever possible. These periods of relative internal calm and harmony would be interrupted occasionally by brief periods of disruption—of something amounting to internal revolution—during which the move to a new configuration is made (or at least attempted). If this were in fact how organizations change, the chances of finding stable and common configurations would be much enhanced.

---

[4]Piecemeal, incremental change may, however, be quite suitable for loosely-coupled, independent variables. Also, multifaceted and concerted incremental change may be sufficient to move firms effectively between many empirically derived configurations (see Introduction to Part IV).

A vivid example of a revolutionary change occurred at Volkswagen-werk AG between 1971 and 1973, after Rudolf Leiding succeeded Kurt Lotz as the new chief executive. To counter the proliferation of unrelated models and stem the sharp declines in market share and profits, Leiding undertook several decisive measures. First, he developed a new product-line strategy, introducing several complementary new models to replace the flagging "Beetle" and several other unsuccessful lines of cars. Second, he changed the manufacturing strategy, effecting economies of production wherever possible by assembling cars in underdeveloped countries. He also reduced the diversity of product lines and laid off many workers. Leiding spent a great deal to finance these strategies, in the process radically chang-ing the debt structure of Volkswagen. Finally, he began to deemphasize certain declining international markets. These measures were accom-panied by widespread administrative and structural changes intended to facilitate implementation of the new strategies. New divisions and product groups were established, and planning, budgeting, and scanning pro-cedures were instituted. More attention was also paid to developing a better group of second-tier managers and to improving interdepartmental and interdivisional collaboration.

Evidence for Common Configurations and the Viability of the Approach of Synthesis

So far, we have argued that the traditional "analytical" contingency approaches are inadequate, and we have proposed searching for common configurations using the approach of synthesis. We argued that this ap-proach could be feasible only if configurations were common and relatively small in number. Finally, we presented some theoretical arguments to sup-port the view that common configurations could in fact be found. But the deciding factor in establishing the viability of the approach of taxonomy and synthesis must be the strength of the empirical evidence supporting the existence and predictive utility of configurations. Supplying such evi-dence will be the primary task of the next three major sections of the book. The content of these sections is outlined in the pages that follow.

A thin stream of research has already begun to produce tentative empirical evidence for the existence of common configurations. Perhaps the first study of note that suggested the existence of configurations is that by Joan Woodward (carried out in the 1950s but published in 1965). It is interesting that Woodward took an analytic perspective at the outset, devel-oping what she believed to be a continuous scale of technology—ranging from the production of units to customer requirements, through mass production, to the continuous production of fluids. She then attempted to study its relationships to various attributes of structure. Some of these relationships proved to be linear. For example, the span of control of chief executives and the ratio of managers to nonmanagers increased along her scale. But a number of relationships were clearly nonlinear. To take some examples, the mass producers in the middle of the scale proved to have the highest first-line-supervisor span of control and the smallest proportion of skilled workers, and this was the only region of Woodward's scale that she felt could be described as exhibiting bureaucratic structure. In other words, viewed in terms of a single scale of technology, Woodward's results proved confusing. (Indeed, the scale itself has proven confusing, with debates raging about what it really means.)[5] But viewed from the perspective of three basic types of organizations, or configurations, Woodward's conclusions fell neatly into place. Each type demonstrated an integral cluster of attributes, and the more successful firms seemed to conform most strongly to the central tendencies of each cluster. Woodward's descriptions of unit-, mass-, and process-production firms have been widely discussed ever since.

In the same vein, we can find a number of other studies—all much cited—that uncovered configurations of attributes of organizational structure and situation. An early one was that of Burns and Stalker (1966, first published in 1961), who found "mechanistic" structures in textile firms dealing with stable environments, and "organic" structures in electronics firms found in dynamic environments. Lawrence and Lorsch (1967) found similar structures respectively in container firms facing simple and stable environments, and plastics firms facing complex and dynamic environments. Indeed, of interest is the strong apparent kinship between Woodward's mass producers, Burns and Stalker's mechanistic firms, and Lawrence and Lorsch's container companies, all corresponding to what we earlier called machine bureaucracy, and Woodward's process firms, Burns and Stalker's organic firms, and Lawrence and Lorsch's plastics companies, all corresponding to what Mintzberg, in Chapter 3, calls adhocracy. The work of Miles and Snow (1978) has sought to classify organizations according to their strategies, structures, and managerial styles. Although based on empirical data, this study too presents a typology derived conceptually.[6] Very recently Chenhall (1983), Hambrick (1983a; 1983b), Hambrick and Schecter (1983), Galbraith and Schendel (1982) and Gartner, Vesper, and Mitchell (1982) have also derived taxonomies or tested typologies.

Part II of this book (Chapters 3 through 5) builds upon some of the preceding typologies. Chapter 3 presents Mintzberg's typology of five structural configurations, introduced earlier, which was developed to synthesize the published research on organizational structuring.

---

[5]Woodward first considered it one of technological complexity; Hunt (1970) and Harvey (1968) disagreed, the latter calling it one of product change or "technical diffuseness"; Starbuck (1965) characterized it as one of "smoothness of production"; later, Woodward (Reeves and Woodward, 1970) described it as one of increasing impersonalization of control.

[6]Others have generated typologies of configurations theoretically but not empirically (except in the sense of trying to integrate the findings of empirical research). Among the best known are those of Parsons (1956, 1960), Etzioni (1961), and Blau and Scott (1962).

In contrast to typologies, which are derived conceptually but not in any rigorous empirical fashion, taxonomies are derived formally, normally using multivariate analyses like those described in Chapter 2. In Chapter 4 we derive an empirical taxonomy of strategy making in context, based on a diverse sample of firms. Variables of environment, structure, strategy making, and performance were examined. By using a multivariate technique to generate the taxonomy, and a related hypothesis-testing method to establish its generality and stability, ten tightly defined configurations or "archetypes" were found. There was much statistically significant clustering in the data.

Chapter 5 reports a second study in which 36 lengthy organizational histories were divided into briefer intervals of transition. Variables describing strategy-making, structure, environment, and performance were used to characterize each transition. Again, predictively useful clustering was found, indicating, in essence, that there may be utility in searching for "configurations across configurations," so to speak, common patterns of transition leading from one configuration to another in the life of an organization. Chapters 3 through 5 show that the approach of synthesis is quite feasible, that it can result in predictive and useful typologies and taxonomies of organizations and their strategy-making behavior. These chapters illustrate that there is ample evidence for the existence of configurations—not only of state, but of state, situation, and process, even of transition.

In Part III (Chapters 6 and 7), configurations are used to make predictions about the behavior of firms. The accuracy of samplewide predictions is compared to that of those specific to the individual configurations. These comparisons reveal gross discrepancies that strongly point to the need for deriving taxonomies or typologies *before* studying the relationships among environmental, structural, and strategy-making variables. It seems that many such relationships vary in nature, direction, and levels of statistical significance as we move from one type or configuration to another.

For example, in Chapter 6 it is shown that the influence of many information-gathering, decision-making and structural variables upon the rate of product/service innovation is opposite in conservative and entrepreneurial firms. The conservative firms require sophisticated information systems and analytical decision-making techniques in order to apprise executives of the need to innovate. The result is a positive correlation between these variables and innovation. In sharp contrast, an opposite, but no less significant, relationship is demonstrated in risk-embracing entrepreneurial firms. Here, information-processing and decision analysis informs managers of the need to curtail superflous innovation in order to conserve resources. Thus, relationships are influenced dramatically by the contexts in which they occur. Chapter 7 pursues a similar theme. The nature and determinants of entrepreneurial behavior are shown to differ radically in three types of configurations. Part III then points strongly to the need for different predictive models in different configurations. The superiority of the approach of synthesis to that of samplewide "analysis" is strongly supported.

We argued earlier that organizations tend to evolve in a peculiar manner, claiming that there would be two common phases of corporate history: the first, long periods of adhering to or simply extending an existing configuration; the second, brief intervals of concerted, quantum change signaling the move toward a new configuration. This pattern causes a relatively small number of configurations to appear, rather than the vastly overwhelming numbers that would exist if organizations were continually changing in piecemeal fashion. Part IV (Chapters 8 through 10) presents a more thorough theoretical discussion and two empirical studies that support this quantum view of change.

In Chapter 8, detailed arguments are developed for the relative efficacy of quantum structural change. Chapter 9 then presents a longitudinal study of structural change that lends strong support to these arguments. The focus is on the relationship between structural change and performance. Firms that have undergone revolutionary structural changes are compared with those that favored piecemeal and incremental approaches. Revolutionary change was defined as being, first, of a quantum nature—that is, concerted or multifaceted as opposed to piecemeal—and second, dramatic—that is, rapid and extreme. Samples of successful firms showed a great propensity to undergo revolutionary structural change, whereas unsuccessful firms were more apt to favor piecemeal and incremental approaches.

Whereas Chapter 9 compares structural change in successful and unsuccessful firms, Chapter 10 examines change patterns in strategy making and structure common to all kinds of firms. We found that there was a tendency for organizations to undergo two types of periods. In the most common periods of "momentum," firms reinforced or extended their past structures and strategy-making practices, adhering to previous directions of evolution. Where changes did occur, these were extrapolations or continuations of earlier developments, and tended to happen simultaneously across many variables, presumably to keep them in some thematic and functional—that is, configurational—alignment. Less common but more dramatic were the periods of "reversal." Here, organizations reversed the direction of change in many variables of strategy making and structure simultaneously, in what seemed an attempt to reach a broadly different configuration.

The studies reported in Parts II to IV provide support for the existence of configurations. They are, of course, too tentative to be conclusive. But, together with the other evidence and theoretical arguments presented, they lead us to the conclusion that configurations, molded by selective and adaptive forces and preserved by economic ones, can be highly functional phenomena for organizations as well as for the researchers who choose to study them.

CONFIGURATION AND COGNITION

Now that we have focused upon objective characteristics of configurations, it might be useful before we close the chapter to argue for the "subjective" or cognitive convenience that configurations offer—for both theoreticians and practicing managers.

Even as untutored visitors to an art museum, we are able to glance at a painting, appreciate its form and structure, and take away impressions of its mood, shape, and perhaps theme. We first appraise our stimulus holistically, roaming over the canvas with our eyes to take in the extensive qualities of the painting. Afterwards, our attention might be directed to appreciating particular areas of the canvas or specific qualities of it—the coarseness of its brushstrokes, the intensity of its hues, the flow of its lines.

In a basic sense then, our first impressions are ones of synthesis. That is how we first appreciate a painting, and comprehend its basic message. We are unconsciously effecting a synthesis that employs components or attributes only so far as they configure into a comprehensible whole. Only subsequently might we begin to *analyze* the attributes individually, to consider their role in making up that whole.

If we lived in a world controlled by a malevolent deity, he might have constituted human beings so that analysis would always have to precede synthesis in cognition, even in the viewing of paintings. He might force us to go over a canvas one square inch at a time, and then somehow to combine a myriad of these fragments to obtain some idea of pattern. In such a world, either paintings would be very small or museums very empty.

To be sure, analysis and synthesis are both necessary phases of scientific activity. Analysis defines the components or attributes of a phenomenon and measures them; synthesis combines these into integrated images, conceptions, or configurations, identifying patterns and forming generalizations. Then analysis returns to test these generalizations and deduce their logical consequences. But the purpose of science is insight, much as is the purpose of painting. In other words, just as the painter paints to enlighten the observer, so too does the researcher study to enlighten the practitioner. And we believe that the practitioner—in the case of organization theory, the line manager, staff specialist, or consultant—perceives much as does the visitor to the museum.

Synthesis forms the basis of the practitioner's perception: It must precede, condition, and inform his analysis. Disjointed analysis by itself provides only glimpses of fragments, whose context-free states obscure their meaning. Findings may be statistically significant, but not conceptually so. They become elusive, float away, inhibit rather than foster understanding. The fewer the fragments and the more distant one from another on the invisible canvas, the more difficult it is to get a realistic image of that canvas—to make any sense of things.

Our world of organizations is very complex, and the fragments uncovered by research from the perspective of analysis are very distant from one another. Hence, the images offered to the practitioner have been very incomplete. Our point is that configurations developed from the perspective of synthesis, by providing more complete images of spheres of reality, may be more compatible with patterns of human cognition than are linear relationships, developed from the perspective of analysis, which seek to explain components more than composites. People deal with a complex world by compartmentalizing it in terms of images or clusters, by putting its many attributes into various envelopes, each of which is a convenient storehouse of related information, with its own label. This is what we mean when we use the words *model, stereotype, kind,* and *type*.

Take, for example, the label "democracy." It could, of course, mean the amount of freedom a citizen has along some continuum, a view compatible with that of analysis. But we suspect that within most minds, the label more accurately represents a configuration of mutually supporting attributes, such as due process, freedom of speech, a free press, universal suffrage, the "social contract," and so on. In the complex world of organizations, populated by practitioners who think in terms of such envelopes, we believe the role of the researcher and theorist is to offer synthesis, holistic concepts, composites and configurations.

The notion of configuration can help us to overcome the problem of the blind men, each of whom touched a different part of the elephant and then argued about the nature of the beast. It can open the eyes of the researcher to the study of whole beasts, each a logical combination of its own characteristics, similar to all the members of its own species yet fundamentally different from those of other species. The research that the book presents points the way, suggesting that studies of many organizational attributes, of process as well as state and situation, ideally over time and reinforced by anecdotal data—what we have called research from the perspective of synthesis—will lead to more complete, more accurate, and more useful theories by which to comprehend our complex world of organizations.

2

Discovering
Configurations

INTRODUCTION

This chapter is concerned with the methods that have been used, and might be used, to discover organizational configurations and the typologies and taxonomies in which they are embedded. We begin with a brief review and critique of the better-known typologies and taxonomies. From this, we derive methodological prescriptions that have guided the typology of Chapter 3 and the taxonomies of Chapters 4 and 5. Because the book is devoted primarily to making the case for configuration, it concentrates on the presentation of empirical evidence, not upon method. But the methodologies of taxonomy generation and testing have received very little attention from organizational theorists. Thus, to broaden the reader's knowledge, the largest part of this chapter is devoted to a general discussion of taxonomic methods. *Owing to the technical nature of much of this material, the general reader might wish to skim through it, focusing mainly on the conclusions.*[1]

Two approaches have been used to discover configurations. The first identifies configurations or types exclusively on the basis of conceptual distinctions. The resultant *typologies* are, in a sense, of an *a priori* nature; they are generated mentally, *not* by any replicable empirical analysis. The

---

[1]First courses in statistics and linear algebra are needed to master much of the material in this chapter.

second approach seeks *taxonomies* of organizations. These are derived from multivariate analyses of empirical data on organizations. Typically, organizations or aspects of their structures, strategies, environments, and processes are described along a number of variables. Attempts are then made to identify natural clusters in the data, and these clusters, rather than any *a priori* conceptions, serve as the basis for the configurations. Typologies and taxonomies can both identify predictively useful configurations. The former have been by far the more common, however. The next section refers very briefly to several notable typologies in the literature.

TYPOLOGIES

Max Weber (1947) first referred to organizational types when he derived his classification of social domination. He discussed the ideal types of patrimonial, feudal, and bureaucratic organization, showing how each type could be characterized by a number of mutually complementary, or at least simultaneously occurring, attributes. For example, the bureaucratic form was more efficient and emphasized rational behavior, legal types of domination, and the extensive use of bureaucratic rules and procedures. Talcott Parsons (1956, 1960) erected his typology of organizations on the basis of their chief function for society. His four types include organizations with economic goals, those with chiefly political goals, integrative organizations, and pattern-maintenance organizations. Etzioni's (1961) typology is one of compliance relationships in organizations. Three types of employee involvement are matched with three types of executive power in a nine-cell matrix. The diagonal of the matrix is said to represent the only three congruent or viable types, which are called coercive, utilitarian, and normative. Blau and Scott's (1962) typology of organizations is based on "who benefits" most from them. Katz and Kahn (1966) have founded their own categorization upon genotypic functions, isolating productive, maintenance, adaptive, and managerial-political organizations. Finally, Perrow's (1970) and Thompson's (1967) typologies are based upon organizational technology. Most of these studies show cohesion among the attributes within types and make important distinctions among types. But no attempts were made by their proponents to gather empirical data to support any of these typologies.

Some typologists, however, have been concerned with testing the discriminatory power of their schemes. Having classified organizations using preestablished criteria, they compare them using descriptive statistics. For example, Joan Woodward (1965) showed how her trichotomized technology dimension predicted many collateral differences among firms. Unit/small-batch, large-batch/mass, and continuous-process firms were quite different from one another in their spans of control, A/P ratios, skill requirements, power distributions, and so on. Burns and Stalker's (1961) "organic" and "mechanistic" firms were also shown to differ a good deal in their attributes of structure, process and environment. [A thorough review of these and other typologies is given by Carper and Snizek (1980)]. Finally, Miles and Snow (1978) have classified their sample of organizations according to their product-market strategies and found their four primary types to differ in many of their process, structural, and decision-making style variables. Although this second group of typologists has made use of empirical data, they all defined their types in advance. That is, they generated their classificatory criteria conceptually rather than through any formal and replicable empirical analysis.

Carper and Snizek (1980) have criticized previous typologies, claiming that "there are virtually as many ways to classify organizations as there are people who want to classify them. Consequently, it is fairly easy to find a single dimension on which a typology can be based and which will . . . support any given philosophical position" (p. 70). They go on to highlight the lack of any basic agreement as to which variables should be used in constructing an optimum typology, and conclude that too many typologies are based upon only one or two organizational variables. We are largely in accord with these criticisms, recognizing with the authors, however, that the field is indeed young and that the typologies cited have been extraordinarily fruitful bases for the generation of hypotheses, models, and theories.

In our view, the typologies have all been a bit too narrowly focused. They have, or seem to have, isolated extremely suggestive configurations, but often the configurations are not sufficiently encompassing to serve as a basis for reliable prediction or prescription. This is precisely the conclusion drawn by Hall, Haas, and Johnson (1967) in their empirical appraisal of the Blau and Scott (1962) and Etzioni (1961) typologies. The narrowness also hinders integrating the different typologies, since there is so little overlap among them. This problem contributes to the noncumulative nature of much organizational research. Unless there is an attempt to integrate many of the different typologies—to focus on a broader array of variables—typologies will continue to reveal only isolated, fragmented, and irreconcilable slices of organizational reality.

The typology presented in Chapter 3 may help to unify many of the previous structural typologies. It is based upon an extensive survey of the literature on organizational structures and attempts to synthesize many of the research findings of the past two decades in deriving its five structural types. A great number and wide range of variables are used to characterize each type. In this way, it was intended to build upon previous typologies, to unify their insights, and to derive a scheme that is more firmly rooted.

TAXONOMIES

This book is mostly concerned with taxonomies rather than typologies. The essence of the quantum view is that there exists clustering among organizational variables that is statistically significant and predictively useful, and that reduces the variety of organizations to a small number of richly defined types. An excellent way of establishing this is by performing empirical studies that uncover predictive regularities in organizational data—regularities that lead to the discovery of truly common types. We shall attempt to determine how closely previous taxonomies adhere to the approach of synthesis advocated in Chapter 1.

A few authors have derived empirically based taxonomies using very many variables. Pugh, Hickson, and Hinings (1969) derived a taxonomy of structures of work organizations from a factor analysis of 64 structural variables. Using three independent structural factors—structuring of activities, concentration of authority, and line control of workflow—in their analysis, they were able to derive seven common bureaucratic types. Although this was a promising beginning, the sample used might not have been broadly representative of organizations in general (McKelvey, 1975). Also, nothing was done to ensure that the firms in each of the types would be as similar as possible or to maximize intertype differences. Finally, no allowance was made for the possibility that there might exist nonlinearities in the relationships among the variables. These could have made the results of the factor analysis, a linear technique, quite misleading.

Haas, Hall, and Johnson (1966) employed a very different method to generate their taxonomy of organizations. They used a computer program designed to search through all the organizations in their broad sample to find the one most typical. After the organizations were ranked according to their similarity to the most typical organization, a cutoff point determined which ones would be considered to be in the first cluster. All other organizations were then used to constitute a new sample, upon which the procedure was repeated. This process was continued until all organizations were classified. In this study, a conscious effort was made to derive internally homogeneous classes. But there was no attempt to then gather a new sample of data to see if the same classes would emerge. In other words, the generality of the taxonomy can be called into question.

Goronzy (1969) using methods of numerical taxonomy similar to those discussed by Sokal and Sneath (1963), wrote a computer program to develop his taxonomy. Four suggestive clusters were discovered. But the focus was very narrow; the author took only measures of size and technology into account. Samuel and Mannheim (1970) used an unusual multivariate technique (multidimensional scalogram analysis) to derive their taxonomy of organizational structures, finding six bureaucratic types from a very limited sample of 30 firms. Finally, in one of the most sophisticated studies, Pinto and Pinder (1972) clustered 227 organizational units on the basis of eighteen behavioral dimensions of effectiveness (flexibility, communications, cooperation, and conflict, for example). They found eight homogeneous clusters, varying in size from eight to 65 units, each characterized by a distinct behavioral profile. The clusters predicted rates of growth, technology, work setting dispersion, and so on, variables that were *not* used to generate the clusters. Pinto and Pinder (1972), using the technique suggested by Ward and Hook (1963), ensured that the hierarchical grouping procedure arrived at clusters that were as homogeneous and as mutually distinct as possible.

One of the most surprising results of this survey is the very small number of taxonomies that have been generated. We could find only five, and the review by Carper and Snizek (1980) identified only four of these. The most recent taxonomy is ten years old.[2] Clearly, the field is in its infancy. Thus it is not surprising that most of the taxonomies have a number of serious shortcomings.

First, the selection of variables is very narrow. Generally, only structural or environmental variables are used as the basis for clustering. The organizational characterizations are very incomplete. We never see what configurations might result if strategy, structure, management-style, environmental, and performance variables were mixed.

Second, clusters are usually defined exclusively by measures of central tendency (means or modes of variables) rather than measures of dispersion (ranges, standard deviations). The latter could be very useful in helping to distinguish vital or central from peripheral attributes for each configuration (Pinder and Moore, 1979).

Third, as far as we can tell, only one method and one criterion for grouping is attempted. Although there is much variation across studies, each author uses only one method. This makes it far less likely that the most predictive kind of clustering in the data will be found. Different patterns of clustering require different methods of discovery.

Fourth, most of the taxonomists do not try to establish the stability and generality of their taxonomies. They use up all their data in the generation of the types and have none left for testing them. Would the same clusters occur in slightly different samples? We have no way of knowing. McKelvey (1975) blames this on taxonomists' inattention to matters of sample selection and argues the merits of stratified random sampling. But equally at fault is the failure to carefully define types using one sample, and

---

[2]As we go to press there are a number of very recent taxonomies, most in the form of working papers or theses, that will be of great interest to many readers. These dwell more upon strategic than structural and environmental aspects of organizations but broadly reflect many of the elements of our approach of synthesis. Both the quantity and quality of these works are very encouraging. See, for example, Chenhall (1983), Galbraith & Schendel (1982), Gartner (1982), Hambrick & Schecter (1983), and Hambrick (1983b).

then establish whether the same types emerge in another sample drawn from the same population.

Fifth, much of the work that has gone into taxonomy generation has had a predominantly methodological orientation. More emphasis is given to discussing methods than to describing and interpreting the findings themselves. This is because researchers are often far removed from their organizations. They have only a set of numerical scores and averages to characterize types and their members. In the absence of rich, anecdotal, "soft" evidence, it is hard to discover the meaning of the types and the essence of their configurations, and to elicit their themes and central interdependencies (Miller and Friesen, 1982b).

Finally, there are no attempts to determine whether or not the types or configurations derived are necessary or even useful for prediction. Do different relationships among variables hold in the different configurations? That is, do configurations require distinct predictive models? Can we use a few variables to classify a new firm and then accurately predict other attributes or the scores along other variables on the basis of configuration membership? If the answer is yes to both questions, the utility of the taxonomy is strongly supported. If not, maybe it is necessary to select other variables, broader samples, or more useful clustering methods.

It is clear, then, that most previous taxonomies fall short of pursuing the recommendations we made in Chapter 1 in discussing the approach of synthesis. The narrow range of variables, the failure to closely examine and interpret the configurations and their predictive power, the lack of attention to process and performance, and the failure to use anecdotal material to help understand configurations limit the utility of prior taxonomies. They prevent taxonomies from affording insights into configurations and may not allow us to discover the most parsimonious predictive frameworks.

The taxonomies presented in Chapters 4 and 5 were designed to overcome some of these limitations. They employ a broader selection of variables, seek out the most densely populated clusters so that as few configurations as possible encompass the largest number of firms, investigate the stability of the configurations across different samples, and collect anecdotal data that provide valuable detail on the configurations. But Chapters 4 and 5 present only two examples of taxonomies in the spirit of the approach of synthesis. There are many other possible methods. It therefore seems appropriate, while we are on the subject, to embark upon a more general, and unfortunately more technical, discussion of methods.

TAXONOMIC METHODOLOGY

We noted in the introduction to Part I that all of our empirical analyses of organizational variables point to complex, nonlinear multivariate relationships. In n-dimensional space these collectively describe a curved surface that is generally of much smaller dimension than the space itself. For example, say we decide to describe 100 firms along 30 variables of environment, structure and strategy. The variables typically will interrelate so that all the firms lie on a 5 to 10 dimensional snake-like surface that meanders through 30 dimensional space. Our objective is to describe such surfaces— to discover the most important regularities among the variables that they disclose. The relatively small dimension of the surface gives rise both to the small number of organizational types and their predictive power. Its curvilinearity indicates that relationships among the original variables will differ from one region of the surface to another. This makes it necessary to search for different types, each with its own relationships, and each corresponding to a small piece of the complex surface. Thus our expectations concerning the nature of the data surface make us believe it likely that the quest for taxonomies will discover predictive types. They also suggest that the search will uncover very different relationships among many of the variables for each of the major types.

Q versus R Approaches to Taxonomy

In generating taxonomies, it is possible to use a Q or an R approach. The first seeks relationships among cases. The second, more traditional, approach seeks relationships among variables. Although both may be useful, we favor Q approaches on the overwhelmingly common occasions when some of the multivariate relationships are expected to be nonlinear. To see why, we can compare two methods of generating a taxonomy.

A common approach would be to perform an R-type factor analysis of n variables. Assume that we find m factors. Bifurcation of the factors would yield 2^m types, which could serve as the basis for the taxonomy. This procedure might be acceptable if the data were multivariate normal and if one could find no clustering of points in the data space. But in most data sets, such conditions do not occur. For example, the data could lie near a curve such as the one in Figure 2-1.[3]

When the data are curvilinear in a complex manner that cannot be anticipated or easily discovered, Q technique can be used to construct "box-like" regions around the data in the space. This helps to disclose, through piecemeal approximation, the basic structure of the data surface. Whereas a bifurcation of the three variables in Figure 2-1 would give 2^3 groups, the construction of box-like regions would give only three. The Q approach, by using a grouping technique and subsequently reverting to the raw scores

[3]In three dimensions, such a curve would be easily detected, but in twenty or so dimensions, if the curve constituted a 3 to 5 dimensional snake-like surface, the nonlinear relationship would be difficult to discover. The nonlinearity of the data can be established by examining the correlations among variables for different sets of score ranges. If the data in one such box-like region shows a significantly different correlation matrix from the data in another, nonlinearity is indicated.

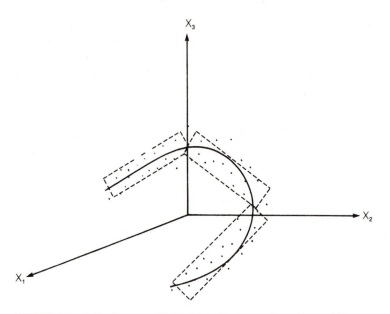

FIGURE 2-1   A Scattergram Divided into Regions.   From Danny Miller and Peter Friesen, "Archetypes of Organizational Transition", *Administrative Science Quarterly* 25 (June 1980).

that define the regions, can thus sometimes afford greater parsimony than an *R* approach. It *directly* seeks out the densest clusters of firms.

Another advantage of *Q* over *R* technique when there is nonlinear clustering is the greater precision of the definition of variable ranges within groups. One can discover which variables vary much within a specific region and which ones hardly vary at all. Samplewide bifurcation of all variables is an unnecessarily crude approach. Also, where *R*-factors instead of variables are used, *R* technique is even more crude, as factors may not explain much variance and may differ in their explanatory power from one group to another. An *R* approach to taxonomy can result in many empty categories. Not all combinations of the variables (or *R*-factors) are equally probable. The *Q* technique strives to focus on the most common types. It is easily the best approach for discovering the curvilinear surfaces that so frequently characterize data on organizations.

We shall discuss some general problems in taxonomy generation and some possible strategies for dealing with them. There are three key classes of questions that must be dealt with when applying Q-techniques to organizations:

1. *Which measures of similarity should be used to compare organizations?* Is the score pattern or intercase correlation all that is relevant in comparing the score profiles of two organizations (score profiles are merely the set of raw scores

across variables for organizations), or should the profile means and variances also be reflected in difference measures? How should each variable be weighted in comparing profiles?

2. *What types of multivariate techniques can be used for grouping?* What are the relative merits of mathematical algorithms, cluster analysis, hierarchical clustering, factor analysis, and multidimensional scaling?

3. *How can the statistical significance of groups be evaluated?* How does one distinguish between chance and valid clustering?

Obviously, the answers to these questions depend in part upon the investigator's research objectives and the nature of the measures and sample. We can only present a number of possible techniques and discuss the advantages, limitations and situational appropriateness of each. Researchers must tailor their approaches to the problem at hand.

GAUGING ORGANIZATIONAL SIMILARITIES

There are many indices that can be used to express the degree of similarity between organizational score profiles. In discussing a number of popular measures of similarity and the advantages and limitations of each, several general cautions should be noted. All similarity measures are summary statistics, and as such, they involve a loss of information. Say we have Firms A, B and C with the following score profiles across four variables (assume each variable is rated on a 1–5 interval scale):

FIRM	V_1	V_2	V_3	V_4
A	4	5	2	2
B	3	4	1	1
C	5	3	3	1

Arriving at a composite similarity score between two firms, described using more than one variable, involves making certain decisions about the weight given to each variable in the index. Should weights be equal, or not? Anytime there exists very substantial intercorrelation among profile variables there is a danger of unconsciously giving too much weight to the underlying factor causing the correlation.

Another problem is deciding whether to standardize score profiles for their means and variances (scatter)—to derive "pure" measures of pattern similarity for constructing relational configurations, or to use raw score profiles to derive unstandardized measures for constructing elemental configurations. In the first case, information on raw scores is lost; in the second, the unstandardized measure is a function of several influences (pattern, means, and scatter) and is thus harder to interpret.

Cronbach and Gleser (1953) discuss several measures of profile similarity. A common one is the D^2 score. A profile pertaining to a firm consists of a set of scores where:

j = any of the variables V_1, V_2, etc., which are n in number;
i = any one of the firms 1, 2, . . . , N; and
x_{ji} = the score of firm i on variable j.

We may regard the x_{j1} coordinates for Firm 1 in n-dimensional space. The more similar the measures of two firms, the closer their points in the space. The dissimilarity of two firms can be taken as the square of the linear distance between their respective points:

$$D_{12}^2 = \sum_{j=1}^{n} (x_{j1} - x_{j2})^2$$

Researchers may wish to standardize this measure by removing differences caused by firm means and variances.

Cattell (1949) has attempted to derive a distance measure, r_p, closely related to D^2, but transformed to have the property of ranging in value from -1 to 1 just like a correlation coefficient. Although r_p contains information on the level and dispersion of profiles, and is preferable to other "pure" measures of pattern association for research that requires the incorporation of such profile attributes, there appear to be no compelling reasons to prefer it to D^2.

For some research questions, profile levels, means, and profile variance may be irrelevant, or the investigator may wish to look at these separately from patterns. Helmstadter (1957), in an excellent review of profile similarity measures, discusses a number of correlational measures that use scores standardized for means and variance. There is the product moment correlation coefficient, perhaps the most familiar measure of association or pattern similarity, which is suitable for interval data:

$$r_s = \frac{\sum x_i' y_i'}{n \sigma_x \sigma_y}$$

where n is the number of variables in the profile, x_i' and y_i' are the corresponding standardized values of the ith variable of each profile, and σ_x and σ_y are the standard deviations of the profiles.

Cronbach and Gleser (1953) describe the use of rank-order correlations such as Kendall's (1948) Tau and Spearman's Rho. In contrast to all previous coefficients discussed, the advantage of these measures is that they require only ordinal information, not interval data.

Sokal and Sneath (1963, pp. 125–41) summarize a set of profile similarity measures that can conveniently be used with nominal data (that is, variables that are scaled in binary terms, such as HAS ATTRIBUTE, DOES NOT HAVE ATTRIBUTE; YES, NO; 0, 1; +, −; and so on). The data consist of n binary (+, −) variables scored for two organizations. For any pair of organizations, the aim is to compare the number of matched variables, m(+, + and −, −) to the number of unmatched, u, variables. There are a number of possible coefficients of matching association that can be used: $(m − u)/n$, $m/(m + u)$, and so forth. Sometimes only positive matches (both organizations in pair have the attribute) are of interest, other times negative matches are of interest (neither organization in the pair possesses the attribute), and sometimes both sorts of matches are useful. Sokal and Sneath (1963) go into considerable detail on the possible matching coefficients and their relative utility for different questions.

The significance of the choice between correlation and D^2 measures becomes clear when we view these as potential inputs to multivariate analysis procedures. Sawrey et al. (1960, p. 670) claim that only correlation measures can be used in factor analysis, but Nunnally (1962) shows that cross-products of D^2 scores can also be factored. Of course these cross-products should be standardized when variables do not have roughly equivalent standard deviations, lest some parameters receive too much weight in the analysis.

The problem of assuring that each variable receives its appropriate weight in D^2 measures is broached by Overall (1964), who is concerned about assigning unintentionally high weights to factors or dimensions underlying those profile variables that are intercorrelated. To assign equal weight to such underlying dimensions, Overall recommends the Mahalanobis (1963) D_m^2 measure. Unfortunately, the Mahalanobis measure is useful only with ratio-scale data and weights unreliable and unimportant factors equally with the major ones. An alternative we prefer to using the Mahalanobis statistic is to run an orthogonal R-type factor analysis and to use the uncorrelated factor scores, rather than the raw variable scores, in profiles. Because of the strong possibility of very relevant curvilinear relations among some variables, we suggest not collapsing variables into factors unless their loadings (i.e. linear relationships) are very high—greater than, say, .80. This policy minimizes the chances of obscuring nonlinear relationships in subsequent analyses as only highly redundant variables would be combined.

We have introduced enough measures of similarity to give the reader an idea of the range of possible choices. Their attributes are summarized in Table 2-1. The measure to be selected should be a function of the investigator's research objectives and the nature of his or her data. Even for ratio scale or interval data, there is no consensus in the literature on whether to include differences in dispersion (variance, scatter) and level (mean) in coefficients of pattern similarity. Although it is true that r's ignore much of

TABLE 2-1:   Comparison of Similarity Measures

		INFORMATION USED[a]	ASSUMPTIONS ABOUT DATA[b]	REQUIRED DATA RELIABILITY[c]	WEIGHTING OF ELEMENTS[d]	M.V.A. SUITABILITY[e]	M.V.A. INTERPRETATION[f]
D^2	Distance	L/S	R	L	V	R	D
D'^2	Mean Adjusted Distance	L/S	R	L	V	R	D
D''^2	Mean & Variance Adjusted Distance	P	R	H	V	A	E
r_s	Product-Moment Correlation	P	R	H	V	A	E
Tau/Rho	Rank Correlation	P	O	L	V	R	E
r_p	Coefficient of Pattern Similarity	L/S	R	L	V	R	D
D_m^2	Mahalanobis Measure	L/S	R	H	C	A	D
Nominal Association Measures	This category is quite variable; see Sokal and Sneath (1963)	L/S	N	L	V	R	D

[a]P means pattern information only, L/S indicates that level and/or scatter is also reflected in measure.

[b]R limits use to ratio scale or interval data, O—ordinal, N—nominal.

[c]L indicates data need not have very high reliability; H indicates the need for high reliability.

[d]V indicates that each profile element or variable is weighted equally (unless researcher explicitly decides otherwise); C indicates that each principle component or dimension is weighted equally.

[e]A indicates measure is suitable for all or most forms of multivariate analysis (M.V.A.); R means that use is restricted (usually to exclude factor analysis).

[f]E means interpretation of M.V.A. is easy; D indicates there might be some difficulty in determining why a particular grouping occurred.

Source: Danny Miller, "The Role of Multivariate 'Q-Techniques' in the Study of Organizations," Academy of Management Review 3 (July, 1978).

the information in the data, more aggregate measures that reflect level and variation may be more difficult to interpret. We suggest that a number of coefficients of profile similarity should be used simultaneously, so that several images of the data can be entered into the subsequent stages of building homogeneous groups. The differences in the resultant sets of groups could prove to be quite informative. We advocate the use of both pure pattern and distance measures when the error in the data is low and factor analysis is to be performed. But pure pattern measures, standardized for variance, should be avoided in cases of high error. Such standardization is computationally equivalent to projecting points representing organizations onto the surface of a hypersphere: increasing the jaggedness of flat profiles that are close to the center of the sphere, and reducing that of profiles with much variance. For a firm that has a fair amount of error and whose variance is low, its location on the surface of the hypersphere is highly influenced by chance (Cronbach and Gleser, 1953, p. 465), and resultant standardized scores of distance or similarity are quite unreliable.

FORMING INTERNALLY HOMOGENEOUS GROUPS OF ORGANIZATIONS

The objective of grouping techniques is to give us some idea of the important patterns to be found among the variables in our snake-like multivarate data surface. Each group of firms should represent an important facet or piece of the surface with its own distinctive relationships among the variables. The advantage of searching for such groups is that the curvilinear surface is often too complex to permit the discovery of useful *sample-wide* multivariate relationships.

Many techniques are available to group together organizations on the basis of the chosen measures of similarity. Some methods are informal and subjective; others involve sophisticated, formal multivariate techniques. No categorization system can be viewed as definitive. The number of groups formed and the grouping criteria employed are always somewhat arbitrary and can be justified only with reference to the research objectives being pursued. The different methods of multivariate analysis yield different groupings given the same data base (Myers and Nicosia, 1968). Thus, it may be useful to try several different multivariate techniques in an attempt to determine what the groupings are revealing. In the end, those sets of groups that most enhance the understanding and predictive ability of the researcher are to be preferred. The two basic aims which all grouping procedures have in common are (1) the attempt to have fewer groups than there are organizations, and (2) once grouping has been achieved, to have companies within a group be, in some important respect, more alike than companies across groups.

Mathematical Algorithms

Fisher (1958) proposed a mathematical algorithm for defining homogeneous groups that minimizes within-group variance. A computer program is described that accomplishes this for samples as large as 200, where at most ten groups are desired. Although Fisher's algorithm may be dated and is inadequate for the needs of most organizational researchers, it does illustrate a class of approaches that may eventually become quite important. Such techniques explicitly define an objective function and seek to maximize or minimize it by varying a concrete set of parameters. Grouping criteria are thus very well defined. In contrast, there can be a psychological danger in using packaged techniques such as factor analysis programs, since there is no obvious need to consider just what is being accomplished by the grouping method.

Cluster Analysis

This term is used to cover a rather broad variety of grouping techniques. According to Tryon and Bailey:

> Cluster analysis is the general logic, formulated as a procedure, by which we objectively group together entities on the basis of their similarities and differences (1970, p. 1).

Frank and Green (1968) and Green, Frank, and Robinson (1967) discuss a typical clustering routine that employs D^2 scores, standardized for both mean and standard deviation. First:

> The pair [of organizations] with the smallest distance is chosen as the node of the first cluster, and the average distance of this cluster is computed.
> Additional points [organizations] are added to this cluster (based on closeness to the last-computed average) until:
> (a)   some prespecified number of points has been clustered;
> (b)   the points to be added to the cluster exceed some prespecified distance-cutoff or threshold number.
> The program next proceeds to the next pair of points which are closest together of all unclustered points, and the above process is repeated. . . .
> The program can be further modified to shift points from cluster to cluster to obtain final clusters which are best in the sense of having the lowest average within-cluster distance summed over all clusters at a given stage in the clustering (Frank and Green, 1968, p. 86).

There are many clustering methods available. These vary greatly in terms of the criteria employed to establish cluster membership and the procedures employed to determine initial, or "nucleus" cluster members. Three common membership rules are exemplified by:

1. *Single linkage clustering*, which first clusters cases (organizations) that are most related, gradually admitting more members into the cluster by lowering the criteria for admission (Sneath, 1957);

2. *Complete linkage clustering*, in which a potential member must have relations—that is, similarity coefficients—at a certain level or above with every member of the cluster (Sokal and Sneath, 1963, p. 182); and

3. *Average linkage clustering*, where admission is based on the average of the similarities of a case with the members of the cluster (Sokal and Michener, 1958).

(Numbers 1 and 2 are "hierarchical" clustering techniques, which are to be discussed in the next section).

In doing research on organizations, investigators interested in establishing very homogeneous groupings might use complete linkage clustering, whereas those who are interested in looser groups might wish to use average linkage clustering. The former researchers might be trying to "control" for certain factors in their investigation, and the latter might merely wish to obtain a general idea of which firms or contexts are most similar.

Some clustering methods identify nucleus cluster members in sequence, starting with the closest firms, adding firms to the cluster until a specified cutoff level is reached, and then finding a new nucleus using the distance between the closest two firms that have not already been clustered (Frank and Green, 1968). Other techniques, such as that used by Sawrey et al. identify several nuclei simultaneously:

> . . . [selecting] groups from a matrix of [distances] between profiles. Based initially on a small number of basic profiles, highly homogeneous groups which are dissimilar to each other are formed. To these homogeneous groups, the remaining profiles in the sample are then compared. As a result of these comparisons, additions are made to one or another of these groups (1960, p. 657).

Tryon and Bailey (1970) and Sokal and Sneath (1963) present some common forms of cluster analysis. The former concentrate on methods that are used with interval data, and the latter refer to clustering schemes that are appropriate for ordinal data. Some methods of clustering are quite complex and require elaborate computer programs (Tryon, 1958a; Schlaifer, 1977); other methods can be performed manually (Kamen, 1970). Clustering can be accomplished using both D^2 measures and correlation coefficients.

Because most cluster analysis programs limit the number of variables they can accommodate, it might be useful to reduce this number by doing an R-type factor or cluster analysis and then using factor/cluster scores. This will:

> . . . secure the gain in generality that such dimensions necessarily possess over individual variables. A greater degree of generality in typological prediction can be expected where a typology is based on cluster-composited dimensions (Tryon, 1958a, p. 140).

Several interesting applications of different types of cluster analysis are contained in Sneath (1957), Boeke (1942), Anderberg (1973),

Hambrick (1983b), Rogers and Tanimoto (1960), Silvestri et al. (1972), and Galbraith and Schendel (1982).

Cluster analysis has several important strengths as a tool for organizational researchers. It is a very flexible approach to grouping because a number of different clustering rules and procedures are available. Both measures of pattern similarity and measures of profile similarity can be clustered. A third and obvious advantage of the technique is its ability to deal with a substantial number of variables and companies. It is also far more convenient and simple to use than a mathematical algorithm. Finally, clustering encourages more effort to tailor the technique to the nature of the research problem than do many of the canned factor analysis programs.

There are a number of inconveniences associated with clustering methods. There are no absolute rules to determine how many clusters should be formed. Each investigator must decide which sets of groups give the most adequate information. If variables are measured in different units, it also becomes difficult to grasp the concept of similarity, as it is made up of "apples and oranges." Criteria for establishing the boundaries or membership criteria of clusters are subjective. Trial and error must be used to find the most homogeneous groups that encompass the largest number of firms. Finally, not much is known about the inferential characteristics of clustering techniques, since little investigation has been made of their statistical properties (Green, Frank, and Robinson, 1967, p. B398).

Hierarchical Clustering

Johnson (1967) suggests a hierarchical clustering procedure that can be used with any profile similarity measure. Figure 2-2 represents a hierarchical clustering output.

FIGURE 2-2   Scheme of Hierarchical Clustering.   From Danny Miller, "The Role of Multivariate 'Q-Techniques' in the Study of Organizations," *Academy of Management Review* 3 (July 1978).

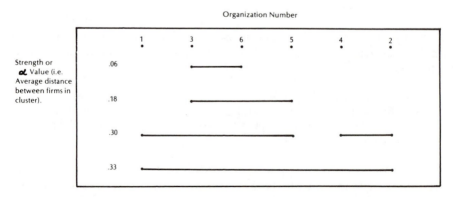

The first clustering (top row) is the "weakest," since each object is a cluster, so that there are six "clusters." The second and third rows show five and four clusters respectively as, first, companies 3 and 6, and then, companies 3, 6, and 5 are grouped. Clustering continues until all groups or units are clustered into one group. Note that clusterings increase hierarchically, since each is obtained by merging clusters at the previous level. With the Johnson procedure, one may replace two or more objects by a cluster and still define the distance between such clusters and other objects or clusters, revealing the structure of the data and the relative degrees of similarity among companies.

Sneath (1957), McQuitty (1960), Ward (1963), and Ward and Hook (1963) explain hierarchical schemes in greater detail, and Johnson (1967) and Schlaifer (1977) have developed computer programs to carry out these procedures. Ward and Hook's (1963) hierarchical scheme employs interval data and attempts to form groups such that the sum of the squared within-group deviations about the group mean of each profile is minimized. Other target objective functions can also be selected.

There appear to be important advantages to hierarchical clustering. First, the procedure takes account of all profiles (that is, similarity scores) at all stages, ensuring the tightest possible groupings. Insights can be derived from the complete hierarchical structure of the profiles that results from gradually and systematically reducing the number of groups in a manner that least impairs the chosen objective function. Fewer arbitrary decisions are required once an objective function has been specified, since "there is no need to define nucleus groups or to set limits to specify the order in which profiles will be added to nucleus groups" (Ward, 1963, p. 79). Another important advantage is that any measure of profile similarity may be used. It is also useful that the "cost" or impact upon the objective function of each grouping step is available; this serves as a guide to help the researcher decide when to stop clustering.

Organizational theorists may, using the hierarchical clustering procedure, attempt to cluster organizations and contexts at various levels of homogeneity. They might then test the stability, generality, and power of several levels of clustering by using some of the techniques suggested in the section on hypothesis testing. Through such an iterative process, the most significant groupings can be discovered. Cluster analysis has been used to study organizations by Hambrick (1983b), Hambrick and Schecter (1983), and Gartner (1982).

Factor Analysis

Factor analysis is a statistical technique for reducing a large number of correlated variables to a small number of generally uncorrelated variables. Our focus will be on Q-analysis (Stephenson, 1936), in which organizations rather than variables are factored. Recall that Q-technique is merely

R-technique using a transposed raw-data matrix. It treats similarities between companies, rather than between variables. Since the process of factor analysis is identical for both techniques, and since readers will probably be quite familiar with R-technique, our discussion will be very brief. Excellent descriptions of factor analysis are available in Harman (1960), Kendall (1957), and Van de Geer (1971). Discussion of Q-technique in particular can be found in Stephenson (1936, 1952, 1953), Bass (1957), and Cattell (1952). Wells and Sheth (1971) present a less technical discussion of factor analysis.

A company, x_j, is expressed as a linear combination of factors, or ideal companies, such that:

$$x_j = \sum_{i=1}^{m} a_{ji}F_i + d_jU_j$$

where a_{ji} is the weight assigned to each factor F_i, and d_j is the weight of the uniqueness factor U_j, corresponding to x_j. If we view an organization as a point, representing its set of scores across all variables in an n-dimension vector space, then it can be shown that organizations that correlate highly with one another will be clustered together in that space. A factor analysis systematically explores this space, attempting to project factors or "ideal companies" into areas that are densely occupied by organizations so that as much variance as possible is explained by consecutive factors. Different factors, if orthogonal, can be used to find uncorrelated groupings of organizations. By definition, any factor that has a number of firms loading highly upon it (that is, organizations that are highly correlated with the factor) will give us groups of firms that are themselves highly intercorrelated and thus similar in terms of score patterns.

Note that factor analysis comprises a family of techniques. Some analyses deal with uncorrelated orthogonal factors, while others, in an attempt to achieve higher loadings and a better fit with the data, use correlated oblique factors. Some techniques attempt to explain all the variance in the original data such that the number of factors equals the number of organizations (principal components analysis). Others attempt only to explain the communality in the data so that there are fewer factors than organizations ("factor" analysis). To make factors more distinctive and therefore easier to interpret as a basis for grouping, various data rotation techniques are available—varimax, quartimax, equimax, and so on—each of which may yield slightly different groups depending on the investigators' grouping heuristic. The importance of a factor is often taken to be measured by the percentage of variance in the original data that is accounted for by that factor. There are several factor analysis computer programs available, the SPSS package being fairly representative (Nie et al., 1975 and updates).

In using factor analysis to form groups, one simply combines organizations with similar loadings across the factors. The advantage of the technique is that like cluster analysis, it is a quick and easy method to use, and it can handle many variables. The rotation techniques also make groupings quite clear where correlational patterns in the original data are varied. Groups formed by orthogonal factoring are usually quite distinctive, at least in terms of score pattern, and thus may be easier to interpret than closely related clusters. There is no need for the user to decide in advance upon the number of groups or the criteria for grouping; so, at least in appearance, the Q-factor analysis may seem more objective than clustering techniques. But this is an illusion, since some decision must be made regarding when to stop factoring or adding new factors; this is usually done according to the percentage of variance explained by the incremental factor. Also, groupings formed on the basis of loadings are quite subjective, since the investigator must develop his own cutoff points and select the method of rotation.

Some limitations of factor analysis are that ratio-scale or interval data and related similarity measures are required; correlation coefficients rather than distance measures are preferred to facilitate interpretation; and only small numbers of organizations can be processed relative to the number of variables. Finally, the implicit assumptions of factor analysts—for example, that underlying factors are invariable across individuals and that communalities can be objectively determined—are questionable (Tryon, 1958b). An interesting use of Q-factor analysis for classifying organizational strategies is given by Chenhall (1983).

Multidimensional Scaling

Multidimensional scaling (MDS) is generally used not as a grouping technique but as a method of discovering the fewest fundamental or underlying dimensions that can be used to describe a set of objects. According to Torgerson:

> The typical problem to be handled by the MDS procedures might be roughly stated as follows: Given a set of stimuli which vary with respect to an unknown number of dimensions, determine (1) the minimum dimensionality of the set and (2) projections of the stimuli (scale values) on each of the dimensions involved (1958, pp. 247–48).

Although its aims are similar to R-factor analysis, it has the advantage of being able to use ordinal data in the form of $N(N - 1) \div 2$ similarity measures for N companies. MDS can replace many ordinal variables with a smaller set of dimensions that possess interval metric properties, and that can then be used in a Q-factor analysis to discover groupings of firms. One advantage of using MDS is that the ordinal data are shaped into a format suitable for a more demanding and easy-to-interpret form of analysis. Also, in contrast to R-factor analysis, the optimal number of dimensions can be determined when the program is given a suitable objective function (Kruskal, 1964a and b). A problem with MDS is that it may be difficult to interpret the nature of the underlying dimensions discovered, since these are not obviously related to the original set of variables. Their nature must be inferred from the array of companies along each dimension. Readers interested in MDS are referred to detailed accounts by Torgerson (1958), Shepard (1962), and Kruskal (1964a and b). For MDS computer programs, see Young and Torgerson (1967) and Kruskal, Young, and Seery (1973).

Occasionally, when MDS reveals only two or three key dimensions along which to plot organizations, the technique can serve directly as a grouping procedure, particularly if an eyeballing technique reveals a clustering of company points in the two- or three-dimensional space. Since the dimensions from MDS have interval scale properties, an F-test can be used to verify the significance of groups by comparing within-group variance to between-group variance.

Recap of Grouping Techniques

Table 2-2 summarizes the characteristics of the grouping techniques that have been presented. The choice of methods must depend on the nature of the scales and measures used by the researcher, the sample size and number of variables or factors used, the index of similarity, and, above all, the natural patterns in the data.

It might be instructive to illustrate several patterns of multivariate data that can occur, and some methods that would be useful for discovering them.

Assume that we have scores for twenty cases or companies along three variables, A, B, and C. Data patterns such as those in Figure 2-3 might arise. The three-dimensional grids show four possible configurations in the data. Each data point represents a company whose scores on the three variables can be read off the three axes.

The first pattern shows a highly significant negative correlation between variables A and B for the whole sample (this appears to be the most meaningful sort of homogeneity of the data), and a tendency toward randomness along variable C. Simple correlational methods would be perfect for analyzing these data and there would be no need to split up the sample into homogeneous groups. For example, grouping with inverse (Q) factor analysis would project the data onto the plane orthogonal to the 45° line and then would show two vectors or factors emanating from the origin and projected onto a hypersphere through the densest clusterings of data points. The loading of a company on a factor would be calculated as the distance of the point projected on the hypersphere from the factor axis. The closer the point or "company" is to the factor, the higher the loading.

TABLE 2-2: Comparison of Grouping Techniques

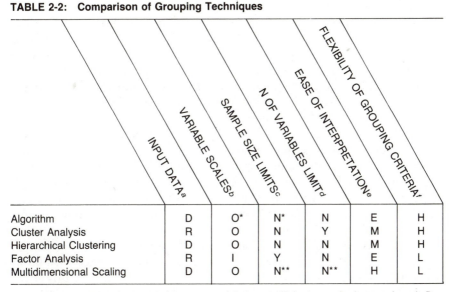

	INPUT DATA[a]	VARIABLE SCALES[b]	SAMPLE SIZE LIMITS[c]	N OF VARIABLES LIMIT[d]	EASE OF INTERPRETATION[e]	FLEXIBILITY OF GROUPING CRITERIA[f]
Algorithm	D	O*	N*	N	E	H
Cluster Analysis	R	O	N	Y	M	H
Hierarchical Clustering	D	O	N	N	M	H
Factor Analysis	R	I	Y	N	E	L
Multidimensional Scaling	D	O	N**	N**	H	L

[a]R = cross-product, covariance, or correlation coefficients required, or preferred, D = any data are suitable.

[b]I = interval scale required, O = ordinal or better, N = nominal or better.

[c]Y = (yes) sample should be < 50, N = sample can be > 50.

[d]Y = (yes) number of variables should be < 20, N > 20.

[e]"Ease of interpretation" of groups is a subjective and conditional category. Author's best guesses are represented by E = usually easy, M = moderate, H = hard.

[f]The flexibility (or range of choice) in selecting one's own grouping criteria are noted by H = highly flexible, L = not very flexible.

*Depends on algorithm used.

**Yes, if used as grouping method.

Source: Danny Miller, "The Role of Multivariate 'Q-Techniques' in the Study of Organizations," *Academy of Management Review* 3 (July, 1978).

FIGURE 2-3 Multivariate Data in Three Space: Four Possible Cases. From Danny Miller, "Toward a New Contingency Approach" *Journal of Management Studies* 18 (January 1981).

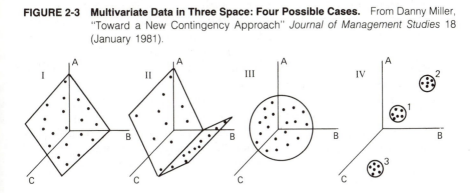

A problem is that since the factor analysis cannot find the best possible origin (for instance, in this case, one of the corners of the plane), it paints an overcomplex picture of data that really has a simple structure. Most types of cluster analysis would pose similar problems. The Q-factor analysis would group companies according to the correlations among their score patterns, while most cluster analyses would group companies according to some distance measure. The groupings of firms would be different in both cases. If a researcher were interested mainly in predicting one variable from the others, a cluster or Q-factor analysis would not provide very useful categorizations. Categories would be superfluous, since all the data could be handled by the same predictive model. Thus, one should compare the predictive utility of two types of approaches: a linear samplewide "R" approach that groups variables according to their similarities, and a "Q" approach that groups cases or companies and does not rely upon assumptions of multivariate linearity.

The second graph shows a simplified version of a very common type of clustering. Here there appears to be an obvious advantage to splitting the sample. Yet no standard multivariate technique can always do the job by itself. The advantage of splitting the sample is apparent, since the relationship between variables A and B depends upon which subsample of data we use. For one half of the sample, the relationship is negative; for the other, it is positive. Segmenting the sample into parts that are homogeneous in their relationships among the variables will be useful for prediction. But Q-factor analysis, because of its fixed origin and its method of standardizing all points by projecting them onto the hypersphere, will not always be able to distinguish between the two "subsamples." Indeed, the factors for our second case might not be very dissimilar to those of the first case. There is a need therefore to examine carefully the raw-score patterns of firms that were grouped by a multivariate procedure. This might reveal a systematic difference within some of the groups. In our example, we might find two subgroups of companies that all load highly on a factor having extremely different scores on variable B. They may be separated by a gulf in which no "mid-range" scores occur on that variable. This may be a sign of the need for further splitting the sample. A cluster analysis procedure might directly reveal at least two groups that are on the distinct planes. Whether the two-stage factor analysis procedure is used or the one-step cluster analysis, the groups should be analyzed using correlational or regression techniques in order to determine their predictive significance. In this case, very different models will emerge for the two groups.

The third graph of Figure 2-3 shows still another problem, one for which there is no remedy. The data scatter randomly, and any grouping will be relatively useless for prediction. Such a situation might be indicated by many factors, each of which explain a small percentage of the variance, or by clusters that are both loose and immediately adjacent to one another (that is, there are no notable discontinuities in the distances between points). When this happens, it is usually because variables have been chosen that are empirically unrelated. The only recourse is to reconceptualize the research to change the variable set.

The final graph of Figure 2-3 shows a situation that would be detected with most cluster analysis methods, but not with Q-factor analysis unless we look at means and deviations (groups 1 and 2 might load highly on the same factor). We see that firms with similar raw variable scores cluster together closely and are rather far away from firms in other groups. Many cluster analysis procedures can discover this. The predictive utility of groups would then be based on raw variable scores. That is, once we know the group a firm is a member of, we can predict its scores fairly accurately. Regression or correlational methods might not disclose any linear relationships among the variables that have any predictive utility either within groups or for the total sample.

Clearly, methods of analysis must vary depending upon the nature of the data. Since this cannot be known in advance, particularly when there are many firms and variables, researchers should not be afraid to experiment with alternative grouping techniques. Of course there is no guarantee that meaningful prediction will be forthcoming from any of the techniques. However, experimentation might reveal a regression relation to be the best predictor in our first case, two regressions, one for each subsample, in the second case, nothing in the third case, and raw scores in the fourth case. The use of multiple methods will improve one's chances of finding the most distinctive facets or segments of any nonlinear data surface.

Predictive Accuracy, Aberrations, and Category Size

A configuration can be represented by a class or category of some type that is defined by the relationships or scores along a series of n variables. It might be instructive to examine some of the things we can manipulate to get predictive categories, and to discuss problems that may arise. Assume we have chosen five variables to describe company score patterns and are willing to say that patterns are meaningfully similar when their raw scores are alike. How alike should the scores have to be to make patterns members of the same class? What percentage of firms in the sample should fall into one or another class? How many classes should we have? All these questions are interrelated. What is more, they cannot always be reconciled to discover useful taxonomies. In fact, the problems will show that our confidence in the possibility of coming up with predictive categories is based completely upon our empirical data and our arguments regarding the existence of configurations, not upon the nature or the logical properties of the taxonomic process.

The degree of similarity required among category members is exclusively a function of the predictive accuracy desired by the researcher. If category membership must be presumed to have very exact implications, then patterns within each category must be extremely similar. A less demanding level of accuracy will permit larger categories. Figure 2-4 illustrates this. We can define category size by the score ranges or "regions" along the five variables, as shown by the dashed lines in both graphs. The graph 1 region allows us to infer more about category members than the graph 2 region and thus increases predictive accuracy. Unfortunately, it includes fewer patterns (pattern B does not fit) and thus forces us either to have more categories or allow a larger percentage of outliers. Neither of these situations is without cost. In the first instance, an unwieldy number of categories makes categorization a bit cumbersome, but much more important, it makes generalization difficult. That is, there may be very many categories, each with very few members, and we begin to operate in a theory-free realm, taking each case as an idiosyncrasy. On the other hand, a large percentage of outliers makes prediction impossible for many firms. Outliers cannot be categorized, and predictions are based on category features. So, even though small categories preserve predictive accuracy so that membership has many precise implications, unless the data are very structured it is possible to have an unwieldy number of sparsely populated categories, or a superabundance of outliers.

Things are not necessarily better if we decide to adopt larger categories, such as those shown on graph 2. Although fewer categories are necessary to include most of the data and the number of outliers decreases, predictive accuracy is lost. Class membership comes to have few implications.

Since the problems mentioned above increase in their severity with the degree of randomness in the data and the number of unrelated vari-

FIGURE 2-4   Predictive Accuracy and Category Size. From Miller, "Toward a New Contingency Approach."

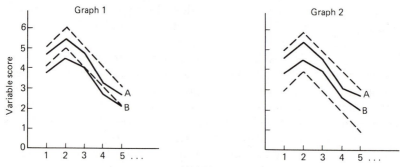

ables, we should emphasize the importance of trying to use variables that are at least conceptually—or better still, empirically—interrelated. To further minimize problems, it is best to construct categories around the regions that are most densely populated with score patterns. Where categories are few, tight, and collectively include a large percentage of the data, they can serve as useful bases for configurations, being both manageable in number and predictive. All taxonomies must be tested to ensure that they possess this sort of predictive utility.

HYPOTHESIS TESTING

It is most discouraging that the application of multivariate grouping techniques is often carried out without any attempt to determine the statistical significance of groups (Schuchman, 1967). Any grouping derived from the multivariate techniques discussed should be viewed as a very tentative and perhaps completely fortuitous ordering of the data until both the stability and the predictiveness of groups have been verified. Our concern here will not be with the tests of significance of factors in factor analysis, since large sample sizes are usually required, and stringent assumptions are made about the normality of the data (Ahmavaara, 1954; Harman, 1960; Rao, 1955). These conditions often do not hold in organizational research, and where they do, it is simple for investigators to apply the appropriate techniques. This section suggests several ad hoc approaches that can be used by researchers who have derived their taxonomies by any technique whatsoever. Once the tentative membership of groups is specified, the testing process can be made independent of the technique used. Thus it is permissible to use multivariate techniques that are not exactly appropriate for the type of data if the significance of the groups is tested by an entirely independent procedure.

To ensure that groups are stable and have generality, one can perform the same grouping technique on separate data samples to test whether similar groups recur. Chapters 4 and 5 develop such a procedure to test simultaneously the stability and tightness of groups. Groups are generated using Q-factor analysis on a random sample of the data base. Then regions such as those of Figure 2-4 are constructed. The boundaries of the regions are usually the ranges of the raw scores of the variables in the original groups. Regions contain information on both score levels and patterns, even though the factor analysis is performed using only correlational data. Thus no information is lost, since one can revert back to the inital raw variable scores of the organizations that belong to specific groups. Having constructed regions based on the initial groups of companies, each can be tested for its stability and density. This is done by comparing the percentage of firms *in a new sample* that fall into the region to the chance proportion of score patterns or sites that could be expected to fall into the region given its size. The appendices to Chapters 4 and 5 present alternative methods for calculating this latter proportion. If a simple binomial test of proportions indicates that the first proportion is significantly larger than the second, then groups can be said to be stable and statistically significant.

Some researchers are interested only in score patterns and not in score levels—that is, in relational rather than elemental configurations. Then "regions" can take the form of hypothesized patterns described, for example, in terms of whether a particular variable is above or below the mean across all variables for a company. The frequency of the pattern can be tested on a new sample of data only once the distribution of scores for each variable has been determined. Rather than assuming that data are normally distributed, the researcher can write a computer simulation program that generates artificial data that conform to the statistical null hypothesis. Comparison of the actual data with many samples of simulated data shows whether the former are improbable. If so, the hypothesis that was simulated can be rejected. The advantages of developing a knowledge of the probability distributions of the data are that no erroneous assumptions are made and that ordinal and nominal data can be tested.

UNIFYING THE CONFIGURATIONS
OF A TAXONOMY

We have stressed that configurations may collectively describe a snakelike nonlinear data surface such as that of Figure 2-1. The configurations are represented by the interlinked box-like regions that meander through the space in a complex way. The surface is often of a much lower dimension than the space, simply because of the multivariate relationships. This gives rise to the predictive quality of configurations. Thus, it might be useful to try to describe the surface itself. We may eventually wish to move from a configuration-based mid-range theory to a higher, more integrated level of conceptualization as we try to chain the pieces of the snake together.

We believe that the empirical configurations ("archetypes") of Chapters 4 and 5 are different parts of the same nonlinear surface defined in the space of variables by the data. Correlations among variables differ dramatically from one configuration to another, attesting to the curvilinearity of the surface. The interdependence among variables would therefore be understated by linear methods such as path analysis and regression. Although there already exist nonlinear methods of data analysis, these all require that the researcher have some *a priori* knowledge about the nonlinearity. They assume that the surface belongs to a known finite-parameter family of surfaces. Thus, there is no way of handling or identifying completely unexpected nonlinearities such as are found in exploratory research.

If it were possible, however, to find such a nonlinear surface, it could serve as the basis for a complete quantitative description of all the data. From it, one might be able to discern how one variable changes when another does, and also how this depends upon the values that still other variables have. One could randomly search for directions on the surface that are "suggestive" about the constraints upon and relationships among the variables describing configurations. A "suggestive" direction might show, for example, that if variable A increases, variables C, D, and E must decrease, while others are not affected. The directions impose constraints upon firms and describe the most common complexes of scores that occur as firms travel through the n-dimensional space.

With the help of linear algebra incorporated into computer programs, we might begin to uncover and describe the nonlinear surface as follows. We could start with a flat surface that has the same dimension as the curved data surface. The flat surface would have an orthogonal coordinate system on it. Then we could map the flat surface onto the curved one, bending it and stretching it as needed, but not tearing it. Once the mapping has been accomplished, the resulting coordinate system on the nonlinear surface would be curved and no longer orthogonal. However, since it was only stretched and bent, never torn, the surface would still show which data points—that is, which score patterns—were close to each other and therefore similar. It would also reveal where the configurations (the densely packed clusters of score patterns) touched each other, as well as which ones were separated by other configurations.

Trial-and-error heuristics could be employed using a time-shared computer system to find independent informative or "suggestive" directions in each configuration on the curved surface. Suggestive directions would reveal the constraints upon and relationships among the variables. The coordinate curves can be forced by the mapping to run parallel to the suggestive directions and to curve so as to join the directions of one configuration with those of another. The result would be a natural coordinate system for the nonlinear surface forming the minimum number of interdependent variables that describe the data. The next section presents this procedure mathematically.

Toward a Procedure for Identifying Nonlinear Surfaces

An m-dimensional surface in R^n can be represented as the range of a function $f: R^m \to R^n$. Since the surface is an empirical one, we can assume that it is smooth, although the data might define several surfaces each of which could have a different dimension. We could check for this by investigating one surface at a time and then seeing if all the data are approximately included in it. If not, we would repeat the procedure on the next surface.

The m-dimensional surface represented by f can be approximately represented by a continuous piecewise linear function $F: R^m \to R^n$. Also, F can be made to differ from f as little as desired. Our task is to construct F. At present we can suggest a procedure for doing this that is feasible only for small m. It is presented chiefly to clarify the challenges encountered, not as a practical method.

Our procedure will make F into a continuously invertible function. Then if we make the domain of F a cubical region, we can use its orthogonal coordinate system to establish spatial relationships on the data surface. Unfortunately, a cubical domain is computationally inefficient compared to a simplicial region. We gain the advantages of both kinds of domains by representing F as a composite of two functions, one with a cubical domain and the other with a simplicial domain. First we discuss the use of the cubical domain.

The most convenient domain for the function $F: R^m \to R^n$ would be a standard cube defined by the origin ϵ_o and the points $\{\epsilon_i | i = 1, \ldots, m\}$ of the unit orthogonal basis vectors. Let us denote by X the set of points in the standard cube. The standard simplex will be denoted Y and is the set $Y = \left\{ \sum_{i=0}^{m} \lambda_i \epsilon_i \middle| \sum_{i=0}^{m} \lambda_i = 1, \lambda_i \geq 0 \right\}$, which is the convex hull of the set $\{\epsilon_i | i = 0, \ldots, m\}$. Also, let the surface in R^n on which the data lie be denoted Z. Then we can construct $F: X \to Z$ by factoring it through Y. That is, $F = F_2 \circ F_1$ where $F_1: X \to Y$ and $F_2: Y \to Z$. The function F_1 will be a piecewise linear homeomorphism between the standard cube and the standard simplex. An example in two dimensions is shown on Figure 2-5.

Here, F_1 is defined on the two overlapping domains X_1 and X_2 by two functions F_{11} and F_{12}, which are identical on the overlap $X_1 \cap X_2$. That is,

FIGURE 2-5   A Homeomorphism from the Standard Cube to the Standard Simplex. From Danny Miller and Peter Friesen, "The Longitudinal Analysis of Organizations," *Management Science* 28, no. 9, (September 1982: Institute of Management Sciences).

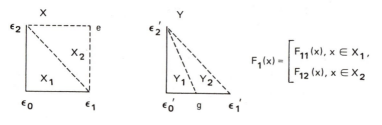

$F_{11}(\epsilon_o) = \epsilon'_o, F_{11}(\epsilon_2) = \epsilon'_2$, and $F_{11}(\epsilon_1) = g$. Then X_1 is mapped onto Y_1 using the fact that $x \epsilon X_1$ implies that x is a convex combination of ϵ_o, ϵ_1, and ϵ_2. Thus we can make $F_{11}(x)$ the same convex combination of ϵ'_o, g, and ϵ'_2. Similarly, F_{12} can be defined on X_2 with $F_{12}(\epsilon_2) = \epsilon'_2, F_{12}(e) = \epsilon'_1, F_{12}(\epsilon_1) = g$.

Although there is always a homeomorphism between X and Y, F_1 may not be the best one, since in higher dimensions its construction becomes complicated. For example, the three-dimensional cube would have to be divided into five tetrahedra. Therefore, it may be that a nonlinear function would be easier to compute. In any event, an algorithm is needed to construct the homeomorphism F_1 for any dimension.

Now we turn our attention to the second of the two functions of which F is composed. The function F_1 is purely a mathematical device. It is the second factor, F_2, that has to incorporate the empirical information. If F_2 is to be piecewise linear and also accurate, the domain Y must be broken up into a number of subdomains, on each of which F_2 will be linear. To make F_2 continuous, its linear pieces that are on adjacent subdomains must be identical where the subdomains overlap.

A systematic way of dividing Y into subdomains is by repeated barycentric subdivision through the barycentric coordinates of the body, faces, and edges of Y. Two repetitions of this procedure when Y is two-dimensional are shown in Figure 2-6 and Figure 2-7, respectively.

The first task in constructing F_2 is to define one of its linear segments. We can choose a subsimplex of Y near the center on which to construct the first linear piece of F_2. Let the corner points of this subsimplex be denoted $y_0, y_1, \ldots, y_m$. Then we may select an arbitrary point z_0 on the data surface Z, by taking the average of the data points in a sphere to ensure that z_0 is in the surface. Principal components analysis of the data in a sphere around

FIGURE 2-6 First Barycentric Subdivision.

From Miller and Friesen, "The Longitudinal Analysis."

FIGURE 2-7 Second Barycentric Subdivision.

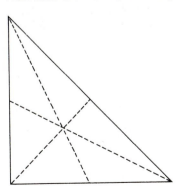

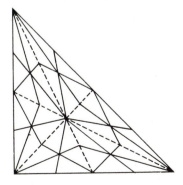

z_0 will find the tangent space of Z at z_0. The analysis will generate a basis, $\{d_i(z_0)|i = 1, \ldots, m\}$, for the tangent space. The basis allows us to specify a simplex around z_0 in the tangent space using the points $\bar{z}_0, \bar{z}_i, i = 1, \ldots, m$ where $\bar{z}_0 = -\dfrac{1}{4} \displaystyle\sum_{j=1}^{m} d_j(z_0)$ and $\bar{z}_i = d_i(z_0) - \dfrac{1}{4} \displaystyle\sum_{j=1}^{m} d_j(z_0)$ for $i = 1, \ldots, m$.

These points in the tangent space can be moved onto the manifold Z by taking the average of the data points in a sphere around each of $\bar{z}_0, \bar{z}_i, i = 1, \ldots, m$. These average points on the manifold will be denoted $z_0', z_i', i = 1, \ldots, m$. Finally, the first linear piece of F_2 can be specified on the simplex generated by the corner points $y_0, y_1, \ldots, y_m$ in the subsimplex of Y. We set $F_2(y_i) = z_i'$ for $i = 0, \ldots, m$. Any point y in the subsimplex can be represented as a convex combination of its supporting simplex, $y = \displaystyle\sum_{i=0}^{m} \lambda_i y_i$ for some $\lambda_i \geq 0$, such that $\displaystyle\sum_{i=0}^{m} \lambda_i = 1$. F_2 is specified in the subsimplex by setting $F_2(y) = \displaystyle\sum_{i=0}^{m} \lambda_i F_2(y_i) = \displaystyle\sum_{i=0}^{m} \lambda_i z_i'$.

Once the first linear piece of F_2 has been constructed, it must be connected to its neighboring linear segments. The procedure for making one such connection is described in the following paragraphs. The procedure can be extended over the whole simplex, one neighboring subsimplex at a time.

There is a simplex adjacent to the one on which F_2 has been constructed. The adjacent simplex has the corner points $y_0', y_1, \ldots, y_m$, which are the same as those of the previous simplex except for one, y_0'. We want to extend F_2 continuously to this simplex. To do this, we select a point $p_0 \in Z$, defined by $p_0 = \dfrac{1}{m} \displaystyle\sum_{i=1}^{m} z_i'$. Next we perform a constrained principal components analysis by finding the principal component vector for the data in a sphere around p_0. The vector is constrained to be orthogonal to the linear variety generated by $z_i', i = 1, \ldots, m$. Let this vector be $d(p_0)$. Then we can construct a reference vector lying outside of the simplex $z_i', i = 0, \ldots, m$ where the reference vector is $p = p_0 + (p_0 - z_0')$. Define a vector on the tangent space at p_0 by $r = p_0 + d(p_0)$ if r is closer to the reference vector p than is $p_0 - d(p_0)$. If not, let $r = p_0 - d(p_0)$. Then define $\bar{r}$ as the average of the data points in a sphere around r so that $\bar{r}$ is in the data manifold. Finally, set $F_2(y_0') = \bar{r}$. F_2 is linearly extended over the whole simplex generated by $y_0', y_i, i = 1, \ldots, m$ in the same way as for the previous simplex. If y is a point in the latter simplex, then $y = \mu_0 y_0' + \displaystyle\sum_{i=1}^{m} \mu_i y_i$ for some $\mu_i \geq 0, i = 0, \ldots, m$ where $\displaystyle\sum_{i=0}^{m} \mu_i = 1$. Thus, $F_2(y) = F_2\Big(\mu_0 y_0' +$

$$\sum_{i=1}^{m} \mu_i y_i \Bigg) = \mu_0 F_2(y_0') + \sum_{i=1}^{m} \mu_i F_2(y_i) = \mu_0 \bar{r} + \sum_{i=1}^{m} \mu_i z_i'.$$ If y is on the re-

gion of overlap between the two simplices, then $\mu_0 = 0$ and $F_2(y) = \sum_{i=1}^{m}$

$\mu_i z_i' = \mu_0 z_0' + \sum_{i=1}^{m} \mu_i z_i'$, which is the same value given to the linear piece in

the previous simplex. Therefore, as we desired, F_2 is continuous on the boundary between the two simplices.

This construction has to be extended over simplices adjacent to ones where F_2 has already been defined until F_2 is extended to all of Y. Once this has been done, F is defined by $F = F_2 \circ F_1$ and contains all the information that is contained in the data about relationships among the variables.

Once the function F has been constructed, we can make better use of the cubical domain by looking for improvements in the component function F_1. We can do this by searching for a coordinate system X' and a homeomorphism F_1' that make a more natural function $F' = F_2 \circ F_1' : X' \to Z$. This function would make the coordinate lines of X' reflect any natural or suggestive directions that may occur in Z. That is, as a point x travels along a coordinate line in X', its image $F(x)$ should travel along a natural direction in Z. Such a procedure may help to disclose nonlinear multivariate relationships describing common structural, strategic, and environmental configurations.

CONCLUSION

Organizational taxonomies are rare, and as yet represent valiant but rather crude attempts at classification. They do not go far enough in isolating predictive configurations or in pursuing the approach of synthesis. We believe, however, that future taxonomies can be improved by incorporating the following recommendations.

First, the types or configurations identified in taxonomies should characterize organizations in as broad and rich a manner as possible. This can be done through larger and wider-ranging selections of variables, the focus on subunits as well as whole organizations, and the use of in-depth studies or anecdotal data to extract insights from the numerical results. It is hard to make specific suggestions concerning the choice of variables. We have urged that dimensions of environment, strategy, managerial process, change, and performance be used in addition to those of structure. The selection of variables might, for example, be guided by the recommendations of McKelvey (1975, 1978) and Pinder and Moore (1979). This should produce more suggestive configurations whose genesis, dynamics, internal interdependencies, and performance implications are better understood.

The characterization of organizations can also be made richer by gathering and comparing data from numerous departments (Pinder and Moore, 1979). This will be especially useful in organizations whose structures, processes, and environments differ substantially from one department to another. A final strategy for obtaining more insights into configurations is to go beyond the numerical output by performing in-depth studies of representative focal organizations, or by using an anecdotal data base composed of detailed organizational histories. These can go a long way in helping to fill out and interpret the quantitative findings.

Our second major recommendation is that multiple methods be used in the attempt to discover the most revealing clustering in the data. Taxonomies must be predictively useful. A few attributes should allow the classification of new organizations, such that many of their remaining features can be accurately predicted on the basis of class membership. Thus, we must find the smallest set of tightly defined groups that have the highest density of members—the highest ratio of class population to class size. To do this, we must try an assortment of similarity criteria and grouping methods, since different patterns in the data require different methods of discovery.

A third suggestion is that greater care should be taken to establish the generality of taxonomies and their stability under different data bases. Taxonomies should be replicable under changes in sample composition. Progress towards this goal can be made by adopting the stratified random sampling methods advocated by McKelvey (1975). It would also be helpful to generate taxonomies using one sample of organizations and then to test their predictiveness upon a different group of organizations. The methods discussed in the section on hypothesis testing can be used to accomplish this.

This chapter has made it apparent that our orientation is somewhat positivistic. We are very concerned with the predictive capacity, replicability, and generality of taxonomies. This is somewhat unusual for researchers who have espoused the "holistic" standpoint that is incorporated in the approach of synthesis. Diesing (1971) has portrayed the holist as believing that "the characteristics of a part are largely determined by the whole to which it belongs and by its particular location in the whole system. . . . The concepts used must be relatively concrete and particularized, close to the real system being described, rather than abstract mathematical concepts . . . [or those] that grow out of a testing instrument" (pp. 138–39). Holists claim that "only the human observer is perceptive enough . . . to draw the proper implications from the complex data coming from human systems" (p. 141). Diesing (1971, p. 140) characterizes the *opposite* standpoint as "a belief in the primary importance of being 'scientific.'"

We are convinced that there needn't be any conflict between the holistic and scientific modalities. In taxonomies, the strengths of both approaches can be brought to bear. By employing quantitative variables, multivariate grouping techniques, and statistical sampling and testing procedures, our powers of pattern recognition are greatly enhanced. It becomes possible to derive replicable, stable, and predictive taxonomies and configurations. But once taxonomies have been derived, they permit a more thorough, intuitive, and subjective exploration of each of the configurations. For example, in-depth studies of representative organizations and anecdotal data bases can afford rich insights into the internal dynamics, formative processes, and performance implications of each of the configurations. Taxonomies, then, should marry the virtues of the holistic and the scientific approaches. Chapters 4 and 5 present taxonomies that were intended to accomplish just that.

Part II

TYPOLOGIES
AND TAXONOMIES
OF ORGANIZATIONS

Having dealt in Part I with the merits of the approach of synthesis, it is appropriate that we now examine its actual results in the form of some typologies and taxonomies of configurations. We use the term *typology* to refer to classification schemes or sets of configurations that have been derived without a formally collected and quantitatively analyzed data base. Typologies are exclusively the products of the concepts and intuitions of theoreticians. Although they are often based on empirical experience, typologies are generated subjectively. They are not replicable in any strict sense. A dozen typologists would probably generate a dozen typologies of the same phenomena.

When we use the term *taxonomy,* on the other hand, we refer to a classification scheme or set of configurations that has been derived from a formal data base using replicable, quantitative techniques. Typically, organizations or organizational phenomena are described by numerical scores across a series of variables. These score patterns are analyzed using multivariate statistical procedures in an attempt to discover significantly common configurations. In theory, any taxonomist starting with the same measurement scales, organizational population, and classificatory methods and standards, would arrive at the same taxonomy, that is, the same characterization of the data surface.

Using preexisting concepts and established habits of pattern recognition, typologists impose order upon the world of organizations. They make distinctions and erect relationships on the basis of many years of experience. Taxonomists, in contrast, are more responsive to their immediate data bases and are constrained by the patterns to be found therein. While typologists are limited only by their imaginations and the richness and maturity of their concepts, taxonomists are also limited by what they find. This is not to say that taxonomies are necessarily more objective or more scientifically useful than typologies. Taxonomies are influenced by many subjective decisions concerning the selection and operationalization of variables, the choice of samples and classificatory criteria, and the selection of statistical procedures. The major difference between taxonomies and typologies is simply that only the former are replicable by other researchers.

The approach we advocate favors both conceptual typologies and empirical taxonomies. Each has its own merits and shortcomings. Typologies tend to be more elegant and neat. The number of ideal types is small, they are made to differ greatly and systematically from one another, and they often display a great deal of harmony in the relationships among the elements within each configuration. In short, typologies are often beautifully constructed. This makes them memorable and easy to understand. They are especially useful as pedagogical tools and as vehicles for representing crucial organizational relationships and themes. But typologies can have shortcomings. First, their strengths and weaknesses are very much those of the typologist—they are exclusively a product of her artistry, knowledge, and conceptual skills. Second, typologies are only a first step in science. Their merits must be established by testing the predictive power of their distinctions and the accuracy of their representations. They require supplementary empirical studies to determine whether or not reality is truly being captured.

Taxonomies avoid some of these problems, or at least they should. Because they are constructed by searching for statistically significant patterning in the data, they go beyond simple impressions. There is an attempt to achieve scientific rigor. Whereas the typologist can always come up with a scheme of one sort or another, taxonomists will often be frustrated by an absence of meaningful or significant clustering in their data. If they have selected the wrong variables or the wrong samples, they may find a daunting degree of obscure variety. In short, taxonomists can always be disciplined by their data, and this weeds out many unpromising categorization schemes and false impressions. All taxonomies should therefore have proved their predictive capacity and generality.

But taxonomies are not free of problems. As we mentioned, they are only as relevant as their variables and samples allow them to be. Also, reality is often messy, so we cannot expect most taxonomies to be as elegant, as parsimonious, as memorable, or as pedagogically appealing as the best typologies. The number of configurations or types is larger, the differences between them are not always very clear, and the connections among the elements or variables within a given type may not be easy to understand.

Part II presents one typology and two taxonomies. Chapter 3, by Henry Mintzberg, describes a typology of five structural configurations derived from a review of the literature on organizational structuring. The five types described are the Simple Structure, the Machine Bureaucracy, the Professional Bureaucracy, the Divisionalized Form, and the Adhocracy. Their most critical parts are described, as are their methods of coordination. In addition, the "design parameters" examined compare the types according to the levels of specialization and formalization of positions, the training of members, the use of liason devices and control systems, and the nature of decentralization. Also treated are "contingency factors" such as age and size, the technical (production) system, the environment, and the locus of power. Mintzberg shows how the five types differ systematically along all these dimensions according to the central themes of each configuration. Configurations are shown to be far more than the simple sum of their parts. Indeed, an adequate understanding of each of the five types comes only when we consider how the dimensions combine and interact. This chapter indicates the pedagogical utility of typologies, as well as the theoretical insights they afford.

Chapter 4 describes an empirically and quantitatively based taxonomy. Ten significantly common configurations or "archetypes" of strategy making in context are presented. A sample of 81 businesses were described along 31 variables of strategy, structure, information processing, and environment. A multivariate statistical procedure was then used to discover common types in samples of successful and unsuccessful firms. The generality and stability of the types were established, and very significant clustering was found. In fact, four failure archetypes and six successful archetypes were discovered that collectively encompassed over 85 percent of the sample. The failure archetypes show how dysfunctional relationships among features of environment, information processing, strategy, and structure led to corporate problems. The successful archetypes reveal the nature of the complementarities among these four classes of variables that seem to account for the major strengths of many organizations.

It will be noted that the configurations of the taxonomy are not as few, as integrally constructed, or as precisely contrasted as those of Chapter 3. They do, however, show a good deal of order among the variables, since a small number of configurations account for a large fraction of the sample. The findings also reveal that relationships among environmental, structural, and strategy-making variables seem to vary as we move from one archetype to another. In other words, although structure in the form of tight and common configurations was discovered in the data, it was not the kind of structure supporting samplewide relationships among variables—the type sought out by proponents of the traditional contingency approach. Therefore, parsimonious taxonomies seemed to be not only possible, but necessary for accurate prediction.

Chapter 5 is in many ways the most complex of Part II. It presents a taxonomy of how organizations change their strategies, structures, and information-processing methods over time. First, 36 organizations were studied by examining histories that had been written about them in the form of detailed books, strings of articles, and press clippings. The lengthy histories were divided into 135 briefer intervals of transition using a specially devised scoring procedure. Twenty-four variables describing changes in strategy making, information processing, structure, environment, and performance were used to characterize each transition. Transition archetypes were then identified using a statistical procedure similar to that of Chapter 4. These were validated upon a new data base of 50 transitions of Canadian firms. Again, predictively useful clustering was found, indicating that nine common transition archetypes collectively encompassed 86 percent of the transitions in the published data, and 54 percent of the Canadian sample. The transition archetypes reveal that organizations very commonly follow certain paths in their evolution. But these paths are very different from one another. Organizations follow diverse evolutionary sequences. As was true for the archetypes of strategy making of Chapter 4, the transition archetypes illustrate that organizational reality is too complex to be captured by samplewide relationships. But there does seem to be sufficient structure in the data to allow methods of taxonomy to isolate configurations that collectively apply to a large fraction of organizations.

3

A Typology
of Organizational
Structure

The "one best way" approach has dominated our thinking about organizational structure since the turn of the century. There is a right way and a wrong way to design an organization. This approach is best captured in Colonel Urwick's famous principle of the 1930s that "no supervisor can supervise directly the work of more than five, or at the most, six subordinates whose work interlocks" (Urwick, 1956: 41). But "one best way" thinking continues to the present day, for example in the activities of consultants who believe that every organization needs MBO, or LRP, or OD.

A variety of failures, however, has made it clear that organizations differ, that long-range planning systems or organizational development programs are good for some but not others. Just as it would be foolish to restrict a foreman to a span of control of six assembly-line workers whose work interlocks, so too is there little sense in forcing formal planning on a firm that must remain highly flexible in an unpredictable market (as many firms discovered during the early days of the energy crisis).

And so recent management theory has moved away from the "one best way" approach, toward an "it all depends" approach, formally known as "contingency theory." Structure should reflect the organization's situa-

This chapter, authored by Henry Mintzberg is drawn from two articles, "Configurations of Organizational Structure," in H. Meltzer and W. R. Nord, *Making Organizations Humane and Productive* (New York: John Wiley, 1981) and "Structure in 5's; A Synthesis of the Research on Organization Design," *Management Science* (1980) 322–41, which themselves are based on *The Structuring of Organizations: A Synthesis of the Research* (Englewood Cliffs, N.J.: Prentice-Hall, Inc., 1979).

tion—for example, its age, size, type of production system, the extent to which its environment is complex and dynamic. To cite some of the more established relationships, larger organizations need more formalized structures—more rules, more planning, tighter job descriptions; so do those in stable environments and those in mass production. Organizations in more complex environments need higher degrees of decentralization; those diversified in many markets need divisionalized instead of functional structures.

This chapter argues that the "it all depends" approach does not go far enough, that structures are rightfully designed on the basis of a third approach, which might be called the "getting it all together" or, as described in Chapter 1, the "configuration" approach. Spans of control, types of formalization and decentralization, planning systems, and matrix structures should not be picked and chosen independently, the way a shopper picks vegetables at the market or a diner a meal at a buffet table. Rather, these and other parameters of organizational design should logically configure into internally consistent groupings. Like most phenomena—atoms, ants, and stars—characteristics of organizations appear to fall into natural clusters, or configurations.

We can, in fact, go a step farther and include in these configurations not only the design parameters but also the so-called contingency factors. In other words, the organization's type of environment, its production system, even its age and its size, can in some sense be "chosen" to achieve consistency with the elements of its structure. The important implication of this conclusion, in sharp contrast to that of contingency theory, is that organizations can select their situations in accordance with their structural designs just as much as they can select their designs in accordance with their situations. Diversified firms may divisionalize, but there is also evidence that divisionalized firms have a propensity to further diversify.[1] Stable environments may encourage the formalization (bureaucratization) of structure, but bureaucracies also have a habit of trying to stabilize their environments. And in contrast, entrepreneurial firms, which operate in dynamic environments, need to maintain flexible structures. But such firms also seek out and try to remain in dynamic environments in which they can outmaneuver the bureaucracies. In other words, no one factor—structural or situational—determines the others; rather, all are often logically formed into tightly knit configurations.

When the enormous amount of research that has been done on organizational structuring is looked at in the light of this conclusion, much of its confusion falls away, and a convergence is evident around five configura-

---

[1]See R. P. Rumelt, *Strategy, Structure and Economic Performance* (Division Research, Graduate School of Business Administration, Harvard University, 1974, pp. 76–77); and L. E. Fouraker and J. M. Stopford, "Organizational Structure and Multinational Strategy," *Administrative Science Quarterly*, 1968: 47–64.

tions, which are distinct in their structural designs, in the situations in which they are found, and even in the periods of history in which they first developed. They are labeled Simple Structure, Machine Bureaucracy, Professional Bureaucracy, Divisionalized Form, and Adhocracy. This chapter describes them and seeks to show their relevance in the design and functioning of organizations.

To understand the five configurations, we must first understand each of the elements that make them up. After reviewing the various elements briefly, we shall show how all of them cluster together to form our five configurations.

THE ELEMENTS OF THE FIVE CONFIGURATIONS

Organizational structure becomes a problem when more than one person must coordinate different tasks to get a single job done. That coordination can be effected in five basic ways:

Direct supervision. One person gives direct orders to others and so coordinates their work, as when an entrepreneur tells different machine operators to make specific parts of an assembly.

Standardization of work processes. One person designs the general work procedures of others to ensure that these are all coordinated, as when a methods engineer specifies how an assembler should bolt a fender onto an automobile.

Standardization of outputs. One person specifies the general outputs of the work of another, as when headquarters tells a division manager to generate sales growth of 10% in a given quarter so that the firm can meet its overall growth goal.

Standardization of skills. A person is trained in a certain way so that he or she coordinates automatically with others, as when a surgeon and an anesthesiologist perform together in the operating room without having to utter a single word.

Mutual adjustment. Two or more people communicate informally among themselves to coordinate their work, as when a team of experts meet together in a space agency to design a new rocket component.

Different parts of the organization play different roles in the accomplishment of work and of these forms of coordination. Our framework introduces five basic parts of the organization, shown in Figure 3-1 and listed below:

The *operating core* is where the basic work of producing the organization's products and services gets done, where the workers assemble automobiles and the surgeons remove appendixes.

The *strategic apex* is the home of top management, where the organization is managed from a general perspective.

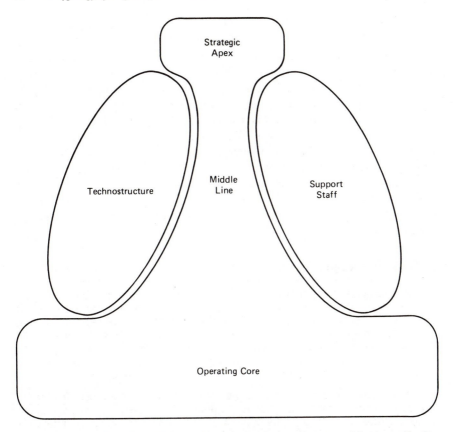

FIGURE 3-1   The Five Basic Parts of the Organization.   From Henry Mintzberg, *The Structuring of Organizations* (Englewood Cliffs, N.J.: Prentice-Hall, Inc., 1979).

The *middle line* comprises all those managers who stand in a direct line relationship between the strategic apex and the operating core; among their other tasks, the managers of the middle line (as well as those of the strategic apex) carry out whatever direct supervision is necessary.

The *technostructure* includes the staff analysts who design the systems by which work processes and outputs are standardized in the organization.

And the *support staff* comprises all those specialists who provide support to the organization outside of its operating workflow—in the typical manufacturing firm, everything from the cafeteria staff and the mailroom to the public relations department and the legal counsel.

The division of the labor of the organization into different tasks and the achievement of the various kinds of coordination among these tasks are accomplished through the use of a set of "design parameters," which are described in Table 3-1.

These parameters include (1) for the design of specific positions: the extent to which their tasks are specialized and their procedures formalized (by job descriptions, rules, and the like), and the extent to which the positions require formal training and indoctrination; (2) for the design of the hierarchy: the bases on which units are grouped (notably by function performed or market served) and the size of each of the units (that is, the span of control of its managers); (3) for the fleshing out of the hierarchy through lateral relationships: the use of action planning and performance control systems and of "liaison devices" such as task forces, integrating managers, and matrix structure; and (4) for the design of the decision-making system: the extent to which power is delegated down the chain of authority (called vertical decentralization) and out from that chain of authority to nonmanagers—operators, analysts, and support staffers (called horizontal decentralization).

TABLE 3-1:   The Design Parameters

Job specialization refers to the number of tasks in a given job and the worker's control over these tasks. A job is *horizontally* specialized to the extent that it encompasses few, narrowly defined tasks, *vertically* specialized to the extent that the worker lacks control of the tasks performed. *Unskilled* jobs are typically highly specialized in both dimensions; skilled or *professional* jobs are typically specialized horizontally but not vertically. "Job enrichment" refers to the enlargement of jobs in both the vertical and horizontal dimensions.

Behavior formalization refers to the standardization of work processes by the imposition of operating instructions, job descriptions, rules, regulations, and the like. Structures that rely on standardization for coordination are generally referred to as *bureaucratic,* those that do not as *organic.*

Training and indoctrination refers to the use of formal instructional programs to establish and standardize in people the requisite skills, knowledge, and norms to do particular jobs in organizations. Training is a key design parameter in all work we call professional. Training and formalization are basically substitutes for achieving the standardization (in effect, the bureaucratization) of behavior. In one, the standards are internalized in formal training as skills or norms; in the other, they are imposed on the job as rules.

Unit grouping refers to the choice of the bases by which positions are grouped together into units, and these units into higher-order units. Grouping encourages coordination by putting different jobs under common supervision, by requiring them to share common resources and achieve common measures of performance, and by facilitating mutual adjustment among them. The various bases for grouping—by work process, product, client, area, etc.—can be reduced to two fundamental ones—by the *function* performed or the *market* served.

Unit size refers to the number of positions (or units) contained in a single unit. The equivalent term *span of control* is not used here because sometimes units

---

continued

TABLE 3-1: Continued

are kept small despite an absence of close supervisory control. For example, when experts coordinate extensively by mutual adjustment, as in an engineering team in a space agency, they will form into small teams. In this case, unit size is small and span of control is low despite a relative absence of direct supervision. In contrast, when work is highly standardized (because of either formalization or training), unit size can be very large because there is little need for direct supervision. One foreman can supervise dozens of assemblers be- • cause they work according to very tight instructions.

Planning and control systems are used to standardize outputs. They may be divided into two types: *action planning* systems, which specify the results of specific actions before they are taken (for example, that holes should be drilled with diameters of three centimeters); and *performance control* systems, which specify the results of whole ranges of actions after the fact (for example, that sales of a division should grow by 10% in a given year).

Liaison devices are a whole set of mechanisms used to encourage mutual adjustment within and between units. They range from *liaison positions* (such as the purchasing engineer who stands between purchasing and engineering), through *task forces* and *standing committees* that bring together members of many departments, and *integrating managers* (such as brand managers), finally to fully developed *matrix structures.*

Vertical decentralization describes the extent to which decision-making power is delegated to managers down the middle line; *horizontal decentralization* describes the extent to which nonmanagers (that is, people in the operating core, technostructure, and support staff) control decision processes. Moreover, decentralization may be *selective*—concerning only specific kinds of decisions—or *parallel*—concerning many kinds of decision altogether. Five types of decentralization may be described: (1) vertical and horizontal centralization, where all power rests at the strategic apex; (2) limited horizontal decentralization (selective), where the strategic apex shares some power with the technostructure that standardizes everybody else's work; (3) limited vertical decentralization (parallel), where managers of market-based units are delegated the power to control most of the decisions concerning their line units; (4) vertical and horizontal decentralization, where most of the power rests in the operating core, at the bottom of the structure; and (5) selective vertical and horizontal decentralization, where the power over different decisions is dispersed widely in the organization, among managers, staff experts, and operators who work in groups at various levels in the hierarchy.

A number of contingency or situational factors influence the choice of these design parameters, and vice versa. These include the age and size of the organization; its technical system of production; various characteristics of its environment, such as stability and complexity; and its power system, for example, whether or not it is tightly controlled from the outside. Some of their influences on the design parameters are summarized in Table 3-2.

TABLE 3-2: The Contingency Factors

Age and Size have both been shown in the research to have important effects on structure. In particular, the older and/or larger an organization, the more formalized its behavior. Moreover, it has been found that the larger the organization, the larger the size of its average unit and the more elaborate its structure; that is, the more specialized its tasks, the more differentiated its units, and the more developed its administrative component of middle line and techno-structure. Finally, Stinchcombe (1965) has shown that the structure of an organization often reflects the age of founding of its industry.

Technical System has been found to affect certain design parameters significantly. For one thing, the more regulating the technical system—in other words, the more it controls the work of the operators—the more formalized is their work and the more bureaucratic is the structure of the operating core. And the more sophisticated the technical system—that is, the more difficult it is to understand—the more elaborate the administrative structure; specifically, the larger and more professional the support staff, the greater the selective decentralization (of technical decisions to that staff), and the greater the use of liaison devices (to coordinate the work of the staff). Finally, Woodward (1965) has shown how the automation of the work of the operating core tends to transform a bureaucratic administrative structure into an organic one.

Environment is another major contingency factor discussed in the literature. Dynamic environments have been identified with organic structures, and complex environments with decentralized ones. However, laboratory evidence suggests that hostile environments might lead organizations to centralize their structures temporarily. And disparities in the environment appear to encourage selective decentralization to differentiated work constellations. Finally, there is a good deal of evidence that diversification of the organization's markets encourages the use of market basis for grouping at high levels, assuming favorable economies of scale.

Power factors have also been shown to have selective effects on structure. Most important, external control of organizations appears to increase formalization and centralization. The need for power of the various members can influence the distribution of decision-making authority, especially in the case of a chief executive whose strong need for power tends to increase centralization. And fashion has been shown to have an influence on structure, sometimes driving organizations to favor inappropriate but fashionable structures.

Note: For references supporting these relationships, see Mintzberg (1979).

CONFIGURING THE ELEMENTS

Up to this point, we have introduced a host of bits and pieces about the structuring of organizations: lots of trees, but still no forests. But a number of forests begin to emerge as we stand back from the specifics and try to perceive the whole picture.

The number 5 appeared frequently in our discussion. There were five coordinating mechanisms, five parts of the organization, and (in Table

3-1) five types of decentralization. In fact, the five configurations bring all of these fives together. Specifically:

> The natural tendency of a *strategic apex* concerned with tight control is to coordinate by *direct supervision;* when that is what the organization needs, *vertical and horizontal centralization* results, and the organization tends to use what we call the *Simple Structure.*
>
> The *technostructure* encourages coordination by *standardization* (especially of *work process,* the tightest form), since it designs the systems of standards; when that is what the organization needs, it accepts *limited horizontal decentralization* to the technostructure, and a configuration called *Machine Bureaucracy* results.
>
> The workers of the *operating core* prefer autonomy above all, which they come closest to achieving when coordination of their work is effected mainly by the *standardization of skills;* organizations that must rely on this form of coordination accept *vertical and horizontal decentralization* to their highly skilled operators and use the *Professional Bureaucracy* configuration.
>
> The managers of the *middle line* try to balkanize the structure, to encourage *limited vertical decentralization* to their level so that their units can operate as semiautonomous entities, controlled from above only by performance control systems based on *standardization of outputs;* when this is what the organization needs, the *Divisionalized Form* results.
>
> And when the *support staff* (and sometimes the operators as well) favor collaboration—the working together in groups whose tasks are coordinated by *mutual adjustment*—and this is what the organization needs, *selective vertical and horizontal decentralization* results, and the structure takes on the form of what we call the *Adhocracy.*

Let us now take a closer look at each of these five structural configurations, whose characteristics are summarized in Table 3-3.

The Simple Structure

As shown in Figure 3-2, the Simple Structure is characterized, above all, by what it is not—elaborated. Typically, it has little or no technostructure, few support staffers, a loose division of labor, minimal differentiation among its units, and a small middle line hierarchy. Little of its behavior is formalized, and it makes minimal use of planning, training, or the liaison devices. It is, above all, organic. Its coordination is effected largely by direct supervision. Specifically, power over all important decisions tends to be centralized in the hands of the chief executive officer. Thus, the strategic apex emerges as the key part of the structure; indeed, the structure often consists of little more than a one-person strategic apex and an organic operating core. Grouping into units—if it exists at all—more often than not is on a loose functional basis. Likewise, decision making is informal, with the centralization of power allowing for rapid response.

TABLE 3-3: Dimensions of the Five Structural Configurations

	SIMPLE STRUCTURE	MACHINE BUREAUCRACY	PROFESSIONAL BUREAUCRACY	DIVISIONALIZED FORM	ADHOCRACY
KEY COORDINAT-ING MECHANISM	DIRECT SUPERVISION	STANDARDIZATION OF WORK	STANDARDIZATION OF SKILLS	STANDARDIZATION OF OUTPUTS	MUTUAL ADJUSTMENT
KEY PART OF OR-GANIZATION	STRATEGIC APEX	TECHNOSTRUCTURE	OPERATING CORE	MIDDLE LINE	SUPPORT STAFF (WITH OPERATING CORE IN OP. AD.)
Design Parameters					
Specialization of Jobs	Little specialization	*Much horizontal and verti-cal specialization*	*Much horizontal specializa-tion*	Some horizontal and verti-cal specialization (be-tween divisions and HQ)	*Much horizontal specializa-tion*
Training and Indoctrination	Little training and indoctri-nation	Little training and indoctri-nation	*Much training and indoctri-nation*	Some training and indoctri-nation (of division man-agers)	Much training
Formalization of Behavior: Bureau-cratic/Organic	Little formalization *Organic*[a]	*Much formalization Bureaucratic*	Little formalization *Bureaucratic*	Much formalization (within divisions) *Bureaucratic*	Little formalization *Organic*
Grouping	Usually functional	*Usually functional*	Functional and market	*Market*	*Functional and market*
Unit Size	Wide	Wide at bottom, narrow elsewhere	Wide at bottom, narrow elsewhere	Wide (at top)	*Narrow throughout*
Planning and Control Systems	Little planning and control	Action planning	Little planning and control	*Much performance control*	Limited action planning (esp. in adm. ad.)
Liaison Devices	Few liaison devices	Few liaison devices	Liaison devices in adminis-tration	Few liaison devices	*Many liaison devices throughout*
Decentralization	*Centralization*	*Limited horizontal decen-tralization*	*Horizontal and vertical de-centralization*	*Limited vertical decentral-ization*	*Selective decentralization*
Contingency Factors					
Age and Size	Typically young and small	Typically old and large	Varies	Typically old and very large	Typically young (Op. Ad.)
Technical System	Simple, not regulating	Regulating but not auto-mated, not very complex	Not regulating or complex	Divisible, otherwise typi-cally like machine bureaucracy	Very complex, often auto-mated (in Adm. Ad.); not regulating or complex (in Op. Ad.)
Environment	Simple and dynamic; sometimes hostile	Simple and stable	Complex and stable	Relatively simple and sta-ble; diversified markets (especially products and services)	Complex and dynamic; sometimes disparate (in Adm. Ad.)
Power	Chief-executive control; often owner-managed; not fashionable	Technocratic and external control; not fashionable	Professional-operator con-trol; fashionable	Middle-line control; fashion-able (especially in indus-try)	Expert control; very fash-ionable

[a] Italic type designates key design parameter.

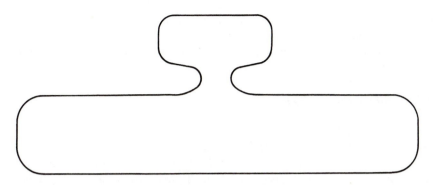

FIGURE 3-2   The Simple Structure. From Mintzberg, *The Structuring of Organizations.*

Above all, the environment of the Simple Structure tends to be at the same time simple and dynamic. A simple environment can be comprehended by a single individual, and so allows decision making to be controlled by that individual. And a dynamic environment requires organic structure. Because the future state of the environment cannot be predicted, the organization cannot effect coordination by standardization. Another condition common to Simple Structure is a technical system that is neither sophisticated nor regulating. A sophisticated system would require an elaborate support structure, to which power over technical decisions would have to be delegated, whereas a regulating one would call for bureaucratization of the operating core. Young organizations and small organizations also tend to use the Simple Structure, because they have not yet had the time, or yet reached the scale of operations, required for bureaucratization. Finally, extreme hostility in their environments forces most organizations to use the Simple Structure, no matter how they are normally organized. To deal with crises, organizations tend to centralize at the top temporarily, and to suspend their standard operating procedures.

The classic case of the Simple Structure is, of course, the entrepreneurial firm. The firm is aggressive and often innovative, continually searching for risky environments where the bureaucracies hesitate to operate. But it is also careful to remain in a market niche that its entrepreneur can fully comprehend. Entrepreneurial firms are usually small, so that they can remain organic and their entrepreneurs can retain tight control. Also, they are often young, in part because the attrition rate among entrepreneurial firms is so high, and in part because those that survive tend to make the transition to bureaucracy as they age. Inside the structure, all revolves around the entrepreneur. Its goals are his or her goals, its strategy his or her vision of its place in the world. Most entrepreneurs loathe bureaucratic procedures as impositions on their flexibility. Their unpredictable maneuvering keeps their structures lean, flexible, organic.

Khandwalla (1977) found this structural form in his research on Canadian companies. Pugh et al. (1969) also allude to this form in what they call "implicitly structured organizations," and Woodward (1965) describes such a structure among the smaller unit production and single-purpose process firms.

The Machine Bureaucracy

A second clear configuration of the design parameters has held up consistently in the research: highly specialized, routine operating tasks, very formalized procedures and large-sized units in the operating core, reliance on the functional basis for grouping tasks throughout the structure, little use made of training and of the liaison devices, relatively centralized power for decision making with some use of action planning systems, and an elaborate administrative structure with a sharp distinction between line and staff. This is the structure Woodward (1965) found in the mass-production firms, Burns and Stalker (1961) in the textile industry, Crozier (1964) in the tobacco monopoly, Lawrence and Lorsch (1967) in the container firm; it is the structure the Aston group (Pugh et al., 1969) referred to as "workflow bureaucracy."

Despite its sharp distinction between line and staff, because the Machine Bureaucracy depends above all on standardization of work processes for coordination, the technostructure, which houses the many analysts who do the standardizing, emerges as the key part of the structure. Consequently, these analysts develop some informal power, with the result that the organization can be described as having limited horizontal decentralization. The analysts gain their power largely at the expense of the operators, whose work they formalize to a high degree, and of the first-line managers, who would otherwise supervise the operators directly. But the emphasis on standardization extends well above the operating core, and with it follows the analysts' influence. Rules and regulations—an obsession with control—permeate the entire structure; formal communication is favored at all levels; decision making tends to follow the formal chain of authority. Only at the strategic apex are the different functional responsibilities brought together; therefore, only at that level can the major decisions be made, hence the centralization of the structure in the vertical dimension.

The Machine Bureaucracy is typically associated with environments that are both simple and stable. The work of complex environments cannot be rationalized into simple operating tasks, and that of dynamic environments cannot be predicted, made repetitive, and so standardized. Thus the Machine Bureaucracy responds to a simple, stable environment, and in turn seeks to ensure that its environment remains both simple and stable. In fact, this helps to explain the large size of the support staff in the Machine Bureaucracy, as shown in Figure 3-3. To ensure stability, the Machine Bureaucracy prefers to make rather than buy—to supply its own support services wherever possible so that it can closely control them. In

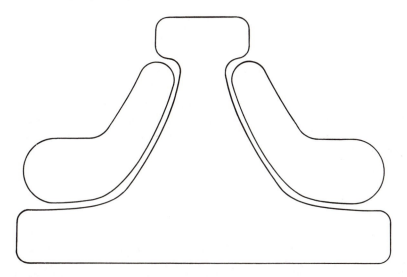

FIGURE 3-3 The Machine Bureaucracy. From Mintzberg, *The Structuring of Organizations.*

addition, the Machine Bureaucracy is typically found in the mature organization, large enough to have the scale of operations that allows for repetition and standardization, and old enough to have been able to settle on the
standards it wishes to use. Machine Bureaucracies also tend to be identified
with regulating technical systems, since these routinize work and so enable
that work to be standardized. But they are not typically found with sophisticated or automated technical systems because, as noted earlier, one disperses power to the support staff and the other calls for organic structure
in administration, thereby driving the organization to a different configuration. Finally, the Machine Bureaucracy is often associated with external
control. The greater the external control of an organization, the more its
structure tends to be centralized and formalized, the two prime design
parameters of the Machine Bureaucracy.

Typical examples of organizations drawn to the Machine Bureaucracy configuration are mass-production firms; service firms with simple,
repetitive work, such as insurance and telephone companies; government
agencies with similar work, such as post offices and tax collection departments; and organizations that have special needs for safety, such as airlines
and fire departments.

The Professional Bureaucracy

Organizations can be bureaucratic without being centralized; that is,
their behavior can be standardized by a coordinating mechanism that allows for decentralization. That coordinating mechanism is the standardization of skills, a reliance on which gives rise to the configuration called

Professional Bureaucracy, found typically in school systems, social-work agencies, accounting firms, and craft manufacturing firms. The organization hires highly trained specialists—called professionals—in its operating core, and then gives them considerable autonomy in their work. In other words, professionals work relatively free not only of the administrative hierarchy but also of their own colleagues. Much of the necessary coordination is achieved by design—by the standard skills that predetermine behavior. And this autonomy in the operating core means that the operating units are typically very large, as shown in Figure 3-4, and that the structure is decentralized in both the vertical and horizontal dimensions. In other words, much of the formal and informal power of the Professional Bureaucracy rests in its operating core, clearly its key part. Not only do the professionals control their own work, but they also tend to maintain collective control of the administrative apparatus of the organization. Managers of the middle line, in order to have power in the Professional Bureaucracy, must be professionals themselves, and must maintain the support of the professional operators. Moreover, they typically share the administrative tasks with the operating professionals. At the administrative level, however, in contrast with the operating level, tasks require a good deal of mutual adjustment, achieved in large part through standing committees, task forces, and other liaison devices.

The technostructure is minimal in this configuration, because the complex work of the operating professionals cannot easily be formalized, nor can its outputs be standardized by action planning and performance control systems. The support staff is, however, highly elaborated, as shown in Figure 3-4, largely to carry out the simpler, more routine work and to back up the high-priced professionals. As a result, the support staff tend to work in a machine-bureaucratic pocket off to one side of the Professional Bureaucracy. For the support staff of these organizations, there is no democracy, only the oligarchy of the professionals. Finally, a curious feature

FIGURE 3-4   The Professional Bureaucracy.   From Mintzberg, *The Structuring of Organizations.*

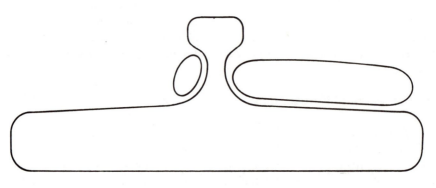

of this configuration is that it uses the functional and market bases for grouping concurrently in its operating core. That is, clients are categorized and served in terms of functional specialties—chemistry students by the chemistry department in the university, cardiac patients by the cardiac department in the hospital.[2]

The Professional Bureaucracy typically appears in conjunction with an environment that is both complex and stable. Complexity demands the use of skills and knowledge that can be learned only in extensive training programs, and stability ensures that these skills settle down to become the standard operating procedures of the organization. Age and size are not important factors in this configuration: The organization tends to use the same standard skills no matter how small or young it is, because its professionals bring these skills with them when they first join the organization. So unlike the Machine Bureaucracy, which must design its own standards, in the Professional Bureaucracy little time and no scale of operations are required to establish standards. The technical system is of importance in this configuration only for what it is not—neither regulating, nor sophisticated, nor automated. Any one of these characteristics would destroy individual operator autonomy in favor of administrative or peer-group influence, and so drive the organization to a different configuration. Finally, fashion is a factor, simply because it has proven to the advantage of all kinds of operator groups to have their work defined as professional; this enables them to demand influence and autonomy in the organization. For this reason, Professional Bureaucracy is a highly fashionable structure today.

The Divisionalized Form

The Divisionalized Form is not so much a complete structure as the superimposition of one structure on others. This structure can be described as market-based, with a central headquarters overseeing a set of divisions, each charged with serving its own markets. In this way there need be little interdependence between the divisions (beyond that which Thompson [1967] refers to as the "pooled" type), and little in the way of close coordination. Each division is thus given a good deal of autonomy. The result is the limited, parallel form of vertical decentralization,[3] with the middle line emerging as the key part of the organization. Moreover,

---

[2]It is interesting to note that in Simon's (1957: 30) criticism in *Administrative Behavior* of the ambiguities in the classical distinction between grouping by process and by purpose, all his examples are drawn from professional work.

[3]"Limited" means that the equating of divisionalization with "decentralization," as is done in so much of the literature, is simply not correct. In fact, as Perrow (1974: 38) points out, the most famous example of divisionalization—that of General Motors in the 1920s—was clearly one of the relative *centralization* of the structure.

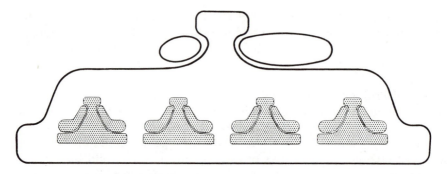

FIGURE 3-5   The Divisionalized Form. From Mintzberg, *The Structuring of Organizations.*

without the need for close coordination, a large number of divisions can report to the one central headquarters. The main concern of that head-quarters then becomes to find a mechanism to coordinate the goals of the divisions with its own, without sacrificing divisional autonomy. And that it does by standardizing the outputs of the divisions—specifically, by relying on performance control systems to impose performance standards on the divisions and then monitor their results. Hence, Figure 3-5 shows a small headquarters technostructure, which is charged with designing and operat-ing the performance control system. Also shown is a small headquarters support staff. Included here are those units that serve all the divisions (such as legal counsel), with other support units dispersed to the divisions to serve their particular needs (such as industrial relations).

Finally, there arises the question of what structure is found in the divisions themselves. Although in principle the Divisionalized Form is sup-posed to work with any kind of structure in the divisions, in fact there is reason to believe, as illustrated in Figure 3-5, that the divisions are driven to use the Machine Bureaucracy. The Divisionalized Form requires the establishment for each division of clearly defined performance standards, the existence of which depend on two major assumptions. First, each divi-sion must be treated as a single integrated system with a single, consistent set of goals. In other words, although the divisions may be loosely coupled with each other, the assumption is that each is tightly coupled within. Second, goals must be operational ones—in other words, lend themselves to quantitative measures of performance control. And these two assump-tions hold only in one configuration, the one that is both bureaucratic (that is, operates in a stable enough environment to be able to establish perfor-mance standards) and integrated; in other words, in Machine Bureaucracy. Moreover, as noted earlier, external control drives organizations toward Machine Bureaucracy. Here the headquarters constitutes external control of the divisions.

One factor above all encourages the use of the Divisionalized Form—

market diversity; specifically, that of products and services. (Diversity only in region or client leads, as Channon [1976] has shown, to an incomplete form of divisionalization, with certain "critical" functions concentrated at headquarters, as in the case of purchasing in a regionally diversified retailing chain.) But by the same token, it has also been found that divisionalization encourages further diversification (Rumelt, 1974: 76–77; Fouraker and Stopford, 1968), headquarters being encouraged to do so by the ease with which it can add divisions and by the pressures from the corps of aggressive general managers trained in the middle lines of such structures. Otherwise, as befits a structure that houses Machine Bureaucracies, the Divisionalized Form shares many of their conditions—an environment that is neither very complex nor very dynamic, and an organization that is typically large and mature. In effect, the Divisionalized Form is the common structural response to an integrated Machine Bureaucracy that has diversified its product or service lines horizontally (that is, in conglomerate fashion).

The Divisionalized Form is very fashionable in industry. It is found in pure or partial form among the vast majority of America's largest corporations, the notable exceptions being those with giant economies of scale in their traditional businesses (Wrigley, 1970; Rumelt, 1974). It is also found outside the sphere of business (in the form of multiverities, conglomerate unions, and government itself), but often in impure form owing to the difficulty of developing relevant performance measures.

The Adhocracy

Sophisticated innovation requires a fifth and very different structural configuration, one that is able to fuse experts drawn from different specialties into smoothly functioning project teams. Adhocracy is such a configuration, consisting of organic structure with little formalization of behavior; extensive horizontal job specialization based on formal training; a tendency to group the professional specialists in functional units for housekeeping purposes but to deploy them in small, market-based teams to do their project work. It relies on the liaison devices to encourage mutual adjustment—the key coordinating mechanism—within and between these teams, and decentralizes power selectively to these teams, which are located at various places in the organization and involve various mixtures of line managers and staff and operating experts. Of all the configurations, Adhocracy shows the least reverence for the classical principles of management. It gives quasi-formal authority to staff personnel, thereby blurring the line–staff distinction, and it relies extensively on matrix structure, combining functional and market bases for grouping concurrently and thereby dispensing with the principle of unity of command.

Adhocracies may be divided into two main types. In the *Operating*

Adhocracy, the innovation is carried out directly on behalf of the clients, as in the case of consulting firms, advertising agencies, and film companies. In effect, there corresponds to every Professional Bureaucracy an Operating Adhocracy that does similar work but with a broader orientation. For every consulting firm that seeks to pigeonhole each client problem into the most relevant standard skill within its given repertoire, there is another that treats that problem as a unique challenge requiring a creative solution. The former, because of its standardization, can allow its professional operators to work on their own; the latter, in order to achieve innovation, must group its professionals in multidisciplinary teams so as to encourage mutual adjustment. In the Operating Adhocracy, the administrative and operating work tend to blend into a single effort. In other words, ad hoc project work does not allow a sharp differentiation of the planning and design of the work from its actual execution.

In the *Administrative Adhocracy*, the project work serves the organization itself, as in the case of chemical firms and space agencies. And here the administrative and operating components are sharply differentiated; in fact, the operating core is typically truncated from the rest of the organization—set up as a separate structure, contracted out, or automated—so that the administrative component is free to function as an Adhocracy.

Figure 3-6 shows both types of Adhocracies, with the blurring of the line–staff distinction in both cases and the truncation of the operating core (indicated by dotted lines), or else, in the case of the Operating Adhocracy, its inclusion in the mass of activities in the administrative center. The figure also shows a partial blurring of the strategic apex with the rest of the structure. This is because in project work, strategy is not imposed from above. Rather, it emerges from the stream of ad hoc decisions made for all the projects. Hence, everyone who is involved in the project work—and in the Adhocracy that can mean everyone in the organization—is involved in strategy making. The key role of the support staff should be underlined here, especially in the Administrative Adhocracy, which houses many of its experts in that staff.

Adhocracy is clearly positioned in environments that are both dynamic and complex. These are the ones that demand sophisticated innovation, the kind of innovation that calls for organic structure with a good deal of decentralization. Disparate forces in the environment, by encouraging selective decentralization to differentiated work constellations, as noted earlier, also encourage use of Adhocracy, notably the administrative kind. Age—or at least youth—is another condition associated with Adhocracy, because time encourages an organization to bureaucratize—for example, by settling on the set of skills it performs best and so converting itself from an Operating Adhocracy into a Professional Bureaucracy. Moreover, because Operating Adhocracies in particular are such vulnerable structures—they can never be sure where their next project will come from—they tend

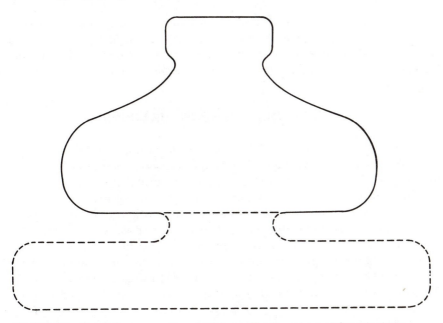

FIGURE 3-6   The Adhocracy.   From Mintzberg, *The Structuring of Organizations.*

to be very young on average. Many of them either die early or else shift to bureaucratic configurations to escape the uncertainty.

Adhocracies of the administrative kind are also associated with technical systems that are sophisticated and automated. Sophistication requires that power over decisions concerning the technical system be given to specialists in the support staff, thereby creating selective decentralization to a work constellation that makes heavy use of the liaison devices. And automation in the operating core transforms a bureaucratic administrative structure into an organic one, because it frees the organization of the need to control operators by technocratic standards. The standards are built right into the machines. In effect, the support staff, being charged with the selection and engineering of the automated equipment, takes over the function of designing the work of the operating core. The result is the Adhocracy configuration.

Finally, fashion is an important factor, because every characteristic of Adhocracy is very much in vogue today—emphasis on expertise, organic and matrix structure, teams and task forces, decentralization without power concentration, sophisticated and automated technical systems, youth, and complex, dynamic environments. In fact, perhaps the best support for Stinchcombe's claim, cited earlier, that structure reflects the age of founding of the industry, comes from the observation that although Adhocracy seems to be used in few industries that were fully developed before World War II, it is found extensively in almost every one that developed since that time. Thus, it is described by Lawrence and Lorsch (1967) in plastics companies, by Chandler and Sayles (1971) in NASA, by Woodward (1965) in modern process production, and by Galbraith (1973) in the Boeing Company. Adhocracy seems clearly to be the structure of *our* age.

BEYOND THE FIVE CONFIGURATIONS

Our five configurations have been referred to in this chapter as ideal or pure types. The question then arises as to where—or whether—they can be found. It is clear that each configuration is a simplification, understating the true complexity of all but the simplest organizational structures. In that sense, every sentence in our description of the configurations has been an overstatement (including this one!). And yet our reading of the research literature suggests that in many cases, the need to favor one of the five coordinating mechanisms introduced earlier draws the organization toward one of the configurations. It is presumably its search for harmony in structure and situation that causes an organization to favor one of the pure types.

Other structures, of course, emerge differently. Some appear to be in transition from one pure type to another, in response to a changed situation. Others exhibit structures that can be described as hybrids of the configurations, perhaps because different forces pull them toward different pure types. The symphony orchestra, for example, seems to use a combination of Simple Structure and Professional Bureaucracy: It hires highly trained musicians and relies largely on their standardized skills to produce its music, yet it also requires a strong, sometimes autocratic, leader to weld them into a tightly coordinated unit. Other hybrids seem to be dysfunctional, as in the case of the organization that no sooner gives its middle managers autonomy subject to performance control, as in the Divisionalized Form, than it takes it away by direct supervision, as in the Simple Structure. School systems, police forces, and the like are often forced to centralize power inappropriately because of the external controls imposed upon them. Would-be Professional Bureaucracies become Machine Bureaucracies, to the regret of operator and client alike.

The point to be emphasized is not that the five configurations represent some final typology, but that together as a set they represent a conceptual framework that can be used to help us comprehend organizational behavior: how structures emerge, how and why they change over time, and why certain pathologies plague organizational design.

4

A Taxonomy

of Strategy Making

in Context

INTRODUCTION

Much has been written about the relationships between strategy and structure, and between structure and environment. The literature has pointed to integral connections among these three categories of variables. Chandler (1962) and Channon (1973) have shown how a strategy of product-market diversification leads to a divisionalized structure; how increased heterogeneity in markets leads to decentralization of decision making and the development of more sophisticated control and coordinative systems. The links between structure and environment are reflected in works by Burns and Stalker (1961), Lawrence and Lorsch (1967), Thompson (1967), Meyer and Associates (1978), and others. A crucial theme of these authors is that there must be a high level of congruence between organization structure and environment. As environments become more uncertain and dynamic, there is a greater need for operating flexibility, for closer interaction and communication among managers, for reliance upon expertise-based rather than position-based power, and for greater variation in the goals and orientations of departments. Performance is said to be greatly influenced by the match between environment, strategy, and structure (see Rumelt, 1974; Miller and Friesen, 1983c; Miles and Snow, 1978; Hambrick, 1982a).

These studies point out two things. First, they show that many variables of strategy, structure, and environment do indeed tend to influence one another, suggesting at least the possibility of their coalescing into common configurations. Second, the literature contains too many works whose authors seem bent upon discovering samplewide linear relationships—those that hold true irrespective of the nature of organizations. As we have already argued, we believe this search is doomed to failure and that the myriad conflicts among researchers bear testimony to this.

We are convinced that relationships among strategy, structure, environment, and performance are too varied and complex to be discovered by traditional research methods. Chapter 1 described how these relationships could differ from one type of organization to another. Indeed, there are probably a number of different paths to success in the same environment, and therefore, substitutability among many elements of strategy and structure. For example, technological innovation may successfully take the place of a niche strategy to cope with a dynamic environment. Thus there is often much latitude for managers to choose their strategies, structures, and even environments (Child, 1972). This becomes particularly apparent when we examine the variety of practices to be found among successful firms operating in the same industry. It seems, therefore, that we must take organizational diversity into account in studying relationships among strategy, structure, and environment.

We tried to do this by developing a taxonomy. This allowed us to search for the most common configurations among our variables, while uncovering important differences among types of firms. Our aim was to discover predictive and stable configurations and to determine whether they had important implications for corporate performance.

METHOD

In Chapter 2, we derived a number of guidelines for the creation of organizational taxonomies. These strongly influenced each of the steps of our methodology.

Scope and Selection of Variables

We criticized previous taxonomies for having too narrow a scope and argued that organizations should be characterized in as detailed and comprehensive a manner as possible. Thus, a broad variety of environmental, structural, and strategy-making variables were selected for study. We employed a rough biological analogy, viewing firms as organisms, which with their structural "anatomies" and strategic "behavioral repertoires" had the task of surviving a specific set of environmental challenges. Performance would ultimately reveal whether the match between anatomy, behavior, and environment was a successful one. We can define some representative components within each of these three categories.

The external environment of a business organization can be described in many ways, but we were most concerned with the challenges that it poses for organizations and the extent to which these have recently waned or intensified. Dynamism, hostility, and heterogeneity were selected as three aspects of external challenge. Dynamism refers to the unpredictability of competitor behavior, customer tastes, and technologies. Hostility encompasses the severity of competition, resource shortages, and economic problems. And heterogeneity is reflected by diversity of markets that requires variation among departments in administrative practices.

To meet these challenges, the firm must evolve a suitable structural and information-processing apparatus. Structure is characterized by dimensions such as the distribution of authority for decision making, the reliance upon staff and technocratic personnel, the differences among departments in their goals and methods, and other variables. The use of management controls and budgets, the practice of environmental scanning, and the intensity of communications across subunits and levels were selected as relevant dimensions of information processing. The literature has suggested the key roles that these dimensions play in adapting to environments and implementing strategies. The reader will already have obtained many insights into their significance from the discussion in Chapter 3.

But structural devices are not the only ones that help firms to cope. The behavioral repertoire manifested by strategies and strategy making are also important. These can take the form of the amount of product-market innovation performed, the degree of risk taking, and whether firms try to lead or follow competitors. They may also constitute the amount of analysis and planning supporting key decisions, or the attention given to developing an explicit and integrated strategy. Ultimately, the success of the adaptive effort must be measured by the firm's performance. This was gauged by growth in profits and sales and return on equity relative to the competition. Our variables are defined in Appendix 4-2.

The Data Base

In Chapter 2, we noted the importance of having recourse to rich anecdotal data to provide insights into configurations—to put flesh on the bones of the numerical results. This caused us to select a rather unorthodox and somewhat biased data base consisting of case studies of 81 companies. Appendix 4-1 describes the data base and the manner in which we derived ordinal numerical scores for our 31 variables. The use of two independent raters to assign scores along the variables ensured that the data were reliable. As a further precaution, a number of firms were approached to verify that the information presented in the cases was accurate. The rich and detailed anecdotal information available for each firm ultimately helped us to identify the central themes and unifying processes of our configurations.

Discovering the Configurations

Appendix 4-1 describes the multivariate and algebraic techniques used to discover and test our configurations. Here we shall present only a brief sketch of our method, mainly to reveal its conformity to the recommendations of Chapter 2.

A sample of 52 firms was split into successful and unsuccessful groups on the basis of performance. Q-type (inverse) factor analysis was used to cluster each group of firms. Factor loadings revealed six clusters in the successful group of firms and four clusters in the unsuccessful group. By plotting the score patterns along the 31 variables that fell into each group, we were able to obtain the score ranges and modal scores for each cluster. These ranges defined regions in a 31-dimensional Cartesian product space in the manner discussed in Appendices 4-1 to 4-5. A new sample of 29 firms was then gathered, and a computer program was used to classify these firms into the ten regions corresponding to each of the clusters. Firms that did not fit into any of the regions were called outliers.

The statistical significance of each of the clusters or regions was established by comparing the proportion of the new sample of firms fitting into the region to the proportion of the Cartesian product space occupied by the region. Where the former proportion was significantly greater than the latter (and it always was by several orders of magnitude), regions were deemed to be significant and given the name *archetypes*. Ten archetypes occupied only one ten-thousandth of the space but encompassed almost 90 percent of the samples of firms (see Appendix 4-5).

A subsequent field study of 52 different firms by Kets de Vries and Miller (1980) established the robustness of the archetypes derived from the published data base. Over 80 percent of the firms in the new sample corresponded to one of the ten archetypes.

The objective of these procedures was to ensure that archetypes were predictively useful, stable, and possessed of generality. That the population density of each region was great was attested to by the comparison of proportions. This implied that many firms could be described by relatively few archetypes. The stability or generality of the taxonomy was established by classifying the new sample of firms, a sample that was *not* used to generate the regions. The case for configuration made in Chapter 1 seems to be vindicated by the taxonomy.

Although the broad selection of variables, the anecdotal data base, and the rigorous hypothesis-testing procedure give our taxonomy a number of advantages over earlier ones, we cannot lay claim to any final or decisive set of configurations. Taxonomies are merely tools for providing us with insights into organizations. Other researchers will wish to characterize organizations differently than we did and to make different distinctions among them. They must search for new taxonomies that are better suited to their purposes.

In the descriptions that follow, the central tendencies of each configuration are discussed. The accounts are based not only on the scores along variables within each type but on the detailed case reports and articles that constituted the data base. Tables 4-1 and 4-2, shown later in this chapter, respectively summarize the features of the unsuccessful and successful archetypes.

THE UNSUCCESSFUL ARCHETYPES DESCRIBED

F_1: The Impulsive Firm (13.5% of the Total Sample)

> These firms illustrate what happens when controls and structures are too primitive for the level of expansion and diversification. Tremendous growth has dramatically escalated the environmental challenges and administrative complexity facing firms. But structures and information systems are inadequate, in large part because the firms continue to be dominated by a few top men who are too busy to do anything about mounting problems and who are reluctant to share the management job with others.

This most dramatic failure archetype is also one of the most common. The scenario is simple. A highly centralized firm, dominated by an aggressive leader, has grown rapidly and diversified broadly, often through the acquisition of companies in new industries. At first the strategy is successful. Care is taken in evaluating new prospects, which are normally in closely related industries. Every move is critical at this early stage, and this elicits much scrutiny in approaching new ventures. Also, the firm is still sufficiently simple and the entrepreneur or leader quite knowledgeable about its industries and markets. But things begin to change. The success of the expansion and diversification strategy leads to unwarranted and uncritical confidence in its merits. New acquisition targets are not examined as closely as before, and there is more of a tendency to purchase weaker companies in unrelated industries. These require a good deal of work and investment to make them successful and to integrate them with existing operations. Firms also establish divisions in other countries and introduce new products, the prime goal being rapid growth. Finally, executives eager for expansion move into far more turbulent developing markets, markets for which the firms are not designed. The net effect of these measures is to make the environment very challenging and complex. New markets and industries are often much more dynamic and competitive than the old ones, and they collectively encompass much more heterogeneity in consumer tastes, production technologies, and competitive behavior.

By taking these bold risks, the companies have in many ways badly *overextended* themselves. The powerful leaders have singlehandedly evolved a rather complex patchwork of new companies, markets, and products that are quite difficult to control and monitor given the meager administrative framework. Because growth has occurred rapidly and, of late, haphazardly, mistakes are made and resources become depleted by misguided ventures. Also, there is not enough managerial talent to administer the expanded enterprise. Bold expansion and reckless major projects have caused the firm to face serious new challenges that it is not prepared to meet.

But why has this condition been reached? The issues of power and control appear to be central. The leader is reluctant to let others have an influence in strategy formation, and he frequently tries to intervene in administrative matters that he simply hasn't the time or ability to pursue. He and a few of his top-level advisors cannot alone control, monitor, or effectively administer the empire they have built. Yet they are reluctant to delegate responsibility and necessary authority to other levels of management. A vicious circle occurs: Top managers do not delegate, therefore they are extremely overworked, thus they cannot make effective decisions about acquisitions and new ventures; as a result, these ventures run into trouble—requiring still more time from the top managers. In spite of the growing problems with failing subsidiaries and disastrous new product ventures, the program to acquire and expand continues unabated, further eroding precious resources and leading to still greater administrative problems.

Other reasons for the difficulties of the F_1 firms are their inappropriate structural and ineffective information systems. We have just mentioned the problems of overcentralization and lack of delegation. These are particularly serious because the highly differentiated nature of departments and divisions often causes them to work at cross-purposes. Their efforts are not integrated by an effective committee structure or by anything else. When departments and divisions run into trouble, their problems are beyond the talents and knowledge of the top levels of management. Also, divisional managers fulfill only an operating role; they generally haven't either the ability or the authority to deal with the problems posed by the increasingly competitive and dynamic environments.

The information-processing system contributes to these difficulties. There are no effective controls to apprise top managers of the problems in the divisions. So expansionary behavior goes on at the top when resources are already being seriously depleted by divisional operating problems. Financial and management information systems are badly needed. Also, even though scanning of the environment does occur, it is of the wrong variety. Scanning is done by head office staff searching for more acquisitions and diversification prospects. But it is rarely performed by the divisions themselves to discover customer wants and competitor innovations, or to guide the development of more relevant strategies. Finally, internal communications are poor. Lower-level managers resent their powerlessness and fear that the poor performance of their divisions will cost them their jobs. They are more interested in concealing than in supplying information to top managers.

A final problem of F_1 firms resides in the nature of their strategy making. Because top executives are overworked and must handle many problems and crises, decisions are made quickly and impulsively: The seat-of-the-pants style of management prevails. There is much risk taking but very little attempt to analyze risks or appraise the strengths and weaknesses of individual projects. Since only few people are involved in policy making, mistaken assumptions tend to go unquestioned, and carelessness goes unchecked. Finally, decisions are often disjointed because they are made so impulsively and because strategies are too vague to guide actions. Little effort is made to plan or to integrate decisions across ventures or over time.

To summarize, the firm has grown very complex and diversified as a result of the aggressive expansionary efforts of its dominant top executives. But growth is reckless and is never properly harnessed, integrated, or consolidated by an adequate administrative, structural, or information-processing apparatus.

A prime example of the F_1 firm was the Automatic Sprinkler Corp. of America (*Fortune*, May 1, 1969). Harry Figgie, Jr., took over a small, ailing fire-equipment company and within five years had converted it into an extremely diversified conglomerate. Between 1963 and 1968, sales had grown from $23 million to $325 million. In both 1964 and 1965, Figgie acquired four firms, most in related industries. In 1966, he bought eleven new firms in unrelated industries. By late 1966, Figgie was paying 20 times earnings for firms that at best had shown lackluster performance and demonstrated few competitive advantages, and at worst were plagued with all sorts of marketing, production, and labor problems.

Figgie had a very small head office, of which he was the dominant figure and prime strategist. Although he had shown great skill as a "turnaround expert," the very rapid pace of expansion allowed him too little time to properly assess and carefully integrate the new acquisitions. Also, Figgie was buying firms in industries that had few complementarities with existing operations and about which he knew very little. The result was that several problem-ridden firms were acquired. The inadequacy of existing control and information systems hid the problems of subsidiaries from the head office, so that corrective measures were slow in coming. As a result, profits, which for the first few years had risen rapidly as a result of the acquisitions, fell even more precipitously as the myriad unanticipated problems came home to roost.

F_2: The Stagnant Bureaucracy (12% of the Sample)

These are highly bureaucratic organizations that have become bound up with past traditions and outdated product lines. A previously placid and simple environment has lulled the firm to sleep. The top management is emotionally committed to the old strategies, and the information systems are too feeble to provide it with evidence of the need to change. The lower-tier managers who are convinced of this need are ignored and alienated.

These firms have become tottering anachronisms. Their managers are bent upon selling products that have long fallen out of favor, or are committed to serving declining markets. Typically, the competition have long since changed their offerings or have gone on to more lucrative endeavors.

A part of the problem might be that markets had remained stable, simple, and uncompetitive for so long. Firms tended to be well positioned in these stable environments, quite often holding on to a very substantial share of the market. There were no real incentives to innovate, since high profits were forthcoming when the firm was simply adhering to a standard and narrow product line and producing this line as efficiently as possible. Operations were accordingly made quite routinized, standard, and formal, the orientation being much like that of the machine bureaucracy discussed in Chapter 3. Because operations were simple and stable, there was no need to delegate decision-making authority. So power in these functionally organized firms is quite centralized. In the absence of the need for change, this structure can be very efficient. Resources are not wasted in the pursuit of superfluous administrative innovations or product novelties.

When the market changes, however, this orientation becomes a very great liability, particularly because it entails an *internal* focus that is exclusively bound up with efficiency. This precludes an awareness of the external conditions that necessitate change. In other words, the bureaucratic orientation, however functional in the short run, may contain within it the seeds of organizational stagnation. Another reason why managers fail to see the need for extensive change is that the firms have done so well with their old ways over long periods. Any environmental changes that the managers do become aware of are written off as fads or anomalies that will quickly pass and allow the firm eventually to succeed once more with its traditional approach. Moreover, the power to change resides in the hands of veteran managers who have vested interests in the old strategy and so are least likely to change it. Change would involve something of an admission of past incompetence.

A very high level of conflict is generated between older, upper-level and younger, lower-level managers in these organizations. It is the younger line managers who are closest to the customers and markets and who are therefore most keenly convinced of the need to change. But because power is centralized, they must obtain approval to initiate any significant innovations. This they almost inevitably fail to get because of the conservative attitudes at the top. As a result, disillusionment sets in, and the firm loses some of its most promising middle managers to more progressive competitors.

The information-processing system of the firm is also deficient, in part because of the mechanistic legacies of the past, and in part because lower levels despair at the attitudes of their superiors. For example, although some scanning of markets is done at lower levels, this information is not acted upon. There is little use in sending the information up the line, and too little authority resides at lower levels to allow significant changes to be made in response to the information. As for organizational controls, they exist to provide upper levels with information on production efficiency. They do not, however, supply data that point to the real problem facing the companies—namely, the lack of an up-to-date product mix. Firms are *already* expert in the efficient manufacture or provision of products or services that won't sell. Finally, internal communications are poorer than in any other archetype. This is due to the divergence in values at the different levels of the firm, and the mechanistic orientation that emphasizes forms, memos, and reports rather than face-to-face contacts or meetings.

As we have already mentioned, strategy making is characterized by extreme conservatism, a strong bias against innovation, and dominance by a number of old-line executives who share their decision-making power with very few others. It is hard to determine whether decisions are made analytically or intuitively, since so few important decisions actually get made. Suffice it to say that established traditions dominate and guide decisions far more than do any contemporary deliberation or discussion. There is a very conscious product-market and production strategy and a great reluctance to deviate from it.

The stagnant bureaucracy is a firm whose top managers fail to allow it to live in the present or adapt to the current exigencies of the marketplace. Traditional strategies are clung to, as are the structural and interpersonal orientations that were appropriate to much simpler and stabler times. Since lower and middle echelons are powerless to help redirect the firm, human disillusionment and corporate demise result.

A good example of a stagnant bureaucracy was Eastern Air Lines during the 1950s (*Fortune*, July 1964). Eastern was run by the autocratic and flamboyant flying ace, Eddie Rickenbacker, from 1935 until 1959. Although Rickenbacker was a rather charismatic person, his financial conservatism was legendary. This did little to damage Eastern in the early years, when the firm had a monopoly on a number of highly profitable routes. But trouble started when the environment, which had been munificent in the extreme, began to get tougher. The CAB opened some of Eastern's routes to other competitors, and the age of the jet was dawning. Eastern, which had held slavishly to the same routes, services, methods, and equipment, was painfully unprepared to meet the challenge. The firm, because of its former monopoly, was not used to competing. Also, his earlier successes made Rickenbacker reluctant to change the old policies. As a result, Eastern continued to provide substandard service, had a lackluster marketing effort, flew the shorter, less profitable routes, and bought airplanes that were quickly becoming obsolete. Rickenbacker's penny-pinching ultimately cost the firm a great deal of money.

A rather similar example of the F_2 bureaucracy was the United Air Lines of the late 1960s, run by George Keck. A cautious loner who thrived on bureaucratic procedures and jealously guarded decision-making power, Keck alienated many of his employees and allowed United to fall behind the times (*Fortune*, March 1972). Tremendous financial losses resulted, in part because of the lethargy and unresponsiveness that had come to pervade the company.

F_3: The Headless Giant (8% of the Sample)

F_3 firms are loosely coupled and diversified fiefdoms of highly independent departments or divisions. There is a grave dearth of leadership, and consequently, no clear strategy emerges to guide the firms or to chart their future. There is a tendency to drift without any sense of direction or mission. The parts of the firm pursue endeavors that are by no means complementary and operate without much regard for one another. No central authority exists to control, monitor, or correct operations that have gone awry.

These firms are more legal entities than true organizations. Their parts are unified by common ownership and control rather than by any concerted goals, operating interdependencies, or collaborative relationships. What is unique about these corporations is their leaderlessness. There is no one to take charge of the extensive and diverse operations. The firms are large, internally differentiated, and often geographically dispersed. They are no longer run by the people who built them or even by those who presided over any important projects or transitional periods. In some sense, these firms are between true leaders, and consequently, they are in a state of limbo in which they drift aimlessly. The focus is exclusively on routine, day-to-day matters, much as it is in the stagnant F_2 firms. Little innovation or change takes place, and the firms muddle through, functioning with blind automaticity.

Most of the administrative activity takes place at the divisional or departmental levels. The managers of this echelon are highly independent—so much so that subunits often operate at cross-purposes without any interference from higher-level administrators. For example, divisions will introduce new products that compete with those of other divisions, duplicating costly developmental expenditures and narrowing the potential breadth of target markets. In cases where firms are structured according to function rather than by industry, there is a great deal of difficulty in getting managers to cooperate with one another. The department heads are about equally powerful, and each may have ambitions of filling the leadership vacuum at the top. This competitive spirit, coupled with the absence of any authority to thwart it, channel it, or arbitrate in disputes, stymies interdepartmental collaboration. As a result, complex projects founder or are avoided. This restricts the firm to intrafunctional changes that are at best minor and inconsequential, and at worst downright disruptive of other departments. The tendency is therefore to muddle through with existing methods, markets, and products. Firms drift, and nothing much changes except the external environment.

Much in line with the description above, the information-processing and coordinative apparatus of such firms is quite underdeveloped. Information in the F_3 archetype is seen as a source of power, as something middle-management careerists can use to make themselves seem superior to their adversaries in other departments. Knowledge is used as a weapon to obtain more resources from the head office or to move up the hierarchy. It is far too rarely used for combatting the external competition. Although some divisions and departments may individually have adequate information systems, the reluctance to share information ensures that companywide information networks are badly neglected. Little information flows to the top, and even when it does reach that level, there is no one with enough inclination or capacity to act upon it. Communications between departments and divisions are particularly rare, there being an absence of any coordinative apparatus that serves anything but a symbolic function.

Because of these internal weaknesses, the firm is unable to adapt to an environment that has become much more competitive, dynamic, and heterogeneous. The fragmented departments of the firm try to deal with problems as they arise. But they haven't the financial, technical, managerial, or knowledge resources individually to make changes of sufficient scope to ameliorate the most pressing conditions.

We have delayed discussing strategy, since no strategy can be identified. All we see are individual decisions being made, but these do not unite into any intelligible or consistent pattern. Some divisions or departments try to expand or innovate, while others consolidate or stagnate. In either case, very little is accomplished, because necessary collaboration is thwarted and resources are not forthcoming. Top managers are merely caretakers, and they hoard resources and veto most significant projects.

Some generalizations can be made, however, concerning the *process* of strategy making: Little innovation takes place in products or services offered; there is almost no effort to adapt to changes in the markets; crises are handled sequentially as they crop up; decisions are made from a subunit rather than a corporate perspective; and it appears that decisions at the divisional level are often driven by political ends. Long-range planning is absent, as is any explicit consideration of product-market strategy. The head-office staff are mainly concerned with financial, legal, and personnel matters and with statutory reporting and government lobbying. They simply do not focus on the analysis or selection of products or markets.

To recap, F_3 firms are for most purposes leaderless. They are a federation of loosely coupled departments or divisions, each of which operates quite independently of the other units or the firm as a whole. This fragmentation and leadership vacuum makes for a rather aimless organization, one in which the focus is upon day-to-day operating matters and the handling of pressing issues. Strategies and long-run plans are ignored as the firm "muddles through."

One of the world's most prominent headless giants was Société Générale de Belgique (*Fortune*, February, 1969). The firm was really a loose conglomeration of widely diversified, financially interlinked companies that operated in the banking, mining, steel, chemical, petroleum, and electrical industries. Société Générale was one of the largest and oldest corporations in the world. It was hopelessly tradition-bound and became too accustomed to operating as a monopoly, both in Europe and in Africa. Because of the financial structure of the firm, it was isolated from stockholder criticism. It also dwarfed its competitors in most areas. But its rigid traditions and awkward structure left it unprepared for the new challenges posed by the declines in some of its industries, the nationalization of some African properties, and the threat of Common Market competition.

Société Générale was run by a head office of 125 people, most of whom were aides to the governor, vice-governor, or the nine directors. Each of the directors was the chairman or president of one or more groups of companies. But every director focused his attention only on his own industry, having an extremely parochial orientation. The head-office staff was far too small to control the vast array of subsidiaries. Only the governor set overall policy. But he hadn't the power to implement it, since he relied upon the directors for contributions to the central treasury and was himself elected by them. As a result, there was no effective coordination or guidance from the top. The member firms went their own ways. It was impossible to take money out of poorly performing sectors to invest in more promising areas, since the powerful directors losing funds would protest. The firm began to suffer as foreign companies moved into growing markets that Société Générale had neglected. It was stuck with a group of enterprises so archaic that the overall rate of return on capital was lower than the yield on government bonds.

Allis-Chalmers Manufacturing Co. also went through a period as a headless giant during the 1960s (*Fortune*, November 1967). It drifted along conservatively, in all directions, as its myriad divisions independently pursued their own, often conflicting, ends.

F_4: The Aftermath (5% of the Sample)

> These firms have been in trouble for quite a long time. They have already suffered severe damage in the form of depletion of resources, loss of markets and reputation, and occasionally, the departure of managerial talent. A new team has taken over and is trying to effect a turnaround and restore corporate health. But scarce resources, the inexperience of the new executives, and an inadequate administrative infrastructure seem to doom efforts at revival.

The histories of these firms vary considerably. They have all gotten themselves into trouble, but in rather different ways. Some have gone through the F_1 stage, in which thoughtless expansion has badly depleted resources and impelled entry into highly threatening or unprofitable markets. Others have passed through the stagnant F_2 phase and have allowed competitors to pass them by. They have spent so long catering to a declining segment of the market that they find themselves left with too few financial, production, or administrative resources to allow an easy recovery. Whatever their history, all F_4 companies are now very weak.

As a result of executive retirements, a corporate takeover, or a revolt among the shareholders, a new team of managers takes control. Top executives are replaced, as are the heads of some departments. Unfortunately, the new team of managers is generally inexperienced, often coming from outside the industry or being propelled to the top of the organization before having had much training. Typically, because a crisis requiring decisive action has been reached, a few of the new executives are placed firmly in charge and given the power to make all key decisions. In other words, power is tightly centralized at the top of the firm, in the hands of one or two newcomers.

Because of the crisis situation, there is a great need to act—in some cases, to consolidate product lines and get out of weak markets; in others, to raise capital, rebuild plant and equipment, or introduce a more up-to-date and competitive line of products and services. But it is very difficult to accomplish these things given the dearth of available resources. Consequently, the only changes that can be made must be inexpensive and piecemeal. For example, part of a production process may be changed, or a single product may be redesigned. A new promotional campaign might be initiated, or an extremely inefficient plant shut down. But unless they are very wisely selected, these stopgap measures accomplish too little to materially affect performance. Many of these actions might have helped had they been implemented five years earlier; but they are either too peripheral or too costly to be effective now.

The problem of a very narrow range of possible remedies is aggravated by the inexperience of the new managers and their failure to listen to some of the old hands who have remained with the company. The veterans are often wrongly held to be responsible for the state of the firm and the current problems. Their advice is therefore not taken seriously, even when it shows a good deal of sagacity about the nature of the industry and customers. Experienced managers are thus lost as a potentially valuable resource. This loss is not insignificant, since the inexperienced group prove unequal to their task, not simply because they lack resources but because they know so little about what it takes to restore effectiveness.

The new managers are impulsive, and because they are faced with a crisis, they jump at making immediate changes without first trying to uncover the roots of their problems or to predict the consequences of their actions. The result is that too many resources are squandered making ineffective peripheral changes, while scant attention is paid to the most crucial weaknesses. For example, one firm went into a completely new and highly risky line of business in order to quickly recoup losses. It forfeited a small fortune in the process and was forced into receivership. Another company introduced a new product that required entirely different marketing procedures. Adherence to the old ways of selling prevented the new offering from becoming profitable.

These examples show two flaws in the strategies pursued in the F_4 archetype. The first is that too many risks are taken in making changes that may not be at all critical to success. The second is the incompleteness of the changes. New elements are *grafted* piecewise onto what is essentially the old strategy, and a rather incongruous and conflicting melange of methods and approaches results. There is no integration of the old and the new, while, of course, resources are insufficient to allow wholesale replacement of the old. Ultimately, a bad situation deteriorates still further.

Although it may be secondary in explaining the F_4 syndrome, it is interesting to look at the administrative climate. Typically, a sharp division is made between new managers and veterans. The first group has all the power; the second, although nominally left in charge of some rather vital functions, has almost none. In other words, power is centralized. Also, the two groups are rather different in orientation: The new people often have backgrounds in finance and accounting; the veterans are experts in production and marketing. The goals, methods, and values of these groups are quite different, so that in a sense, there is a high degree of differentiation in the structure. But the imposed power inequalities, coupled with the lack of effective coordination and integrative devices, allow differentiation to serve as a divisive force rather than as a managerial resource. The new group locks itself away, making decisions without the benefit of advice from those who know best. Moreover, it meddles incessantly in low-level operating matters that it should be leaving to others.

There are also problems with information-processing practices. Scanning of markets is minimal, since executives are in too much of a hurry to act and are not sure of what environmental conditions they should be looking at to begin with. The state of management controls is primitive, and even though efforts are being made to implement more of these, the new controls are ineffective. First, there is resistance to them from old-line managers. But perhaps more important, the controls gather only financial data that tell executives what they already know. What is lacking is the qualitative information that reveals *which* things are going wrong and *why*, the type of information that is most easily conveyed in meetings and face-to-face contacts among members of different departments. But the conflicts and communication barriers created by the distrust and the power imbalance among new and old managers prevent the generation or exchange of this kind of information.

To conclude, F_4 firms start off in poor condition and become even worse off after a few years. The new, inexperienced managers are engaged in a trial-and-error process of trying to influence performance. They have no clear strategy but tinker with assorted innovations, many of which are ineffective, costly, and in conflict with existing elements of strategy. Instead of using some of the managerial resources in the firm, the new group isolates itself, preferring to make decisions on its own. Many F_4 firms simply go bankrupt or are absorbed in mergers.

Examples of the F_4 archetype were Franklin National Bank (*Fortune*, October 1974) and Wheeling Steel (*Fortune*, July 1967). In both instances, poor performance had badly depleted financial and capital resources, so that the turnaround options were quite limited. Also, the new managers who entered to save the day were inexperienced or badly lacking in industry expertise. They tended to alienate other managers within the company and to carry out remedial programs that were incomplete, wide of the mark, or overambitious.

The main features of the unsuccessful archetypes are summarized in Table 4-1.

Bivariate Trends among the Unsuccessful Archetypes

Now that we have discussed the failure archetypes, it might be useful to show how some of the relationships among environmental, organizational, and strategy-making variables were a function of the context in which they occurred.

The literature often suggests a positive correlation between centralization of authority and risk taking (Normann, 1971; Thompson, 1967). The F_1 firm is dominated by a powerful chief executive who, in making bold moves, is unimpeded by more cautious managers. At the opposite end of the spectrum, the F_3 firm has no leader with sufficient power to embark

TABLE 4-1: Summary of Features of Unsuccessful Archetypes

	RELATION TO ENVIRONMENT	STRATEGY	STRUCTURE	INFORMATION PROCESSING	POWER	DECISION MAKING	FUNCTIONAL FOCUS
Impulsive F_1		OVEREXTENSION	TOP-CENTERED, DIFFERENTIATED				
	Select environment via acquisitions	Rapid expansion & growth via acquisition	Divisionalized Centralized Differentiated Not integrated	Very poor controls	All at the top—with the entrepreneur	Impulsive Simplistic Risky Bold Unplanned	None—perhaps most attention to "new ventures" by financial staff
Stagnant F_2		ULTRA-CONSERVATISM	RIGID, BUREAU-CRATIC				
	Ignore environment	Produce yesterday's product efficiently	Functional Centralized Monolithic Mechanistic Formal	No scanning Blocked internal communications Alienation of middle management	All at the top—with aging conservative	Conservative Reactionary Tradition-bound	Production
Headless F_3		MUDDLING THROUGH	LEADERLESS, DIVERSIFIED				
	Different divisions have different relations with environment	Drifting, focus on day-to-day issues	Divisionalized Extremely decentralized Fragmented Political Uncoordinated	Poor communications Lack of control over subunits	Dispersed among middle managers	Fragmented Conflicting Politically motivated	Varies among subunits
Aftermath F_4		GRAFTING & GROPING	MAKESHIFT				
	Adapt to it, in piecemeal, incomplete manner	Attempt turnaround via piecemeal innovations—grafting onto old strategy	Functional Centralized Few resources Differentiated	Schism prevents hierarchical and horizontal communication and collaboration Poor controls	With new top-level managers	Impulsive Trial & error Risky Unplanned	Varies with background of new leaders

upon a decisive course of action. Decisions tend to be incremental because of limited resources, and because bold actions might be vetoed by conservative managers with equal power. The F_4 firm falls somewhere between these extremes, with resource restrictions being a far more salient constraint upon risk than the dispersal of authority. So investigators not making distinctions among archetypes might erroneously conclude that centralization promotes risk taking. (The important roles played by strategies and resource scarcities in influencing risk taking and centralization in some archetypes would presumably be ignored.)

But the positive correlation discovered by investigators whose samples consist mostly of F_1, F_3, and F_4 firms might be questioned by researchers whose sample comprised F_2 and, say, F_3 types. F_2, the stagnant bureaucracy, is dominated by a very powerful leader. But the leader, a bastion of conservatism committed to the old ways, effectively dampens any innovative initiative. In a sample of F_2 and F_3 firms, no relationship—or perhaps a slightly negative one—would surface between centralization and risk taking. The hazards of samplewide analysis are brought home.

Confusion can also arise in examining the relationship between environmental heterogeneity and centralization in firms that perform poorly. F_1 has high heterogeneity and high centralization scores, mainly because powerful executives have boosted diversity through an aggressive growth, diversification, or acquisitions program. In F_4, heterogeneity is much lower and centralization slightly lower. A sample consisting mostly of F_1 and F_4 firms might therefore show a positive relationship between the two variables. But an opposite result would be obtained from a sample composed of F_3 and F_2 firms. In F_3, there is a leadership gap, and competing power factions grow up in the organization. Thus, a decentralized firm faces a heterogeneous environment. In F_2, a centralized firm faces a homogeneous environment. So a negative correlation would occur among the variables. The archetypes illustrate the treacherous nature of simple generalizations and the importance of viewing relationships within their corporate contexts.

Let us now turn to the successful archetypes.

THE SUCCESSFUL ARCHETYPES DESCRIBED

S_{1A}: The Adaptive Firm under Moderate Challenge (13% of the Total Sample)

These simple and undiversified firms are dominated by a powerful chief executive. In dealings with a competitive but stable market, the major weapons are the low prices or convenience of the products and services offered. Most innovations are marginal and incremental, although firms are always slightly ahead of the competition. Decision making is informed by a good knowledge of markets and costs and is characterized by the leader's informally consulting with his subordinates. Structures are organized by function, quite centralized, and in the main undifferentiated but well and informally integrated.

In recent years, S_{1A} firms have encountered increasing levels of challenge in their external environments. Dynamism has been boosted slowly by the greater number of product and service innovations in the industry, and hostility, particularly as manifested by price competition and tougher economic conditions, has also intensified. Indeed, hostility has reached a fairly high level, so that the firm is continually challenged in its interaction with competitors. What is most significant about these environmental trends, however, is that in spite of the changes, the environments have remained relatively placid and predictable, and also quite undiversified. Typically, firms tend to be in very well established industries such as banking, machine-tool manufacturing, and automobile retailing, where the level of product or service innovation is moderate. The main challenges come from service and price competition and business-cycle fluctuations.

The two main strategies of these firms are to keep prices down and to develop attractive products. In making products appealing, the emphasis is not, however, on major design or technological improvements or on radical departures from tradition, but on catering to the wishes of customers. This is done by establishing better product warranties, situating sales outlets in convenient locations, providing good after-sales service, and tailoring products to the needs of specifically defined groups of customers. For example, one bank introduced special financial services for clients in the volatile construction industry, and a car dealer provided excellent service facilities. Because the firms exist in relatively stable settings, product-market innovation is of a gradual and incremental nature. Although, *relative to competitors*, such firms are innovative and given to being the first out with most changes, these are not major departures from established business methods, product lines, or markets. They mainly complement previous orientations.

In S_{1A} firms, the chief executive plays a highly central role, not only because of his formal authority but through his personal influence. First, strategies are created almost entirely by the leader and are often closely tied to his goals and expertise. Firms whose leaders possess marketing backgrounds emphasize advertising and sales promotion, whereas those run by accountants focus on cost control and the maintenance of profit margins. Also, the leader acts as the central coordinator, ensuring through personal intervention that the different subunits operate in harmony. His own directives, more than any formal rules, policies, or committees, unite the efforts of departments to achieve the most salient goals. Clearly, then, the administrative focal point is the leader. Thus, the strengths and weaknesses of the firm closely parallel those of its central actor.

In order to devise more responsive strategies to cope with environmental challenges, rudimentary but effective intelligence systems are employed. The predominant emphasis is upon vigilance through formal cost controls. Because competitive conditions place financial resources at a premium, costs are closely monitored to maintain efficiency and margins. Controls have the added advantage of allowing prices to be trimmed to the most competitive levels. Another practice of S_{1A} firms is to informally scan their environments to discover competitive threats and customer buying habits. This is usually done by top managers and enables them to tailor products to market conditions. However, because the stable environments are easy to monitor, controls play a more crucial role than scanning in the intelligence effort. Firms also benefit from free and open internal communications in which the leader seeks out the opinions of well-informed lower-level managers to help in making strategy. Managers, in turn, frequently approach the leader with their own suggestions and ideas.

The structures of the S_{1A} firms are simple and only moderately bureaucratic. Because the environment is predictable and homogeneous and because product lines are not very broad or differentiated, the organization itself tends to be somewhat monolithic. There is not much need for scientists, engineers, or other technocrats so necessary to the more innovative enterprises. Therefore, goals, methods, and decision-making orientations do not differ a great deal from one department to the next. This keeps down the amount of conflict among subunits. The relative simplicity of operations also makes it quite functional for power to be highly centralized in the hands of the top executive and perhaps a handful of close administrative associates. The simple structure of Chapter 3 is recalled.

In spite of this centralization, well-established policies and clear strategies ensure that line managers receive very few countermanding orders from the leader when making operating decisions. Strategies are formulated consciously and pursued explicitly. They are carefully selected on the basis of the industry parameters within which the firm must operate. However, strategies are not inflexible or tradition-bound and are subject to regular but contained reassessments. Analyses of past practices and broad considerations of their adequacy in the light of evolving market conditions are surprisingly frequent. These often take the form of bull sessions involving several tiers of managers and have the effect of ensuring that strategies are *adaptive*—that is, responsive to external events and trends.

To summarize, S_{1A} firms are simple and centralized. They cope by incrementally adapting their products to changing markets, selling at competitive prices in good locations, and tailoring their offerings explicitly to precisely defined segments of the market. The leader is the main strategist but is careful to track performance, scan the environment, and solicit the opinions of other managers to make sure that strategies remain relevant.

An example of the S_{1A} firm was the Citizens & Southern National Bank of Georgia, headquartered in Atlanta (*Fortune,* November 1969). The bank was run by Mills Lane, Jr., a flamboyant and strong executive who focused on the marketing end of banking. Lane, a major shareholder whose grandfather founded C & S, emphasized extra service at slightly higher prices. His entry into areas such as factoring, real estate loans, corporate accounts, and international business took advantage of the most salient opportunities in the market. It made C & S one of the fastest-growing and most profitable banks in the state. In an often dull but increasingly competitive industry, C & S commonly led its competitors, pioneering the use of bank credit cards and "instant money." Although these customer conveniences were incremental innovations rather than bold departures from tradition, they were very effective.

The bank's structure was highly centralized, with Lane often running the bank as a one-man show. Frequent informal meetings were a principal means of coordination and direction. Lane met with his key officers at 7:00 every other morning, and each Wednesday he conducted his "sunrise service," meeting with all the bank's officers to try to keep them enthusiastic and dedicated. Although strategies were largely a product of Lane's intuitions, they were often analyzed and made explicit to others during the many meetings. The bank had a rather sophisticated accounting system, one of the first to adjust earnings by expected loan and security losses. This provided managers with good performance estimates, allowing problems to be spotted early.

S_{1B}: The Adaptive Firm in a Very Challenging Environment (12% of the Sample)

These are rather complex organizations that exist in competitive and dynamic industries. The emphasis is upon dramatic product innovations that involve complicated and risky projects and pioneering technologies. This requires a sophisticated but flexible organization structure and the recruitment of a diverse group of consultants, managers, and scientists. The emphasis is upon fruitful collaboration that results in the firms becoming leading innovators in very challenging markets.

The S_{1B} firms are bold and aggressive innovators operating in environments that are exceptionally challenging and turbulent. Typically, they are found in industries such as semiconductors, military electronics and aircraft, and artificial fibers and chemicals. Such environments are very dynamic and unpredictable, and the main competitive weapon of firms is their ability to rapidly and effectively produce innovations in product designs as well as production technologies. Indeed, the major preoccupation of the S_{1B} firms is with innovation.

Whereas the S_{1A} firms have settled upon their product lines, market niches, and modus operandi, things are not so ordered and stable for members of the S_{1B} archetype. Outside, the environment is very dynamic, and this condition has been in effect for quite a while. The dynamism is caused by rapid changes in the product lines of the competitors and the shifting needs and desires of customers. It is also caused by the rapidly changing production technologies. Environmental hostility too is a challenge, particularly where firms race to beat each other to the marketplace in introducing wide-ranging innovations, or try to outbid one another on large contracts that involve the design and production of new products.

There are three principal methods used in S_{1B} to cope with this environment: They are reflected by the firm's information-processing behavior, its structure, and its strategy-making processes. Let us look at the last of these factors first. Innovation is pursued with a vigor not found in any of the other archetypes. It is manifested not by small, incremental design changes but by assertive, radical, and dramatic ones. The introduction of nylon and the advent of the first microprocessor computer chips are illustrative of the innovations pursued. Often, products are so distinctive that entirely new production processes must be created and new markets opened up and cultivated. The emphasis is on leading competitors, not following them, and great financial risks are taken in the attempt to accomplish this. Fortunately, resources are plentiful, so that major projects can be funded.

The process of strategy making that gives rise to such innovations is a highly participative one, with different functional areas and levels of the hierarchy collaborating intensively to solve the myriad problems that arise. The emphasis is on *analysis* rather than intuition, as much time is spent on feasibility studies, pilot projects, and the careful planning of each stage of the innovation. It may seem strange that long planning horizons are adopted in turbulent environments, but these are quite necessary, given the complexity of some of the innovations and the time required to commercialize them and bring them to market.

In order to innovate effectively and cope with new environmental challenges, S_{1B} firms have adopted rather special structural and information-processing devices. Structures are of an *organic* nature, similar to those of the adhocracies discussed in Chapter 3. Much power is centered in the hands of the experts who are responsible for research and development. The innovative task and administrative burdens are too complex and weighty for power to be tightly centralized. Although the top executive maintains control over the general policies of the firm, the broad interpretation and execution of the policies are the province of middle-line managers. Delegation of authority for routine operating matters is complete. Aside from decentralization and delegation of authority, another structural feature is the great number of, and heavy reliance upon, technocrats such as scientists, engineers, accountants, and consultants. These people help shoulder the burdens of innovation. Structures tend to be very highly differentiated, in that the methods, time horizons, goals, and procedures are very different among departments. Scientists in the R&D department have very little in common with production supervisors or marketing managers in the way they must carry out their jobs. But collaboration is necessary among all these individuals owing to the broad scope of the innovations being worked upon. Products are often so novel that they impose new production and marketing parameters, and these must be worked out jointly by the different departments. Thus, there is much use of standing cross-functional committees and task forces to facilitate interdepartmental collaboration.

Information-processing systems also tend to be very highly developed in S_{1B} firms. Substantial efforts are devoted to scanning the environment, developing sensitive management controls, and facilitating internal communications across different levels of the hierarchy. The scanning is done formally as well as informally to keep abreast of new technologies and to track customer and competitor behavior. Market and industry surveys are performed, and technocrats are recruited who are intimately familiar with the complex technologies and sciences relevant to the firm. Management controls take the form of cost centers, elaborate cost-accounting systems, sophisticated capital-budgeting procedures, and rigorous program-planning and evaluation procedures. Finally, communications among departments and between the various levels of management are open and frequent. Complex innovation projects involve many false starts, problems, and reversals, and these can be resolved only by quick, free, and generally informal collaboration among different experts and managers. The sophistication and intensiveness of scanning, control, and communication activity cause us, somewhat presumptuously, to liken S_{1B} structures to the human brain and call them *cerebral*.

When Intel Corp. started operations, there was not yet any market for its major product line—semiconductor memory components (*Fortune*, November 1973). Intel pioneered in the development of large-scale integration circuits and microcomputers that could hold thousands of instructions and perform complex tasks. These would revolutionize the computer industry and find a broad range of other applications. In fact, the new products helped Intel's sales grow from almost nothing in 1968 to about $60 million in 1973. Intel was run by two highly accomplished scientists, Robert Noyce and Gordon Moore, who had contributed fundamental breakthroughs leading to the development of integrated circuits. These managers owned 27 percent of the company, had extensive experience in the semiconductor industry, and had substantial backing from the wealthy venture capitalist Arthur Rock. Even though the firm started with an ample sum of capital and an impressive stock of technological expertise, it faced tremendous engineering problems, not only in designing a microminiature memory chip but, perhaps even more significantly, in producing it. Also, many other firms, such as Advanced Memory Systems, Cogar Corp., and Mostek, soon entered the industry to try to beat Intel to the marketplace with the best chip. The race was on.

Intel emerged the champion. By some sophisticated engineering breakthroughs and the use of new materials, their 1103 memory chip became by far the most popular on the market. Intel was able, because of the new materials, to effect production economies that far exceeded those of the competition.

Intel's continued success in a turbulent, dynamic, supercompetitive market stems from a number of factors: its technical and production expertise, its excellent understanding of markets and customers, and its very sophisticated internal controls that ensure efficient operation and top-quality products. The organizational structure is very decentralized—the performance of middle managers is monitored carefully, but they have a great deal of operational freedom. The engineer in charge of a project could buy a $250,000 tester by simply signing for it, provided it was in the budget. There was also a great deal of effort devoted to scanning the environment for threats and opportunities and assuring effective collaboration among departments. The focus continues to be on technological leadership and market acceptance, and the firm remains one of the most successful in the industry.

S_2: The Dominant Firm (7.5% of the Sample)

> Dominant firms, the largest, strongest, and most established firms in their industries, are generally immune from very serious challenges by competitors. They have glowing performance records, key patent rights, and are dominated by a top tier of executives whose power is largely based on their past successes. The consequence is that structures are highly centralized, and that strategies of the past are adhered to rather closely. Since initial strategies involved product innovation, this tradition tends to be continued, ensuring that product lines are usually kept very much up to date.

The dominant firms are not as common as many of our other types. Indeed, they are probably over–represented in our sample because of the extent to which they have been glamorized in the business literature. As their name would suggest, dominant firms exert a good deal of control over their markets. They are far bigger than their competitors and also more experienced, and this has allowed them to enjoy a good deal of success. So has their treasury of long-running patents on key products and processes. Indeed, it is not uncommon for such firms to have high price–earnings multiples for their shares precisely because of their excellent past records. These firms are infused with confidence in their ability to continue to lead their markets. Moreover, whereas the S_{1A} and, to a lesser extent, the S_{1B} firms worked hard to respond to their external environment, S_2 firms act upon and to a degree control and manipulate their environments. They are the big fish that the competitors must worry about.

Although dominant firms tend to be large and powerful, they are not very diversified and operate in fairly homogeneous environments. Some of these firms are in moderately dynamic industries such as computers and office equipment, but the dynamism is created mostly by the firms themselves rather than by the competition. Indeed, the external sources of challenges and complexity are quite mild compared to those existing in other archetypes.

The past successes, great resource strength, and simple environments of the S_2 firms have important repercussions upon their strategies and structures. First, they allow the leaders to play a very dominant role. Their brilliant performance records contribute to their unchallenged authority, making them enshrined heroes. Moreover, an absence of competitive and economic threat makes it possible for the leaders to hoard much of their authority. They are not in a position of having to surrender power to others in order to get help in coping with crises. In fact, although these firms are large, it is not uncommon for the top executives to interfere directly in the handling of some minor operating problems. Indeed, a preoccupation with *hierarchically* derived power often filters down to the lowest levels. The dominance of the leaders is much like that which occurs in the S_{1A} archetype, the major differences being the larger size of the S_2 firms and the greater tendency for their executives to meddle in the most routine matters.

Another repercussion of the favorable history and relative strength of the S_2 firms is their proactive nature and their tendency to *extrapolate* past strategies. Success breeds imitation, and in this case, the firms imitate themselves. This is not to say that they do not innovate to alter their product lines. It simply means that they continue to pursue their previous strategic orientations. In this case, it is one that actually stresses technological and product improvement. S_2 firms may be the first out with new and sometimes quite novel products. But these innovations, unlike those of the S_{1B} firms, are not made in response to competitor or customer demands. They are mainly an expression and affirmation of the credo or corporate philosophy of the top executives. This credo and its resulting strategy are quite explicit. They permeate the company and are continually reinforced by slogans, meetings, and internal literature. In short, the firm is ideologically committed to an established strategy of product innovation.

Innovations are not, however, made blindly. Although they may at times be a bit superfluous and absorb a good deal of the firms' rather sizable reserves of slack resources, product-line changes are in fact quite responsive to the needs of customers. Considerable effort is devoted to the careful design of products so that they incorporate features that thorough market research has shown to be attractive. Also, there is a great deal of emphasis placed on providing customers with quick and reliable after-sales service. Customer loyalty is most ardently pursued. Finally, marketing is very aggressive—much attention is paid to preserving the lion's share of eligible clients.

Turning to the information-processing apparatus, we find that it is somewhat less developed than that of the S_{1B} archetype, particularly when it comes to internal communications. Communications are mainly in a top-down direction because of the emphasis placed upon hierarchy. Also, the actions of competitors are not tracked all that closely, so occasionally, the firms receive some nasty surprises. Finally, despite a myriad of formal controls and sophisticated budgeting procedures, the overriding innovation philosophy allows cost overruns to be quite common. But we must be careful not to paint too negative a picture of information processing in the S_2 archetype. Upward communication may sometimes be impeded, but cross-functional collaboration necessary for the execution of complex innovation tasks tends to be quite good. As for environmental scanning, the firm compensates for its ignorance of competitor behavior with its excellent knowledge of customer needs. Finally, it is not the absence of management controls but rather the grandiosity of some of the ventures that causes cost overruns.

To summarize, the S_2 firms have more of an inward than an outward focus. Their leadership and past history induces them to be more given to doing things their own traditional way than to following the actions of others, and their environments are such that this strategy can be pursued quite successfully.

A classically dominant firm was the Xerox Corp. of the 1960s (*Fortune,* July 1962, November 1965, September 1974). Xerox is famous for the wall of patent protection it has given its copiers, the most sophisticated in the field. The ability of the model 914 copier to quickly produce dry and sharp copies made it the most profitable product ever manufactured in the United States. Sales volume in the copying market was $200 million in 1960, and it grew to $700 million by 1965, with Xerox being the principal beneficiary as well as the instigator of this growth. The firm's machines, which accounted for 38 percent of the market in 1963, accounted for 61 percent in 1965. Xerox's cash flow per share grew from less than 50 cents to over $7.00 in about five years.

The firm was dominated by Joseph Wilson, the chairman and CEO, who took over the leadership from his father in 1946. He devised the ingenious pricing policy by which the copiers were rented out and customers were charged according to the number of copies they produced. That way, Xerox could depreciate its copiers, lowering the tax burden. Each 914 copier, which cost $2,000 to build, brought in more than $4,000 a year, in large part because Xerox sold aggressively to the high-volume sector of the market. The superior product, the strong sales force, and the pricing policy were major factors in the firm's success. Even though other firms, such as Pitney-Bowes, Litton, Olivetti, S. C. M., 3M, and Addressograph-Multigraph, were beginning to enter the market, all their machines could make copies only with special coated paper. This gave Xerox a tremendous advantage of convenience. Thus it had little to fear from competitors.

Xerox's success gave it little incentive to change its strategies. The marketing formula remained intact for many years. But the firm sought continually to make significant improvements to its product lines, introducing faster duplicating machines and smaller desktop copiers. Xerox also began to move gradually into foreign markets, perhaps the fastest growing of all.

Another excellent example of the dominant archetype was the IBM of the mid 1960s, when it undertook to introduce the new 360 series of computers, making obsolete its own product line as well as those of most of the competitors. Under the dynamic and often autocratic leadership of Watson and Learson, the firm incurred grave cost overruns in introducing the 360 line. It jumped too far ahead of the market a bit too quickly. But ultimately, IBM produced an excellent product that was well received and beautifully adapted to the needs of the largest segment of its market.

S_3: The Giant under Fire (5% of the Sample)

Giants are among the most complex and elaborate firms in our sample. They operate in many mature markets, most of which are highly competitive and quite different from one another. These firms are decentralized, so that a good deal of power falls into the hands of the managers of product divisions. Much effort goes into controlling and coordinating divisions through the use of sophisticated information systems, task forces, and coordinative committees. The result is that strategies never change very rapidly or boldly, and much analysis and discussion precedes any innovations. Their caution causes such firms to mostly be followers rather than leaders in their industries.

In no other successful archetype must firms face such a dramatically escalated level of challenge in the environment. Nowhere else are the dangers and complexity facing the firms so difficult to deal with. First, S_3 firms are in traditional industries such as packaged foods, automobiles, and chemicals, where the rate of growth is slow and markets are nearly saturated. Second, economic conditions have made the firms increasingly vulnerable to foreign competition and business-cycle fluctuations. Finally, for the first time in years, consumer tastes are shifting in a major way, making it difficult for the firms to avoid implementing major changes in their product lines. In other words, dynamism and hostility have grown. Another important challenge comes from the fairly high levels of heterogeneity in markets. There is substantial geographical dispersion and much product diversification, so that different production and marketing techniques are required in different markets.

In spite of these rather substantial difficulties, these firms seem to be coping reasonably well. They possess a number of advantages that allow them to do this. First, they are large and somewhat diversified. Their size provides them with the resources necessary to take them through periods of adversity, and their diversification allows them to be nurtured by at least some of their markets during such intervals. Another advantage is that the firms are well established and have favorable reputations. This gives them some superiority over most of their adversaries, particularly in the segments of the market where brand loyalty exists. Also, like the S_2 firms, those in S_3 tend to be richer and more diversified than their domestic competitors. They are better able to survive under tough circumstances and, in fact, often take market share away from competitors during the lean years. However, S_3 firms cannot dominate their markets the way their S_2 counterparts can: Their size and resource advantages are limited, and they lack crucial patents.

But these size and resource factors are not the only ones that allow S_3 firms to succeed. Their strategies and particularly their structures seem to help as well. Because markets are diverse, structures are generally decentralized; the firm is divided into semiautonomous divisions whose managers are responsible for many strategic as well as operating decisions. These managers are experts in their particular markets, and they have substantial authority for selecting the product lines and marketing practices of their divisions. The control exercised by the head office is principally of a financial nature. Large-scale capital projects must be approved centrally. Also, the head office closely assesses the profitability of the divisions, changing top-level personnel when necessary. The structures of S_3 firms correspond closely to the divisionalised form discussed in Chapter 3.

Because of the decentralized nature of operations and the high levels of challenge, great stress is placed on the development of effective information-processing systems. But these systems are more formal than those of most other archetypes. Scanning is done through market-research studies and is often performed by departments at the head office and divisional level that have been especially established for this purpose. Management controls take the form of sophisticated and computerized information systems, a regimented capital-budgeting and planning aparatus, and detailed cost-accounting systems. These systems tend to be the province of multiple departments and are the chief means by which the head office exercises control over and coordinates the efforts of the divisions. Finally, there is an elaborate system of communications—but the emphasis is upon cross-functional rather than interdivisional or hierarchical communication. These communications tend to be highly formalized through the use of specialized standing committees that meet regularly to discuss specific problems or projects. There are also frequent meetings between head-office and divisional personnel, mostly for the purposes of assessing major projects or reviewing performance. In order to maintain this elaborate system, many technocrats such as financial experts, information-systems designers, cost accountants, and management consultants are needed. In essence then, in the S_3 archetype, the information-processing network serves not only to inform managers of external conditions, but to integrate, coordinate, and control the efforts of the many diverse subunits. Indeed, to a large degree, the formal information-processing network of the S_3 firms plays an integrative role similar to that of the leader in the S_{1A} firms.

The strategy and strategy-making modes are rather consistent with the elaborate structure. As we noted earlier, it was the initial strategy of product-market diversification that necessitated the divisionalized structure to begin with. Once the structure is set up, however, it seems itself to begin to influence strategy and strategy making. Because of the division of the firm into semiautonomous parts, and because there is centralized financial control, no one individual has enough power to singlehandedly determine strategy. Risky and dramatic moves are thwarted by a system of checks and balances and the elaborate committee structure that plays a role in major decisions. The firm tends to be as bold as its most conservative committee. Thus, adherence is in large part to traditional product-market strategies; changes are generally of an *incremental* nature. For example, moves to diversify are always tentative and usually take the form of small alterations to existing lines of products or limited geographical expansion rather than the introduction of radically new lines. Strategies become institutionalized by years of tradition and by the many written policies and guidelines that attest to their very explicit and conscious nature. This conservatism is reinforced by hostile environments that can mete out severe punishments for impulsive and risky ventures and therefore demand that resources be used sparingly.

Decision making is characterized by reason and thoroughness. Care is taken to analyze projects by subjecting them to the scrutiny of staff experts and the full weight of the committee structure. This is true for decisions at the head office and at the divisional levels. The collective expertise of a great many managers is brought to bear in making major decisions. Although this reduces dangers, it also seems to act as something of a damper on risk taking and proactiveness. There is more conservatism, a greater tendency to let other firms lead the way with innovations. But by the same token, S_3 firms make certain that innovations *are* imitated if and when they should prove to be successful for competitors. In that way, they remain adaptive while letting others take the greatest risks.

To summarize, S_3 firms are large, complex, and decentralized. They deal in a diverse and competitive environment and require a very sophisticated structural and information-processing apparatus to allow them to cope. Strategies tend to be cautious and are made analytically, often with the participation of many executives. Incremental and imitative rather than dramatic and innovative moves are most common.

The I.T.T. of the early and mid 1970s (*Fortune*, September 1972) is quite reminiscent of the S_3 firm (this was *after* it reduced its rate of corporate acquisitions). I.T.T. dealt in a complex and uncertain environment, having to cope with intense competition in some of its industries. A new antitrust ruling severely limited the scope for acquisitions and required I.T.T. to divest a significant fraction of its operations. But I.T.T. was still well diversified, having acquired a large number of subsidiaries in many different types of service and manufacturing industries. The chief executive, Harold Geneen, was internationally known as a manager's manager. By establishing extremely sophisticated management information systems and a highly responsive divisionalized structure, Geneen kept very tight control over operations. His Office of the President consisted of staff financial and industry experts who regularly and intensively appraised the performance and plans of the divisions. The staff carefully scrutinized all major capital-expenditure proposals. I.T.T.'s extensive committees and frequent management meetings served as key coordinative devices. To avoid nasty surprises, the controllers of the divisions, rather than reporting to the head of the division, reported to the corporate controller.

Few of I.T.T.'s divisions made very radical or bold product innovations. But they did keep their lines up to date. The committee structure seemed to foster caution in the divisions, but it also forestalled moribund conservatism. The Office of the President continued to revitalize the firm by selectively making acquisitions in the most promising industries.

Other firms that were representative of the S_3 archetype were the H. J. Heinz Co. of the late 1960s and early 1970s, and the General Motors of the same era. Both firms were divisionalized, placed great emphasis upon information systems and elaborate committee structures, had complex and diversified operations, and pursued conservative and cautious product strategies. They also faced heterogeneous and competitive environments. The firms were moving from an era in which they had been dominant to one in which economic conditions, government constraints, and international competition were beginning to pose serious challenges.

S_4: The Entrepreneurial Conglomerate (7.5% of the Sample)

These firms are in many ways extensions of the rather bold and ingenious men who built and continue to run them. The emphasis is upon rapid growth through the acquisition of other firms, and this generally brings an extremely diverse set of markets. It also requires divisionalized structures and the extensive delegation of operating authority. Elaborate control and information-processing systems are employed to ensure unity of effort.

The sagas recounting the development of these firms make interesting reading. Typically, they begin with a young entrepreneur obsessed with a dream of building a business, and culminate in the description of a great enterprise that has achieved remarkable rates of growth under the direction of the very same man. Certain periods in the histories of Boise Cascade, Gulf & Western, and Textron are illustrative of the genre.

The most interesting aspects of these organizations are their strategies. The dominant emphasis is upon rapid growth in lucrative markets through the acquisition of other firms. Growth rates accelerate, causing the price–earnings multiples of the shares to rise. This enables the growth strategy to continue, as it becomes cheaper to buy firms with lower multiples through the exchange of stock. The strategy is pursued until the firms become extremely large and diversified, and this is their status when they become members of the S_4 archetype.

Here again we have an example of firms acting upon and manipulating rather than (or at least more than) reacting to their environments. The entrepreneur looks for attractive industries to enter and, upon finding them, begins to purchase firms that have already established themselves in these industries. Sometimes there is an effort to find the most successful firms that can be purchased, but often, especially when cash resources are scarce and managerial resources plentiful, the entrepreneur will take over firms that are in trouble. The management of these companies is replaced, usually by bright young professional managers who are then charged with turning the firms around.

Frequently, S_4 firms are highly levered, as entrepreneurs are by no means reluctant to take calculated risks. Because these leaders have a large share of ownership in their firms and have established excellent track records, their power for strategy making goes unchallenged. The charisma of the leaders also contributes to their influence. Thus, no one interferes as the entrepreneur undertakes chancy and large-scale projects. The more entrepreneurial the top executive, the more entrepreneurial the S_4 firm. So personality is a key factor determining the nature of this archetype.

Because these firms have grown complex and diversified, they have had to evolve an elaborate structure, one that is in some respects like that of the S_3 firms. First, the organization is split into divisions specializing in particular industries, with the top divisional manager responsible for the direction of production, marketing, and personnel functions. Second, there is a reliance upon head-office planning groups and interdivisional committees to coordinate operations, allocate funds, and appraise divisional performance. Finally, extensive use is made of financial and M.I.S. consultants and sophisticated information systems to allow the head office to control and monitor its divisions. Close scrutiny is given to the operating results of divisions and to their capital projects, and meetings between head-office and divisional personnel are frequent.

But there are also major differences between the S_4 and S_3 structures. The most important is that S_4 firms are quite centralized, particularly in terms of power for strategy making. The entrepreneur hoards much of this power, sometimes causing conflicts with independent-minded divisional executives. Although there may be an extensive head-office advisory staff of experts in finance, marketing, and venture management, they have very little formal authority, and their influence on the entrepreneur fluctuates with that person's preferences and interests. Also, divisional managers are mostly charged with looking after the normal functioning of their divisions. Large expenditures, attempts at diversification, or new product/service innovations not only must be approved by the entrepreneur; they are generally initiated upon and designed according to his or her instructions.

Another key difference between S_3 and S_4 is in the purpose of the information-processing apparatus. In S_4, there is far more emphasis on scanning the environment to identify attractive new markets, industries, and candidates for acquisition. The goal is not so much to discover what current customers want or what competitors are doing as to find attractive new areas where competition is weak and markets are growing rapidly. The control systems are oriented to giving the entrepreneurs the information they need about the performance of their "portfolio" of divisions. These systems are designed more for head-office than for divisional use. Also, communication systems in S_4 firms are a bit more informal than they are in S_3 firms. The entrepreneurs often initiate divisional visits and meetings spontaneously. Their long personal acquaintances with divisional managers have established a high degree of rapport with these people, who themselves often initiate contacts with the entrepreneurs. The tendency is to meet informally and to organize conferences and temporary task forces, rather than to evolve the formal, sophisticated, and permanent committee structure of the S_3 companies.

Finally, we come to the mode of strategy formulation. We have already mentioned the proactiveness and riskiness of many decisions. What is notable is that these decisions, although they are often initiated and approved by one central actor, are not usually made impulsively. There is a great deal of effort devoted to analyzing projects and potential acquisitions and in planning their integration with the company. A highly trained head-office staff helps the entrepreneur to ensure that major decisions are carefully appraised. Sophisticated techniques of financial and market analysis are carried out, and as much as possible is done to make bold decisions less hazardous.

To recap the essential features of S_4, we have a diversified growth- and acquisitions-oriented business dominated by a venturesome and ambitious entrepreneur. A decentralized structure is used to cope with diversity, even though the entrepreneur holds onto much of the strategy making power. A diligent attempt is made to identify opportunities, monitor the performance of divisions, and provide top-level decision makers with relevant analyses to support their decisions and projects.

The December 1965 and October 1969 issues of *Fortune* tell the story of Boise Cascade, a fairly representative S_4 firm. Between 1957 and 1965, chief executive Bob Hansberger increased sales volume eightfold to make Boise rank among the biggest companies in the forest-products industry. Profit growth was almost as impressive. This was largely achieved by an aggressive series of acquisitions and an energetic internal expansion program. Growth was at times forced and disconnected, but during the mid-1960s, things were going well. Strategic decisions were made by a three-man Office of the President dominated by Hansberger. Any of the three executives could commit Boise to an acquisition. They prided themselves in making major decisions very quickly. A prime function of theirs was seeking out acquisition candidates and ensuring that the acquired firms ran in a smooth and coordinated way.

Hansberger, within ten years, had taken a failing timber firm and converted it into a successful, vertically integrated organization. He started by building a small kraft pulp and paper mill and a corrugated-box plant to use its product. He then acquired a chain of lumberyards. But soon the pace of acquisitions quickened, and the new subsidiaries were in businesses further and further removed from traditional forest products. Thirty-three acquisitions were made in twelve years, as the firm moved from lumber to paper, to packaging, to building materials, and finally to housing. As a result, the debt-to-equity ratio became quite high. A great deal of attention was paid to achieving complementarity between acquisitions and existing operations: One unit often used, salvaged, or marketed the products of another. Also, much sophisticated financial and marketing analysis was done by the head office in assessing acquisitions.

The organization was centralized, in that the president's office made all key corporate decisions. Headquarters had to approve all capital expenditures over $10,000. However, almost every one of the hundreds of small units in the company was established as a profit center. Each manager had a good deal of discretion over the operating decisions of his area, but the very sophisticated computerized management information systems allowed top management to keep close tabs on things and to assess managers by their financial performance. Rigorous budgeting and planning procedures were also used, and there was a good deal of communication between the head office and the eight major divisions as they worked together on major problems. A great deal of effort was devoted to strategic planning, industry studies, and the analysis of competitors. In the 1970s the firm ran into trouble as it became more impulsive, making risky, ill-considered acquisitions in several strange industries. Clearly, some S_4 firms become F_1 firms.

S_5: The Innovator (5% of the Sample)

> These are typically smaller companies whose strategy is to find and occupy a niche of the market that has been left open by competitors. Firms enter interstices of the market where their size and inexperience are not disadvantageous. They typically remain simple and undiversified, ensuring that they continue to dominate their niches through the frequent generation of product innovations.

It is interesting that although the environments of S_{1A} and S_5 firms are somewhat similar, the strategies for coping with them are very different. Instead of closely tracking and adapting to what the competitors are doing or meeting competitors head-on with price cutting and small product or service modifications, S_5 firms have decided to sidestep the competition. Because they are generally smaller and weaker than their competitors, and because they have not established any solid reputation in the markets dominated by competitors, a decision is taken to avoid any direct confrontation with the competition by sticking to a carefully defined peripheral segment of the market.

Two well-known examples of this strategy were pursued early in the history of the Polaroid and Control Data companies. These firms opened up new and unexploited niches of the market. In the first case, this was the instant photography field, which had been neglected by other firms that hadn't the imagination or the technical or innovative resources to enter it. In the second case, it was the very large-scale scientific computing market, which had not yet been developed by the other mainframe manufacturers, for much the same reasons.

Firms appear to succeed not only because they have avoided segments of the market where they would have been at a disadvantage, but also because they have elected to cultivate segments where they have strengths that can be maintained for a long time. These usually take the form of a superior ability to design products and innovate for a small niche of the market. This talent and its focused application to a narrow set of customers make it undesirable for larger and more diversified competitors to compete directly with S_5 firms. The competition thus concentrates on a broader market that is less troublesome to serve.

The S_5 firm is very much under the control of its top executive, often the founder of the firm and an originator of the niche strategy. Thus, power to make strategic decisions is highly centralized, and this degree of centralization is facilitated by the leader's intimate knowledge of the market. Also, since the firm remains quite undiversified, there is no real pressure for divisionalization or administrative decentralization.

However, because of the emphasis placed on product innovation, there is much need to give scientists, engineers, and other technocrats and middle-level managers a good deal of discretion over their work. The experts must be free to pursue their ideas and to work in a climate that fosters creativity. This requires that they have authority and are not encumbered by bureaucratic strictures. These considerations drive structures to incorporate some of the informality, extensive delegation, and open communication characteristic of the S_{1B} archetype, although important differences remain between the two types. For example, S_5 firms are far more centralized and directed from the top. The chief executive is the custodian of the niche strategy and he guards that role very zealously. Others must innovate within the bounds dictated by this strategy and this strategist. In that sense, the firm is *encephalized,* since most of the intelligence and guiding function are situated at the very apex of the structure.

The information-processing functions of the S_5 firms are very different from those of the other successful archetypes. First, they are informal and relatively unsophisticated. In fact, they are deemphasized. Since these firms have avoided the competition, there seems to be no need to monitor their behavior very carefully. Thus, scanning is not an important activity except as performed by the R&D department to identify promising scientific or technological developments. Second, there is not much need for sophisticated formal controls—costs do not have to be carefully monitored, since profit margins are usually high. Also, there are no diverse or differentiated operations whose performance must be measured, since a functional basis for organization prevails. Finally, internal communications take place informally. There are task forces and spontaneous cross-functional and interlevel consultations but not many regularly scheduled committees. The innovations of the S_5 firms require flexible and quick consultation and collaboration, not an elaborate coordinative apparatus.

More than for any other archetype, strategy and decision making are performed intuitively rather than analytically. When the leader likes an idea, it tends to get implemented, without much thought being given to master plans, cost–benefit analyses, or the generation of alternatives.

In some cases, it seems clear that innovation occurs simply for its own sake and because it falls within the image or ideology that the leader has for the firm. Because of this image, the design and R&D departments are the strongest functional areas, and this helps place the balance of power firmly behind innovation. Any cautionary gestures from the more cost-conscious production and marketing departments can thus be easily ignored. Strategy is determined here mainly by ideology and the uneven distribution of power. This allows firms to be extremely innovative, risk-embracing, and proactive, facilitating continued dominance of the niche. But it also allows for too little planning and too narrow a point of view in making key decisions.

To summarize, the S_5 firms are innovative and pursue a niche strategy. They have simple structures and a primitive information-processing system while being highly centralized. Decisions are made on the basis of the intuition and ideology of innovation-oriented leaders.

One of the best examples of an innovator was the Control Data Corp. of the mid 1960s (*Fortune,* April 1966 and February 1968). With a revenue of only 4 percent of that of their largest competitor (IBM), Control Data made a successful assault on the market for very large computers. It was able, through the superb research and development organization run by Seymour Cray, to open up and to corner the special market for scientific computers. This market comprised nonbusiness customers such as government agencies and universities. Control Data succeeded by hitting IBM where it was weakest.

The firm was really run by two men: Willian Norris, one of its founders and the chief executive, and Seymour Cray. Both boldly pursued a product-development strategy that was years ahead of the competition. C.D.C. was highly centralized, with Norris making all the major marketing, production, finance, and acquisition decisions. The research department, independent and geographically removed from headquarters, undertook an extremely ambitious engineering venture in developing the 6600, the most powerful and sophisticated computer in the world. Specialists collaborated intensively to design the radically new product. But they badly underestimated the time it would take to debug the 6600 and had to pay heavy penalties for late delivery. This compounded the already substantial burdens of the development costs. Also, C.D.C. was late in developing software and support services for customers. They were far more adept at understanding and pioneering new technology than in divining the needs of their potential clients. They were better designers than marketers. But ultimately, the power and speed of the 6600 saved the day, and C.D.C. went on to make major inroads into the market.

The main features of the successful archetypes are summarized in Table 4-2.

Bivariate Trends among the Successful Archetypes

The archetypes just described serve collectively as an antidote to the simplistic conclusions that are often projected about the relationships among variables of strategy, structure, and environment. These relationships seem very much a function of the archetypes in question. This theme will be explored more formally and rigorously in Chapters 6 and 7, but it is worth making some illustrations using the successful archetypes we have just described.

Let us take the relationship between environmental dynamism and the sophistication of organizational intelligence and communication systems. The more dynamic the environment, the greater is said to be the

TABLE 4-2: Summary of Features of Successful Archetypes

	RELATION TO ENVIRONMENT	STRATEGY	STRUCTURE	INFORMATION PROCESSING	POWER	DECISION MAKING	FUNCTIONAL FOCUS
Adaptive #1 S_{1A}	Adapt to environment Power on a par with competition	**ADAPTIVE** Low cost/price Incremental change Efficiency	**VIGILANT** Functional Monolithic Coordination by leader	Personal, informal controls	At apex, charismatic leader	Intuitive & analytical Conscious strategy	Production & marketing
Adaptive #2 S_{1B}	Adapt to environment Lead competitors somewhat	**ASSERTIVE** Bold innovations that are hard to imitate New technologies	**ORGANIC-CEREBRAL** Functional Technocratic Differentiated Integrated	Scanning environment Open internal communications Committees for collaboration	Dispersed through the firm	Analytical Planning Risky Bold	R&D, engineering
Dominant S_2	Manipulate the environment Dominate the competition	**EXTRAPOLATING** Up-to-date & appealing products Excellent service "Ideology"	**HIERARCHICAL** Functional Technocratic Hierarchical Committees for innovation	Scanning customers Collaborative framework for innovation	At apex, hero	Based on old strategy and ideology	Marketing New-product development

Giant S_3	Adapt to environment Follow competitors	INCREMENTAL Some incremental innovation & imitation to keep lines current Diversification Some geographical expansion	DECENTRALIZED Divisionalized Differentiated Elaborate & formal committee structure	Elaborate M.I.S., control systems, profit centers, cross-functional & interdivisional committees	At level of divisional managers—shared with top	Analytical Traditional Cautious	Sometimes marketing (since industries mature)
Conglomerate S_4	Select environment by diversification and acquisitions	EXPANSION Purchase firms in attractive industries and manage them	CHARISMATIC Divisionalized Centralized Differentiated Elaborate & informal collaborative mechanisms	Controls and info. systems, scanning for ventures, and informal meetings	At apex, entrepreneur	Analytical & intuitive Bold	Finance, M.I.S.
Niche Innovator S_5	Create new segment of environment	NICHE Niche strategy—innovation within niche	ENCEPHALIZED Functional Centralized	Crude Open communications to facilitate innovation	At apex, founder-expert	Analytical Bold	R&D, engineering

need for open interdepartmental communications, sophisticated scanning and control systems, and elaborate integrative devices. (Authors such as Thompson, 1967; Lawrence & Lorsch, 1967; Burns & Stalker, 1961; Aguilar, 1967; Wilensky, 1967; Galbraith, 1973; and many others have long stressed this theme.) If we were to concentrate on four particular archetypes and had samples composed mainly of their member firms, such a relationship would no doubt be found. Specifically, S_{1B} and S_3 have very dynamic environments and perform a great deal of intelligence activity in order to cope, whereas S_2 and S_{1A} face less demanding environments and do, indeed, place fewer resources into organizational intelligence and information processing. However, archetypes S_4 and S_5 spoil this neat relationship. In S_4, intelligence activity, rather than being determined by dynamism, seems mostly a function of the diversity of the environment and the expansion program being pursued by data-hungry entrepreneurs. The S_5 firm, because it possesses the capacity to devise important product innovations, does very well in a dynamic environment with only a rather modest intelligence effort. Thus it seems that intelligence is not the only way to deal with dynamism—there may be substitutability among the different coping methods. Furthermore, it is debatable whether a keen intelligence effort *causes* firms to enter more dynamic environments because it identifies growing markets and innovations—this seems true in S_4 and perhaps in S_2—or whether the dynamism prompts firms to adopt sophisticated information-gathering and -disseminating methods to reduce uncertainty—this seems to appy in S_{1B} and S_3. The world of organizations appears to be too complex to explain by viewing a few simple relationships across a broad variety of firms.

To further support this point, we can examine the relationship between centralization of decision-making authority and the risk-taking behavior of firms. Most of our types collectively show a positive relationship between these variables: Archetype S_3 is conservative and decentralized, while S_4, S_{1A}, and S_5 are bold and centralized. This is in accord with much of the literature (see Collins & Moore, 1970; Normann, 1971; Miller, 1979). But S_{1B} cannot be subsumed under this relation, since the turbulence and complexity of its environment have prompted both decentralization and bold innovation. There exists the dual need to parcel out authority to innovators and to take risks in major new product-development efforts. S_2 firms are another exception, in that they are centralized owing to the past successes of their leaders. However, because these firms are so dominant, they feel little pressure to change their previous strategies and become ideologically conservative.

Finally, we can look at the relationship between environmental heterogeneity and centralization of authority. The classical literature and most of our archetypes suggest a negative relationship (Chandler, 1962; Channon, 1973; Thompson, 1967). For example, whereas S_3 has decentralized to cope with substantial heterogeneity, S_{1A}, S_2, and S_5 are more centralized, perhaps in part because they face less heterogeneous environments. But archetypes S_{1B} and S_4 again destroy the simplicity of the relationship. In S_4, centralization of power in the hands of an aggressive entrepreneur has allowed him to enter new markets, thereby *increasing* environmental heterogeneity. In this case, centralization has fostered heterogeneity rather than heterogeneity causing decentralization. S_{1B}, on the other hand, has both moderate heterogeneity and moderate centralization scores. Here, perhaps, the environment's dynamism has induced more decentralization, while its challenging nature restrains managers from straying too far afield in their pursuit of markets.

To conclude, the "exceptions" seem to present as many insights into administrative behavior as the general tendencies. Because these exceptions are consistent and predictable within particular types, they can be discovered using methods of taxonomy. They need not and should not be overlooked by an exclusive focus on the broad-brush analyses of entire heterogeneous samples.

CONCLUSION

The ten archetypes show the intricate and multifaceted nature of relationships among organizational environments, structures, and strategies. Each scenario is elaborate, and the interdependencies among the variables reveal complex networks of mutual causality among a large number of elements. The significance of elements is determined by their relationships to a broad context of other elements. What is more, the interdependencies among elements seem to vary from one archetype to another. Those whose business it is to make generalizations about organizations might be disappointed by these findings. It appears that no recipes, rules of thumb, or simply expressed contingencies are adequate to describe or prescribe organizational behavior for a diverse sample of firms. The world is too complex to allow us to combine very different types of firms and yet say anything very useful about what they have or should have in common.

But we think that this cloud has a silver lining. Even though firms may not collectively exhibit the kind of pattern that can be discerned by statistical methods lumping together many types, there is a good deal of harmony and order in what we have found. A rather small number of stories and descriptions seem to pertain to a rather large number of organizations. The same scenarios or patterns among elements keep occurring again and again. It is this type of consistency or order in organizational data that can allow us to predict and prescribe by using methods of numerical taxonomy as a first step in analysis.

In other words, once we find the homogeneous clusters among elements that describe common configurations or archetypes, it becomes possible to study each configuration to try to understand the central forces and multivariate interdependencies that best characterize it. This may help develop insights that can be used to guide managers and theoreticians alike. Some of the very recent work by Chenhall (1983), Hambrick (1983b), Hambrick and Schecter (1983), Galbraith and Schendel (1982) and Gartner (1982) strongly bear out these conclusions.

5

A Taxonomy
of Organizational
Transition

INTRODUCTION

Chapter 3 argued that there are several common and integral configurations that typify a large number of organizational structures. Chapter 4 isolated ten very common archetypes of strategy making and their contexts, and again there was much order and patterning in the data. A small number of common types exhausted a large fraction of the sample of firms studied. Given that the number of stable states was so circumscribed, it seemed likely that the transitions that link these states would also be quite limited in variety. Just as there are common structures and strategic orientations, there are likely also to be common evolutionary patterns that characterize the development of organizations. The research described in this chapter tries to discover if this is indeed the case. It embarks upon a quest in search of archetypes of organizational transition.[1]

The literature on organizations provides some support for the idea that there are common transition scenarios that are relevant to a large number of organizations. The work by Chandler (1962), Channon (1973), and Rumelt (1974) shows how organizations go through phases of history in which changes in strategy lead to changes in structure. Typically, as firms diversify their product lines and move into new markets, their ad-

[1]The authors gratefully acknowledge the support of the Social Sciences and Humanities Research Council of Canada for Grants #S76-0379, #410-77-0019, and #410-80-0071. We thank also the Government of Quebec for FCAC Grant #EQ1162.

ministrative tasks become more complex. This forces them to change from a functionally based structure to a divisionalized one, a transition that usually involves many collateral changes in controls, information systems, integrative practices, and so on.

The work done on the organizational life cycle and the product-market life cycle also highlights the orderly nature of organizational evolution (Kimberly & Miles, 1980; Quinn & Cameron 1981). The theme of this literature is that changes that occur in organizations follow a predictable pattern, which can be characterized by developmental stages. The work by Adizes (1979), Greiner (1972), Kimberly (1979), Miles (1980), and Scott (1971) highlights sequential stages of development that occur as a hierarchical progression that is not easily reversed, and that involve a broad range of organizational activities and structures (Quinn & Cameron, 1981, p. 1; Lavoie & Culbert, 1978). A number of typical progressions are said to occur as firms move through stages of birth, growth, maturity, and diversification. We believe that this literature provides important clues concerning how organizations develop and points strongly to the structured nature of that development. Of course, different authors have looked at different variables and sequences. But they almost invariably emphasize a single developmental sequence that is expected to pertain to most organizations.

This goes somewhat against the grain of the approach of taxonomy. We believe that different organizations not only differ in their current stages of development, but may in fact follow rather different developmental sequences (Miller & Friesen, 1983b). These will vary as a function of leadership, strategy, industry, and so on. Some organizations may, for example, spend almost no time in the birth or growth phase. Steel mills and paper manufacturers are typical of these. Other organizations may remain small and simple forever; these are generally in purely competitive industries such as retailing and farming. Finally, instead of there being a progression from a functional to a divisional orientation in response to strategic diversification, we might find the reverse movement as firms consolidate their product-market foci and centralize control (Miller & Friesen, 1983a).

To reflect this diversity, it was necessary that we explore briefer periods of transition rather than entire life cycles. In this way, the periods could be chained together differently to reflect the variety of organizational developmental sequences. The problem was how to find these transition periods, ensure their generality, and establish their predictive importance.

To do this, we initiated a study in which many features of the approach of synthesis that were advocated in Part I are exhibited. First, there is the selection of a broad array of environmental, structural, information-processing and strategy-making variables. Second, care is taken to make distinctions among the different types of transitions in the attempt to derive a parsimonious taxonomy. Third, organizations are studied over time to obtain insights into causal networks and organizational dynamics. And finally, parts of the data base are anecdotal in nature, allowing us to probe more deeply in interpreting the quantitative results that were derived.

METHOD

The Concept of Transitions and the Selection of Variables

In Part I, reasons were given for expecting regularities in the adaptive behavior of organizations. The historical accounts that compose part of our sample seem to show that these regularities are brought about by imbalances and incongruities among environmental, organizational, and strategy-making variables. For example, a strategy of diversification or acquisition may lead to great administrative burdens that promote decentralization, formal controls and profit centers, more planning, and more delegation of authority. Increasing environmental hostility or dynamism may prompt product or market innovation, which in turn might require more analysis and scanning activity, more technocratization, and freer internal communications. In other words, it seems that an initial key event or decision causes an imbalance that either requires or facilitates a series of subsequent environmental, organizational, or strategy-making changes. After these adjustments have been made, the stress or predilection toward change is reduced until the next major unsettling incident. A *transition* is a package of changes that occur between the onset of the imbalance or stress and the time when some equilibrium or tranquil interval is reached. The selection of variables and the heuristic device for isolating transitions in the data base were determined by this view of organizational adjustment.

As we saw earlier, interaction among environmental, structural, information-processing, and strategy-making variables can richly characterize the adaptive process. We have employed essentially the same variables in this study as in Chapter 4. Differences were due to the inability to accurately measure some variables in our longitudinal data base. For example, we could not get very good assessments of team spirit or conflict. Also, variables such as *past* dynamism, *past* hostility, and *past* heterogeneity of the environment were deleted, since these were automatically reflected by the present focus on change. Appendix 4-2 presents the definitions of the 24 variables selected for this study.

Data Bases and Scoring Procedures

Three distinct data bases were used in the research. The unusual nature of the first necessitated the use of the others. Because we decided to focus on organizational adaptation as it takes place over time, and because a broad sample of firms was needed to allow generalizations, it was necessary to perform longitudinal research on many organizations. The only manageable way to do this was to employ detailed published organizational histories in the form of books or lengthy series of cases covering at least twenty years of continuous history. Because of the problems of interpreting, scoring, and analyzing the data from such a sample, it was necessary to employ, in addition, questionnaires that solicited information from executives who played key roles in the corporate histories. Finally, we used questionnaires that gathered similar data on a new and different sample of firms to test the validity, reliability, and generality of the findings ("data base 3").

First we shall deal with the published data base ("data base 1"), since it is the most unusual. Miller and Friesen (1980a) list some sources constituting this data base. In order for studies to be retained in our sample, they had to contain sufficient information for raters to be able to score 90 percent of the scales of the 24 variables. Historical accounts were chosen rather than textbook cases intended to illustrate organizational dysfunction. The scoring proceeded in two steps—the identification of transition periods, and the scoring of the 24 variables at the beginning and end of these periods. Both steps were performed by two independent raters, each of whom was well acquainted with case analysis, had read many organizational histories, and possessed doctoral-level training in management policy and organizational theory. A total of 135 transition periods were selected from the published accounts of 36 firms. Although the average number of transition periods for each firm was between three and four, one firm had a long and eventful history and yielded twelve transition periods, whereas another yielded only one.

The choice and definition of a transition period must always involve a degree of arbitrariness. The principal guide was the researchers' intuitions about what might be interesting about the adaptive process. Organizational adaptation is complex and can be studied from many perspectives. The goal here was to study the more intricate, challenging, and nonroutine type of adaptation—the type that has a consequential influence on the way the variables of structure, strategy making, and environment interact over time. We wished to identify common transitions or "packages" of change, and to discover some details about their nature and genesis. Single variable changes were important only as they interrelated to compose more complex, holistic, and revealing scenarios of adaptation. A transition was measured by the *changes* in the scores for the 24 variables over the transition period.

The problem of how to select the right transition period is not easily solved. If the period is very brief, only small and simple changes are apt to surface, and these are not our topic. In contrast, if the period is very long (and defined by changes along the 24 variables computed by comparing scores at the beginning and end of the period), reversals in the direction of change in many variables are concealed. It is of course hazardous to standardize the length of a period, since rate of change varies. To rescue the situation, a compromise was effected: A heuristic device for conditional scoring was employed by two independent raters.

Raters were told to begin or end a transition period during a tranquil interval just before any of the following critical decisions or events: (1) the replacement of a top executive (president of CEO); (2) the introduction of a new product or market strategy; (3) the decision to build a major new facility or to adopt a significantly different production technology; (4) a major change in distribution, promotion, or pricing strategies and techniques; (5) modification of organizational structure and the distribution of authority; (6) a change in the external environment caused by competitor strategies, technological obsolescence, economic booms or recessions, and so on; (7) acquisitions, mergers, or the addition of new departments; or (8) a change in administrative practices pertaining to such issues as control and information systems, or planning methods. The focus was on major changes; that is, those that would result in a change in any of our variables. Periods were continued for at least four years to allow significantly complex adaptive scenarios to emerge. If this did not result in a change along at least four variables, the period was extended until such a change occurred. Termination would occur before the end of four years if a change that happened during the period was reversed (for example, if increased centralization were about to decrease in the same period). This was done to capture the high and low points. A period could not be terminated at a time when two or more variables were changing, unless offsetting changes were about to occur. That is, periods were to begin and terminate when things were relatively tranquil. No gaps were left between periods; the beginning of one constituted the termination of another. For 86 percent of the cases, the boundaries were agreed upon by the raters. When there was disagreement, the shorter period was used to avoid obscuring offsetting changes. On an average, periods were about six years in duration, the shortest being eighteen months, the longest twenty years. Changes did not usually occur throughout the transition period. They often took place during the first two or three years, after which very little occurred.

The way in which the chronology was segmented into transition periods was designed to allow the most common types of transitions to emerge. The establishment of period boundaries at tranquil intervals helps to segregate unrelated-change scenarios and allows the transition to go to completion. Of course, the heuristic device is not perfect, since a boundary must be erected when offsetting changes are about to occur. Since the transition periods derived using this rule vary in duration, we cannot draw conclusions or make meaningful distinctions about rates of change. This shortcoming was inevitable given the objectives of the research and the constraints they imposed.

The second step in analyzing data base 1 was to assign scores to the firms for each of the 24 variables at the beginning of each transition period. The independent raters, who were never in communication with one another, were given no special instructions except to pay strict attention to the definitions of the variables and to assign scores from 1 to 7 to indicate where the firm stood in relation to others in the rater's experience, higher to much higher (5 to 7), lower to much lower (3 to 1), or median (4). Raters were given from twenty to thirty diverse histories to read to get a suitable basis for comparison. A random half of the periods were rated by both raters independently. The Spearman correlation between raters was excellent, being .874 for a sample of 65 periods spanning 36 organizations. In only 4 percent of the cases did scores differ by more than two points on the seven-point ordinal scale. Missing data represented only about 3.8 percent of the possible scores. After all scoring had been completed, scales of the two raters were averaged if there was disagreement.

The units of analysis for the research were not, however, the static variable scores but the transition scores. A *transition score* is the difference between scores at the start of two temporally adjacent periods. There are 24 of these for each period, barring any missing data. Scores are computed to be arrayed along the seven-point ordinal scale using the formula $V_i = ((v_{i2} - v_{i1})/2) + 4$, where v_{i1} is the score at the beginning of the period for variable i, v_{i2} is the score at the end of the period (that is, the beginning of the next period), and V_i is the transition score. This standardization was effected to make scores correspond to those in a questionnaire data base.

A second data base was used to establish the accuracy of the published data, and the procedures and results of this exercise are given in Appendix 5-1.

Finding the Archetypes

The 24 transition scores defined each period or pattern of transition. We wished to cluster these patterns into homogeneous groups to identify common configurations. For this purpose, an inverse or Q-type factor analysis was performed on a randomly selected half of data base 1. This resulted in nine tight groups of patterns that were used to define bounded regions in the data space according to the procedure already described in Appendix 4-1. The regions themselves are given in Appendix 5-3. The remaining half of data base 1 as well as all of data base 3 (see Appendix 5-5) were then classified into the regions (or as outliers) using a computer program. We calculated the expected proportion of companies falling into each of the nine regions given their size. A Poisson test of proportions showed that most of the regions contained significantly more members than could be expected by chance for both data samples. The statistically significant regions or groups defined *transition archetypes*. These were shown to be densely populated and therefore predictively useful. Archetypes were also stable across different data bases and period definition procedures. A complete discussion of the methods used to identify, define, and test the significance of the transition archetypes is given in Appendix 5-2.

THE ARCHETYPES DESCRIBED

To conserve space, we present in detail only the six transition archetypes that were statistically significant in *both* our samples of data. Briefer descriptions of the remaining three archetypes, which are less densely populated, follow. The descriptions are based on evidence contained in data base 1. These accounts provide a level of detail and richness that goes beyond what is portrayed in the raw-score patterns and allow us to derive more complete descriptions of organizational dynamics than would the discussion of solely numerical output.

Archetype descriptions are presented by discussing the attributes and forces that seem to most strongly convey the prevailing threats, opportunities, organizational context, and managerial approaches. We use terms such as *scanning, analysis, multiplexity,* and *futurity* according to their definitions in Appendix 4-2. In order to make the accounts of the archetypes as interesting and informative as possible, there is some bias toward dramatization. The reader should bear in mind that each transition may represent either an amelioration or a deterioration in a firm's condition. This depends largely on the initial state of the firm and the magnitude of the changes. As a perusal of the regions in Appendix 5-3 will reveal, there is latitude for variation in each archetype.

In order to relate our findings on transitions to the results of Chapter 4, we discuss the static archetypes that seem most likely to be associated with each of the transitions. Since we have no empirical data on this because of the different data bases used in the two studies, this part of our discussion is based entirely upon our intuitions. The features of the most significant archetypes are summarized on Table 5-1 which appears later in the text.

T_2: Entrepreneurial Revitalization (32% of the Sample)

A new chief executive attempts to revive his enterprise by increasing innovation, pursuing new market opportunities, and devising more adaptive strategies. Power gravitates toward the CEO as he studies markets and primes the structural and information processing apparatus to facilitate the revitalization.

The T_2 transition describes the comprehensive and often dramatic movement away from traditions, conservatism, and rigidity and toward adaptiveness, vigilance, innovation, and diversification. The incentives for change may be very great. Sometimes corporate profitability has declined as a result of the firm's failure to keep its product lines and administrative practices up to par. Products may not be suitable to new competitive conditions and customer needs, and so market share begins to dwindle.

Occasionally the incumbent CEOs recognize the need for change; more frequently this realization comes to their successors. At first, these executives arrogate more power to themselves and attempt to get more information about the sources of the difficulties. They set up new or improved control and information systems and encourage internal communications. Different divisions or functional areas are put in closer touch with one another to deal with the problems. Perhaps most important, there is a concerted effort to track the external environment—to discover the new market forces in order to be able to adapt to them.

Although intelligence activity may stem from a recognition of the need to address vague, undefined difficulties, it seems to result in a more focused conception of what the problems really are. It also serves as a forceful impetus to develop a new set of strategies and to change, often drastically, the nature of the firm's business and its structure.

The greatest changes involve the modes of response to the external environment. Companies become more aggressive and innovative in dealing with competitors and more imaginative in meeting the needs of customers. That is, proactiveness and product-market innovation are increased. Moreover, there is less aversion to taking risks. As a consequence, product lines become broader and more diverse and change more frequently. This increases the administrative complexity of the task of running the firm. It is not surprising, then, that we find more delegation of authority to lower levels, more technocratization, and more extensive and highly developed intelligence systems.

The informal intelligence devices established to more clearly define the problem become formalized and institutionalized. For example, spontaneous scanning procedures developed out of individual initiatives are transformed into a more formalized set of information-gathering and - processing programs. Ad hoc committees become standing committees, and executive performance appraisals become routine and systematized. These activities usually call for a higher level of expertise than was hitherto available to the firm, and so the level of technocratization (professional staff as a percentage of total employees) increases.

This increased administrative sophistication and awareness of problems seems to result in a more analytical and multiplex decision-making style. In other words, the pressures for change and the administrative (intelligence and structural) devices established to implement change result in a more considered and thorough approach to making key decisions. If the attitudes and devices that prompt or facilitate the initial changes become firmly established, the organization can become more adaptive and sensitive to market forces for a long time.

It is interesting to contemplate how the T_2 transition may relate to the particular static archetypes that we introduced in Chapter 4. Certainly, it is possible for many types of firms to pass through each kind of transition. But we feel that there exist some natural polarities that may serve as more frequent starting and ending points for each archetype. For example, since T_2 reveals increases in innovation, diversity, centralization, information processing, and analysis, it seems to represent a movement *towards* the S_4 archetype—that is, toward the Entrepreneurial firm. The latter is highly centralized, is in the process of constant expansion, innovation, and diversification, and has rather sophisticated intelligence systems. Companies moving from the F_3 Headless Giant, the S_3 Giant Under Fire, or even the F_4 Aftermath toward the S_4 Entrepreneurial firm might all be undergoing the entrepreneurial revitalization of T_2. Power becomes more consolidated under a leader who desires more innovation and diversification but who, at the same time, wants to avoid costly mistakes. So analytical, integrative, and information-processing activities are enhanced to cope with the risk and complexity of the new projects.

The F_3 Headless Giants seem especially *in need* of entrepreneurial revitalization, since they may be missing precisely what the S_4 firms have the most of: strong leadership, an aggressive and unified product-market strategy, and an information-processing system that effectively controls and integrates the efforts of subunits and divisions. All the conjectures we make about the relationships between static and transition archetypes are summarized on Table 5-2, later in this chapter.

During the 1960s, International Paper underwent a period of revitalization (*Fortune*, March 1969). The firm had been somnolent for many years until a new chief executive was appointed. He began to expand capacity, modernize plant and equipment, move into high-margin consumer products, and beef up the marketing organization. He also started to more systematically exploit I.P.'s vast tracts of timber and to enter the real estate business. Hundreds of millions of dollars were spent on the move into more lucrative fields, to break I.P.'s exclusive reliance on the cyclical, highly competitive paper industry. The substantial borrowing that took place represented another departure from the conservative past.

The diversification strategy required a new structure. Accountability for the profits of various product lines was shifted from the production to the marketing group. The effectiveness of the reorganization was boosted by installing a computer-based standard cost system that helped to determine the optimal product mix for the firm and to assess the performance of the new profit centers. Also, the new CEO, Edward Hinman, was less autocratic but more influential and active than his predecessors. He was at the same time much more responsive to the needs of the divisions and subsidiaries. Clearly, a major revitalization of I.P. was under way.

T_3: Consolidation (6% of the Sample)

The objective is to conserve resources and to stem losses. Unprofitable products are abandoned and market scope is reduced. This is facilitated by improved cost controls and greater attention to budgeting. Conservatism increases and power disperses as entrepreneurs are replaced by teams and committees.

The T_3 scenario is usually triggered by a perceived need to retrench and consolidate. For example, the firm may have diversified too quickly into several unprofitable areas, or resources may have been taxed owing to overexpansion. The decline in profits and the sense that the firm is out of control causes the realization that some sort of change is necessary. For some firms, it is the bankers who become alarmed at the consequences of a rash expansion and acquisition program. For others, shareholders are the instigators of a more conservative policy. Still a third type of organization relies on the natural succession processes to replace an aggressive, entrepreneurial leader with a chief executive who perceives a need for greater conservatism.

Once the entrepreneur is replaced, decision-making power becomes more dispersed throughout the firm. The organization builder is often replaced by a more conservative professional manager or "inside man." Sometimes, more than one executive is needed to replace the entrepreneur, and occasionally, several committees are formed to make decisions that had been the exclusive prerogative of the chief executive.

The new group recognizes the need to slow down and to consolidate operations. Often a period of growth and diversification has left the firm with a number of unprofitable subsidiaries or product lines. Managers are aware that internal controls are needed to identify the weak operations, and these are implemented soon after the new managers arrive. Controls increase the complementarity of decisions, since key actions are placed under the scrutiny of multifunctional committees or other bodies, ensuring that plans and actions of different departments do not conflict. Also, numerous staff experts are recruited. Because the emphasis is on becoming more efficient, operations that are not complementary to the main lines of business or are unproductive may be terminated. The intent is to curtail expansion into new product lines or new markets until corporate health has been restored. Thus, the level of product-market innovation usually decreases considerably. New managers are less proactive. They are still learning the business and are more inclined to follow rather than lead competitors. So it is not surprising that the new group of professional managers takes fewer risks than the entrepreneurs who preceded them. They are consolidators, not builders. Whereas the entrepreneurs had a conscious and relatively explicit corporate strategy, the new team of executives is less sure of what corporate objectives should be and is too busy attempting to stabilize the company to develop a clear new strategy. Because the policies of expansion and diversification give way to a more placid orientation, strategies become less explicit and less conscious. The emphasis is on short-term measures rather than long-term master plans.

Again there appear to be natural associations between the static archetypes and T_3. In particular, the F_1 Impulsive firms seem to be much in need of a phase of consolidation. Many have expanded and diversified too rapidly, and their leaders have hoarded too much power and too many tasks. It has become essential to weed out poor products and unprofitable divisions, to recruit a larger and more influential head-office staff, and to allot more decision-making authority to divisional and functional managers. All of this happens during consolidation. Other appropriate consolidating measures that occur in T_3 and that should benefit Impulsive firms are boosting intelligence activities and attenuating the level of risk taking. The first change ensures greater awareness of problems and inefficiencies in the diversified operations and allows better control over divisions. The second avoids the commitment of substantial resources to ventures that the company can no longer afford.

Occasionally, S_4 Entrepreneurial firms and S_5 Innovative firms might also benefit from a period of consolidation. Both types are so highly centralized that some of their top executives are overloaded with work. Also, the S_4 firms may diversify excessively, while the S_5 firms tend to perform too much product innovation. In both cases, there may be a need to further delegate power, recruit more executive talent, and consolidate product lines and markets. In the S_5 type, there may also be improvements necessary in the intelligence network to provide better data on the environment, and in S_4, a boost in intelligence could be useful in the form of more formal control and information systems to monitor and channel divisional activities.

Although F_1, S_4, and S_5 might have a natural and functional proclivity to consolidate, the process of consolidation itself may lead firms to become more like the S_3 Giant Under Fire, and, in extreme cases, more like the F_3 Headless Giant. This can occur as a result of the dispersion of power and the avoidance of risk or innovation. Strictly speaking, the F_3 position should *not* be reached via consolidation from S_4 or S_5, since this would require a decline in organizational intelligence, something that does not happen during consolidation. But starting from F_1, which has a very low level of intelligence, consolidation might lead to F_3 because of the decentralization and reduction in risk and innovation. Thus, although the effects of consolidation may often be salutary, this is not always the case. To take the most extreme example, what a debacle it would be if the F_2 Stagnant Bureaucracy or the F_3 Headless Giant were to consolidate. Stagnation and leaderlessness would be severely aggravated in each case.

A very well known example of consolidation occurred at General Motors between 1910 and 1915, after William Durant's first term in office (Chandler, 1962, pp. 138–99). Durant, in the immediately preceding years, had taken a number of small independent car and parts manufacturers and assembled them into a loose confederation. He was primarily an aggressive salesman and an organization builder. But by making it grow too fast, he overextended the new organization and caused a severe cash squeeze. To obtain funds, Durant had to turn over the management of the company to several bankers after signing a five-year voting trust agreement.

The bankers curtailed further expansion and began to bolster the internal organization. They consolidated a number of subsidiaries, concentrating production in a few big plants. They also integrated some of the smaller manufacturing operations, combined the three truck makers, and united some parts producers into one plant. James Storrow, the chairman of the new Finance Committee and the spokesman for the banking group, worked to ensure better control over and more cooperation between the subsidiaries. He relocated the general offices from New York to Detroit and installed a new president whose role it would be to help determine broad policy and achieve effective coordination. The chiefs of all of the major subsidiaries were expected to aid the president in these tasks. Purchasing, accounting, and production departments were set up at the head office to produce better cost and profit information and to provide a more rational basis for decision making. An engineering department was also established to improve automobile designs and production processes, and to help plant managers with technical problems. Finally, a series of interdivisional committees was set up to coordinate and improve communication among the subsidiaries.

Because of the independence of the entrepreneurs who ran the subsidiaries, these administrative innovations had little effect. Too much power still resided with these people, and they resisted complying with the new procedures. Also, the new head office was still too small to control the vast industrial empire that Durant had assembled in so short a time. Thus the consolidation was only partly effective.

T_4: Toward Stagnation (16% of the Sample)

A weaker, more conservative group of leaders push the firm towards stagnation. Strategies become unresponsive and vague, as structures become more mechanical. Passivity reigns. Adaptation is neglected, markets are ignored, vigilance declines, and administrative units begin to drift apart.

The T_4 transition archetype centers around a change in leadership; bolder, more assertive leaders give way to more passive, conservative ones. Sometimes a change occurs in the personality of the top manager, who, growing older, becomes more content with past practices and is less willing to change the organization or its product-market orientation to better meet new conditions. More often, however, the T_4 transition is initiated under a change of CEOs. New executives take a "wait-and-see" attitude. Their reaction to their ignorance of the firm and its environment is very different from that of managers presiding over the T_2 or T_3 transitions. Whereas the latter respond by carefully studying the organization and the administrative task, gathering information wherever possible, the T_4 executives abdicate some of their responsibility and power to those who report to them and are more conservative in their approach to new projects.

The immediate consequence of such an attitude is diminished control over operations. Departments become more independent. As a result, they are more likely to pursue mutually conflicting policies, since the leadership vacuum reduces the amount of coordination and guidance from the top. There is also less exploration of the environment, since the top level of management performs a caretaker role more than a strategic one. Instead of ensuring that the firm is in the right areas of the market by examining emergent trends and opportunities, managers are more likely to handle routine operating problems or crises as they develop. The result is a decrease in adaptiveness and market expertise.

Other interesting aspects of the T_4 archetype are the reduced emphasis on product-market innovation, risk taking, and proactiveness, and the increase in traditions. Again, it appears that the reduced expertise and the growing insecurity or complacency of top management play an important role in boosting conservatism. Insecurity stems from the ignorance of a new CEO; complacency is usually the product of a commitment to past practices by an executive who implemented them and enjoyed their initial success. In either case, the CEO is reluctant to initiate or direct meaningful reorientations of the firm. Normally, since such decisions were made at the top in the past, there is a time lag before divisions take over the innovation and strategy-making initiative. Meanwhile, the firm tends to drift. To the extent that the environment changes, strategies become anachronistic.

As increasingly alienated and independent divisions bear a greater amount of the innovation and strategy-making burden, conflicting decisions and plans become more prevalent. Where the adaptive effort is carried out by lower-level units rather than a central authority, innovations tend to be more piecemeal and incremental. A CEO can decide to enter a radically new market, but a division manager may only be allowed to "fill out" his product line, and a marketing manager may only modify a product subject to the limitations placed on him by his production counterpart.

A final point of interest is the reduced analysis and multiplexity of strategic decision making. Restricted information processing (less scanning, controls, and communication) may account in part for this. More information might trigger better analysis and broaden perspectives of problems. A dearth of information seems to occasion the reverse. But the issue is more complex than this. In a central office that deals explicitly with strategy-making and corporate reorientation, there is frequently a good deal of thought devoted to the conceptualization and execution of major decisions. In contrast, where a caretaker attitude prevails, most decisions are apt to be of an operating nature and require less intensive study. Unfortunately, this passive, unreflective approach tends to be extended to the occasional major decisions that arise.

The stagnation transition can represent a movement toward the F_2 Stagnant Bureaucracy or the F_3 Headless Giant archetype. Weakened or conservative leadership, reduced information processing, declining innovation, and redistribution of power to the divisions are very consistent with the characteristics of F_3. Therefore, the progression toward stagnation might be quite a dangerous one. Of course, this need not always be the case. Successful archetypes such as the Entrepreneurial S_4 firm or the Adaptive S_{1B} firm might actually benefit from a reduction in the rate of expansion or innovation, and S_4 in particular might benefit from greater dispersion of decision-making power. Probably neither firm would benefit, however, from the reduction of information-processing and decision-making rationality that occurs during the move toward stagnation. Only in cases of dramatic risk taking and centralization would the benefits from reducing these excesses more than offset the costs of reduced intelligence.

Sears, Roebuck moved toward stagnation between 1929 and 1932 (Chandler, 1962, pp. 278–348). After a period of dramatic expansion and many store openings, it became obvious that growth had to stop. Too many administrative problems had become manifest. Sears was using its mail-order structure to administer its stores, and the needs of the two types of units were completely different. The mail-order buyers knew little about the urban markets in which the stores were situated. Yet they had the power to stock the stores with merchandise that was not moving. Consultants were called in to devise a new structure. They established five territorial divisions to supervise both mail-order and retail sales. But this plan failed, since the lines of authority and communication were unclear. Indeed, Sears was now left with both a functional *and* a territorial organization, neither of which was cooperating with the other. The territorial officers knew the needs of their units but hadn't the personnel or the power to fulfill them. The functional chiefs still had authority for purchasing and pricing but had too little knowledge of urban markets. The resultant conflicts stymied the organization to the point where it became impossible to adapt to changing market conditions or to innovate significantly. The focus was on routine problems rather than overall strategy, and no central leadership emerged to resolve the issue. As a result, the firm drifted aimlessly as competitors began to gain ground.

T_5: Toward Centralization, Boldness, and Abandon (14% of the Sample)

> The spirit of entreprenuership grows as innovation, diversification, and expansion take on greater importance. But caution and intelligence activity decline and strategies begin to mirror more closely the personal goals of a powerful leader rather than the realities of the marketplace.

The T_5 archetype has its roots in the consolidation of leadership power by an executive or group of executives who have extensive experience with the company. Over the years, the executives assiduously have gathered around them a team of managers and directors who see things from the same perspective. The people at the top proceed increasingly to make most of the key decisions themselves without subjecting their judgments to the scrutiny of others. The CEO or the top team has ambitious plans for the organization. These may involve the acquisition of new firms, the creation of dramatically new product lines or services, or the entry into new foreign or domestic markets. There is an atmosphere of growing optimism, and there remain fewer administrative checks and balances available to mitigate the greater risks undertaken by the leaders.

Previously, a more diffused distribution of organizational power required that plans and proposals be justified to other executives. This generally prompted more thorough discussion and investigation of decisions and problems. Such analysis becomes less necessary as actions are subject to diminished scrutiny. The decline in analytical activity, coupled with the development of "pet" strategies—that is, strategies that reflect what certain executives want rather than what is best—result in a less adaptive company. No longer are strategies as appropriate to the requisites of the marketplace.

The diversification of the firm causes greater administrative complexity. New divisions or departments are added, and these must be assimilated into the organization. But because executives are so involved in the process of expansion, they neglect this task of integration. Also, perhaps because operations are more diversified and complex and because controls are not developed for the new areas of business, integration declines. Decisions in the new areas are more likely to detract from or disrupt those in the established fields.

Clearly, the T_5 transition may often represent a movement toward the F_1 Impulsive type. All the trends are there: the centralization of power, the tendency of top executives to make decisions on the basis of untutored whim, and the aggressive expansion and diversification that can easily overtax administrative resources.

To take two somewhat more benign examples, the T_5 transition could also lead toward the S_2 Dominant or S_4 Entrepreneurial archetypes for firms starting in the S_{1B} Adaptive or S_3 Giant archetypes respectively. The past successes of an S_{1B} firm may allow its leader to gather more power and encourage him to become committed to the strategy of intensive innovation. The firm therefore begins to move towards S_2—that is, to run more automatically, to become more centralized and boldly innovative, and to apply less scrutiny to new projects and decisions. This is especially likely to happen if competitors weaken, or if past successes boost resources so much that the firm can more readily dominate its markets.

The movement from the S_3 Giant to the S_4 Entrepreneurial archetype may also be reflected by the T_5 transition. A change in leadership may allow a new group to consolidate power and to reverse the firm's conservative orientation. Here, the emphasis is upon diversification into new markets. A potential danger is that the new group of executives might favor informal (S_4) over formal (S_3) information systems at a time when the expansion and complexification of markets could render the former inadequate.

To summarize, the T_5 transition can lead to organizational growth and renewal in the hands of a bold cadre of leaders. But it can be taken to extremes, crippling organizational intelligence and overtaxing resources.

An example of the T_5 transition took place during Donald Kircher's last years with the Singer Manufacturing Company (*Fortune*, August 1976). When Kircher became chief executive in the 1950s, he converted a somnolent, static sewing-machine company into a well-controlled international concern with a fine line of attractive products. But Kircher, a dominating personality from the start, began to show signs of hubris. His confidence and his power grew as a result of his past successes, and he decided to thoroughly modernize Singer. He wished to take the firm into new fields, such as aviation electronics and advanced data processing.

Kircher's forcefulness, his autocratic nature, his past successes, and the substantial cash reserves of the company allowed him to launch his diversification program without any resistance from the board or from other managers. He boldly moved into new industries in which Singer had absolutely no expertise, often by acquiring firms that had serious problems and substandard products. The new acquisition candidates were not properly assessed, and a few were purchased impulsively. Also, the existing information systems and management structure were wholly inadequate for controlling, monitoring, and appraising the performance of the new divisions. Problems were allowed to get completely out of hand, since no one at the head office knew about them, or even understood their significance once the facts came to light. Because of the flurry of activity surrounding the new operations, the traditional sewing-machine business was neglected. Singer began to fall behind with its marketing and design efforts, and its manufacturing efficiency did not measure up to that of the competition. Also, the new ventures drained the firm of capital and imposed a burdensome debt structure. In short, too much was done too quickly and impulsively, at the instigation of one central actor. Singer has still not completely recovered from the ravages of this era.

T_7: Maturation (10% of the Sample)

> As firms mature they face more challenging, complex, and diverse environments. They respond by increasing the sophistication of the administrative structure—establishing profit centers, divisions, coordinative committees, and elaborate information systems. This entails decentralization which often makes for a more gradual and cautious adaptive effort.

The T_7 archetype represents a maturation of sorts. It heralds the transition to a more professional management approach, often from an entrepreneurial one. As firms grow older and larger, and face more complex environments, there is a greater need to delegate some of the decision-making tasks to functional and lower-level managers, to professionalize and institutionalize the intelligence-gathering and information-processing functions, and to integrate the efforts of decision makers by formal means such as committees and planning sessions. It is not only the organizational growth and development sequence that causes this transformation. The new approach may also be motivated by the ill effects of a period of rapid diversification or a major new-product introduction. Such events often prompt the setting up of new divisions that require a greater degree of autonomy than the more established departments, particularly if the new area of endeavor is very different from the old ones.

The T_7 firms are most adept at assuming the mantle of maturity. The formerly dominant CEOs or their replacements recognize the need for major changes in the structure and modus operandi of the firm. This awareness is very prominent, lucid, and compelling, and concerted efforts are devoted to effecting the required transition. A multifaceted plan is adopted to change the organization.

The first change that normally occurs is the boosting of the intelligence system. Whereas managers may have gathered information quite informally on their own, systems and departments are set up to gather certain types of information routinely and to disseminate this information to the appropriate decision makers. Also, formal inventory controls, profit centers, cost-accounting systems, and quality controls are implemented. To improve cross-functional communications, various committees—ad hoc and standing—are established. The elaborated intelligence system is useful given the firm's decentralization and diversification. It helps monitor the new operations and educates the new divisional decision makers.

Another major change that takes place involves the style of decision making. Whereas in the past, entrepreneurs would make bold and intuitive decisions mostly on their own, the decision-making process now becomes increasingly decentralized and analytical, with divisional or departmental personnel deciding most issues within their sphere of expertise and devoting more time and effort to these tasks. Where issues require a broader perspective, committees are convened so that a variety of viewpoints are brought to bear. This increases the multiplexity of decisions and ensures that actions in different areas are complementary. Also, the interaction among decision makers encourages discussion of overall goals and plans, and, as a result, strategies become more conscious and more clearly defined.

Not all trends in the T_7 archetype have positive connotations. Some of the initiative and leadership of the company is lost as decision makers become more risk-averse. There is less likelihood that the firm will be proactive and beat competitors to the punch in introducing new products and broaching new markets. The routinization and systematization of functions bring bureaucratic momentum, traditions, and resistance to change. Also, the greater tendency to subject decisions or proposed courses of action to a forum introduces a measure of conservatism, since managers must come prepared to defend their actions.

The T_7 transition leads in the direction of the S_3 Giant archetype. It represents the movement toward a more divisionalized, decentralized, and well-integrated organization. S_3 can be reached via T_7 as S_{1A} or S_{1B} adaptive firms become more conservative and differentiated, or as S_2 or S_5 firms become more decentralized and diversified while developing their information-processing apparatus. The movement through the maturation process of T_7 is described by authors such as Chandler (1962), Channon (1973), and Rumelt (1974), as well as some of the life-cycle researchers (Quinn & Cameron, 1981). It is a common transition to make for firms that have become more diversified and complex and must move toward a divisional structure. Thus we should find that S_3 is reached from many successful archetypes by moving through T_7.

The types of firms that might benefit most from the T_7 transition are overcentralized, too aggressive, excessively diversified for their administrative structure, and inadequately integrated. The F_1 Impulsive firm fits this description. Those attempting to effect a turnaround strategy for the Impulsive firm might do well to study the T_7 transition.

Chandler (1962) discusses a T_7 transition that occurred during the 1920s at General Motors when Alfred Sloan radically redesigned the structural apparatus, converting GM from a loosely coupled set of subsidiaries to a market-based, integrated organization. Under the new divisional structure, managers were made accountable for the profits of particular product lines. Sloan also appointed group executives to supervise the work of several divisions and to set overall policies. A strong general office was established to coordinate and appraise the divisions. Everywhere staff activities were bolstered, especially in the financial and accounting areas to facilitate the control, assssment, and planning of operations.

T_8: Troubleshooting (6% of the Sample)

Troubleshooting often occurs after a firm has undergone a major shock—a financial loss, a sharp reduction in sales, or an aborted takeover bid. The emphasis is on finding out what went wrong and why. A top executive or committee is accorded much power to carry out its investigation and to take preliminary corrective action.

The period of troubleshooting is somewhat similar to that of consolidation, but there are major differences. During the former period, there is a greater increase in the centralization of power by the chief executive and a more pronounced improvement in intelligence effort devoted to discovering just what is wrong with the firm. Whereas the consolidators escalate their firefighting activity, troubleshooters, under the direction of a strong leader, begin to work harder to uncover the *roots* of the difficulties. This is done by doing more scanning, priming control systems, and improving internal communications. Interestingly, delegation of authority for operating matters is reduced, usually because middle managers cannot be fully trusted to discharge their functions competently. Decision making becomes more analytical, and the resultant decisions are better unified and much more complementary. They also tend to take into account more viewpoints and considerations than was true in the past. Risk taking, innovation, and proactiveness are reduced, as in the case of consolidation, and strategies are left vague pending the outcome of the investigation.

T_8 seems to be a general-purpose transition for firms that find themselves in trouble because of a lack of leadership, poorly conceived innovations, overexpansion, or failing divisions or product lines. We should thus find troubleshooting occurring from time to time in many static archetypes, particularly those that are diversified, innovative, decentralized, or lacking in controls. The F_3 Headless firms might benefit from the emphasis on more centralized leadership, better controls, and integration. There might be occasions when excessive innovation in S_{1B} Adaptive firms requires a similar transition.

An interesting period of troubleshooting took place at du Pont between 1920 and 1922. The firm had been expanding rapidly during the war, entering a wide variety of new businesses. But it was becoming apparent that du Pont's structure was quite inadequate for its given state of diversification and complexity. One marketing department couldn't possibly handle the selling job for all the different products. For example, du Pont's consumer goods demanded more extensive advertising and a larger distribution network than did their tonnage goods. A committee was appointed to study the problem. They undertook a methodical, rational study of markets and the practices of other firms. The committee found that other firms were making money in the finished-goods areas where du Pont was incurring losses. Committee members expressed concern that under the functional structure, no one was responsible for the profitability of a given line. It was recommended that product rather than function become the basis for organization. A new executive committee was proposed to oversee a divisional structure. This was an extremely radical proposal at the time, and top executives in the firm resisted its implementation for over a year. But the hard-hitting recession of 1921 conclusively revealed the need for the new structure.

The main features of the preceding transitions are summarized on Table 5-1. The expected links between the six most statistically significant transition archetypes and the static archetypes of Chapter 4 are given in Table 5-2.

T_1: Fragmentation (3% of the Sample)

Our last three archetypes are described only briefly, because their ability to be generalized is more limited. To include as much information as possible in the descriptions, variable names and their modal scores are given on a scale of 1 (great decrease), through 4 (no change), to 7 (great increase). These scores are presented in parentheses.

The T_1 archetype is given the appellation "Fragmentation" because it represents a disintegrative phase of corporate history. The subunits of the organization acquire more power, and there is less leadership and direction coming from the top (centralization, 3; delegation, 5). This leads to a decline in communication (3) among units, each of which has more tendency to become an independent domain paying less attention to integrating (3) its decisions to ensure complementarity. Often the leadership vacuum is caused by the departure of a strong manager, who is replaced by a much less experienced (industry expertise, 3; tenure, 3) and less forceful team. Because subunits are not used to making top-level strategy, there is more concern for operating matters than for strategic decisions and plans (consciousness of strategy, 3; futurity, 3). Strategies all tend to be based on tradition (5), past practices, and intuition. They are therefore less adaptive (3), less multiplex (3), and less analytical (3).

T_6: Initiation by Fire (6% of the Sample)

Major tribulations may be suffered by firms that must deal with great and discontinuous changes in their environments, particularly when the firms are not used to having to change their methods, structures, and strategies. Environmental dynamism (5), hostility (6), and heterogeneity (5)

TABLE 5-1: Most Significant Transition Types

	RELATION TO ENVIRONMENT	STRATEGY	STRUCTURE	INFORMATION PROCESSING	POWER	DECISION MAKING
Entrepreneurial Revitalization T_2		REVIVAL	BUILDING			
	Adapt to it more quickly	More innovation, diversification	More technocrats & delegation	Increased scanning & communication	Towards apex	Sensitive, analytical
Consolidation T_3		RETRENCHMENT	COMMITTEES			
	Reduce its scope	Pruning, cost cutting	More participative mgmt.	Internal controls bolstered	Disperses throughout org.	More conservative and integrated Short-time horizon
Toward Stagnation T_4		WAIT-AND-SEE	FRACTURED			
	Begin to ignore it	Drifting, no strategy	More fragmentation among departments	Reduced vigilance	Moves down to depts. & divisions	More complacent, less adaptive, crisis management Risk aversion

continued

TABLE 5-1: Continued

	RELATION TO ENVIRONMENT	STRATEGY	STRUCTURE	INFORMATION PROCESSING	POWER	DECISION MAKING
Centralization, Boldness . . . T_5	Manipulate it	EXPANSION Diversification, innovation	OVERLOAD Divisionalization, disintegration	Controls diminished	Moving towards the top	More impulsive, risk-embracing & intuitive
Maturation T_7	Adapt to it more slowly	INCREMENTAL ADAPTATION More gradual product-market renewal	PROFESSIONALIZATION Profit centers Committees for integration Bureaucratization	More sophisticated and formal scanning & controls	Delegation downwards	More analytical, consultative, multiplex and conservative
Troubleshooting T_8	Study it	PROBLEM ANALYSIS		Improved info. gathering to discover problems	Power centralized during crisis	Careful and considered

TABLE 5-2: Transitions and Static Archetypes

TRANSITION	LIKELY SOURCES		LIKELY DESTINATIONS	
T_2: Entrepreneurial Revitalization	F_3:	Headless	S_4:	Entrepreneurial
	S_3:	Giant		
T_3: Consolidation	F_1:	Impulsive	S_3:	Giant
	S_4:	Entrepreneurial	F_3:	Headless
	S_5:	Innovative		
T_4: Stagnation	S_{1B}:	Adaptive	F_2:	Stagnant Bureaucracy
	S_4:	Entrepreneurial	F_3:	Headless
T_5: Centralization, Boldness, & Abandon	F_2:	Stagnant	F_1:	Impulsive
	S_{1B}:	Adaptive	S_2:	Dominant
	S_3:	Giant	S_4:	Entrepreneurial
T_7: Maturation	S_{1A}, S_{1B}:	Adaptive	S_3:	Giant
	S_2:	Dominant		
	S_5:	Innovative		
	F_1:	Impulsive		
T_8: Troubleshooting	F_3:	Headless	Various	

have increased, and some relatively inexperienced managers are trying to cope. They begin to scan (5) their environments to more precisely define the threats, to delegate more power to knowledgeable people (centralization 3, technocratization, 5), and to innovate more to adapt to the new conditions (innovation, 5; risk taking, 5; and proactiveness, 5). Managerial inexperience is evidenced by the spottiness of the adaptive effort. Delegation of operating authority is slow to come about, few improvements are made in internal control (4) and communication (4) systems, and intuitive, short-run tactics preclude the development of a more conscious (3) and integrated (3) strategy. Normally these omissions might not be critical, but here the more challenging environment takes its toll (resources, 3; success, 3) in spite of the firm's efforts.

T_9: Formalization and Stability (8% of the Sample)

There is very little change evidenced in this last archetype. Existing strategies and procedures become formalized and standardized, so that operating authority can be delegated further (5). Managers become more experienced with the stable organizational practices and can therefore be trusted to perform in line with expectations. Also, concrete standards can be set up to discover and correct deviations in managerial behavior because of the predictability of the operations. Past and mounting success (5) and the resultant buildup in resources (5) are in part responsible for the greater reluctance to change and to take risks (3). The more enduring terms in office (tenure, 5) of the top executives may be another reason for the continuity.

It should be remembered that since we are dealing with transition scores along the variables, the periods may be very diverse in their raw scores. That is, firms that are bold, centralized, or intuitive can undergo the very same transitions as those that are conservative, decentralized, or analytical.

CONCLUSION

We see each of the transition archetypes as both potentially promising and hazardous. Just as Hedberg, Nystrom, and Starbuck (1976) show organizations balancing on a multidimensional seesaw, trying to avoid various excesses, the transition archetypes may be seen to represent a trend toward moderation or toward a dangerous extreme, depending upon the starting position of the firm and the magnitude of the transition. Although we have too often used value-laden expressions in our descriptions of the archetypes, mainly to make them more interesting and memorable to the reader, such statements are often misleading. For example, the "toward stagnation" type does not by any means always result in stagnation. Where the transition occurs in a firm that was overly aggressive and innovative and had high degrees of intelligence and rationality, the stagnation influence may be constructive. In contrast, where this transition proves to be extreme in the magnitude of change or occurs in an unvigilant company, there may be some real dangers. It is therefore unrealistic to expect performance to be well correlated with the nature of the transition.

What the transitions do tell us is that changes tend to come in packages. Given a few changes of a certain type, a host of secondary alterations is likely to follow. Thus, firms in trying to achieve balance by, say, reducing commitment to an explicit strategy, will have to watch that an imbalance is not created by the deterioration of interunit linkages, a phobia toward (or excess of) innovation, or a leadership gap. Organizations are complexes of interrelated systems. One change provokes another. Striving for balance along one dimension may be harmful if it creates excesses or imbalances in others. By finding out more about transitional tendencies, the designer of organizations can better understand the requisites of organizational change and the natural tendencies that must be built upon or combatted to improve organizational functioning.

Perhaps the most arresting finding of this study is that the same types of transitions keep cropping up with impressive frequency in an extremely diverse sample of firms. Furthermore, there do not appear to be a very great number of common transition types. Therefore, it might eventually be possible to discover the fundamental building blocks underlying the dynamics of organizational change.

Although the findings of this chapter are of an exploratory nature, the predictive utility of transition archetypes looks promising. To the extent that archetypes are stable, few, and tight enough to preserve the essential features of transitions, the scores on some of the variables may be used to identify the related archetype and thereby to predict scores on most of the other variables.

If there is one central lesson that issues from this research, it is that we must pay more attention to organizational diversity. We believe that it is wrong for researchers to look at organizations from a purely deterministic "organization-adjusting-to-the environment" point of view (Child, 1972). While it is certainly true that some of the transitions portray environment as an incentive for changes in organization structure, strategy, and decision-making style, it is equally true that past strategic choices and modes of behavior influence the nature of the environment, that strategies influence structure (Chandler, 1962), and that structure constrains strategic choice (Hedberg, Nystrom and Starbuck, 1976). Any study of organizations and their relationships to the environment, or, more specifically, any research into the nature of functional and dangerous response patterns to specific challenges and settings must consider multiple configurations among many environmental, organizational, and strategy-making dimensions. This argues for broadly conceived multivariate taxonomies. The prime need is to get away from looking at unitary relationships among elements of structure, and to stand back and try to understand a multiplicity of fundamental response patterns of organizations, in all their complexity.

We would like to conclude with a plea for more longitudinal studies of organizations. Benson (1977) and Hall (1976) have respectively argued for and demonstrated the utility of a focus upon organizational dynamics. Although many studies of the anatomy of organizations have brought rewards, it is time to begin to undertake "physiological" explorations. Only then can we begin to understand the etiology of dysfunction and move toward more informed prescription.

Part III

Introduction

CONFIGURATIONS
IN PREDICTION

Part III presents two empirical studies that demonstrate the advantages of using typologies in making predictions. In Chapter 1, we argued that it was hazardous to examine heterogeneous samples of organizations in attempting to discover relationships among variables of strategy, structure, and environment. The compositions of such samples are bound to influence results, since relationships among the variables vary considerably among groups of different firms. We also made this point in Chapter 4, showing how the relationships between environmental dynamism and organizational intelligence, for example, seemed to differ according to the set of archetypes we chose to examine. In this section of the book, we present two empirical studies that establish this theme more rigorously than do our earlier accounts. It is shown that if we take care to make distinctions among organizations before trying to predict relationships, far more accurate results will emerge than if we lumped very different types of firms together and performed statistical analyses upon the total sample.[1]

Two areas of research are examined, each of which has generated a good deal of controversy. The first searches for the determinants of inno-

---

[1]To return to our geometrical representation of Chapter 2, we believe that rich characterizations of organizations in terms of their strategies, structures and environments will show considerable clustering among the variables. But many of the relationships will be nonlinear. The data will often be arrayed in n-dimensional space to form a snake-like nonlinear surface of much smaller dimension than the space itself. Taxonomies will isolate types that represent distinct segments of the surface or snake (see Appendix 4-1). Each of these can show very different relationships among the variables.

vation. Why are some firms so active in introducing new products and processes while others fail even to imitate the unmistakable advances of their competitors? Debates have appeared in the literature over the past two decades on the roles of environmental, structural, information-processing, and decision-making variables in promoting innovation. Some researchers have pointed to the importance of particular organizational variables, only to have their results contradicted by subsequent research studies. The nature of the archetypes discussed in Chapter 4, together with the typologies of others, have led us to conceive of two very different models of product innovation that would seem to be applicable to two very different types of firms or configurations.

The *conservative* model assumes that innovation is performed only reluctantly in response to serious challenges. It therefore predicts that innovation will be boosted by environmental variables that represent these challenges, and by information-processing, structural, and decision-making variables that help managers to recognize and cope with them. For example, the model predicts that the higher the level of environmental dynamism, the more innovation there will be to keep up with changing markets. Also, the greater the amount of scanning and analysis of the environment, the more likely it is that managers will recognize the sizable gap between their own firms and the competition, and will therefore be motivated to innovate. In other words, the conservative model predicts that there will be positive correlations of innovation with environmental dynamism, scanning, analysis, and other factors that either necessitate innovation or create an awareness of that necessity. The conservative model is expected to apply to samples of conservative firms—those that require prompting in order to change and that therefore generally have fairly low levels of innovation.

In sharp contrast, the *entrepreneurial* model of innovation supposes that innovation is aggressively pursued because of the ideologies, policies, or beliefs of top managers. It predicts that the level of innovation will normally be very high unless decision makers are given some concrete and pressing incentive to slow down. Thus, negative correlations are expected to occur between innovation and the variables that can provide such warning. These include scanning and analysis—precisely those variables that were predicted to *boost* innovation in the conservative model. The research reported in Chapter 6 shows each of the models to be strongly supported in samples of conservative and entrepreneurial firms respectively. Many of the conflicts in the literature can apparently be explained by the failure to make distinctions between different types of firms in predicting innovation.

Chapter 7 examines the determinants of entrepreneurship in three very common types of companies or configurations. The literature on entrepreneurship has typically focused upon one type of organization: that owned and run by a founding leader who boldly marshals the factors of production to build an innovative enterprise. We believe this scope to be excessively narrow. Entrepreneurship is a concept that can be made relevant to many types of firms if we are careful to make distinctions among them. We have tried to do this by redefining entrepreneurship to encompass organizational risk taking, proactiveness, and innovation; essentially to encompass the processes of market and organizational renewal. We conjectured that the factors determining entrepreneurship would vary as a function of the nature of the firm or configuration. In small, *simple*, centralized firms, entrepreneurship would be determined by the characteristics of the top executives: their power, their personality, and their knowledge of markets and products. In larger, more bureaucratic, *planning*-oriented firms, functioning is more mechanical, and the emphasis is on efficiency and smoothness of operations. Here, entrepreneurship must be planned, regular, and systematized—that is, incorporated explicitly into product-market strategies. The explicitness and completeness of strategies that allow for orderly innovation are expected to boost the entrepreneurial behavior of planners. Finally, in the more complex, decentralized, technocratic, *organic* firms, the emphasis is upon adapting to the external environment. In these firms, entrepreneurship is predicted to be a function of environmental challenges and structural conditions: the former because they require entrepreneurial behavior, the latter because they facilitate it.

The theme of Chapter 7 is the same as that of Chapter 6; namely, that the identification of common configurations is a critical first step in predicting organizational relationships. The two chapters use different typologies to show how robust the theme is. Chapter 6 bifurcates the sample into composite types that are loosely based upon some of the archetypes discussed in Chapter 4. Since there were ten archetypes but only 52 firms in this sample, we did not have sufficient data to be able to use each of the individual types. In Chapter 7, the sample is split into three to obtain a typology based on Mintzberg's (1973) strategy-making modes and three of the structural types he discusses in Chapter 3.

6

Innovation in Conservative
and Entrepreneurial
Configurations

INTRODUCTION

There is much controversy in the literature on organizational innovation. According to Downs and Mohr (1976, p. 700):

> Perhaps the most alarming characteristic of the body of empirical study of innovation is the extreme variance among its findings, what we call instability. Factors found to be important for innovation in one study are found to be considerably less important, not important at all, or even inversely important in another study. This phenomenon occurs with relentless regularity. . . . In spite of the large amount of energy expended, the results have not been cumulative.

Of the 38 propositions bearing directly on the act of innovation cited by Rogers and Shoemaker (1971, pp. 350–76), 34 were supported in some studies and found to receive no support in others. The four consistently predictive propositions were treated in very few studies.

We believe that in research on product innovation, many of the conflicts in the literature have been caused by the failure of researchers to take into account the nature of the configuration of the firm and the strategy or philosophy behind innovation. Some executives decide that regular and extensive innovation in product lines, services, and product designs should be a vital element of strategy. In Chapter 4, we saw that *entrepreneurial* S_4, S_5, and F_1 firms try to obtain a competitive advantage by routinely making dramatic innovations and taking the concomitant risks. But other organizations are run by more conservative managers who may view innovation as costly and disruptive to production efficiency. *Conservative* firms such as F_2 or S_3 seem to innovate only when they are seriously challenged by competitors or by shifting customer wants. The thesis of this chapter is that the impact upon product innovation of environmental, information-processing, structural, and decision-making variables will vary significantly and systematically among entrepreneurial[1] and conservative firms; that future research on the determinants of innovation must consider organizational configuration.

Based on previous empirical research, this chapter develops distinct arguments concerning the determinants of innovation in conservative and entrepreneurial firms. It then presents data from a diverse sample of 52 Canadian business firms that show how different are the correlates of product innovation for both kinds of firms. The scope of the research is limited to innovations in product lines, product designs, and services offered. It does not extend to technological or administrative innovations. Only business firms are studied. Our arguments or findings may not hold for other types of organizations. Finally, although we sometimes talk about the "determinants" of innovation, the direction of causality is always in doubt and, strictly speaking, we should refer only to "correlates" of innovation.

The Conservative Model of Innovation

The literature on product development, although fraught with conflict, seems to point preponderantly to a conservative model of innovation. The model implies that innovation is not a natural state of affairs, that it must be encouraged by challenges and threats, and that it requires a particular type of structure and an effective information-processing system to make conservative managers aware of the need for change. We contend that the conservative model will apply to firms that perform little innovation or risk taking. These are reminiscent of the "reactors" of Miles and Snow (1978), the F_2 Stagnating and S_3 Giant firms of Chapter 4, and the "adapters" of Mintzberg (1973). Here, innovation is performed infrequently and, perhaps because of its disruptive nature, reluctantly.

The conservative model suggests that innovation will take place only when there are felt pressures. It postulates four types of prerequisites, or at least strong facilitators, of innovation. First, there must be environmental *challenges* before innovation occurs. For example, because they create a need for innovation, factors such as environmental dynamism and hostility would be expected to correlate positively with innovation. Second, there

---

[1]The term *entrepreneurial* is used here in its broadest sense, that is, to refer to bold risk taking and high levels of innovation, *not* to owner-managed or small, centralized companies.

must be *information* about these challenges brought to key decision makers by effective scanning and control systems. Third, there must be an *ability* to innovate that is created by adequate resources, skilled technocrats, and structural devices. And finally, there must be decision-making *methods* appropriate for innovation projects. For example, the extent to which key decision makers analyze innovation-related information and use it for planning and strategy development is expected to correlate positively with innovation. As we shall see, many of the findings in the literature seem to support our conservative model. What follows are some specific predictions implied by this model.

Environmental Variables.   Myers and Marquis (1969) found that 53 percent of the product and technological innovations in their sample came in response to market, competitive, or other external environmental influences. The more *dynamic* and *hostile* (that is, competitive) the environment, the greater the need for innovation and the more likely it is that firms will be innovative. When competitors' products change rapidly or when customer needs fluctuate, the conservative model hypothesizes that innovation will be common. In stable environments innovation is less likely to be necessary (Burns and Stalker, 1961). Environmental *heterogeneity* may also be germane. Firms operating in many different markets are likely to learn from their broad experience with competitors and customers. They may borrow ideas from one market and apply them in another. Diversity in personnel, operating procedures, technologies, and administrative practices increase with environmental heterogeneity (Peters, 1969). According to Wilson (1966), the greater the diversity of the organization, the greater the probability that innovations will be proposed, and the greater the likelihood that organization members will conceive major innovations.

Information Processing Variables.   Burns and Stalker (1961) have argued that mechanistic structures impede innovation and organic structures facilitate it, in part because the former have much less information processing capacity. Subsequent literature has shown that there are at least two types of information processing categories that can influence innovation. Aguilar (1967), Baker, Siegman, and Rubenstein (1967), Utterback (1971), Keller and Holland (1975), and Tushman (1977) have called attention to the role of *scanning* the environment, claiming that a primary limitation on a firm's innovativeness is its ability to recognize the needs and demands of its external environment. Perceived market needs were discovered to account for 75 percent of the ideas for innovation (Baker et al., 1967). This was confirmed by the work of Carter and Williams (1957), Myers and Marquis (1969), Mueller (1962), and the survey of Rogers and Shoemaker (1971, pp. 372–73). *Controls* are also said to facilitate innovation. Controls that monitor task performance and financial results may identify areas of weakness and encourage remedial innovations (Rosner, 1968; Downs, 1966, p. 191).

Structural Variables. Several structural variables have also been shown to promote innovation. One is *centralization* (or concentration) of authority for decision making. According to James Thompson (1969, p. 25):

> . . . dispersal of power is important because concentrated power often prevents imaginative solutions of problems. When power meets power, problem solving is necessarily called into play. . . Dispersed power, paradoxically, can make resources more readily available to support innovative projects, because it makes possible a large number and variety of subcoalitions. It expands the number and kinds of possible supporters and sponsors.

Hage and Aiken (1970) seem to concur. But Richard Normann (1971) disagrees, claiming that major innovations, which he calls "reorientations," were made in companies that either were family-owned or otherwise had a strong concentration of power. Victor Thompson (1969) also claims that only a powerful leader is able to overcome resistance to change and to make bold innovations. Rogers and Shoemaker's (1971, p. 384) review indicates that Victor Thompson's (1969) and Normann's (1971) positions are those most strongly supported by previous studies.

Technocrats and professionals such as scientists and engineers possess the knowledge and training that often make them most capable and motivated to discover new products and processes. Professional employees may best be able to recognize the need for change (Hage and Aiken, 1970, p. 33). Therefore structures that have a high percentage of influential technocrats will tend to be the most innovative.

Mohr (1969) has emphasized the need for organizational *resources* in promoting innovation. Most major innovations are too costly to be undertaken by organizations that are short of financial capital. Abundant material, capital equipment, and human resources are also necessary. For example, some kinds of innovation require laboratories, scientists, and financial resources. New-product introductions often entail large expenditures on R&D, test-marketing and changes to production facilities.

The final structural dimensions that we shall consider have been introduced by Lawrence and Lorsch (1967). They are *differentiation* and *integration*. For our purposes, the first will refer to the extent to which an organization's products require different marketing and production methods and procedures [our indicants of this scale will differ from those of Lawrence and Lorsch (1967)]. Hage and Aiken (1970) have argued that the existence of very different groups in the firm will make available more varied sources of information for developing new programs. Complex innovations require a diversity and richness of inputs that is most likely to be available in differentiated organizations (Wilson, 1966; Thompson, 1969). But differentiation causes debilitating conflicts among subunits and departments unless there are *integrative* devices to ensure effective collaboration. It is necessary to keep departmental parochialism to a minimum. In carrying out complex new-product innovations, it may be necessary for members of the R&D, marketing, finance, and production departments to work together intensively. Unless there are integrative devices such as task forces, interdepartmental committees, integrative personnel, or matrix structures, collaboration is difficult and conflicts and mistakes result (Lawrence and Lorsch, 1967; Galbraith, 1973).

Decision-Making Variables.   The final set of variables that can stimulate innovation in conservative firms describes the way executives use and process information in decision making. Given that the organization gathers the appropriate information about the environment and about organizational performance through its scanning and control systems, and assuming that this information is communicated to the right decision makers, it is still necessary for the information to be properly *used* and evaluated. For example, if conservative executives ignore conditions or cues that signal the need to innovate, then innovation will not take place. The more that *analysis* is performed by key decision makers—that is, the more they search deeply for the roots of problems and try to generate the best possible solution alternatives—the more likely it is that opportunities for innovation will be discovered and pursued. Managers who make seat-of-the-pants decisions are unlikely to spend the time and effort required to recognize the need for innovations (Lindblom, 1968).

Planning horizons (or *futurity*, as we shall call the variable) are also very likely to influence organizational innovation. Executives who are concerned with putting out fires will be too preoccupied with matters of the moment to be able to assess the long-term adequacy of their product lines and product designs. They may therefore fail to perceive the need for innovation. The more future-oriented the firm, the greater the concern with change and innovation (Ansoff, 1965; Andrews, 1980).

Our final variable is *consciousness of strategy*. It concerns the degree to which strategies have been explicitly considered and deliberately conceptualized. Executives whose attention is devoted exclusively to nonstrategic matters tend to muddle through and are much less likely to engage in product innovation (Mintzberg, 1973; Miles and Snow, 1978; and Chapter 4, type F_2). But where there is a concerted attempt to decide upon the product-market orientation of the firm, there is a greater likelihood that target markets will be defined more broadly. Consideration is given to goals and opportunities, and therefore to programs of innovation.

The Entrepreneurial Model of Innovation

In sharp contrast to the conservative model, the entrepreneurial model applies to firms that innovate boldly and regularly while taking considerable risks in their product-market strategies. The entrepreneurial strategy might be followed, for example, by Collins and Moore's (1970) and Mintzberg's (1973) "entrepreneurial" firms, Miles and Snow's (1978) "prospectors," and the S_{1B} Adaptive, S_4 Entrepreneurial, and S_5 Innovative firms of Chapter 4. According to the entrepreneurial model, innovation is seen as good in itself—as a vital and intrinsically desirable part of strategy. The entrepreneurial model postulates that firms will innovate dramatically unless there are certain key obstacles that get in the way. First, innovation will be very high unless good scanning or control systems reveal it to be too expensive or wasteful. That is, there may be *negative* correlations of scanning and controls with innovation. Second, effective analysis of decisions, futurity, and the explicit consideration of strategy will also guard against the natural tendency toward innovative excesses. Here again we expect to find negative correlations. Third, because strategy is expected to be the main driving force behind innovation, the role of environment as a stimulus for innovation will be reduced. However, since innovation can by itself induce environmental dynamism and heterogeneity, there should still be positive correlations between innovation and environment. Finally, the frequently observed positive correlation between innovation and structural factors such as technocratization and differentiation should prevail, but at a lower level of significance than for conservative firms. This is again because goals and strategy, not structure or environment, are expected to be the prime causes of innovation in entrepreneurial firms. Now we can derive some specific predictions that follow from the entrepreneurial model.

Environmental Variables. For entrepreneurial as for conservative firms, environmental variables are expected to relate positively to innovation. Entrepreneurial firms are often found in *dynamic* and *hostile* environments because their venturesome managers prefer rapidly growing and opportune settings, those that have high risks as well as high rewards. Such firms may even be partly responsible for making the environment dynamic by contributing their own challenging product innovations (Peterson and Berger, 1971). Because innovation prompts imitation, the more innovative the firms, the more dynamic and competitive their environments can become. Innovation is also likely to be positively correlated with *heterogeneity*, because firms that innovate are more apt to come up with products and services that can be exploited in different markets (Chandler, 1962). Notice that in entrepreneurial firms, unlike conservative firms, innovation may *cause* dynamism, hostility, or heterogeneity, rather than the other way around. If so, the greater latitude for strategic choice (for example, the ability to innovate in stable environments) will cause correlations between innovation and environment to be lower in entrepreneurial samples than in conservative samples.

Information-Processing Variables. Traditionally, the effect of information-processing variables upon innovation has not been clear. Although there have been numerous empirical studies, these often conflict. For example, Rogers and Shoemaker (1971, pp. 373–74) found 46 studies that showed early adopters of innovations to have greater exposure to information channels than did later adopters, but fourteen studies did not support this finding. They also found that twelve studies showed that earlier adopters scan or seek information about innovations more than later adopters do, while two studies contradicted this. We believe that for studies of business firms, this conflict can be resolved by examining the role of strategy. Although we postulated that samples of conservative firms would show positive correlations between innovation and information processing, an opposite relationship might hold in entrepreneurial samples. Some entrepreneurial firms may have a tendency to innovate too much. A proclivity toward taking risks and an innovation-embracing ideology can cause firms to squander resources in the pursuit of superfluous novelty. An effective *control* framework can flag the need to reduce the scope and expense of projects and to slow down an overly rapid pace of innovation. *Scanning* the environment to monitor the more parsimonious strategies of competitors is also expected to have a dampening effect upon innovation as opportunities for resource savings are discovered.

Structural Variables. For much the same reasons as those presented in the discussion of the conservative model of innovation, most of our structural variables are predicted to have a positive correlation with innovation in entrepreneurial firms. The only qualifier we must add is that, in general, the positive relationships between structure and innovation should be weaker in the entrepreneurial sample. This is because the innovativeness of entrepreneurial firms is believed to be determined more by the strategy of the firm and the aims of its venturesome top managers than by structure. It would not be surprising to find some entrepreneurial firms that have a tendency to innovate a great deal even though their structures are less than ideal for this according to the literature supporting the conservative model.

The *integration* variable should be negatively correlated with innovation in entrepreneurial samples. Integrative devices such as committees, task forces, and integrative personnel bring important facts to bear upon decisions. The innovation proposals of enthusiastic but reckless executives are apt to be defeated by those whose aim it is to ensure effective resource management and efficiency.

Decision-Making Variables. The variables of *analysis, futurity,* and *consciousness of strategy* are expected to correlate negatively with the degree of product innovation. Essentially the same rationale presented in the discussion of information-processing variables also applies to these predictions. Analysis, planning, and the deliberate attempt to explicitly formulate strategies will provide the firm with a better knowledge of its opportunities and excesses. Any tendency to overemphasize product innovation should therefore be curbed by these activities.

METHOD

The Variables and Questionnaires

In order to test the predictions derived in the last section, we employed a lengthy questionnaire to gather information on variables of environment, information processing, organization structure, decision-making style, product innovation, and risk taking. The questionnaire is available from the authors. All scale items were averaged for each variable to obtain the final scores. Table 6-1 presents the construct reliability measure of each of our variables. In every instance, the Cronbach alpha measure (which averaged .74 for all variables) well exceeded the guidelines set up by Van de Ven and Ferry (1980, pp. 78–82) for measuring organizational attributes.

Data Sample

Our data sample consists of 52 business firms that range in size from sales of less than $2 million to those of over $1 billion. Mean sales are $237 million and the standard deviation is $649 million. The average number of employees is 2,270. Firms are in industries as varied as retailing, furniture manufacturing, broadcasting, pulp and paper, food, plastics, electronics, chemicals, meatpacking, publishing, construction, and transportation. No industry represents more than 10 percent of the sample. Still, we cannot pretend here to have a random sample, since its geographic area is restricted to the Montreal region, and because firms were chosen by teams of second-year M.B.A. students according to their personal interests. However, because of the broad representation of types and sizes of businesses, and because no one type of firm dominates the sample, these exploratory findings should have quite a high degree of generality.

TABLE 6-1: Means, Standard Deviations, and Cronbach Alphas

VARIABLES	CONSERVATIVE SAMPLE N = 29		ENTREPRENEURIAL SAMPLE N = 18		TOTAL SAMPLE N = 52		CRONBACH ALPHA
	MEAN	S.D.	MEAN	S.D.	MEAN	S.D.	
Environment							
Dynamism	3.7	1.3	4.4	1.6	3.9	1.4	.74
Heterogeneity	3.5*	1.6	4.7*	1.4	4.1	1.6	.84
Hostility	3.9**	1.1	4.7**	1.0	4.2	1.1	.55
Information Processing							
Scanning	4.6	1.3	4.8	1.4	4.7	1.4	.74
Controls	4.3	1.5	4.6	1.9	4.4	1.7	.69
Structure							
Centralization	5.2	1.0	4.9	1.5	5.1	1.2	.79
Technocratization	3.4**	1.3	4.9**	1.7	4.0	1.7	.69
Resources	4.4	1.4	4.2	1.2	4.3	1.3	.68
Differentiation	2.8**	1.7	4.6**	1.4	3.5	1.7	.88
Integration	4.8	1.2	4.9	1.0	4.8	1.2	.71
Decision Making							
Analysis	3.9	1.0	4.3	1.5	4.0	1.3	.62
Futurity	3.8	1.4	4.5	1.4	4.1	1.5	.83
Consciousness of strategy	3.4*	1.6	4.5*	1.4	3.9	1.6	N/A†
Product Innovation	2.3**	0.8	5.3**	0.8	3.5	1.6	.77
Risk Taking	3.0**	1.0	4.7**	0.8	3.6	1.2	.91

* and ** signify that the sample means differ significantly at the .05 and .01 levels of significance using a two-tailed *t*-test.
†Only one scale was used to measure this variable.

All responses to the questionnaire were obtained by interviews. This ensured that executives could have any vague items explained to them and removed any problem of missing data. Although it is difficult to estimate a response rate, most interviewing teams were able to obtain cooperation from the first company they contacted.

All respondents used in the analysis had the rank of divisional vice-president or higher. In 67 percent of the cases, more than one respondent per firm completed the questionnaire. The ratings of the highest-ranking respondent were always used. In 73 percent of the cases, the data were supplied by the chief executive. Interrater reliability was adequate across all the variables. In cases of diversified and divisionalized companies, each division was treated as a separate entity to ensure that questions could be answered unambiguously. Thus, five of the "firms" in the sample were really divisions rather than autonomous organizations. In every case, the divisions represented profit centers and were controlled on the basis of their financial performance.

To carry out our analysis, we had to split the sample into two groups that were unambiguously conservative and entrepreneurial. Two dimensions were used in the split: innovation and risk taking. Firms whose scores on innovation and risk taking averaged less than or equal to 3.5 on the 7-point scales were classified as conservative (innovation and risk taking were positively correlated with a product moment coefficient of .51 in a sample of 52). Such firms tended to be risk-averse and engaged in relatively little product innovation. Firms whose score on innovation and risk taking averaged greater than or equal to 4.5 on the 7-point scales were classified as entrepreneurial. Firms with average scores of greater than 3.5 and less than 4.5 tended to be in a grey area. They manifested high risk taking and low innovation, or vice versa, and therefore were deleted from the *subsample* analysis. They simply could not be unambiguously classified.

FINDINGS

Distinctions between Conservative and Entrepreneurial Types
mmmm164

We called our subsamples "conservative" and "entrepreneurial," and must now justify these appellations. We cannot from our data directly determine the underlying management philosophies or motives of the firms in these groups. However, it is possible to determine whether the partitioning of the sample based upon risk taking and innovation produced other intergroup differences among the variables—differences that are consistent with our typology of conservative and entrepreneurial firms.

The figures in Table 6-1 reflect the characterizations given conservative firms by the literature. Low differentiation, market homogeneity, and unconscious strategies are in line with the features of the types that served as a conceptual genesis for our conservatives. These were principally the F_2 Stagnant firms of Chapter 4, and Mintzberg's (1973) "adapters." The conservatives' features make sense in the light of their avoidance of risk taking and innovation. A low level of innovation forces firms to operate in environments that are neither very dynamic nor challenging. It requires very few scientists, engineers, or other technocrats. Also, firms can be relatively undifferentiated because environments are fairly simple and homogeneous. Finally, the tendency to adhere to established products and practices makes rare the need to explicitly reconceptualize strategy or to plan far into the future.

Our characterization of entrepreneurial firms was loosely based upon Chapter 4's S_4 Entrepreneurial Conglomerates, and F_1 Impulsive types, Miles and Snow's (1978) "prospectors," and Mintzberg's (1973) "entrepreneurial" organizations. We thus expected the entrepreneurial sample to display many of the collateral characteristics of these firms. From Table 6-1, we can see that again this expectation is fulfilled. Most notable are the significantly higher degrees, relative to conservatives, of environmental hostility and heterogeneity, organizational differentiation, technocratization, and consciousness of strategy. The rate of growth in sales for the entrepreneurial firms from which we could obtain data averaged 14.7 percent per annum for the last three years of operation. This is significantly higher (at the .10 level) than the 8.2 percent rate of growth for conservatives, and this finding too is consistent with the characterizations in the literature.

It is not hard to surmise possible reasons for the subgroup differences. For example, entrepreneurial firms may operate in more heterogeneous markets and become more differentiated as a consequence of their innovativeness. Innovations can lead them into new and different fields. Also, a high level of technocratization might be necessary to help such firms innovate and cope withtheir more hostile and diverse environments. Finally, attention to product strategy and futurity may be high because major innovation projects force firms to consider where they have been and where they wish to be strategically.

Our subsample statistics are thus consistent with the concepts of conservative and entrepreneurial configurations. We are therefore tentatively justified in applying the interpretations and predictions derived from our two models to the respective subsamples.

Correlational Analysis

We can now begin to test the predictions of the conservative and entrepreneurial models of innovation. Some of the findings are to be found in Table 6-2, which presents the product moment correlations between product innovation and all other variables for conservative and en-

TABLE 6-2: Product Moment Correlations with Innovation

VARIABLES	CONSERVATIVE SUBSAMPLE[a] N = 29	ENTREPRENEURIAL SUBSAMPLE N = 18	TOTAL SAMPLE N = 52	SIGNIFICANCE LEVELS OF DIFFERENCES IN r's BETWEEN SUBSAMPLES (FISHER TRANSFORM)[b]
Environment				
Dynamism	.32**	.36*	.36***	NS
Heterogeneity	.36**	.28	.49***	NS
Hostility	.33**	.25	.43***	NS
Information Processing				
Scanning	.27*	-.36*	.08	.05
Controls	.38**	-.41**	.07	.005
Structure				
Centralization	.15	.25	-.03	NS
Technocratization	.18	.15	.44***	NS
Resources	.13	-.30	-.05	.09

166

Differentiation	.26*	−.09	.48***	NS
Integration	.11	−.33*	−.03	.09
Decision Making				
Analysis	.13	−.39**	.09	.05
Futurity (planning)	.41***	−.67***	.20*	.001
Consciousness of strategy	.47***	−.47**	.33***	.001

[a]The symbols *, **, and *** respectively indicate that the correlation coefficient is significant at the .10, .05, and .01 levels of significance.

[b]We wished to determine if the correlation coefficients of both subsamples represented populations having the same true correlation p. We tested the hypothesis using the ratio:

$$\frac{Z_1 - Z_2}{\sigma(Z_1 - Z_2)}$$

where Z_i represents the Fisher transformed value of the correlation coefficients r_{xy} such that:

$$Z = 1/2 \log_e \left(\frac{1 + r_{xy}}{1 - r_{xy}} \right)$$

and:

$$\sigma(Z_1 - Z_2) = \sqrt{\frac{1}{N_1 - 3} + \frac{1}{N_2 - 3}}$$

trepreneurial configurations and for the total sample. It is obvious that many of the predictions of the respective models are strongly confirmed. We shall discuss the findings for each class of variables.

Environmental Variables. Our discussion predicted that there would be significant positive correlations between environmental variables and innovation for both configurations. Strategic choice rather than environmental pressure was expected to play the greater role in promoting innovation in entrepreneurial firms; the opposite was expected for conservative firms. The implication was that correlations between environment and innovation would therefore be higher for conservatives. Although our results were consistent with this conjecture, they cannot be unambiguously interpreted. All correlations are significant at or beyond the .05 level in the conservative sample, but only one correlation is significant at beyond the .10 level in the entrepreneurial sample. Unfortunately, we cannot make too much of these differences, since none are statistically significant using Fisher's Z statistic. This result should be held in abeyance, however, pending the examination of our multiple regression models.

Information-Processing Variables. Both the information-processing variables show the predicted significant differences between the conservative and entrepreneurial configurations. *Scanning* serves to bolster innovation in firms that are classified as conservative. Attempts to gather information from the environment may make managers aware of the disadvantages of their own product lines and the superiority of the product lines of competitors. Scanning can also point out changing customer desires and buying patterns. In other words, it demonstrates the need for innovation to conservative managers.

The entrepreneurial firms show an opposite relationship between scanning and innovation. A significantly *negative* correlation is manifested. We expected this finding to be caused by information that induces highly innovative and risk-embracing executives to slow down. Scanning may reveal that competitors succeed without introducing many new products, that they cut costs by taking advantage of long production runs, product standardization, and the "economies of stability." Market research may show that customers favor established brands, or pay attention to price and quality more than variety and novelty. The effect of such information might be to reduce superfluous and expensive product innovation.

The same duality in the findings occurs when we examine the relationship between the use of organizational *controls* and innovation. Controls may stimulate innovation in conservative firms, but curb innovative excesses in entrepreneurial firms. It is interesting that the relationship between controls and innovation is greater than that between scanning and innovation. Controls provide concrete quantified information that is hard to dismiss or to rationalize. Controls may indicate to entrepreneurial executives that a great deal of money has been spent on innovation and that very little return has been forthcoming. They may show that reserves of capital have been badly depleted, that productivity and efficiency have fallen, or that scrap rates have escalated because of too much product-line novelty or change. In conservative firms, controls may reveal significant declines in market share, a dramatic reduction in the sales of older, more obsolete products, and declining profitability.

Structural Variables.   Modest support has been found for the predictions of Normann (1971) and Rogers and Shoemaker (1971, p. 384), who postulated that *centralization* is positively correlated with innovation. The reasons for this prediction were given earlier. However, we hesitate to place much reliance on the finding, since none of our coefficients is significant at the .10 level, and the negative samplewide correlation coefficient appears to confuse things. Perhaps in some types of organizations, centralization boosts innovation while in others it serves to obstruct it. Chapter 7 will produce more definitive findings on this point.

Technocratization is positively correlated with innovation in both subsamples as well as in the total sample. This is in line with most of the predictions in the literature (Hage and Aiken, 1970; Zaltman, Duncan, and Holbek, 1973). It is interesting that the samplewide correlation is much more significant than the correlations of the conservative and entrepreneurial subsamples. This may be because the conservative firms are less technocratized *and* less innovative than the entrepreneurial firms. When the subsamples are combined a very positive correlation results.

The finding on *resource availability* surprised us at first. We predicted a positive correlation with innovation for both subsamples, but got a negative one for the entrepreneurial firms. Perhaps this is because among very high innovators, resources are depleted by too much expenditure on new designs and new products. Among the more restrained innovators in the entrepreneurial sample, resources are less apt to be squandered. This confirms the notion that many entrepreneurial firms tend to overspend on innovation and that scanning and control devices are required to inform managers of the hazards of this practice. Collectively, the results so far seem to be telling a story that is consistent with our models.

We predicted that *differentiation* would correlate positively with innovation, but more so in the conservative than in the entrepreneurial configurations. This is essentially what we found. Differentiation is positively and significantly correlated with innovation in the conservative sample. But in the entrepreneurial sample there is actually a slightly negative correlation between the variables.

We also found that *integration* may facilitate innovation somewhat in the conservative firms and restrain it in the entrepreneurial firms. The first relationship is not surprising. It has been widely predicted in the literature (Lawrence and Lorsch, 1967; Galbraith, 1973). Innovation requires the collaboration of various departments and groups of specialists in order to generate ideas for new products, and to plan and actualize their design, production, and marketing. However, the relatively low correlation coefficient for innovation and integration in the conservative sample seems to indicate that integration sometimes is not a very key factor in innovation. Perhaps some conservative firms wait so long to innovate that they are finally forced into it. They must eventually come up with new products even if they do not have adequate integrative mechanisms to do so effectively.

As we expected, in entrepreneurial configurations, integration seems to behave like an information-processing device. It can serve to warn executives of the dangers or costs of excessive innovation. This might happen as, say, cross-functional committees enable production managers to resist pressures from marketing or R&D departments to introduce new products. There is a freer exchange of information, so departments that must bear the brunt of too much innovation will be capable of communicating their difficulties to other departments. Remedial action may then be taken more quickly.

Decision Making Variables.   We hypothesized that the decision making variables would behave very much like the information-processing variables. They would boost innovation in conservative configurations and curb excessive innovation in entrepreneurial ones. Again the findings strongly support the prediction. *Analysis, futurity,* and *consciousness of strategy* formulation correlate positively with innovation in conservative firms and negatively in entrepreneurial firms. Analyzing decisions, carefully weighing alternative courses of action, planning future activities, and explicitly formulating strategy cause a greater awareness of the problems and opportunities facing the firm. In sluggish, conservative firms this tends to increase innovation, and in overly innovative firms, it reduces it.

Multiple Regression Analysis

In order to test the models further, multiple regressions were run on the conservative and entrepreneurial subsamples. Because the number of variables included in the regression is quite high relative to the sample size, the results of our analyses will be tentative. Regression was not used to discover the best predictive equation but rather to crudely control for the influences of the independent variables when trying to establish differences between the two subsamples. The regression results confirmed the correlational findings and explained a very high percentage of the variance in our dependent variable of innovation. Stepwise regression procedures were used to obtain the best models with our variables. A partial F statistic of 1.0 was used as the cutoff point to ensure that only the most predictive variables would be included. For the conservative sample, the best equation was:

INNOVATION =
−1.74 + .25 Dynamism + .26 Hostility + .11 Scanning
+ .26 Futurity + .16 Consciousness of Strategy

Partial F ratios for the variables were 12.4, 9.5, 2.6, 13.3, and 5.7 respectively, with 1, 27 degrees of freedom; all but the third were significant at beyond the .05 level. The R^2 was .678, the multiple R was .823, and the adjusted R^2 was .608. The overall F statistic was 9.67 which is significant at beyond the .01 level with 5, 23 degrees of freedom.

Essentially, then, the conservative model was strongly supported. Environmental, information-processing, and decision-making variables were significantly and positively related to innovation in samples of conservative firms.

For the entrepreneurial sample, we obtained the following regression equation:

INNOVATION =
3.74 − .17 Scanning − .14 Controls + .20 Centralization
+ .27 Technocratization + .30 Differentiation − .31 Futurity
− .15 Resources

Partial F ratios for the variables were 2.1, 3.1, 4.9, 9.8, 7.2, 7.7, and 1.6 respectively, with 1, 16 degrees of freedom. All but the first and last were significant at beyond the .10 level. The R^2 was .785, the multiple R was .886, and the adjusted R^2 was .634. The overall F statistic was 5.21, which is significant at beyond the .01 level with 7, 10 degrees of freedom.

The entrepreneurial model is strongly supported. It is notable that whereas environmental dynamism and hostility were significant predictors in the conservative regression model, no environmental variables approached significance in the entrepreneurial model. Perhaps, then, strategic goals and top-executive motivations are more important than environment for promoting innovation in entrepreneurial firms. This is consistent with the significant relationship between centralization and innovation. Powerful entrepreneurial top executives can more easily implement bold innovations than can those who must share power with their more conservative counterparts. The observed levels of significance for variables of technocratization and differentiation probably result from the tendency for experts and more complex structures to boost innovation, or vice versa (Burns & Stalker, 1961; Lawrence & Lorsch, 1967). Finally, the negative regression coefficients that were expected for information-processing and decision-making variables were also borne out.

Curvilinear Regression Analysis of the Combined Sample

The correlational and regression results suggest that there might be a curvilinear relationship of information-processing and decision-making variables with the level of product innovation. At low levels of innovation, there should be a positive correlation between innovation and information-processing or decision-making variables, while at high levels of innovation, a negative relationship would be manifested. An inverted U-shaped curve such as the one in Figure 6-1 is expected to result. The regression equation that reflects this relationship is $Y = \alpha + \beta_1 X - \beta_2 X^2$, where the dependent variables are scanning, controls, analysis, futurity, and consciousness of strategy, and the independent variables are innovation and innovation–squared. The results of the analyses are given in Table 6-3. They are based upon data from all 52 firms in the sample.

For all but one regression, the additional variance explained by the X^2 term is statistically significant at beyond the .05 level. This is shown by the second partial F statistic for each equation. The appropriateness of the curvilinear function appears to be unquestionable. The inverted U shape of the curve is indicated by the negative beta coefficients for all the second-order independent variables.

An examination of the information-processing variables of equations 1 and 2 of Table 6-3 reveals that the total F statistics are only significant at about the .10 level. This may indicate that there is some substitutability among the variables of scanning and controls in influencing innovation. In some cases, controls may flag the need to boost or curtail innovation; in others, scanning may serve this purpose. If so, we should expect that when we perform regression using an information-processing composite variable that is formed by taking an average of scanning *and* control scores, the

FIGURE 6-1   Innovation, Information Processing, and Decision-Making.

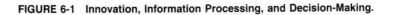
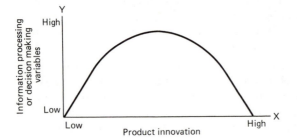

TABLE 6-3: Results of Curvilinear Regression Analysis

GENERAL FORM: $Y = \alpha + \beta_1(\text{Innovation}) + \beta_2(\text{Innovation})^2$

1. Scanning =	$2.61 + 1.25I - .16I^2$		
$F\dagger =$	4.3** 4.0**	Total $F = 2.2$	$R^2 = .08\dagger\dagger$
2. Controls =	$1.85 + 1.57I - .20I^2$		
$F =$	4.8** 4.5**	Total $F = 2.4^*$	$R^2 = .09$
3. Analysis =	$2.60 + .85I - .10I^2$		
$F =$	2.4 2.1	Total $F = 1.3$	$R^2 = .05$
4. Futurity =	$.97 + 1.81I - .22I^2$		
$F =$	9.3*** 7.9***	Total $F = 5.2^{***}$	$R^2 = .17$
5. Con. Str. =	$-.09 + 2.20I - .25I^2$		
$F =$	12.8*** 9.6***	Total $F = 8.5^{***}$	$R^2 = .26$
6. I.P. Comp. =	$2.23 + 1.41I - .18I^2$		
$F =$	7.2*** 6.7**	Total $F = 3.6^{**}$	$R^2 = .13$
7. D. Mkg. Comp. =	$1.16 + 1.62I - .19I^2$		
$F =$	11.9*** 9.6***	Total $F = 7.0^{***}$	$R^2 = .22$
8. Total Comp. =	$1.59 + 1.54I - .19I^2$		
$F =$	12.1*** 10.3***	Total $F = 6.6^{***}$	$R^2 = .21$

*, **, and *** indicate the statistical significance of an *F*-test at the .10, .05, and .01 levels respectively.

†In all cases, the partial *F* statistic is given for the "innovation" and "innovation squared" independent variables, with 1, 49 degrees of freedom. The total *F* applies to the whole regression analysis and has 2, 49 degrees of freedom.

††Although the R^2 statistics are small, this is not a serious problem, since we are not using the regressions to predict the scores along the dependent variables. We merely wished to show that the relationship between innovation and intelligence variables is of the inverted U type.

significance of the results will be boosted. Equation 6 shows that this is exactly what happens.

The decision-making variables of futurity and consciousness of strategy manifest very significant curvilinear relationships with innovation (see equations 4 and 5). The analysis variable does not, perhaps because it displayed only a very modest positive correlation with innovation in the conservative sample. Nonetheless, the overall finding for the decision-making composite variable (formed by taking the mean score of analysis, futurity, and consciousness of strategy) shown in equation 7 is highly significant. Again, there may exist some substitutability among the variables.

Finally, we decided to take a total composite of all five variables relating to information processing and decision making. Again, the curvilinear relationship between the composite and innovation variables is highly significant, as we can see from equation 8. In all except equation 3, our predictions were well-supported.

An essential difference between conservative and entrepreneurial firms can be seen in two representative examples from our sample. Both firms had been losing money for over two years and had called in management consultants. They each benefited from an identical remedy: The consultants installed information systems that not only provided better data on costs and efficiency, but regularly provided managers with information on customer behavior, competitor actions, and other industry developments. The reactions of the two firms to their information system were completely opposite. The managers at the conservative firm came to realize that they had let the competition pass them by—that their product lines were no longer very desirable to younger consumers. They soon began to place more emphasis on new product development. In the entrepreneurial firm, the information system showed managers that their competitors were achieving excellent market penetration with half the number of new products. Executives undertook a consolidation that was to save a considerable fortune.

CONCLUSION

Two very different models of innovation were proposed and tested. Each seemed to be substantially borne out in different corporate configurations. The "conservative" model views product innovation as something done in response to challenges, occurring only when very necessary. The model predicts that innovation will not take place *unless* (1) there are serious challenges, threats, or instabilities in the environment; (2) these are brought to the attention of managers and consciously analyzed by them; and (3) structural, technocratic, and financial resources are adequate for innovation. In short, positive and significant correlations were expected between innovation and environmental, information-processing, decision-making, and structural variables. The predictions of the conservative model were supported for our subsample of conservative firms.

A very different "entrepreneurial" model was also proposed. This model predicts that innovation is a favorite strategy; that it will be boldly engaged in unless there is clear evidence that resources are being eroded by the pursuit of unprofitable novelty. This model postulates that innovation will tend to be excessive and extremely *high* unless (1) information processing (scanning and control) systems warn executives of the dangers of too much innovation, and (2) analytical and strategic-planning processes and structural-integration devices do the same. In other words, negative correlations of innovation with information-processing, decision-making, and structural-integration devices were expected. The entrepreneurial model also predicts low-order positive correlations of innovation with environment and only moderately positive correlations with structural devices. Goals and strategies rather than environment or structure are seen to be the key impetuses to innovation. Most of the predictions derived from the entrepreneurial model were borne out in our subsample of entrepreneurial firms.

A central message of this research is that taxonomies have key predictive implications. The determinants of product innovation in firms are to a great extent a function of the type of configuration being studied. The impact of information processing, decision making, and to a lesser degree, some environmental and structural devices, appears to be a function of the type of firm and its chosen strategy. Many of the conflicts in the innovation literature that have been highlighted by Rogers and Shoemaker (1971), Downs and Mohr (1976), and Zaltman et al. (1973) show promise of being resolved when we begin to make distinctions among configurations in studying the relationships between innovation and its context.

On a somewhat more practical plane, the research suggests that in addition to making remedial efforts to stimulate innovation in stagnating firms, it might also be useful to take care that innovation does not become an end in itself. It is necessary to ensure that the rate of innovation does not outstrip its utility or the organization's ability to pay. If the speculations of Chapter 10 are correct, there may be a tendency for any organizational trend to have momentum—that is, to feed upon itself, perhaps being protracted past the point of usefulness. This might be true of the drift toward excessive conservatism *or* excessive entrepreneurialism. Practitioners should begin to focus upon the second danger as well as the first.

7

The Determinants
of Entrepreneurship
in Three Configurations

INTRODUCTION

Entrepreneurship can be defined and studied in a broader, less restrictive manner than tradition seems to indicate. There has been a strong tendency to identify entrepreneurship with a dominant organizational personality, generally an independent-minded owner-manager who makes the strategic decisions for his firm (Cole, 1946; Redlich, 1949; Hartman, 1959; Collins and Moore 1970; Shapero, 1975). The emphasis has been upon the innovative abilities of this individual, and generally, the entrepreneur as actor has been the focus of the research. This chapter shifts the emphasis somewhat, looking at the entrepreneurial activity of the *firm*. With the growth and increased complexity of organizations, there is a constant need for renewal, innovation, risk taking, and the pursuit of new opportunities. These activities often go beyond the efforts of one key manager. The entrepreneurial role stressed by Schumpeter (1934) is socially vital, but it can be performed by entire organizations. It can easily exceed or even circumvent the contributions of one crucial actor. In some firms, organizational

Adapted from Danny Miller, "The Correlates of Entrepreneurship in Three Types of Firms," *Management Science* 29, No. 7 (July 1983) 770–791.

The author would like to thank Professors Peter H. Friesen, Manfred F. R. Kets de Vries, Henry Mintzberg and Jean-Marie Toulouse for their comments on an earlier draft of this chapter. This research was supported in part by grant EQ 1162 of the Government of Quebec, and by John Labatt Ltd.

renewal is performed by a traditional entrepreneur. In others, it is the province of a head-office "planning" or "ventures" department. And in still other organizations, it may be performed at lower levels of the hierarchy in R&D, engineering, marketing, or even production departments. But what is most important is not who the critical actor is, but the *process* of entrepreneurship itself and the organizational factors that foster and impede it. These are the foci of the chapter. The theme, once again, is that different predictive models are needed to explain adaptation in different organizational configurations.

Previous literature causes us to treat entrepreneurship as a multidimensional concept encompassing the firm's actions relating to product-market and technological innovation (Schumpeter, 1934; Cole, 1946; Cooper, 1973), risk taking (Collins and Moore, 1970; Kets de Vries, 1977), and proactiveness (Miller and Friesen, 1978; Mintzberg, 1973). An entrepreneurial firm is one that engages in product-market innovation, undertakes somewhat risky ventures, and is *first* to come up with "proactive" innovations, beating competitors to the punch. A non-entrepreneurial firm innovates very little, is highly risk-averse, and imitates the moves of competitors instead of leading the way. We can tentatively view entrepreneurship as a composite weighting of these three variables. A statistical justification for this will be presented later.

Much has been written on the determinants of entrepreneurship. Different works stress different determinants. For example, Shapero (1975), Collins and Moore (1970), Collins, Moore, and Unwalla (1967), Kets de Vries (1977), and Toulouse (1980) have stressed the importance of personality factors, psychodynamic characteristics, and the sociocultural background of the chief executive in fostering entrepreneurial behavior. In contrast, March and Simon (1958), Burns and Stalker (1961), V. Thompson (1961), J. Thompson (1967), and Hage and Aiken (1970) have called attention to the environmental and structural aspects of the firm that seem to promote innovation and entrepreneurial activity. Finally, Ackoff (1970), Mintzberg (1973), and Miller and Friesen (1978) have stressed decision-making and strategy factors.

Not only do authors place varying emphases upon the different determinants of entrepreneurship; debates also abound about the effect of a given variable. Take the case of centralization. Thompson (1967), Normann (1971), and Hage and Dewar (1973, p. 285) argue that centralization will promote innovation, the latter being vital to entrepreneurship. According to Thompson (1967, pp. 153–54):

> . . . diffusion of power to the point where no inner circle emerges with sufficient stability to give direction to the organization . . . [may result in] administrative behavior [which is] problem oriented, not aggressive, and . . . safety oriented, not innovative.

But a very different message issues from another body of literature. Burns and Stalker (1961), Thompson (1961), and Litwak (1961) point out the advantages that expertise-based power and extensive delegation of decision-making authority have in *promoting* innovation. We shall try to show that this conflict and many others in the literature are due to the failure to distinguish among types or configurations in examining the determinants of entrepreneurship. The central theme of this chapter, as well as its main finding, is that the correlates of entrepreneurship vary in a systematic and logical way from one configuration to another.

The chapter is structured as follows: First we briefly describe three common but very different types of firms and predict the determinants of entrepreneurship for each. We then proceed to describe our variables and to validate our typology of firms using hypothesis testing and analysis of variance techniques. Finally, we present our findings on the correlates of entrepreneurship for each type of configuration.

CONFIGURATIONS AND THEIR
ENTREPRENEURIAL CORRELATES

Our first task was to arrive at a predictive typology of firms that would focus upon *common* but very *different* types. We wished the typology to include environmental, structural, and strategic variables, since these have all been shown to influence entrepreneurship. Unfortunately, we could not use the types derived in Chapter 4, since our sample was too small to be divided into ten groups. The work by Mintzberg (1973, 1979) posits far fewer types. His three modes of strategy making and his five structural configurations of Chapter 3—three of which relate quite naturally to his strategy-making modes—served as a promising basis for our typology. Aside from the broad scope, a key strength of Mintzberg's work is that it represents the outcome of an exceedingly thorough and widely acclaimed synthesis of the literature on policy and organizational theory.

But there were some problems in using Mintzberg's types. A major shortcoming is that they have not been empirically validated. Thus, it was necessary for us to establish the generality and predictiveness of his typology. Second, Mintzberg did not directly make the link between his strategy-making modes and his structures. This task fell to us. Fortunately, Mintzberg (1973) discusses the environmental and structural contexts of each of his strategy-making modes. A third problem was that it would have been impossible to accurately and parsimoniously measure all of Mintzberg's (1979) structural attributes in a questionnaire study such as ours. Thus, we have focused mostly upon his (1973) environmental and strategy-making variables and have employed rough surrogates for only a subset of his structural variables of Chapter 3. Fourth, each of the three types had to be defined to allow considerable variation in the degree of entrepreneurship—our dependent variable. Finally, because leader personality has been shown to be critical to entrepreneurship (Shapero, 1975; Miller, Kets de Vries, and Toulouse, 1982), we decided to go beyond Mintzberg's work to take this into account.

As a result of these problems, our three types are only loosely based upon those discussed in Mintzberg (1973) and in Chapter 3. It is suggestive of the generality of the typology, however, that each type recalls many of the ones described by other organizational theorists. Essentially, our *Simple* firms are those that pursue Mintzberg's (1973) "Entrepreneurial" mode of strategy making and possess his "Simple" structure. Our *Planning* firms are those that have adopted his "Planning" mode of strategy making and his "Machine Bureaucracy" structure. Finally, our *Organic* firms conform to Mintzberg's (1973) "Adaptive" mode of strategy making and suggest his "Adhocracy" structure. Although these types do not exhaust the population of business firms, they do tend to be rather common and quite different from one another, and this is all that we needed for our typology. We anticipated that the determinants of entrepreneurship would be different for each of the three types.

Type 1. Simple Firms: The Leadership Imperative

These are small firms operating in homogeneous environments and generally run by owner-managers. Ease of entry makes markets hostile, and the small size of these firms leaves them susceptible to threats from competitors. Power is highly centralized in the hands of one or two top administrators. This is often practical, since firms tend to be so simple and undiversified. One person can usually master their intricacies and effectively control them. According to Mintzberg (1979, p. 306):

> The *simple structure* is characterized, above all, by what it is not—elaborated. Typically, it has little or no technostructure (e.g., planning and control personnel), few support staffers, and minimal differentiation among its units. Coordination is effected largely by direct supervision.

Strategy making in these firms tends to be intuitive rather than analytical. It is performed by people who have a "feel" for their business, not by staff planners or technocrats. There is generally little planning, time horizons are short, and the focus is upon operating matters rather than visionary master plans (Filley and House, 1969). Finally, strategies are not explicitly or formally elaborated but reside as the implicit and often vague visions of the leaders.

In Simple firms, we expect there to be a "leadership imperative" driving entrepreneurship. This is largely because the orientation of the firms is tied so closely to one central actor. Three prime factors, all of them leadership-related, are expected to determine the level of entrepreneurship. These include the personality, the power, and the store of knowledge of the leader.

> *Hypothesis 1.1:* Because the leaders are the driving force behind the Simple firms, their personalities will be a key determinant of entrepreneurship. Their *"locus of control"*[1] (Rotter, 1966) may be especially crucial. The work of Miller et al. (1982) and Shapero (1975) shows that "internal" leaders, those confident of their ability to control their environment, are the most likely to be entrepreneurial.
>
> *Hypothesis 1.2: Centralization* of decision-making power is also expected to be positively correlated with entrepreneurship. Where the leaders have arrogated most of the power to themselves, they are freer to embark upon innovations and entrepreneurial ventures (Wilson, 1966; Sapolsky, 1967; Normann, 1971).
>
> *Hypothesis 1.3:* In small Simple firms, the chief executives often act as the brain. We propose that the more knowledge they have about emerging markets, products, and technologies, the greater the number of innovative ideas they will have and the higher the level of entrepreneurship. Two key sources of such ideas will be environmental *scanning* (Aguilar, 1967; Carter and Williams, 1957) and discussions with *technocrats* (Hage and Aiken, 1970; Miller, 1971).

To summarize, in small, centralized firms, entrepreneurship is predominantly influenced by the leaders: their personality, their power, and their information. They are in a position sufficiently powerful to override structural and environmental obstacles to entrepreneurship. They can also resist entrepreneurial activity in the face of environmental incentives and structural pressures.

Type 2. Planning Firms: The Strategic Imperative

The emphasis or objective of Planning firms is smooth, efficient, and regular functioning. Such firms try to buffer themselves even from their rather stable and predictable environments, to function with a machinelike harmony. This aim tends to be reflected by the structure of the organization, principally by the use of elaborate control and planning systems, the extensive use of structural integration devices such as committees and task forces, a low to moderate level of interdepartmental differentiation, and a powerful central group of managers and technocrats who dominate decision making. Typically, the firm has an abundant store of slack resources.

According to Mintzberg (1973), there are three central *strategy-making* features characterizing the planning mode: the analyst plays a major advisory role in strategy making; there is a systematic analysis of the costs and

---

[1]The terms italicized in our hypotheses are the names of the variables we measured in our data base.

benefits of competing proposals; and there is a careful integration of decisions. The stable environment allows a somewhat mechanical orientation, making it easier and safer for the firm to buffer itself from external uncertainties. It is too difficult to plan or to use sophisticated control systems when the ground rules keep changing.

What factors are likely to determine entrepreneurship here? Some might be tempted to say that these firms will be anything but entrepreneurial. But Planning firms often pursue a systematic and orderly process of innovation and product-market renewal. We anticipate that entrepreneurial activity will be mainly a function of the strategy pursued by Planning firms—hence our title, "the strategic imperative." Specifically, we hypothesize the following (variable names are italicized):

> *Hypothesis 2.1:* The *explicitness* and *integration* of product-market strategies are likely to be the critical factors influencing entrepreneurship. Vague and disjointed strategies increase the natural danger that Planners will begin to focus exclusively on internal matters such as operating efficiency.[2] If there is a clear and well-articulated product-market strategy, it draws attention to the big picture: the distinctive competence of the firm, its ultimate mission, its business scope, and present and future target markets (Ansoff, 1965; Steiner, 1969).[3]
>
> *Hypothesis 2.2:* Because power is centralized, the *locus of control* of the chief executive is again expected to be important, as was the case in the Simple firms.
>
> *Hypothesis 2.3:* Planners' efforts to buffer themselves from their environment make them far less responsive to it (Burns and Stalker, 1961; Mintzberg, 1979). Thus we predict that environmental *dynamism* and *hostility* will *not* correlate significantly with entrepreneurship for samples composed of Planners.
>
> *Hypothesis 2.4:* Only planned, regular, and predictable entrepreneurship is palatable to Planners. This can be as easily undertaken by firms with "mechanistic" structures as those with "organic" ones (the former

---

[2]In the Simple firms, an explicit strategy is not needed to induce innovation. The dominant leader's private visions of the future are enough to guide the firm. But in the larger and more complex Planning firms, many managers must be involved in decision making. Unless product-market strategies are articulated explicitly enough to guide these managers, the firm can lose its sense of direction and thus begin to ignore product-market posture. The Planner's natural compulsion to pursue efficient and mechanical operation will then thwart entrepreneurship, and the status quo will prevail. The focus becomes operations instead of mission, maintenance instead of progression.

[3]It can be argued that product-market strategies might be explicit and integrated but still oriented toward the status quo. There can, in other words, be an explicit strategy of conservatism. But we think this is unlikely in the case of most Planners. Any focus on product-market mission by the many staff technocrats and experts will induce them to be more concerned with seizing innovative opportunities and avoiding obsolescence. Decisions tend to be made analytically in these firms, and product-market analysis will tend to lead to product-market entrepreneurship (Ansoff, 1965). Where product-market strategies are too vague and fragmented to command the attention of managers, the focus will more likely be upon the production and operating problems that are an abiding obsession in Planning firms.

are *centralized,* have restricted hierarchial *communication,* high *integration,* low *differentiation,* and tight formal *controls*). Either type of structure will do. Thus, for Planners, we predict that our structural variables will *not* relate significantly to the level of entrepreneurship. This goes against the predictions of Zaltman et al. (1973), Lawrence and Lorsch (1967), and indeed most of the literature on organizations.

To recap, the level of entrepreneurship in the Planning firms is expected to be largely a function of the explicitness and integration of the product-market strategy. Clear, explicit, well-integrated strategies may make executives focus regularly on the need for product-market renewal. Vague, implicit product-market strategies increase the likelihood that Planners will develop too much of a preoccupation with operating problems and efficiency at the expense of giving sufficient attention to the prospects of products and markets.

Type 3. Organic Firms: The Environmental and Structural Imperatives

These are perhaps the most interesting firms highlighted by recent literature. Their structures correspond roughly to the adhocracies of Chapter 3, as well as Burns and Stalker's (1961) "organic" firms, and Lawrence and Lorsch's (1967) plastics firms. The firms tend to operate in dynamic environments where customer tastes, product-service technologies, and competitive weapons often change unpredictably. Because product-market innovations are common in such firms, managers often find themselves dealing with a diverse array of customers—that is, with a heterogeneous market.

To cope with the very complex setting, these firms adopt a rather organic structure. They try to be responsive to their challenging environments. Adaptation is facilitated by five structural devices. First, much authority is delegated to lower-level personnel. The adaptive task is too difficult to be done exclusively by the top managers. Second, much use is made of technocrats such as scientists and engineers in creating product and technological innovations (Hage and Aiken, 1970). Third, such firms engage in much scanning of the environment to discover important challenges and opportunities (Carter and Williams, 1957). Fourth, they are highly differentiated, as diverse contingencies posed by the environment require individuals and departments with very different abilities (Wilson, 1966; Lawrence and Lorsch, 1967). Finally, there is a need for extensive and open internal communication among organizational members so that they can work jointly on complex innovative projects (Thompson, 1961; Litwak, 1961; Burns and Stalker, 1961).

Strategy making resembles Mintzberg's (1973) "adaptive" mode. It emphasizes careful but quick analysis of issues and is performed by many levels of managers. There may be no time for lengthy studies. Also, planning horizons are not very long because of the turbulent environment. Finally, strategies cannot be explicitly conceptualized or articulated, since they must change rapidly. In fact, complex, detailed, and tightly integrated strategies may be too confining for these firms (Mintzberg, 1973).

Because Organic firms strive to be adaptive, their entrepreneurial efforts will reflect the demands of their environments and the capacities of their structures (hence the "environmental-structural imperative"). More specifically:

> *Hypothesis 3.1:* The more *dynamic* and *hostile* the environment, the more firms will be entrepreneurial. Dynamism and hostility require innovation. Managers try to tailor their entrepreneurial efforts to the demands of markets (Burns and Stalker, 1961; Thompson, 1967).
>
> *Hypothesis 3.2:* Structure will importantly influence entrepreneurship. For example, delegation (*decentralization*) of authority to lower-level experts allows the most knowledgeable people to help the firm adapt and innovate (Hage and Aiken, 1970). The use of *technocrats* increases the store of innovative ideas. Organizational *differentiation* provides the mix of skills necessary to develop these ideas (Lawrence and Lorsch, 1967). And finally, effective and open internal *communications* bring together those with different skills so that they can collaborate effectively on innovative projects (Litwak, 1961; Rogers and Shoemaker, 1971).
>
> *Hypothesis 3.3:* The *locus of control* of the top executive will have *little* influence upon entrepreneurship in Organic firms. Power is decentralized, and the entrepreneurial effort is carried out by many lower-level technocrats and department heads, not by the top executive.
>
> *Hypothesis 3.4:* Whereas in Planning firms, *an explicit* and *integrated strategy* should boost entrepreneurship, this is less true of Organic firms. Consciousness of strategy may unite the efforts of technocrats and help them to work more effectively toward a central goal. But extremely detailed, tightly integrated, long-standing product-market strategies will serve to constrain adaptive behavior and curtail entrepreneurship. They will reduce the flexibility so necessary to Organic firms.

To summarize, the two key determinants of entrepreneurship in Organic firms will be environment and structure. The more challenging the firms' environments, the greater their need to be entrepreneurial; the more organic their structures, the better they are able to recognize and fulfill this need.

Table 7-1 summarizes the anticipated features of the three types of firms and the expected determinants of entrepreneurship in each. It is notable that for each type, a different category of variables is expected to be related to the level of entrepreneurship: In the Simple firm, it is the leader's personality, power, and knowledge; in the Planning firm, it is strategy and leader personality; and in the Organic firm, it is environment and structure.

TABLE 7-1: Expected Type Attributes and Hypothesized Determinants of Entrepreneurship

	SIMPLE: ATT.*	SIMPLE: HYP.**	PLANNING: ATT.	PLANNING: HYP.	ORGANIC: ATT.	ORGANIC: HYP.
Size	c Small***		c Large		Medium	(0)
Locus of Control		(−)		(−)		(0)
Environment						
Dynamism	Medium		Low	(0)	High	(+)
Heterogeneity	Low		Medium		High	(+)
Hostility	High		Low	(0)	Medium	(+)
Organization Structure						
Scanning	Low	(+)	Medium	(0)	High	(+)
Controls	Low		c High	(0)	Medium	
Communication			High		c High	(+)
Resources	Low		c Medium	(0)	Medium	
Centralization	c High	(+)	Medium		c Low	(−)
Technocratization	Low	(+)	Medium		c High	(0)
Differentiation	Low		High	(0)	High	(+)
Integration	Low			(0)	Medium	
Strategy/Decision Making						
Analysis	Low		High		Medium	
Futurity	Low		c High		Medium	
Explicitness of product-market strategy	Low		High	(+)	Medium	(+)
Strategic integration	Medium		High	(+)	Low	(−)
Entrepreneurial Imperative	Leadership (personality, power, and knowledge)		Strategy		Environment & structure	

*Att. stands for attributes of the types. High, Medium, and Low are ranks relative to the other two groups. Where the space is left blank, the authors discussing the types tended to be noncommittal.

**Hyp. signifies hypothesized relationship with entrepreneurship. Signs indicate an expected positive (+) or negative (−) correlation with entrepreneurship on the basis of our hypotheses. (0) indicates that we expect an insignificant relationship. A blank space indicates no opinion.

***Variables preceded by a c are those that were used as classificatory criteria.

METHOD

The Variables and Questionnaires

In order to test the hypotheses derived in the last section, we employed a lengthy questionnaire to gather information on variables of environment, organization structure, decision making style, strategy, and entrepreneurship. The questionnaire is available from the authors. We measured a number of distinct indicants and aspects for each variable to ensure that it would be broadly and thoroughly measured. Scale items were averaged to obtain the variable scores. In every instance, the Cronbach Alpha measure far exceeded the guidelines established by Van de Ven and Ferry (1980, pp. 78–82). The standard of comparison for our scales was all other firms, unless different polarities were specified. The data sample was described in Chapter 6.

There are many ways to describe personality, but we were concerned mainly with factors that relate to entrepreneurship. The literature points very strongly to "locus of control" (Rotter, 1966) as a critical characteristic influencing entrepreneurial behavior. Shapero (1975), Kets de Vries (1977), and Miller, Kets de Vries, and Toulouse (1982) have established that entrepreneurial behavior such as risk taking, innovation, and proactiveness is strongly associated with locus of control. Specifically, the more "internal" the executives—that is, the more they feel they have control over their environment and their destiny—the more entrepreneurial their behavior. In contrast, if they believe that outcomes influencing their lives are principally due to chance or to elements beyond their control, they are much less likely to take risks or to be innovative and proactive. We measured locus of control using Rotter's (1966) well-known internal-external scale.

VALIDATING THE TYPOLOGY

Because Mintzberg's work [(1973) and Chap. 3] was conceptual rather than empirical, it was necessary to establish the predictiveness of the typology. Two methods were used to do this. The first classifies firms using only a few structural and strategy-making characteristics, and then attempts to determine whether the remaining characteristics are in line with those attributed to each type. The second method performs analyses of variance to establish whether the groups of firms are significantly different from one another in the manner predicted.

Let us consider the first method of assessing the typology. Firms were classified into one of the three types (or as outliers) using a selection of attributes that Mintzberg (1973, 1979, and personal communication)

TABLE 7-2: Selection Criteria and Variable Means and Standard Deviations for the Types

Selection Criteria	TYPE 1: SIMPLE FIRMS		TYPE 2: PLANNING FIRMS		TYPE 3: ORGANIC FIRMS		ALL TYPES	
	No. of Employees < 500 Centralization > 5		No. of Employees ≥ 500 Controls Futurity > 4 Centralization & Analysis ≥ 4		Centralization ≤ 4 Technocratization > 4 Communication ≥ 4			
Sample Size	18		18		13		52	
VARIABLES	*M.*	*S.D.*	*M.*	*S.D.*	*M.*	*S.D.*	*M.*	*S.D.*
Sales ($MM)	18	33	405	923	493	518	230	639
No. of Employees (00s)	2	3	44	100	31	36	22	66
Locus of Control of Leader	6.0	2.2	4.4	1.9	4.4	1.6	5.4	3.2
Environment								
Dynamism	4.0	1.8	3.7	1.1	4.2	1.2	3.9	1.5
Heterogeneity	3.4	1.4	4.5	1.3	5.2	1.5	4.1	1.6
Hostility	4.4	1.3	4.0	1.0	4.2	1.0	4.2	1.1

Organization Structure

Scanning	4.3	1.7	5.1	1.3	5.4	1.3	4.7	1.4
Controls	3.5	1.7	5.6	.7	4.9	1.8	4.4	1.7
Communication	5.0	.9	4.9	1.2	4.5	1.5	4.9	1.1
Resources	4.1	1.6	4.9	1.0	4.5	1.2	4.3	1.3
Centralization	6.2	.4	5.0	.8	3.5	.7	5.1	1.2
Technocratization	3.2	1.9	4.6	1.4	5.4	1.1	4.0	1.7
Differentiation	2.7	1.0	4.0	1.7	4.8	1.4	3.5	1.8
Integration	4.9	1.3	5.2	1.0	4.3	1.2	4.8	1.2

Decision Making/Strategy

Analysis	3.6	1.3	4.8	.9	4.7	1.4	4.0	1.3
Futurity	3.4	1.5	5.5	.5	4.2	1.7	4.1	1.5
Explicitness of Product-Market Strategy	3.4	1.9	4.8	1.3	4.2	1.4	3.9	1.6
Strategic Integration	4.5	1.2	4.7	1.0	4.2	1.1	4.3	1.1

Entrepreneurship

Innovation	3.2	1.8	3.8	1.3	4.1	1.6	3.5	1.6
Proactiveness	3.9	2.0	4.9	1.0	4.7	1.1	4.3	1.5
Risk Taking	3.2	1.3	3.9	1.1	3.8	1.1	3.6	1.2
Average (Entrep.)	3.4	1.3	4.2	.8	4.2	1.1	3.8	1.2

deemed central to each. Simple firms were classified according to their small size (< 500 employees) and high centralization of power (score of > 5 on the 7-point scale). Planning firms had to be large ≥ 500 employees) and centralized (score of ≥ 4), and to make use of sophisticated controls (> 4), long-range planning (futurity > 4), and much analysis of decisions (> 4). Finally, Organic firms were classified as those having a low centralization score (≤ 4), open internal communications (≥ 4), and high technocratization (> 4).

With the firms classified using these criteria, the problem was to assess the predictiveness of the typology. In other words, given the classification, is it possible to accurately predict the characteristics of the types summarized in Table 7-2? This was easy to establish. We trichotomized our variables into low, high, and medium ranks. These terms signified that relative to other groups, the average variable score for the type was the lowest of the three, the highest, or "in between" respectively. The variables of size, communication, and centralization did not have to be predicted, since they were used to classify firms. For three variables (controls, technocratization, and futurity) only the *high* rank was used as a classification criterion. It was thus necessary to predict only the low and medium ranks for these variables.

As we can see from comparing Table 7-1 to Table 7-2, 35 out of the 37 ranks (those on Table 7-1 *not* marked with a *c*) were classified correctly. We erred only on the integration variable. The probability of arriving at so accurate a classification under the null hypothesis of ignorance was less than .00001, a most significant *p*-value. Thus our typology seems to be quite predictive.

We can get some intuitive grasp of the predictiveness of the typology by taking the example of the Simple firm. The classification criteria for admission to this category were small size and extremely centralized power. It is encouraging that the group of companies defined by these criteria had all the attributes that were listed on Table 7-1 and in our descriptions. That is, as we can see from Table 7-2, compared to Planning and Organic firms, Simple firms were in a less heterogeneous and more hostile market, and were the least technocratized and differentiated. Their use of control systems was minimal, and their decision making was the least analytical. Strategies were the most vaguely articulated. The same predictiveness was obtained for the Planning and Organic groups.

The second method of validating the typology consisted of a series of one-way analyses of variance. Since the means of variables used to define groups were forced to differ significantly across types, these were of course excluded from our analysis. However, where a variable was used to define only one group, a *t*-test was used to compare the means on that variable for the remaining groups to see if they differed as predicted. The results are presented in Table 7-3. As we can see, the analysis of variance shows the

**TABLE 7-3:   Analysis of Variance and *t*-Tests
for the Three Types for Nonclassificatory Variables[a]**

	F-RATIO[b]	*t*-STATISTIC[c]
Dynamism	1.0	
Heterogeneity	5.7***	
Hostility	1.2	
Scanning	1.8	
Controls		2.3** (29)
Resources	2.9*	
Technocratization		2.5*** (34)
Differentiation	6.1***	
Integration	2.9*	
Analysis	6.2***	
Futurity		1.4* (29)
Explicitness of strategy	5.9***	
Strategic integration	0.8	
Innovation	0.7	
Proactiveness	3.8**	
Risk taking	2.5*	
Entrepreneurship	3.6**	

[a]Variables of size, communication, and centralization were omitted, since these were used to classify firms or were not predicted to differ among types. Variables used to generate groups cannot be used to establish the predictiveness of any typology.

[b]The F-ratio presented has 2, 46 degrees of freedom. The symbols *, **, and *** indicate statistical significance at the .10, .05, and .01 levels respectively.

[c]Where a variable was used for purposes of classification for one group only, the differences in means for the other groups were tested using a *t*-test. The degrees of freedom are presented in brackets.

variable means of groups to be significantly different in the predicted direction according to the *F*-statistic for heterogeneity, resources, differentiation, integration, analysis, and explicitness of strategy. Differences are also significant for proactiveness, risk taking, and average entrepreneurship. The *t*-tests show significant differences along the controls, technocratization, and futurity variables. Thus, our groups of firms have clearcut differences along most attributes. Their characterization as Simple, Planning, and Organic configurations seems to be quite accurate.

FINDINGS

We shall, for purposes of relevance and brevity, focus upon the relationships between the independent variables and our aggregate entrepreneurship variable. The latter is simply an arithmetic average of the 7 items of the innovation, proactiveness, and risk-taking variables. As we noted at the outset, the literature shows entrepreneurship to be a multidimensional concept comprising at least the above three dimensions (Toulouse, 1980;

Kets de Vries, 1977). In general, theorists would not call a firm entrepreneurial if it changed its technology or product line simply by imitating competitors and refusing to take any risks. Some proactiveness would be essential as well. By the same token, risk-taking firms that are financially levered are not always considered entrepreneurial. They must also engage in product-market or technological innovation. Thus, our focus upon the composite dimension seems reasonable.

The Cronbach Alpha coefficient for the 7-item entrepreneurial variable is .88. Also, the correlations between entrepreneurship and its component variables of innovation, proactiveness, and risk taking are .82, .76, and .80 respectively (all correlations are significant at beyond the .001 level). Finally, in 79 percent (114/144) of the cases, correlations that are significant/not significant between aggregate entrepreneurship and the independent variables are significant in the same direction/not significant for innovation, proactiveness, and risk taking.

Where the correlational findings for the aggregate entrepreneurial variable are not representative of most of its component variables, we shall often mention this in the text. Readers who are interested in the relationships between innovation, proactiveness, risk taking and the independent variables can find these in Appendix 7-1.

The correlational and regression results are given in Tables 7-4 and 7-5. Stepwise regressions were run merely to obtain some idea of the unique contributions of the most important independent variables to entrepreneurship. The small sample size of the Organic subsample makes the exact predictor equation somewhat unreliable. A cutoff of 2.0 for the partial F ratio was used to ensure that only the most relevant variables would be included. Before we proceed with a discussion of each hypothesis, it might be useful to summarize the findings. In general, most of the hypotheses are confirmed, and there is a high degree of explanation of the dependent variable for each type.

Simple firms show the expected high correlations of entrepreneurship with locus of control and centralization, as well as with scanning and technocratization. No other correlations are significant. Thus, all variables contributing to entrepreneurship in Simple firms appear to be leader-related—namely, personality, power, and knowledge from scanning and technical advice. Together, locus of control and centralization explain 52 percent of the variance in entrepreneurship.

As predicted, the major correlates of entrepreneurship for the *Planners* are the explicitness of strategy and leader locus of control. Environmental and most structural variables seem to matter hardly at all, with the possible exceptions of technocratization and differentiation. The latter may provide the variety and expertise necessary for innovation. Explicitness of strategy and technocratization together explain 59 percent of the variance in entrepreneurship.

TABLE 7-4: Product Moment Correlations of Variables with Entrepreneurship for Three Types

	SIMPLE FIRMS N = 18	PLANNING FIRMS N = 18	ORGANIC FIRMS N = 13	ALL TYPES N = 52
Locus of Control of Leader	-.66***	-.43**	-.16	-.64***
Environment				
Dynamism	.09	-.06	.52**	.35***
Heterogeneity	.18	.22	.44*	.41***
Hostility	.24	.12	.50**	.26**
Organization/Structure				
Scanning	.41**	.21	-.01	.26**
Controls	.12	.13	-.11	.11
Communication	-.09	.27	.38*	.08
Resources	-.10	-.11	-.18	-.07
Centralization	.40**	-.06	-.60**	-.01
Technocratization	.51**	.36*	.53**	.46***
Differentiation	.19	.34*	.10	.46***
Integration	.31*	-.11	.00	.10
Decision Making/Strategy				
Analysis	-.10	.20	.42*	.19*
Futurity	.15	.10	.37*	.25**
Explicitness of strategy	.24	.69***	.43*	.39***
Strategic integration	.02	.33*	-.31	-.09
Entrepreneurship				
Innovation				.82***
Proactiveness				.76***
Risk taking				.80***

*, **, and *** indicate that the correlations are significant at the .10, .05, and .01 levels respectively.

TABLE 7-5:   Multiple Regressions for Entrepreneurship in the Three Types of Firms*

Simple Firms:

Entrepreneurship = .31 − .35 Locus of Control + .84 Centralization
Beta: −.61   .29
    Partial F: 11.1   2.5
        Overall F = 8.03, d.f. 2,15, p = .005, R = .72, R^2 = .52, Adj. R^2 = .45

Planning Firms:

Entrepreneurship = 1.40 + .41 Explicitness of Strategy + .19 Technocratization
Beta: .68   .33
    Partial F: 17.1   4.1
        Overall F = 10.9, d.f. 2,15, p = .005, R = .77, R^2 = .59, Adj. R^2 = .54

Organic Firms:

Entrepreneurship = 3.2 − .96 Centrali-   .53 Explicitness   .40 Techno-
                            zation   +   of Strategy +   cratization
        Beta: −.57   .65   .41
            Partial F: 13.3   19.6   6.7
            Overall F = 13.8, d.f. 3,10, p = .001, R = .91, R^2 = .82, Adj. R^2 = .76

---

*In adding variables to the regression, a cutoff point of 2.0 was used for the partial F ratio. Variables not meeting this criterion would not explain a significant amount of variance even at the .10 level.

Finally, for *Organic* firms, many structural, decision-making, and environmental variables seem to correlate with entrepreneurship, whereas locus of control does not. Again, this generally conforms with our predictions. Table 7-5 shows that collectively, centralization, explicitness of strategy, and technocratization explain 82 percent of the variance in entrepreneurship.

DISCUSSION

Simple Firms and the Leadership Imperative

The findings presented in Tables 7-4 and 7-5 leave little doubt that leadership-related factors are those most correlated with entrepreneurial activity in the Simple firms. These are of at least three varieties: the leaders' personalities as portrayed by their locus of control scores, their power, and their knowledge of markets and products. We shall discuss each factor in turn.

Hypothesis 1.1.   Our first hypothesis is strongly borne out: Locus of control is indeed very significantly correlated with entrepreneurial activity in the Simple configuration. The more "internal" the leaders—that is, the more they believe events to be subject to their own control and influence—the more likely it is for their firms to undertake entrepreneurial projects. This is consistent with the findings of Shapero (1975) and Miller, Kets de Vries, and Toulouse (1982). In contrast, "external" leaders will feel that events are beyond their influence; they will be more passive in dealing with their environments. Since leaders dominate the Simple firms so thoroughly, their personalities are a critical factor—indeed, according to our findings, the *most* critical factor—in determining entrepreneurship. As we can see from Table 7-4, personality far overrides the effect of environmental, structural, and decision-making factors upon entrepreneurship in the Simple firms. Here, entrepreneurship requires an entrepreneur.

Hypothesis 1.2.   Hypothesis 1.2 correctly predicted that centralization would correlate with entrepreneurship in the Simple firm. The more powerful the leader, the more entrepreneurial the company. This supports the arguments of Hage and Dewar (1973), Normann (1971), and Thompson (1967), cited earlier, but not those of Burns and Stalker (1961), Thompson (1961), and Litwak (1961). Having leadership divided among several partners of a small firm can paralyze action when there are dissenting views. The partners may veto one another's proposals so that no entrepreneurial programs can be implemented. In contrast, where a leader has unchallenged authority, he can confidently make entrepreneurial decisions without having to be concerned about their ultimate acceptability to other managers. We shall see that things are very different in Organic firms.

Hypothesis 1.3.   As expected, we found a positive correlation between scanning and entrepreneurship. Because in Simple firms the entrepreneurial task usually falls upon one person, his knowledge of the environment—that is, of customer wants, sources of supply, and competitor strategies—will provide the information necessary for an aggressive competitive strategy.

There is also a positive correlation between technocratization and entrepreneurship. Where leaders are frequently in touch with scientists, engineers, or even marketing experts, they are more likely to become informed of new-product opportunities and to engage in entrepreneurial activity. Also, technocrats enjoy working at the forefront of their fields and want to develop professionally. They may thus try to sell the entrepreneur on new ideas so that they can have more variety and challenge at their jobs (Hage and Aiken, 1970; Zaltman et al., 1973).

Moving beyond our original hypotheses, it is noteworthy that in the Simple configuration, entrepreneurship is so very tied up with the leader's personality, power, and information that *almost nothing else seems to count.* Neither environment, structure, nor decision-making styles seem to correlate with entrepreneurship. Simple firms could be entrepreneurial in stable environments and conservative in dynamic ones. Environment just did not seem to matter. During the course of interviews, the chief executives of several small firms claimed not to belong to any industry. They said their firms were unique and followed a niche strategy. Industry parameters were not viewed as constraints. Entrepreneurship seemed to be much more a function of the leader's goals and character than of external events.

The structural variables so often identified in the literature as facilitators of entrepreneurship also seemed extraneous in the context of the Simple firm. For example, internal communication, differentiation, and integration were uncorrelated with entrepreneurship. One possible explanation for this is that in Simple firms, acts of entrepreneurship and innovation also tend to be simple. They do not involve complex projects requiring the collaboration of diverse groups of specialists. The simplicity of innovations allows for simple structures. Entrepreneurship can be the province of one person. For the same reason, the analytical, future-oriented, integrated strategies advocated by Ansoff (1965), Ackoff (1970), and Steiner (1969) seem to play no role in boosting entrepreneurship in Simple firms. These techniques are required mainly when the innovative project is complex to design and administer.

To conclude, our hypotheses about the Simple firm are borne out. The use of the phrase *leadership imperative* to describe the genesis of entrepreneurship seems appropriate. Two of our Simple firms were both clothing retailers, yet their commitment to entrepreneurship could not have been more different. Nor could the personalities of their proprietors. The first man was passive, shy and insecure. His major ambition was to keep his firm solvent. He had inherited the business from his father over twenty years ago. His modest goals were reflected in the conservative and unchanging operations of the company. In spite of having outlets in excellent locations, market share had been falling because of the narrow, outdated line of garments and the stodgy nature of the premises. The second proprietor was a young entrepreuneur who had founded his business only seven years ago and watched it become one of the largest in the city. He was an active, sociable and aggressive man who constantly updated his wares and tailored services to the needs of his customers. A quick glance inside any of the stores of these businesses would have revealed a good deal about their respective proprietors.

Planning Firms and the Strategic Imperative

Earlier, we postulated that for Planners, two types of obstacles would have to be surmounted before entrepreneurial activity could take place. The first is the tendency to focus exclusively inward in the pursuit of efficiency and operating stability. The second is the proclivity to become monolithic, to concentrate only upon the production function of the firm. The first tendency can produce an automaticity of operation that causes entrepreneurial activities to be neglected. The second may accord too much power to those who dislike the disruptive nature of organizational or product-market renewal.

Our results in Tables 7-4 and 7-5 show that there are four safeguards against both tendencies; the two most significant ones, explicitness of strategy and top-executive locus of control, were hypothesized. The others, differentiation and technocratization, were not.

Hypothesis 2.1. There are indeed high correlations of entrepreneurship with the explicitness of strategy and strategic integration variables. Sporadic, disruptive bursts of unpredictable innovation may be unpalatable to Planners. But regular, predetermined entrepreneurial activity that follows an explicit master plan can be more readily systematized and prepared for. It can be fit more easily into the operations of the "machine," since its scope and methods are carefully defined to begin with. Instead of having to adapt to uncertain and unforeseen challenges, the firm can broaden its product-market field in a planned and consistent direction. This approach was used by firms such as I.T.T. (Sampson, 1973) and IBM (Rodgers, 1969). However, it can occur only where strategies are explicitly articulated, well established, and integrated.

When product-market strategies have been explicitly formulated, and when these established strategies strongly and regularly guide decision making, executives will continually be reminded of the broader objectives of the firm. They will think more of product-market renewal and of the need to incorporate entrepreneurial activity in an orderly way (Ansoff, 1965). The tendency toward conservatism will have been combated as growth and opportunities are pursued as vigorously as the efficiency and stability of internal operations.

Hypothesis 2.2. As predicted, another correlate of entrepreneurship in the Planning configuration is the leader's locus of control. Because strategy-making power is quite centralized, the personality of the top executive plays a key role in determining entrepreneurship, for the reasons given in the discussion of the Simple firm. The CEO can overcome the obstacles of automaticity and a monolithic staff with innovative directives. It is notable, however, that the correlation between locus of control and entrepreneurship is less significant in Planning firms than in Simple firms, probably because Planning firms are more elaborate and many people besides the CEO get involved in strategy making. The leader's role and influence are reduced, so his personality is no longer quite so critical. Locus of control is not, however, correlated with the innovation component of entrepreneurship in Planning firms (see Appendix 7-1). Innovation is a complex process in large firms and so is likely to be influenced by the qualities of technocrats and R&D departments. Although the leaders can individually set the tone for risk taking and competitive aggressiveness, their personalities must be complemented by the skills of others in order to boost innovation.

Hypothesis 2.3.   Hypothesis 2.3 is supported: The environment does not serve as a stimulus to entrepreneurship. Planning firms try to operate mechanically. Thus, they buffer their operating cores from the environment (Mintzberg, 1979). Extensive controls, plans, and close subunit integration induce smooth and regular functioning, while a stable, munificent environment and ample slack resources make such functioning possible. Litwak (1961) discusses the inability of such rule-bound, mechanical structures to respond to nonroutine events. The organization starts to ignore the environment by design, erecting elaborate and rigid "castles" (Hedberg, Nystrom, and Starbuck, 1976). This in turn causes it to ignore the environment by necessity, since there is no longer sufficient flexibility to adjust to unpredictable external pressures.

Possible exceptions to this tendency can be found in the significant relationships shown in Appendix 7-1 between innovation and environmental hostility and heterogeneity. We believe these to be due, at least in part, to the effect of the large organization upon its environment rather than vice versa. That is, by innovating, many firms enter into different segments of the market, boosting heterogeneity. They also create greater challenges for competitors, who usually decide to fight back. So competition escalates.

Hypothesis 2.4.   Hypothesis 2.4 was only partially confirmed. As we predicted, most structural variables do not correlate significantly with entrepreneurship in the Planning configuration. The regulated and planned entrepreneurial projects of Planners may be just as compatible with mechanistic as with organic structures. To our surprise, however, two structural variables did seem to be important to entrepreneurship: differentiation and technocratization (see Table 7-4).

Differentiation allows a greater diversity of talent and experience to coexist within the organization. When managers collectively are familiar with different product lines, technologies, and areas of expertise, their diverse bank of experience may help them to generate and implement entrepreneurial ideas (Hoffman and Maier, 1961; Wilson, 1966). Familiarity with a variety of markets can combine with knowledge of assorted production techniques and design procedures to suggest interesting innovation opportunities. Conservatism can also be combated by hiring technocrats such as scientists and design engineers. These people may constitute an effective pressure group that lobbies *for* change in the face of the production and work-flow design people who lobby against it (Zaltman, Duncan, and Holbek, 1973).

But these results are highly tentative. It is true that correlations of entrepreneurship with differentiation and technocratization were significant at the .10 level. However, we can see from Appendix 7-1 that the correlations were not significant for the proactiveness and risk-taking components of entrepreneurship. In other words, technocratization and differentiation are correlated *only* with the innovation component of entrepreneurship. Perhaps this is because in Planning firms, technocrats rather than chief executives are responsible for most of the innovation. Innovation may be greatly facilitated by technocrats and by the diversity of managerial personnel. But risk taking and proactiveness are more strongly influenced by the explicitness of product-market strategy and the personality of the leader.

It is now possible to summarize the findings for the Planning configuration. We stressed earlier that Planners make an effort to buffer themselves from their environments. Thus, they do not gear their levels of entrepreneurship to the external circumstances they face. Instead, entrepreneurial activity depends upon *internal* initiative. We argued that this initiative comes largely from the product-market strategy and the personality of the leader. The "strategic imperative" seems to be borne out for the Planning configuration.

One of our Planning firms religiously pursues five year product development plans. Although it has at times been notoriously unresponsive to customer demands and competitors' actions, its regular and programmed innovations serve to continually revitalize its product mix. Performance stays surprisingly buoyant in spite of the insularity of this enterprise. Products are very well-designed and extremely economical to manufacture. The organization does indeed run like a machine; but occasional well-chosen changes in the program seem to dramatically extend its operating life. Many of our Planners do not have such explicit new product development plans. They are far more apt to ignore innovation and stagnate as they concentrate primarily on producing efficiently.

Organic Firms and the Environmental/Structural Imperatives

Hypothesis 3.1. We hypothesized that Organic firms would be adaptive; that they would tailor their levels of entrepreneurial activity to the demands of the environment. This process is strongly reflected in the results shown in Table 7-4. Dynamism and hostility are significantly correlated with entrepreneurship. This finding is not surprising. It is much in line with the predictions of Burns and Stalker (1961) and their followers (Miller, 1971; Harvey and Mills, 1970; Cooper, 1973; Downs, 1966, p. 172). Indeed, researchers have come to expect that organizations will adjust to challenges by innovating and updating their strategies. What *is* surprising is that Organic firms are the *only* ones in our sample that seem to gear their innovative and entrepreneurial responses to their environments. Simple firms and Planning firms do not.

It is interesting also that environmental heterogeneity is related to entrepreneurship. But here, the direction of causality is especially ambiguous. It may be that market heterogeneity gives managers broader experience so that they perceive more entrepreneurial opportunities. Firms may begin to apply lessons learned in one market to their other markets. Conversely, entrepreneurial activity may cause growth in product lines or entry into more diverse markets, thereby boosting heterogeneity.

Hypothesis 3.2.   The hypothesis that many structural variables would correlate highly with entrepreneurship in Organic configurations was generally confirmed. Organic firms face the most dynamic and hostile environments, and, unlike Planners, make deliberate efforts to be open and responsive to the challenges they face. This involves quick responses that cannot be well planned or programmed, and requires ad hoc collaboration among diverse groups of specialists and technocrats as new products or technologies are developed. An Organic structure thus becomes critical in mediating between environment and entrepreneurship. Table 7-4 shows that many structural variables seem to be correlated with entrepreneurship. Technocratization, delegation of authority, and open internal communications, all seem to induce firms to engage in entrepreneurial endeavors. They make decision makers aware of the need for change and provide the expertise, resources, and collaborative framework necessary to achieve it.

It is instructive that *de*centralization rather than centralization is related to entrepreneurship in the Organic firms. This is the opposite of what we found for Simple firms and vindicates the predictions of Burns and Stalker (1961), Read (1962), and Thompson (1961). It seems the controversy over the influence of centralization shows hope of being resolved if we control for the type of firm. Where the firm and the innovative task are simple, having one powerful leader in control speeds things up and avoids political obstacles to change. But where the adaptive task and the environment are as complex as they are in Organic firms, it is impossible for the leader to effectively shoulder a major portion of the burden of entrepreneurship. It is necessary for authority to be shared with those who are in the best position to devise, understand, and implement innovations. Power is useless to entrepreneurship when capability is lacking.

We were quite surprised that scanning and differentiation did not correlate more highly with entrepreneurship and are at a loss to explain this convincingly. Most of the firms in the Organic sample scored high on these variables. Perhaps, then, the threshold levels of the variables were attained, and they could no longer induce or facilitate entrepreneurship.

For example, it may be that once differentiation is high enough to combat any monolithic tendency that lies in the way of innovation, it ceases to have any effect. Certainly, further research is needed on these questions.

Hypothesis 3.3.   Hypothesis 3.3 was also confirmed. Decision-making power is diffuse in Organic firms. Thus the personality of the leader does not have a significant effect upon entrepreneurship, which is performed by many people at many levels of the organization. The chief executives do not dominate Organic firms as they do Simple or Planning firms. Entrepreneurial activity seems then to be mainly a function of the nature of the environment and the adequacy of the organization structure for innovation. It is not determined by personality.

Hypothesis 3.4.   We can turn now to our final hypothesis. We expected that an explicit and well-articulated product-market strategy would help to give managers of Organic firms some common vision of where to go, thereby facilitating collaboration among those working on entrepreneurial endeavors. Such a strategy helps to avoid fragmentation and divided goals, and thus ensures a more concerted entrepreneurial effort. This indeed seems to be consistent with the figures of Table 7-4. The strategic integration variable may have the opposite effect, however. It reflects the extent to which an *established* strategy tends to guide decision making and is resistant to change. In Organic firms, the turbulent environment dictates that strategies must constantly be revised and updated. Strategies cannot be rigid without becoming anachronistic and interfering with the process of innovation (hence the weak negative correlation). Recall that strategic rigidity and stability were not obstructive in the calm settings of the Planners. Perhaps they made entrepreneurial product-market objectives that much clearer and more compelling. But rigidity seems out of place in Organic firms and may hinder their adaptive efforts.

The decision-making variables of analysis and futurity also appear to be significantly associated with entrepreneurship. It may be that Organic firms become entrepreneurial only in order to meet and exploit external challenges. This requires a careful analysis of the environment, the methodical selection of the best plan from among different possible courses of action, and the prediction of market-related factors. Decision-making variables have much the same effect as communication, centralization, and technocratization in helping the firm to better understand and cope with external contingencies.

To conclude our discussion of the Organic configuration, we should point out that the focus upon an environmental-structural imperative for entrepreneurship is incomplete. All environmental and most of the predicted structural variables did in fact correlate with entrepreneurship. But the decision-making variables of analysis and futurity seemed also to be important, as did the two strategy variables. *All* classes of variables seemed to be related to entrepreneurship in Organic firms.

Perhaps this is because the Organic firms have so many interdependencies among all classes of variables. Given that their goal is to adapt to the environment, the nature of environment will influence structure and strategy. Strategy and structure can in turn influence decision making and entrepreneurship. In other words, in Organic firms, there may be a tightly interdependent constellation of variables. For example, highly dynamic and uncertain environments will breed technocratic, decentralized, organic structures, flexible but well-articulated strategies, a great analytical effort to master uncertainty, and a high level of entrepreneurship. In stable and more predictable environments, most of these variables will shift. There will be fewer technocrats, more centralization, less internal communication, less analytical decision making, more rigid strategies, and less entrepreneurship.

One of our Organic firms is in the chemical industry. It had once concentrated almost exclusively on industrial chemicals but recently had entered the more dynamic and competitive plastics business. The concerted effort to adapt to this new industry by becoming more entrepreneurial changed everything. R&D soon came to take precedence over production. The structure was overhauled to disperse more authority to scientists and operating managers, to emphasize collaboration among the major functional departments, to stress team decision-making, and to facilitate the exchange and analysis of information. Strategy, structure, and environment all changed together to support more innovation.

CONCLUSION

In our discussion, we have often referred to entrepreneurial "determinants" and "imperatives." These terms were used simply to make our conjectures more coherent. Unfortunately, the correlational data give us no adequate grounds for inferring causality. There remains much uncertainty about the direction of influence between entrepreneurship and the "independent" variables. There can, however, be little doubt about the truth of the central thesis of the chapter—that entrepreneurship is integrally related to variables of environment, structure, strategy, and leader personality, and that these relationships vary systematically and logically from one type of firm or configuration to another.

It is instructive to turn back to Table 7-4 and examine its final column of correlations. As we can see, any samplewide analysis would have concealed the dramatic differences that occurred among our three configurations. The aggregated sample reveals, for example, that there is a strong relationship between locus of control and entrepreneurship. But the relationship holds true only for Simple and Planning firms; it is not true for

Organic firms. Similarly, environment is shown to have many significant relationships with entrepreneurship, again bearing out the literature; but most of the significance is due to the adaptive Organic firms. Planners' entrepreneurial activity is not much influenced by the environment.

Another misleading aggregate result is the completely insignificant correlation shown between entrepreneurship and centralization. This seems to have been due to two dramatically opposed results: a significant positive correlation for the Simple firms, and a significant negative correlation for the Organic firms.

The only uniformly significant result is that between technocratization and entrepreneurship. It seems that no matter what kind of firm we are dealing with, the presence of technocrats will boost entrepreneurship. Their scientific interests, expertise, and desire for learning and career development may cause them to perceive and to wish to implement ideas for innovation and organizational renewal. But for this, as well as for many of our other findings, the reverse causal direction is also plausible—namely, that entrepreneurship generates complex innovative projects that require firms to hire technocrats.

The theme of the chapter as well as its central finding seem to have practical importance. Different firms probably do require very different kinds of forces to stimulate entrepreneurship. There appear to be very few panaceas for promoting entrepreneurial activity. In Simple firms, the focus may have to be upon the leader. If he has the wrong personality or inadequate power, entrepreneurship will be rare. In Planning firms, entrepreneurship may best be stimulated by explicit entrepreneurial product-market strategies, strategies that ritualize and systematize innovation and risk taking. This will ensure that entrepreneurship is focused upon, in addition to routine operating matters. It will also minimize the disruptiveness of entrepreneurship, a trait that is particularly unpalatable to firms that try to function mechanically. Finally, Organic firms may tend to be entrepreneurial in proportion to the demands of their environments and the capacities of their structures. Any change agent wishing to stimulate entrepreneurship would probably be wise to focus upon these distinctions.

In retrospect, it is interesting that the findings of the last two chapters may be pointing to the 'relational' configurations that we discussed in our introduction to Part I. The conservative and entrepreneurial firms of Chapter 6 and the Simple, Planning, and Organic types of the present chapter may in some respects be considered relational configurations. They are characterized not only by their scores on particular variables (as are elemental configurations), but also by certain relationships among the variables. Many relationships seem to differ dramatically among the configurations. As the score ranges along the variables get larger for a group of firms and as the key relationships among the variables become stronger and more distinctive, it becomes more convenient to seek out relational rather than elemental configurations.

Part IV

Introduction

QUANTUM CHANGE AS A CONSEQUENCE OF CONFIGURATION

So far, we have argued for the existence of organizational configurations and have discussed their role as the bases for parsimonious taxonomies. We have also highlighted their predictive utility, showing that it is necessary to make distinctions among configurations or types in studying the relationships among organizational phenomena. Essentially, we have painted a picture of a world in which a relatively small number of very common but quite different configurations encompass a rather large fraction of the population of business firms.

Obviously, such a view has important implications for how organizations must change, and conversely, the way in which organizations change strongly influences the plausibility of the case for configuration. Specifically, if organizations changed in a piecemeal and disjointed way, altering elements of strategy and structure quite loosely and independently, they would constantly be realigning their profiles, moving from one state to a randomly different one. The number of states would then proliferate to such an extent that chances for predictive, empirically based sets of configurations would be diminished. On the other hand, if firms remain with a configuration for a long time, and then, concertedly, move to a different configuration, this increases the chances of there being a limited number of common types. This quantum kind of change was indicated by our case for configuration, and, if verified, would in turn support that case.

Because of the variety and complexity of the arguments to be presented in Part IV we shall briefly summarize them. The first set of arguments supports concerted or multifaceted change. Multifaceted change is the opposite of piecemeal change. It is characterized by a number of contemporary changes, whether these be major or minor. Concerted change is just a form of multifaceted change in which the changes are thematically related or orchestrated. Concerted and multifaceted change are both called *quantum* change. The second set of arguments supports *dramatic* change, which contrasts with incremental change. Change that is of both a quantum and a dramatic nature is termed revolutionary. Let us first summarize the arguments for quantum change.

1. Part II presented several taxonomies of configurations. Each seemed to support the notion that configurations tend to be broadly different from one another—that they differed in many respects. The widespread differences among the empirical configurations or "archetypes" of Chapter 4 were caused by a stable and complex form of *interdependency* among the variables. Since many of the variables are integrally related, so must be their changes. Specifically, many variables must change together, and therefore firms will usually change in a multifaceted way. For example, firms moving from a conservative to an entrepreneurial configuration will tend to alter a great many aspects of strategy and structure. So will those within a conservative relational configuration that wish to increase the rate of innovation. This might, for better or worse, induce more scanning, delegation of authority, technocratization, organizational integration, and so on. In other words, quantum change may take place as firms move within a configuration (especially a relational one) or between configurations.[1]

We noted in our earlier geometrical representation that organizational multivariate data in n-dimensional space is expected often to form a snakelike surface of much smaller dimension than the space itself (see Appendix 4-1). Since the surface exhausts the population, when firms change they will move from one part of the surface to another instead of moving randomly through the space. In other words, the movement of firms is restricted. For example, if variable A changes, so must variables B, C and D in their own way to keep the firm on the operative surface. The greater the degree of clustering among the variables, the smaller the dimension of the surface relative to the total space. The smaller the relative dimension of the surface, the more restricted the movement of firms through the space and the more variables must change in a multifaceted way for firms to stay on the surface. This geometry shows the close relationship between configurations and change. The tighter the configurations, the more multifaceted the change.

2. The preservation of specific *functional* alignments within or across configurations might be another factor promoting quantum change. For example, it may be that as variables of differentiation increase, so must

---

[1] Recall that the boundaries of the configurations of Chapters 4 and 5 were somewhat arbitrary. So, at least from the empirical data, there is no need to make a major distinction between intra- and interarchetype change. Both would have to be of a quantum nature because of the multivariate interdependencies.

those of integration (Lawrence and Lorsch, 1967). Piecemeal change might destroy a complementary configuration without having the scope to erect a new one. Here we have a normative argument—perhaps some configurations contain particular kinds of complementarities that are functional and *should* be maintained. In this case, some types of concerted multifaceted change would be more common among successful than among unsuccessful firms. The functionalist would therefore argue for their prevalence. They produce success, therefore they must be common.

3. We can also argue for quantum change by establishing the rarity of its opposite—piecemeal change. We have shown how configurations, even those that are dysfunctional, have a number of mutually supportive attributes. Many things fit together. This can lead to a climate of *resistance to change.* In the short run, anomalous changes may be resisted because they run counter to the ideology of the firm, the values or beliefs of its managers, or even their political interests. In the long run, once an orientation has proved to be decisively dysfunctional, piecemeal change may be inadequate to reestablish success.

The prevalence of dramatic change, the second aspect of revolutionary change, can be supported by a different set of arguments. Although the notion of configurations was used to argue for multifaceted change, it is only of secondary importance in explaining dramatic change. The latter is defined as a great deal of change on a given attribute over a brief interval—for example, a great increase in centralization. Its opposite is incremental change. Two related normative arguments support dramatic change.

1. The major reason for making dramatic changes is economic. Configurations cause change to be multifaceted. But such change is disruptive and very costly. It is expensive to change a great many things at once; confusion results, and fixed setup and retraining costs are incurred. As a consequence, it might be best to avoid making such changes very often—to wait until they are clearly required or amply rewarding. But the resultant delays give rise to the need for dramatic changes. Delays cause very significant discrepancies between desired and actual states, gaps that can be bridged only by substantial changes.

2. Another economic impetus for dramatic change may be that firms in the process of changing are not yet properly adapted to their new surroundings, and at the same time have lost the complementarity among the elements of their old configurations. These disonnant intervals of flux are best gotten through as quickly as possible. Incremental change would simply be too slow. Dramatic change is called for. This is especially true for firms in a state between two functional configurations.

Although dramatic change may be more common than many theorists indicate, we cannot claim that it is predominant. It should prevail mainly where change is multifaceted and organizations economically motivated. The concept of configuration directly implies that there will be quantum change, but not necessarily revolutionary change. The latter will occur principally as a result of the expensive nature of quantum change. In other words, quantum incremental and quantum dramatic (revolutionary) changes are *both* consistent with configurations. But we still think that dramatic changes will happen quite frequently as a result of the economic incentive.

The next three chapters are devoted to developing insights into organizational change. Chapter 8 argues that there are hidden costs in making disjointed and piecemeal changes to organizational structure, even where the purpose is to adapt to a changing environment or a new strategy. It is maintained that stable intervals punctuated by infrequent periods of quantum, and even dramatic, structural change often constitute the most economical strategy. Because of the integral and complementary alignment of elements in common structural configurations, multifaceted structural changes are frequently necessary. But the costs of such changes are very high. These costs, if incurred frequently, may well outweigh the benefits of a closer adaptation or fit with environment and strategy.[2] Therefore, it is often best to delay changing structure and to bunch changes together to make the disruptive interval as rare and brief as possible. These delays allow the mismatch with strategy and environment to become more severe, so that when change does finally come, it must be dramatic.

In Chapter 9, this view is tested upon three samples of data. The samples are bifurcated into successful and unsuccessful groups of firms. It is shown that there are clear differences between the two groups in the way firms change their structures. The successful firms change many elements of structure in concert and also tend to change more dramatically than unsuccessful firms. Specifically, in groups of successful firms, there are more high correlations among changes in uncertainty-reduction, differentiation, and integration variables than there are in groups of unsuccessful firms. Also, the changes along these variables tend to be most extreme in the successful groups. We argue that perhaps this revolutionary approach to structural change is associated with success precisely because there exist common structural configurations.

Chapter 9 examines the differences in approaches to *structural* change between successful and unsuccessful firms. But what about general transitional tendencies among *all* firms, and how must strategy making as well as structure change? These questions are germane, since, in Chapter 4, we identified and argued for common successful *and* unsuccessful configurations, and characterized these configurations using variables of strategy making as well as structure. We begin to provide some answers in Chapter 10.

---

[2]Firms that change in a concerted but gradual way may thereby maintain consistency among their structural elements. Thus they can reduce the cost of internal disharmonies, a significant component of the cost of change. But if firms are *constantly* changing, the remaining costs of change—those of retraining, poor morale, and establishing new administrative procedures—might be prohibitive. Thus, although concerted incremental change is in most cases to be preferred to piecemeal change, it still may often be an uneconomical strategy. It will succeed best when it is infrequently required.

Until now, we have focused mostly on "elemental" configurations, collections of integrally and commonly configured elements. But, as we noted in the introduction to Part I, configurations can also be built of common relationships among variables. The research presented in Chapter 10 gives evidence for relational configurations. The way in which 24 structural and strategy-making variables change is analyzed in a longitudinal study of 26 companies. The question is whether variables tend to exhibit continuity over time—that is, keep evolving simultaneously in the same direction (to preserve a relational configuration)—or whether the direction of change is reversed. We found that organizations resist reversals in the direction of evolution in strategy and structure. Also, there is a tendency for organizational histories to demonstrate two extremes: periods of momentum in which no, or almost no trend is reversed; and dramatic periods of reversal, in which a very great many trends are reversed. The results seem to strongly support the notion of relational configurations. For example, during periods of momentum, firms may tend to become more bureaucratic by simultaneously continuing to increase their use of formal controls, integration, and centralization, while continuing to decrease their informality. The relationships among the variables are thereby preserved.[3] In the much rarer periods of reversal, firms change the direction of evolution among a great number of variables of strategy and structure. They apparently move to a new relational configuration, one that will ultimately be preserved or extended through momentum of its own. Here, perhaps, the bureaucratic firms may decide to become more like the adhocracy, reversing the direction of evolution in controls, centralization, and many other variables in the process of erecting a new configuration.

To conclude, our examination of organizational change provides very tentative but broadly relevant evidence for the existence of different types of common configurations. Results are not always unambiguous, however. The longitudinal analysis of organizations is a process fraught with hazards and difficulties, particularly when performed from a distance on diverse samples of firms. The evidence presented in Chapters 9 and 10 does seem to reveal important patterns in organizational change that support the case for configuration. But many of our conclusions are based upon interpretations of summary statistics and measures. Causes and even causal directions were impossible to establish with any certainty. These chapters and our interpretations should be read with this in mind.

---

[3]These periods of momentum demonstrate concerted quantum change. But we could not say how dramatic the changes were. The data indicated that many intervals of momentum demonstrated brief episodes of dramatic quantum change surrounded by periods of no change. Other intervals of momentum showed quantum change of a gradual, incremental nature. Both these types of quantum change are quite consistent with the nature of relational configurations.

8

Quantum Structural Change in Organizations

INTRODUCTION

A recurrent theme in the literature is that organizations are often slow to adapt to changes in their environments. Significant changes in structure tend to occur quite a long time after the environmental and strategic developments that necessitated them. This is typically viewed as a problem. Many causes have been attributed to the tendency toward sluggish adaptation and resistance to change. For example, Carter (1971), Cyert and March (1963), and Pfeffer (1978, p. 14) have called attention to the adaptive rigidities caused by the avoidance of uncertainty and the fragmentation of the political coalition and its goals. March and Simon (1958) have shown how slack resources can cushion the organization from the need for rapid responses while their programmed natures make operations resistant to modifications. Wildavsky (1972) and Wilensky (1967) have noted that information-processing systems in organizations may tend to perpetuate narrow, self-affirming models of reality so that there is a lack of awareness of the need to adapt. The work of Mitroff and Kilmann (1976) and Clark (1972) suggests how organizational ideologies cause resistance to change. Finally, Miller and Friesen (1980b) have pointed to the role of emotional, cognitive, and power factors as inhibitors of prompt organizational responsiveness. Such delays in structural change are said to eventually require

Adapted from Danny Miller, "Evolution and Revolution: A Quantum View of Structural Change in Organizations," *Journal of Management Studies* 19 (1982) 131–51.

costly and disruptive organizational revolutions as firms try suddenly to reverse their orientations. These revolutions are often taken to be unnecessary evils (Hedberg, Nystrom, and Starbuck, 1976; Starbuck, Greve, and Hedberg, 1978).

We find much praise, therefore, of firms that can be responsive to uncertainty in their environments, particularly when environments are dynamic. Burns and Stalker's (1961) "organic" organizations, Lawrence and Lorsch's (1967) successful plastics firms, Stinchcombe's (1959) "craft" firms, and Mintzberg's (1979) "adhocracies" are praised because of their adaptive capacities. These firms are normally less bureaucratic, less centralized, more technocratized and innovative, and more internally differentiated than most organizations.

The message in the literature is that resistance to change is bad and that firms must be structured to avoid this. But there seem to be two problems with this view. First, firms that are structured for a dynamic environment must, when their markets stabilize, face an adaptive task that is every bit as difficult as that which confronts mechanistic or bureaucratic firms whose environments are becoming more dynamic. No type of structure can remove the need for periodic restructuring. Second, and far more important to our subsequent discussion, the functional aspects of resistance to change are generally ignored and the desirability of piecemeal and incremental change in structure is overemphasized.

If structural configurations are composed of mutually supportive elements, piecemeal changes may cause discrepancies or costly disharmonies. These may have to be corrected by making other structural modifications or by reverting back to the old structure. For example, if product diversity is increased to capture a new market, the firm may decide to decentralize authority or adopt a market-based rather than a function-based structure. But, in isolation, such changes may be inconsistent with existing information systems, bureaucratic devices, spans of control, administrative ratios, and perhaps even technologies. Unless these inconsistencies are remedied, the piecemeal or unitary structural modification may be harmful. We shall argue that there may be hazards in making such piecemeal structural changes; that potentially disruptive changes must be delayed until the cost of not restructuring becomes high enough to justify the widespread structural modifications that may be required to reestablish harmony among structural elements. Thus, adaptive lags must often be long, and piecemeal, incremental change may not be as functional as its proponents seem to assume (see Lindblom, 1968; Braybrooke and Lindblom, 1963; Cyert and March, 1963).

We believe that organizations should often resist structural changes until a critical state of incongruence with the environment is reached. Then a quantum or concerted structural change must occur. As we said earlier, change is of a *quantum* (as opposed to piecemeal) nature when *many* things change together—that is, when structures change in a multifaceted or concerted way. It is *dramatic* (as opposed to incremental) when elements quickly change a great deal. Revolutionary change is of a dramatic *and* quantum nature. Evolutionary change is incremental and piecemeal.

We first present a summary of our argument and then define its scope and terms. We proceed to elaborate upon each of its points, eliciting from the literature empirical and conceptual evidence to support the arguments whenever possible. The next chapter subjects the quantum view to an empirical test.

SUMMARY OF THE REVOLUTIONARY QUANTUM VIEW OF STRUCTURAL CHANGE

1. Typically, organizations must achieve harmony among their elements of structure. That is, structural elements such as technology, the distribution of authority, differentiation and integration, and spans of control must be complementary. These elements are interdependent and must be combined into functional configurations to maximize organizational performance. Thus, many elements cannot change independently without causing costly imbalances. For example, organizational integration must increase with differentiation.

2. The organization must adjust its structure to changes in its environment and strategy. This has been a dominant message in much of the organizational literature over the past two decades.

3. Points 1 and 2 interact to constrain the set of alternatives for constructive structural change. Two costs must be traded off—the cost of the structure being out of kilter with the environment or strategy (C_1), and the cost of destroying or resurrecting complementarities among structural elements (C_2). When long-run estimates of C_1 are less than those of C_2, the structure should not be changed.

4. Because of the interdependencies among structural elements, C_2 costs will often be high. Many elements must change together, and this can be expensive. Such quantum structural change must therefore be delayed until the anticipated long-run C_1 costs are larger than the C_2 costs. Often these delays can be considerable.

5. When change finally comes, it may have to be of a revolutionary nature. The substantial lag in adaptation has created a serious mismatch with the environment or strategy, one that may require dramatic corrective actions.

SCOPE AND DEFINITIONS

Before elaborating upon each of the points above, it is necessary to establish the range of our discussion and to define our terms. Broadly speaking, our concern will be with how organizations should change their structures to adapt to new environments and strategies.

Our focus will be upon business organizations that must vie for material, human, and financial resources in a competitive marketplace. It is quite possible that the functionalism implicit in our approach also pertains to other types of organizations, such as churches, prisons, and the civil service. However, we are at this point reluctant to extrapolate our views to organizations that are not regularly challenged by their interaction with competitors and clients. Following Weber (1947, pp. 139–46), we include in our definition of the organization all its formal members: employees and managers at all levels, including the board of directors. Customers, suppliers, and competitors are considered members of the external environment. Our concern is strictly with formal business organizations that have over 100 or so employees and have a cadre of managers. Many of our variables do not pertain to very small and simple firms.

Because we deal with the problem of structural change, the structural elements or variables we focus upon must be those that can and often have to change as the environment alters. Business firms do not generally metamorphose into churches, or vice versa. Nor do prisons become factories. Therefore, variables such as the *cui bono* (who benefits?) of the Blau-Scott (1962) typology, the modes of compliance and commitment of the Etzioni (1961) typology, or the principal mission of the organization in the Parsons (1956, 1960) typology are not treated. To use the terms of McKelvey's (1978) organizational dendrogram, we are concerned not with structural dimensions that distinguish among organizational classes at the level of "kingdoms" or "divisions," but rather with those that distinguish between the more similar subclasses and orders—the much lower categories that are frequently crossed as structures change. Although we are in no position to give an exhaustive list of relevant structural variables, some representative ones are technology, as described by Woodward (1965), structuring of activities (bureaucratization, formalization, specialization), concentration of authority and work-flow integration (Pugh et al., 1968), vertical and horizontal spans of control, organizational differentiation and integration (Lawrence and Lorsch, 1967), the sophistication of information-processing and coordinative devices (Galbraith, 1973), the mechanistic and organic qualities of Burns and Stalker (1961), and so on. These characteristics must often change in some synchronous fashion, and it is this that makes them of interest to us. Attributes such as specific intra-unit rules and individual task designs are beyond our scope since they can be loosely coupled—that is, they can change independently without threatening performance (Weick, 1969; Aldrich, 1979, pp. 80–86).

Our discussion will focus on changes that occur in structure to make it harmonious with strategy and environment. *Strategy* refers to the product-market scope of the enterprise, its plans for resource deployments, and the nature of its distinctive competences (Chandler, 1962). It is the "match between an organization's skills and resources, the environmental opportunities and risks it faces, and the purposes it wishes to accomplish" (Hofer and Schendel, 1978, p. 11). The *environment* can be described in terms such as the changefulness or dynamism of competitors and customers, their unpredictability or uncertainty, threatfulness or hostility, and diversity or heterogeneity. In all cases, our concern will be with the *changes in the levels* of these qualities. These changes challenge all kinds of firms, mechanistic and organic alike. The environment might change by itself, causing the firm to react, or it may change because the firm's strategy causes it to proactively enter a new environment or to change the old one. Our arguments will not be influenced by whether structural change is the product of a reactive or proactive matching of strategy and environment.

THE QUANTUM VIEW OF STRUCTURAL CHANGE

1. **Structural elements must be combined in a harmonious manner. Most combinations should not and do not occur, because they will hurt performance.**

In nature, although species number in the millions, they are by no means infinitely variable. We find no three-legged creatures, two-headed beasts, or insects that weigh over five ounces. According to Charles Darwin (1859, p. 231), natural selection ensures that "species at any one period are not indefinitely variable, and are not linked together by a multitude of intermediate gradations." In the same way, as we have argued in Parts I and II, there are not an infinite variety of organizational structures. The parts or elements of structure must fit together in a harmonious configuration. While there are, of course, many different types of structural configurations, their variety is circumscribed by the need for complementarity among the elements. Just as a dysfunctional aspect of anatomy can lead to the extinction of a biological species, a conflicting element of structure can cause organizations to fail or to have to take costly corrective action (Levins, 1968; Miller, 1981).

It has been demonstrated empirically that organizations must be constructed in a manner that evidences a complementary alignment among structural variables. For example, Joan Woodward (1965) has shown that, given an organization's technology, it is necessary for features of structure such as spans of control, levels in the hierarchy, the size of the administrative component, and the relationships between task functions to be consistent with that technology. According to Woodward (1965, p. 69):

> It was found that the figures relating to the organizational characteristics of the successful firms in each production category tended to cluster round the medians for that category as a whole, while the figures of the firms classified as "below average" in success were found at the extremes of the range.

Lawrence and Lorsch (1967) found that the levels of organizational differentiation, integration, and conflict-resolution capacity had to covary positively or performance would suffer. More specifically, as the time, goal, task, and interpersonal orientations of subunits became more differentiated, there was a greater need to integrate the efforts of these units using such devices as task forces, standing committees, and cross-functional and interdepartmental committees. Jay Galbraith (1973) has confirmed this finding, arguing that increases in differentiation and uncertainty boost the information-processing task of the organization and require more sophisticated integrative devices, such as integrative personnel and matrix structures.

The empirical findings of Khandwalla (1973, p. 479) are especially revealing. He showed that:

> . . . for a firm to be *effectively* designed, it may have to be . . . high, medium or low [in *all* the sets of structural variables, namely] uncertainty reduction, differentiation, and integration. . . . The larger [the firm], and the more uncertain its external environment, the higher it would have to be along *all three* sets of variables. . . . [The] Gestalt or configuration of an organization is likely to be a more potent determinant of its effectiveness than any of the individual components of this configuration.

Khandwalla (1973) showed that although there was no significant correlation between any one structural variable and performance, successful subsamples demonstrated a good number of significant correlations within the set of structural variables. Unsuccessful firms did not. Success seemed to stem not from the use of any single structural device, but from the combination of appropriate ones. There is little doubt, based upon the empirical evidence, that the integrity of the alignment among structural elements is an important determinant of performance. It therefore follows that unitary piecemeal changes in many elements may create costly disharmonies unless they are complemented by other structural changes.

The nature of the necessary complementarities among structural elements can be illustrated using the example of the classical Weberian bureaucracy that seems to describe Woodward's (1965) mass-production firms, Crozier's (1964) tobacco monopoly, Lawrence and Lorsch's (1967) container companies, Pugh et al.'s (1969) workflow bureaucracy, and the machine bureaucracy of Chapter 3. According to Mintzberg (1979, p. 315), this organization has:

> . . . highly specialized, routine operating tasks, very formalized procedures in the operating core, a proliferation of rules, regulations, and formalized communication throughout the organization, large-sized units at the operating level, reliance on the functional basis for grouping tasks, relatively centralized power for decision making, and an elaborate administrative structure with a sharp distinction between line and staff.

Such organizations, when they are businesses, tend to have mass-production technologies, are large, and are found in mature and stable industries. The rigid, automated technologies are very cost-efficient and take advantage of a great many programmed, formal, standard operating procedures. The routine nature of operations facilitates power centralization: There is no need to delegate much authority to boundary-spanning units, since administrative complexity is generally low. The key challenge is to be efficient, so that only technocrats who design work-flow processes and cost controls are accorded decision-making discretion. There is a strong reluctance to change products or technologies in a major way. Since extensive rules and standardized procedures require stability, firms will not enter dynamic settings and will try to arrange a negotiated environment with their few competitors.

The elements of the configuration are mutually reinforcing. Most changes in only one variable such as controls, centralization, technology, bureaucratization or integrative devices would be dysfunctional unless accompanied by changes in many other variables. For example, a decrease in bureaucratization would conflict with the assembly-line technology. Job specialization, formalization of rules, and the use of standard operating procedures are most efficient given the line technology (Woodward, 1965). Say a shift in strategy requires a new, more flexible custom or small-batch technology to be adopted. It follows that *many other* structural elements will have to change. For example, bureaucratization may have to decrease with the rise in task diversity; task specialization declines, work-flow coordination is effected more by mutual adjustment or standardization of skills than by standardization of work processes, and spans of control must be reduced (Woodward, 1965). Also, formalization decreases, and more authority is vested in middle- and lower-level line personnel and less in technocrats responsible for designing work flow. In this case, one structural change may require that many others occur. Since the parts of the structure are so interdependent, it is difficult to establish any primacy or dependent–independent variable distinction among the elements. As we have argued in Chapter 1, the parts make sense mainly in reference to the whole configuration.

2. The organization must match its structure to its environment and its strategy: The better the match, the higher the performance.

These contentions are so well researched and their truth is so widely accepted that they need hardly be discussed. The basic message of the most prominent contingency theorists is that structure must be tailored to environment. For example, bureaucratic, programmed, mechanistic firms are said to be most effective in stable and predictable environments (Burns and Stalker, 1961). Organic firms or adhocracies are best suited to dynamic or uncertain environments (Schon, 1971). Also, delegation of authority to boundary-spanning units is believed to be most necessary under conditions of environmental turbulence and complexity (Thompson, 1967), whereas more elaborate information-processing and coordinative mechanisms are thought to be required in uncertain markets (Lawrence and Lorsch, 1967: Galbraith, 1977). Countless other such links between organization and environment have been established in the literature.

Structure must also be adapted to strategies. A strategy of product-market diversification may require a divisionalized structure (Chandler, 1962; Channon, 1973; Rumelt, 1974). A high-technology or product-novelty strategy may require an organic structure (Peterson & Berger, 1971). In summary, the firm may have to change its structure in response to an external environmental factor, or it may have to change its structure to better execute a new product-market strategy.

In points 1 and 2 we are not arguing that the same interdependencies among variables exist among very different types of firms, or that the same environmental challenges cause similar structural modifications. We have spent most of the book arguing that the nature of organizational relationships is not all that orderly, uniform, or deterministic. Our main point here is that many structural elements are interdependent in many different kinds of configurations, even though, as we have shown, the nature of those interdependencies may vary a great deal from one configuration to another.

3.   It follows from 1 and 2 that sometimes the organization will face the dilemma of whether to change an element of structure to adapt to environment, or to do nothing and avoid destroying the complementarity among structural elements.

A firm's competitor may begin introducing new products more frequently, so that market share is threatened. The firm may decide to respond by expanding and modifying its product line more frequently to protect itself. But this might necessitate a change, say, from a large-batch to a more flexible small-batch technology, or from a line to a large-batch process. Although this in itself would be expensive, substantial additional costs might accrue if the change destroys complementarities between production technology and other elements of structure (Woodward, 1965, pp. 65–71). Thus, there must be a tradeoff made between two types of costs: that of being inappropriately structured for the environment or strategy, and that of destroying internal complementarities (or establishing new ones).

We are not contending that there will *always* be a conflict between satisfying internal and external constraints. For low performers, a change that responds to external requirements may also entail a more functional alignment among internal factors. Also, there may be a good deal of leeway in changing variables that can be loosely coupled, those that do not have to align closely to other variables. Often, however, this is not the case. The evidence already presented indicates that many structural complementarities are both essential and somewhat fragile. Piecemeal structural adjustments made in response to environmental challenges may unbalance the structural configuration and will be costly unless much of the structure is redesigned to erect new complementarities. The multifacetedness of the latter kind of change will make it expensive. Thus, the dilemma managers must face is often very real.

4. **Some firms should behave like sluggish thermostats: They must alter structure only after a substantial and long-term level of dysfunction is anticipated.**

The projected cost of being mismatched with the environment (C_1) must exceed the cost of either destroying old internal complementarities or the cost of erecting new ones (C_2). Until then, structural change should not occur. This threshold level will determine the period of adaptive lag for significant structural reorientations. Such a situation is rather arbitrarily represented in Figure 8-1. We consider only expected long-run costs as they are likely to be estimated by managers at specific points in time. These are represented by the points that constitute the C_1 and C_2 curves. In other words, the horizontal axis of the graph refers to the time at which the managers make their cost estimates.

The levels, slopes, and shapes of the C_1 and C_2 cost curves will of course vary among firms and contexts. The C_2 curve will often be flat, since it may be possible for managers to derive a rough but stable estimate of the costs of a structural overhaul. The C_1 curve will usually have a positive slope as cost estimates rise with decreasing market shares and the growing conviction that the environmental shift is to be more lasting than had been

FIGURE 8-1   Adaptive Lag as a Function of Cost Tradeoffs

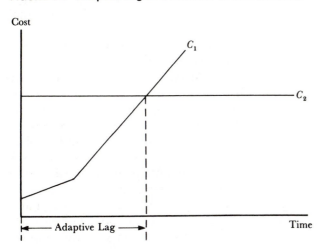

anticipated. The higher the degree of customer brand loyalty and the greater the stability of market shares, the smaller the level and slope of C_1 and the greater the adaptive lag. The more comprehensive and necessary the internal structural complementarities, the more multifaceted change must be and the higher the level of the C_2 curve. This increases the adaptive lag. Thus, the more change is of a quantum or multifaceted nature, the more expensive it is, and the less frequent it should be.

The C_1 curve is, of course, difficult for us to estimate. Where the environment exhibits temporary and erratic changes, the curve might have several sharp kinks or "bumps" as managers shift and reverse their appraisals of long term costs. In most cases, however, the curve will show a positive slope as the costs of being out of tune with the environment make themselves increasingly manifest via corporate financial and market reports, more severe competitor inroads, growing client dissatisfaction, and the like (Miller, 1982, pp. 144–48). In general, the less predictable the environment, the more gradual the slope of the C_1 curve and the longer the delay in adapting. Managers may need much time to become convinced that the changes in an uncertain environment are to be severe and enduring.

The literature seems to bear out the sluggishness of adaptive behavior. In fact, the issue has become a prime focus. Hedberg, Nystrom, and Starbuck (1976) have presented an excellent review of this field. Many possible reasons for sluggish adaptation have been suggested (Starbuck, Greve, and Hedberg, 1978). They range from ideological and political obstacles (Mitroff and Kilmann, 1976; Pfeffer, 1978, p. 14) and blockages in information-processing networks (Wilensky, 1967; Wildavsky, 1971) to bureaupathologies (Thompson, 1961). However, the destruction of complementarities among structural elements has been largely ignored in accounting for such lags. This is evidenced by the fact that in almost every instance, resistance to change is viewed in a highly pejorative light as something that must be combatted.

It might, of course, be argued that adaptive lag is always dysfunctional. Why not change as soon as possible even if it means making major structural alterations? The costs will have to be incurred eventually, so why not incur them before maladaptation to the environment severely weakens the firm? We believe, however, that organizations that change with hair-trigger responsiveness may be exposing themselves to two types of potential diseconomies. The first results from the "incompleteness" of partial or piecemeal structural changes. Because of their conflicts with other structural elements, these changes may incur hidden C_2 costs that exceed the benefits of responding to novel strategies or environments. A second type of diseconomy might occur when the firm *does* undergo a thorough and therefore costly restructuring, but does this too frequently. The environment may be undergoing a change that is temporary or somewhat unpredictable. If the change is temporary, then there is probably no need to make any major moves. It is best to delay acting until one knows whether the environmental transition is of a long-term, unreversable or a short-term, reversable nature. If the course of external change is unpredictable, it may be best to wait for some relatively stable interval of quasi-equilibrium before making structural changes. Otherwise there might be too many disruptive occasions for temporary but costly changes.

> . . . paradoxes inhere in matching an organization to a future environment that has still to be defined: curricula cannot be tailored to the unique needs of unknown students; unspecified customers or suppliers cannot influence strategic planning. [Hedberg, Nystrom, and Starbuck, 1976, pp. 52–53]

5.   Eventual changes in structure must often be dramatic and revolutionary.

We have argued that change may have to be of a quantum, multifaceted nature to preserve or to reestablish complementarities among the different elements of structure. Because of the expense of such multifaceted changes, it is best not to perform them very often. The resultant delays will allow structure to become quite anachronistic. Thus, when change comes, it may have to be dramatic. It may have to be revolutionary in addition to being multifaceted.

It appears that the longer the lag in adaptation, the more disruptive and comprehensive the changes that follow. Descriptions of the extensive changes that take place during revolutionary intervals can be found in Schendel, Patton, and Riggs (1975), White (1969), Chandler (1962), Normann (1971), Starbuck, Greve, and Hedberg (1978), and Chapter 10. In many cases, the changes described have been delayed until the organization is very much out of kilter with its environment. The changes in strategy and structure that take place to combat this are major, dramatic, and costly. Many histories reveal organizations experiencing a revolution as they leap directly and quickly from one structural and strategic orientation to another that is very different.[1] For example, General Motors under Sloan radically changed its structure to emphasize controls and close coor-

---

[1]The literature has demonstrated that some structural types are very different from one another *along many dimensions.* Contrast Burns and Stalker's (1961) organic and mechanistic organizations, Woodward's (1965) line and custom firms, Stinchcombe's (1959) craft and bureaucratic firms, and Lawrence and Lorsch's (1967) plastics and container organizations. The same sorts of widespread differences can be seen among the types in conceptual typologies generated by Perrow (1970), Segal (1974), and Van de Ven (1976), and in the empirically based taxonomies of Samuel and Mannheim (1970), Pinto and Pinder (1972), Haas, Hall, and Johnson (1966), and Chapters 4 and 5 of this text. This phenomenon was dramatically illustrated in Mintzberg's typology of five common structural configurations, presented in Chapter 3. Thus, if the environment changes, some organizations may have to move from one structural type to another that is in many ways different. Many attributes will have to quickly change together in a concerted way if structural hybrids or mutations are very dysfunctional.

dination, and renewed its product-market strategy by rationalizing product lines. The change took place within a few years, from 1921 to 1924 (Sloan, 1964). A similar period of dramatic change took place at Ford Motor Co. after the Second World War. Vivid accounts of corporate revolutions can be found almost every month in periodicals such as *Fortune* and *Business Week*.

EMPIRICAL EVIDENCE

Three of our chapters present empirical studies of organizational change and provide tentative support for the quantum view. One such study has already been reported. In Chapter 5, we showed that organizational change tends to come in packages. The same nine packages or scenarios recurred with remarkably high frequency in a diverse sample of organizational histories. Many scenarios showed a complex, far-reaching process of realignment among environmental, structural, and strategy-making variables. Structural variables tended to change together as firms progressed through periods of transition.

The study to be presented in Chapter 9 shows that when groups of firms from three nations were bifurcated according to their growth and financial performance, the samples of high performers exhibited many high correlations among changes in their structural variables, but the samples of poor performers showed few such correlations. It was also shown that high performers were more apt to make revolutionary and dramatic changes.

Finally, Chapter 10 presents a study showing that changes in the direction of evolution in a set of 21 structural and *strategic* variables occurred together. That is, reversals in the direction of change among variables such as centralization, innovation, technocratization, and so on were likely to happen during the same turbulent interval. Continuity in the direction of change also tended to occur simultaneously among most of the variables. The periods of reversal often reflected a search for new configurations, while those of continuity or "momentum" extended established configurations.

CONCLUSION

This chapter sought to explain structural change as a product of two potentially conflicting adaptive demands: the need to adapt structure to a new strategy or environment, and the need to maintain complementarities among structural elements—to preserve configurations. Normal interdependencies among structural elements require that change be multifaceted. This will make it expensive, reducing its optimal frequency. The resultant delays will in turn require that changes often be dramatic. The next chapter begins to test this view in three large samples of business firms.

We are not arguing that long adaptive lags and revolutions are the best way for all organizations to adapt, or that piecemeal or incremental changes are always inappropriate. This depends on the shape and levels of the cost curves and the manner in which they are determined by the interactions of internal and external complementarities. The point we wish to stress is that organizations, like biological organisms, are complex entities that are by no means infinitely manipulable or malleable. Many piecemeal structural changes have extensive and often negative repercussions because of the tight interdependencies among organizational "parts." The more integral the interdependencies, the greater the need for multifaceted quantum change. The more costly such change, the rarer it will be and therefore the more revolutionary—*ceteris paribus.*

One area requiring a great deal of further research is the question of how structural attributes must be aligned when changing different types of organizations and different kinds of structural variables. Are bureaucracies in greater need of structural integrity than organic firms are? Can the latter have more loosely coupled elements? Also, do variables such as size and technology have more implications for other variables than do say bureaucratization and centralization? These mysteries are worthy of much more attention from organizational theorists.

9

Structural Change
and Performance

INTRODUCTION

There has been very little research done on the efficacy of different approaches to structural change in organizations. Although much attention
has been devoted to discovering the structural requisites of different organizational environments and strategies, not much is known about the way
in which organizations must change their structures. Should firms change
their elements of structure in concert or in piecemeal fashion? In the last
chapter, we argued that in order for structures to be most effective, they
must comprise mutually supportive elements. Changing only one or two
key elements might upset the balance within integral structural configurations, destroying complementarities. We therefore predicted that elements
must change together in a quantum or concerted way. In contrast, others
have highlighted the advantages of making piecemeal, remedial, and disjointed changes. These are said not to be as upsetting, as costly, or as
cognitively demanding as concerted and pervasive changes.

An independent question concerns whether structural changes
should occur rapidly, in large dramatic jumps, or gradually and incremen-

The authors are grateful to the Social Sciences and Humanities Research Council for
grants #410-80-0071 and #410-77-0019 and to the Government of Quebec for FCAC grant
#EQ1162.

tally.[1] We have emphasized the desirability of rare but dramatic intervals of change as these capitalize on the surrounding periods of stability. Periods of multifaceted change are costly and so, perhaps, are best gone through as seldom as possible. Other authors have suggested that minor, incremental changes are less risky and disruptive and more politically expedient. Evolutionary change was defined to be both piecemeal and small. Revolutionary change is concerted and dramatic.

We wished to begin to explore these questions by studying how several diverse samples of firms changed their structures, and by examining the link between organizational performance and the nature of structural change. It is important, however, to discuss the scope and some of the limitations of this research at the outset. First, this chapter is concerned with structural change only. Such change may constitute a reaction to increases or decreases in environmental uncertainty, dynamism, heterogeneity, or hostility, or to changes in the product-market strategies of the firm. It may be reactive or proactive. But our research did not differentiate between the causes of structural change. Consequently, it will not be possible to derive conclusions about the contingencies under which different types of structural change strategies are required. Second, the research focuses upon a broad but carefully circumscribed set of structural variables. The desire to have diverse and representative samples of firms studied longitudinally and the need to focus upon a large set of variables made it impossible to measure variables that each would have required many precise measurement scales. Third, our study of change looks only at the changes that have occurred over an interval; the exact sequencing of the changes within the interval was not established, since there was no practical method for doing this with our large and varied sample of data. Finally, our findings are of an exploratory nature. Even though there seem to be very significant statistical associations between organizational performance and strategies of structural change, our analysis will not allow us to impute any causal relationships.

The chapter is structured as follows: First, two apparently conflicting bodies of literature are examined to gauge their normative implications for structural change. From a liberal interpretation of this literature, hypotheses are derived concerning the performance implications of concerted versus piecemeal, and dramatic versus incremental change. These hypotheses are then tested on three diverse samples of business firms.

---

[1]In general, things change more quickly during periods of dramatic change than in periods of incremental change. That is, the rate of change is faster the more a firm changes during a given period since there are no significant differences in the length of dramatic vs. incremental change intervals. Clearly, however, it is possible for some incremental changes to be rapid, and for some dramatic changes to be quite time consuming.

THE APPROACH OF EVOLUTION

Unfortunately, much of the literature on organizational change deals with strategy or policy change rather than structural change. Therefore, some of the arguments we call upon in this section have been interpreted loosely.

A rather commonly held view of organizational adaptation pictures sensible managers adjusting piecemeal and incrementally, responding locally to individual crises as they arise. The well-known concepts of problemistic search, uncertainty avoidance, and quasi resolution of conflict portray individual subunits of organizations dealing incrementally and disjointedly with one problem and one goal at a time while emphasizing short-run reaction to short-run feedback (Cyert and March, 1963, p. 119). According to Hedberg, Nystrom, and Starbuck (1976, pp. 60–61):

> What an organization should be avoiding is drastic revolutions. . . . Costs such as hostilities, demotivation, wasted energies, illfounded rationalities, and foolish risks can be lowered by nurturing small disruptions and incremental reorientations—by substituting evolution for revolution.

Braybrooke and Lindblom (1963), Lindblom (1959), Day and Tinney (1968), Cartwright (1973), Carter (1971), Starbuck, Greve, and Hedberg (1978), and Vickers (1959) have argued that organizations should generally avoid dramatic, widespread, and concerted change by adapting gradually and incrementally. This was expected to be the most economical and the least disruptive strategy (Quinn, 1980).

Lindblom (1968, pp. 24–25) has suggested that:

> Policy analysts may simplify [an] otherwise impossible goal–setting task by refusing to look very far ahead—focusing instead on the removal of all-too-observable [problems]. . . . [They] will see that policy making is typically a never-ending process of successive steps in which continual nibbling is a substitute for a good bite. . . . At an extreme, one can see the two contrasting possibilities for policy analysis: on the one hand, plan everything to fit with everything else; on the other, plan to break specific bottlenecks as they arise. The first is impossible; the second, though far from ideal, works.

This strategy of disjointed incrementalism may have much to recommend it. It reduces political obstacles to changes and avoids irresolvable arguments about complex goals and values. The focus is upon patching things up and dealing with obvious problems as they arise. There is generally little disagreement surrounding the choice of methods for handling crises. Also, the risk of ruin or great loss tends to be reduced by the making of incremental moves in place of major and far-reaching ones. Incrementalism allows the organization to learn from its previous actions and still be in a position to remedy them. Finally, cognitive strain is reduced by dealing with manageable fragments of reality; by focusing upon bottlenecks and choosing from a short list of well-tried expedients for dealing with them.

Unfortunately, the applicability of this approach to the realm of structural change has not been considered. It may be reasonable to suggest, however, that incremental and piecemeal strategies might offer as many political, economic, and cognitive advantages for changing structures as they do for modifying policies. For example, small structural adjustments that respond to specific and pressing problems are likely to cause the least dissension and conflict. Also, they are more reversible, cheaper, and less disruptive than extensive changes, and are therefore less risky. If small changes do not work out, the organization's survival will probably not be threatened. Finally, small structural changes are less taxing to the imaginations and cognitive capacities of executives. They do not require lengthy periods of analysis or complex and elaborate master plans.

Although we must not put too fine a point on it, the strategy of disjointed incrementalism seems consistent with the views of those who see organizations as loosely coupled systems (Aldrich, 1979; Weick, 1969). It is maintained that different subunits of the organization can change independently, without significantly influencing the other subunits. Therefore, it may be that many elements of structure can be changed locally, and that much adaptation to the environment can be effected independently by organizational subunits.

On the basis of this discussion, then, one might derive predictions concerning the efficacy of structural change. In the first place, concerted change will be less conducive to success than will piecemeal change. Therefore, changes among structural variables will be less correlated among successful than among unsuccessful firms. Second, dramatic changes may be so risky, costly, and politically inexpedient that they are more likely to meet with failure than with success. Samples of firms showing very great (or no) changes may therefore be outperformed by samples of firms that change gradually and incrementally.

THE APPROACH OF REVOLUTION

In sharp contrast to the piecemeal-incremental view, we advocate that changes in structure must often be both concerted and dramatic. These arguments were presented in Chapter 8 and need only be made more concrete and operational in this section.

The Argument for Concerted Quantum Change

Chapter 8 made the case that if there are integral organizational configurations, variables should change in a concerted way—that is, they should change together in a manner that either avoids disharmonies in configurations or that builds new configurations.[2] Of course, in operationalizing the concept of concertedness in an empirical study of many diverse firms, it is essential to avoid focusing upon structural variables whose relationships would vary over time or among different types of firms. Unfortunately, our theme has been that there are very few such variables, that there exists substitutability among different elements of structure, and that there are different structural evolutionary patterns among firms moving between different configurations. Like Khandwalla (1972, 1973), however, we believe that three broad *classes* of variables must change in concert in most firms; these classes are uncertainty reduction, differentiation, and integration. Although the variables *within* these classes are apt to evolve distinctly and interrelate differently in different types of firms, we predict that in *most* firms, changes in one class will probably have to be matched by complementary changes in the other two classes. The precise nature of these changes is, of course, expected to vary across different types of firms.

Recall that Lawrence and Lorsch (1967) found organizational differentiation, integration, and conflict-resolution capacity had to covary positively or performance would suffer. More specifically, as the time, goal, task, and interpersonal orientations of subunits become more differentiated, there is a greater need to integrate the efforts of these units using devices such as task forces and interdepartmental and cross-functional committees. Galbraith (1973) supported this contention, arguing that increases in differentiation and uncertainty boost the information-processing task of the organization and require more sophisticated integrative devices, such as coordinating personnel and matrix structures.

We think that Khandwalla (1973) is roughly correct in his assertion that effective organizations must be high, medium, or low in their use of uncertainty-reduction, differentiation, and integration devices. It follows that *the use of these devices must increase and decrease in concert.* In other words, major increases in strategic or environmental uncertainty or heterogeneity may require the simultaneous adoption of a number of uncertainty-reduction, differentiation, and integration devices. *Uncertainty-reduction devices* may comprise information-seeking and -processing services by staff managers (Aguilar, 1967; Wilensky, 1967), formal structural devices such as delegation of authority and formal policies, programs and procedures (March and Simon, 1958; Cyert and March, 1963), and interpersonal devices such as consultative decision making (Likert, 1961). These devices reduce uncertainty by insulating parts of the firm from the turbulent environment, allowing more efficient and economical operation. Khandwalla

---

[2]In an earlier paper by the authors, entitled "Structural Change and Performance," *Academy of Management Journal,* 1982, 25, 867–92, quantum change was defined to be both concerted and dramatic. Here it is defined only as being concerted. This usage conforms to that in the rest of our chapters.

(1972) argues that organizations, having reduced uncertainty, must respond to the more diverse contingencies brought about by an uncertain or diverse environment by employing *differentiation devices* such as decentralization, differentiation of operating styles, and the use of technocrats. Finally, the coordinative difficulties caused by increased differentiation will require more *integrative devices* such as participative management, sophisticated control systems, computerized information and budgeting systems, and coordinative committees (Lawrence and Lorsch, 1967; Morse, 1970; Galbraith, 1973; Beckhard and Harris, 1977).

Two hypotheses concerning structural change seem to follow from this discussion. If it is true that change must be concerted—that variables of uncertainty-reduction, differentiation, and integration must change together to maintain a complementary configuration—we should find that:

> *Hypothesis 1a:* Changes in uncertainty-reduction, differentiation, and integration variables will correlate more highly in successful than in unsuccessful groups of firms; this will be most true of correlations *between* categories of variables.
>
> *Hypothesis 1b:* The *average* levels of change (the arithmetic average of the variables in a category) among uncertainty-reduction, differentiation, and integration categories will be more highly correlated in successful than in unsuccessful groups of firms.

The Need for Dramatic Change

The presence of organizational configurations, or at least of required covariation among many structural variables, may make it desirable that change take place infrequently, but quickly and dramatically. Periods of concerted change may be very costly and disruptive as *many* elements of structure are being recast. In Chapter 8, we argued that rational organizations should therefore try to delay such periods until they are adequately rewarding—that is, until their benefits are likely to exceed their substantial costs. We also claimed that successful firms will minimize the number of change periods, and move through the periods as quickly as possible. Of course, the delays and the brevity of the transition periods may require change to be dramatic. Thus, effective firms will often tend to be in one of two states: a common state in which they are undergoing very little or no change, and a rarer state in which they will be experiencing far more *dramatic* changes. The model proposed by Greiner (1972) is most consistent with this view.

The proponents of dramatic change would hypothesize that:

> *Hypothesis 2a:* Successful groups of firms will have a larger proportion of extreme change scores (great increases or great decreases) along their variables than will unsuccessful groups.

Hypothesis 2b: Successful groups will have larger standard deviations along the variables than will unsuccessful groups. (Whereas the former will contain firms making very large changes as well as those making no changes, the latter will contain mostly incrementalists making moderate changes.)

METHOD

The Variables and Data

Our data-collection instruments measured structural variables falling into the categories of uncertainty reduction, differentiation, and integration.[3] Each category was further divided into three subcategories of formal structural, interpersonal, and information-processing devices in a scheme that is similar to Khandwalla's (1972). We used one operationalization of the nine categories upon our two questionnaire data bases and another upon our published data base. This was intended to ensure the validity and robustness of the findings. The questionnaire used in the first two research samples employed eighteen scales that measured *changes* in structure. The third sample comprised published data and employed nine variables of structural change (defined in Appendix 4-1). Table 9-1 summarizes the adaptive devices and lists the numbers of the scales in the questionnaire and published data bases that were used to measure these devices. The citations in the table refer to the studies that were most suggestive of the importance of the category for structural adaptation.

Two samples of questionnaire data were collected from Canadian and Australian business firms. A third sample comprised a large set of published histories of business firms, most of which were located in the United States. The Canadian and published samples have already been described in Chapter 5 and in Appendix 5-5. The Australian sample of 60 firms in many diverse industries is described in Miller and Friesen (1982a). The reliability and validity of the data were acceptably high, as these sources report.

In all cases, 7-point scales were used to measure all the structural variables, where, for example, a score of 1 represented a great decrease in the variable over the period being studied, 7 meant a great increase, and 4 indicated no change. Periods were defined to reveal the most significant structural changes, using the procedures discussed in Chapter 5. The scoring heuristic reported there was used to define periods in the published

---

[3]As we can see from Table 9-1, the integration category includes *dual-function* variables, those that serve both to reduce uncertainty and to integrate organizational efforts. These will be split into a distinct fourth category in some of our analyses.

TABLE 9-1: Adaptive Devices Used by Organizations

	UNCERTAINTY REDUCTION	DIFFERENTIATION	INTEGRATION/ DUAL FUNCTION†
Formal Structural Devices	Use of formal rules, policies, and procedures in capital budgeting, personnel management, etc. (March and Simon, 1958). Scales 1 and 2 of questionnaires. Not measured in published data base.	Decentralization, departmentalization, number of staff departments (Thompson, 1967; Khandwalla, 1972). Scales 8, 9, and 10.* Variable 4.**	Use of task forces, coordinative committees, etc., to integrate decisions (Galbraith, 1973). Scale 13.* Variable 7.**
Interpersonal Devices	Group decision making, delegation of authority (Burns and Stalker, 1961). Scales 3 and 4. Variable 1 in published data base.**	Organizational differentiation (Lawrence and Lorsch, 1967). Scale 11.* Variable 5.**	Open internal communications and participative management (Likert, 1961). Scale 14.* Variable 8.**
Information-Processing Devices	Environmental scanning and analysis (Aquilar, 1967; Mintzberg, 1973). Scales 5, 6, 7.* Variables 2 and 3.**	Use of technocrats in decision making (Burns and Stalker, 1961; Perrow, 1970). Scale 12.* Variable 6.**	Sophisticated, computerized control systems (Wilensky, 1967). Scales 15, 16,† 17,† and 18.† Variable 9.**

*Scale numbers are those used for the two questionnaire data bases.

**Variable numbers are those used in the published data base.

†Scales 16, 17, and 18 refer respectively to computerization, long-term planning, and capital budgeting, which, although they are integrative devices, can also be considered uncertainty-reduction devices. Later, these will be called dual-function devices, since they accomplish two purposes.

data base, whereas a standard 5-year interval was used for the Canadian and Australian data.

Performance Evaluation

Each of the three samples was bifurcated into high-performance and low-performance segments. High-performance samples contained only firms that performed well in *both* sales growth and profitability; low-performance samples performed poorly according to both criteria. We measured growth in sales and growth in return on equity during the period.

For the Canadian sample of 50 firms, annual reports or financial statements were obtained covering the period beginning with the first year of the five years and extending two years beyond the end of the period. That is, a total of seven years of data were gathered on growth in sales and growth in equity. The last two years of data were gathered because of the possible lag between a series of structural changes and their performance implications. Logarithmic averages of the growth in sales (revenues) and the growth in R.O.E. were taken for the seven years. Firms that had a growth rate in sales of less than 8 percent (the average rate of inflation for the period) *and* an average decrease in R.O.E. were classified as low performers ($N = 23$). The firms that had exhibited *real* growth in sales and R.O.E. were classified as high performers ($N = 17$). The balance of the sample either had missing performance data ($N = 4$) or experienced a decline in one performance indicator and an increase in the other ($N = 8$). The latter firms were dropped because of the desire to avoid any ambiguity in estimating performance.

In the Australian sample of 60 firms, confidentiality was guaranteed to the firms. We could not identify the firms in the sample and thus had to rely on the reported performance of the respondents. The following questions were asked of the chief executives regarding performance:

Over the last five years, your firm's performance relative to your competitors' in:

i) Growth in sales/ revenues:

Has become poorer vis-à-vis competitors'   1 2 3 4 5 6 7   Has become better

No change

ii) Return on equity:

Has become poorer vis-à-vis competitors'   1 2 3 4 5 6 7   Has become better

No change

Again, fourteen firms in the sample had to be dropped because of conflicting performance ratings in the different indicators or because performance averaged about 4 (no change) on the scales. There were no missing data in this sample. Of the remaining 46 firms, 23 showed scores of 5 or more on both indicators, and the rest had scores of 3 or less on both indicators.

Of the 135 periods in the published data sample, we were able to obtain reliable performance data on 83. Another 29 periods had very clear and marked increases or decreases in both sales and R.O.E., although exact data for each year of the period could not be obtained. The remaining 23 periods could not be rated. Of the 112 rated periods, 89 had unconflicting performance in sales and R.O.E. growth. That is, *both* performance indicators improved or deteriorated. Forty-eight of these firms showed improving sales growth and R.O.E. for the duration of the period plus the following two years, and 41 firms showed declines. The performance criteria for the published sample were the same in inflation-adjusted terms as those for the Canadian sample.

After having divided the three samples, we found that there were no significant systematic differences in industry composition or size between the high- and low-performing groups of firms. Of the eighteen scales used, only one showed significantly different means (at the .05 level) between the high- and low-performing groups in the Canadian sample, and only two scales showed significantly different means in the Australian sample. The most obvious difference between the subsamples seemed to be their financial performance. None of the scales were significantly correlated with performance.

FINDINGS

The findings section is divided into four parts, each of which tests one of the hypotheses. Hypotheses 1a and 1b concern the merits of concerted versus piecemeal change; 2a and 2b focus on the performance implications of dramatic versus incremental change. All hypotheses are presented from the point of view of the advocates of revolutionary change.

Concerted Quantum Versus Piecemeal Change

Hypothesis 1a. Changes in uncertainty reduction, differentiation, dual function, and integration variables will correlate more highly in successful than in unsuccessful groups of firms; this will be most true of correlations between categories of variables.

Product moment correlation matrices were computed for each of the six subsamples. In every instance, the high-performing subsamples exhibited more significant correlations among the changes in the structural variables than did low-performing subsamples. This was true for correlations in the predicted direction at the .05, .01, and .001 levels of significance. Tables 9-2, 9-3, and 9-4 present the correlation matrices for the Canadian, Australian, and published data samples respectively. In each table, the upper rows of coefficients for each variable present the results for the successful, high-performing subsamples (S), and the lower rows present the findings for the unsuccessful (U) subsamples.

Table 9-5 summarizes the number of correlations that are significant at different levels for the six subsamples. The levels of significance for the differences in the number of significant correlations between the subsamples is given in the final column of the table. From the table we can see that the correlational results support the superiority of quantum or concerted

TABLE 9-2: Product Moment Correlation Matrices for the Canadian Subsamples

	UNCERTAINTY REDUCTION							DIFFERENTIATION					INTEGRATION			DUAL FUNCTION			
	1	2	3	4	5	6	7	8	9	10	11	12	13	14	15	16	17	18	
Uncertainty Reduction																			
1. Formal rules & policies in capital budgeting	1.0	90**	−43*	45*	34	44*	25	07	−18	16	07	36	71***	85***	81***	58**	47*	19	S[a]
	1.0	19	07	65***	58**	57**	43*	14	35	25	29	28	−17	34	45*	09	09	33	U[a]
2. Formal rules & policies in personnel management	1.0		−41*	48*	27	34	27	23	−11	07	−03	35	72***	68***	87***	59**	43*	12	S
	1.0		09	15	−10	28	25	51**	09	−09	−10	−16	01	21	22	48**	−07	31	U
3. Constraints limiting managerial discretion			1.0	−19	−22	−23	−46*	−45*	−40	−73***	49	−34	−56**	37	−48*	−69***	−43*	−44*	S
			1.0	−36	−31	12	12	−03	−17	−29	−14	41	−44*	01	09	09	15	12	U
4. Group decision making				1.0	−08	−29	23	39	−54	04	06	56**	57**	40*	46*	43*	30	−22	S
				1.0	52**	34	40*	−22	−16	41*	29	13	25	14	38*	−02	−04	29	U
5. Scanning of markets via formal staff activities					1.0	47*	28	14	−02	26	24	08	27	19	11	19	−13	61**	S
					1.0	45*	10	−24	37*	33	−05	23	05	09	21	02	−29	01	U
6. Informal scanning of markets by managers						1.0	−07	−34	32	27	14	−23	25	37	35	38	30	74***	S
						1.0	32	19	13	−05	05	0	−10	18	19	18	34	14	U
7. Briefings by field personnel							1.0	53**	04	12	−08	31	49*	20	29	49*	10	−10	S
							1.0	−08	−33	16	16	08	03	09	45*	−01	40*	52**	U
Differentiation																			
8. Number of staff departments								1.0	03	09	01	60**	46*	−10	16	46*	16	−07	S
								1.0	11	−01	11	−15	18	41*	25	17	14	18	U
9. Number of profit centers									1.0	23	−18	−52	−27	−40	−01	06	26	28	S
									1.0	07	−20	0	−25	−14	−10	20	−34	43*	U

Variable		10	11	12	13	14	15	16	17	18
10. Delegation of authority for strategic decisions	S	1.0	−45	20	27	26	13	47*	34	55**
	U	1.0	10	48**	56**	41*	62***	40*	05	−06
11. Organizational differentiation	S		1.0	34	−02	−23	−05	−11	−10	−12
	U		1.0	−15	38*	24	21	−26	−41*	47*
12. Influence of technocrats in decisions	S			1.0	62**	48*	34	52*	12	−05
	U			1.0	−14	06	46*	22	0	13
Integration										
13. Formal task forces and committees	S				1.0	74***	78***	79***	44*	22
	U				1.0	42*	45*	16	05	−07
14. Frequency of meetings and communications	S					1.0	75***	55**	41*	18
	U					1.0	−60	15	05	05
15. Formal controls	S						1.0	68***	61**	09
	U						1.0	32	09	17
Dual										
16. Computerization of information processing	S							1.0	58**	26
	U							1.0	−02	−02
17. Long-term planning systems	S								1.0	09
	U								1.0	38*
18. Capital budgeting	S									1.0
	U									1.0

[a] For each variable, the top row presents the correlation coefficients for the successful sample (S), and the bottom row for the unsuccessful sample (U). All decimals are deleted.

*The coefficient is significant in the predicted direction at the .05 level.

**The coefficient is significant in the prediction direction at the .01 level.

***The coefficient is significant in the predicted direction at the .001 level.

The sample size was 17 for the successful subsample and 21 for the unsuccessful subsample.

TABLE 9-3: Product Moment Correlation Matrices for the Australian Subsamples

	UNCERTAINTY REDUCTION							DIFFERENTIATION				INTEGRATION				DUAL FUNCTION			
	1	2	3	4	5	6	7	8	9	10	11	12	13	14	15	16	17	18	
Uncertainty Reduction																			
1. Formal rules & policies in capital budgeting	1.0 / 1.0	67*** / 50**	10 / −26	34 / 23	43* / 30	40* / −20	02 / 27	27 / 45*	−05 / 06	35* / 08	26 / −05	50** / 22	72*** / −08	46** / 14	39* / 23	35* / 58**	38* / 47**	45* / 38*	S[a] / U[a]
2. Formal rules & polices in personnel management		1.0 / 1.0	27 / 13	19 / 24	47** / 10	29 / −27	05 / 24	32 / 17	−20 / 22	17 / 14	04 / 11	59** / 20	58** / 28	41* / 07	30 / 24	27 / 44*	33 / 19	23 / 18	S / U
3. Constraints limiting managerial discretion			1.0 / 1.0	−03 / −03	−04 / 03	10 / −04	22 / 07	46 / −50**	−14 / −10	02 / −10	06 / 35	−22 / 10	19 / 16	−17 / 10	−03 / 18	20 / 28	−29 / −37	−40* / −03	S / U
4. Group decision making				1.0 / 1.0	39* / 16	24 / 44*	27 / 48**	03 / 22	29 / 33	47** / −28	42* / 06	14 / 44*	55** / 36*	11 / 33	40* / 59***	15 / 28	15 / 18	28 / 50**	S / U
5. Scanning of markets via formal staff activities					1.0 / 1.0	24 / −02	−06 / 01	22 / 21	43* / 30	41* / 48**	44* / −05	47** / 56**	51** / 26	57** / 54**	30 / 10	31 / 28	18 / 58**	32 / 11	S / U
6. Informal scanning of markets by managers						1.0 / 1.0	20 / 29	43* / 18	34 / 32	57** / −19	21 / 08	23 / 10	25 / 30	23 / −17	31 / 31	25 / −15	−05 / −02	−02 / 06	S / U
7. Briefing by field personnel							1.0 / 1.0	13 / 07	−11 / −08	03 / −26	−03 / 35*	23 / 08	19 / 40*	15 / 17	11 / 56**	22 / 32	−50 / −05	−25 / 13	S / U
Differentiation																			
8. Number of staff departments								1.0 / 1.0	28 / 33	40* / 01	37* / −47	16 / 07	24 / 11	20 / 02	−22 / 25	21 / 05	13 / 44*	−14 / 17	S / U
9. Number of profit centers									1.0 / 1.0	62*** / 47**	54** / 19	15 / 10	10 / 14	28 / 08	06 / 08	17 / −06	−05 / 51**	−03 / 38*	S / U

232

		10	11	12	13	14	15	16	17	18
10. Delegation of authority for strategic decisions	S	1.0	30	38*	24	43*	41*	37*	35*	23
	U	1.0	01	-07	-14	-01	-30	-01	37*	-18
11. Organizational differentiation	S		1.0	02	52**	23	07	31	11	-01
	U		1.0	07	20	06	42*	41*	-41	-19
12. Influence of technocrats in decisions	S			1.0	48**	87***	32	41*	31	50**
	U			1.0	40*	48**	08	27	23	04
Integration										
13. Formal task forces and committees	S				1.0	49**	42*	51**	27	28
	U				1.0	36*	43*	-06	06	01
14. Frequency of meetings and communications	S					1.0	35*	51**	24	42*
	U					1.0	37*	45*	14	10
15. Formal controls	S						1.0	60***	20	41*
	U						1.0	48**	-04	25
Dual										
16. Computerization of information processing	S							1.0	14	16
	U							1.0	-01	23
17. Long-term planning systems	S								1.0	53**
	U								1.0	35*
18. Capital budgeting	S									1.0
	U									1.0

[a]For each variable, the top row presents the correlation coefficients for the successful sample (S); the bottom row for the unsuccessful sample (U). All decimals are deleted.

*The correlation is significant at the .05 level.

**The .01 level of significance.

***The .001 level of significance.

The sample size was 23 for both the successful and unsuccessful subsamples.

TABLE 9-4: Product Moment Correlation Matrices: Published Data Subsamples

	UNCERTAINTY REDUCTION			DIFFERENTIATION			INTEGRATION			
	1	2	3	4	5	6	7	8	9	
Uncertainty Reduction										
1. Delegation for operating decisions	1.0	33*	22	33*	26*	27*	07	33*	11	S[a]
	1.0	-06	20	50***	-08	06	14	33*	-02	U[a]
2. Scanning		1.0	56***	-11	07	49***	39**	70***	59***	S
		1.0	18	-14	52***	26	27	42**	22	U
3. Analysis			1.0	-03	-03	44***	55***	63***	74***	S
			1.0	19	15	38**	60***	40**	38*	U
Differentiation										
4. Decentralization				1.0	05	02	-05	-02	-15	S
				1.0	-11	-07	-07	-21	-37	U
5. Differentiation					1.0	09	-10	11	-11	S
					1.0	45**	08	15	06	U
6. Technocratization						1.0	26*	39**	30*	S
						1.0	20	30	26	U
Integration										
7. Integration							1.0	31*	50***	S
							1.0	56***	70***	U
8. Communications								1.0	67***	S
								1.0	58***	U
9. Controls									1.0	S
									1.0	U

[a]For each variable in the table, the top row presents the correlation coefficients for the successful subsample (S); the bottom row for the unsuccessful subsample (U). All decimals are deleted.

*The coefficient is significant in the predicted direction at the .05 level.

**The coefficient is significant in the predicted direction at the .01 level.

***The coefficient is significant in the predicted direction at the .001 level.

The sample size ranged between 34 and 40 for the successful sample and between 34 and 40 for the unsuccessful sample when the pairwise

TABLE 9-5: Comparison of Number of Significant Correlations in Subsamples of Successful and Unsuccessful Firms

SIGNIFICANCE LEVEL OF CORRELATIONS	SUCCESSFUL GROUP		UNSUCCESSFUL GROUP		p-VALUE OF INTERSAMPLE DIFFERENCES IN NUMBER OF CORRELATIONS
	NO. OF SIGNIFICANT CORRELATIONS	% OF TOTAL CORRELATIONS IN MATRIX	NO. OF SIGNIFICANT CORRELATIONS	% OF TOTAL CORRELATIONS IN MATRIX	
Canadian Sample					
.001	15	9.8	2	1.3	
.01	13	8.5	8	5.2	
.05	25	16.3	21	13.7	
Total	53	34.6	31	20.3	.003
Out of	153	100	153	100	
Australian Sample					
.001	5	3.3	1	0.7	
.01	19	12.4	15	9.8	
.05	28	18.3	20	13.1	
Total	52	34.0	36	23.5	.02
Out of	153	100	153	100	
Published Sample					
.001	10	27.8	6	16.7	
.01	2	5.6	3	8.3	
.05	8	22.2	3	8.3	
Total	20	55.6	12	33.3	.03
Out of	36	100	36	100	

rather than piecemeal change. In other words, at least from a purely quantitative perspective, successful samples of firms show a higher number of significant correlations among changes in uncertainty-reduction, differentiation, and integration variables than do unsuccessful samples.

But such a gross analysis hides many variations among the findings and does not get to the root of the most pronounced differences between successful and unsuccessful subsamples. Whereas the successful samples exhibit *more* concerted change, they also exhibit qualitatively different types of concerted change. The significant correlations among the subsamples differ not only in number, but also in *nature*.

One of the most important qualitative differences we expected to find was suggested by Lawrence and Lorsch (1967), Galbraith (1973), and Khandwalla (1973). These authors argued that organizational structures have to be balanced in their degrees of uncertainty reduction, differentiation, and integration in order to safeguard performance. If so, the changes *across* these classes of variables should be more highly correlated in successful than in unsuccessful subsamples. For example, firms that fail to boost uncertainty reduction and integration in concert will be penalized. On the other hand, the literature does not suggest as strongly that there should be concerted changes *within* categories of variables. Some of the uncertainty-reduction and integration devices are more substitutable than complementary. For example, long-term planning may be used instead of capital budgeting; formal scanning can be done in lieu of informal scanning.

Table 9-6 shows all successful samples to have a significantly higher proportion of meaningful between-category correlations than do their unsuccessful counterparts. It appears important to performance for changes across uncertainty-reduction, differentiation, integration, and dual categories to be highly correlated. Although there also seems to be some advantage to changing variables within a category in concert, this advantage is modest and never statistically significant. There are on average 78 percent more across-category correlations in the successful than in the unsuccessful subsamples. The corresponding figure is only 30 percent for within-category correlations.

The within–across category distinction that we have made is a crude one. Readers interested in a more refined analysis of differences in the types of concertedness between successful and unsuccessful subsamples are urged to consult Appendix 9-1.

Hypothesis 1b.   *The average levels of change among uncertainty-reduction, differentiation, integration, and dual categories of variables will be more highly correlated in successful than in unsuccessful groups of firms.*

The findings of the last section indicate that we should focus on across- rather than within-category correlations. Now we shall get away

TABLE 9-6: Proportion of Correlations Significant beyond the .05 Level within and between Categories of Variables

	WITHIN CATEGORY CORRELATIONS				BETWEEN CATEGORY CORRELATIONS			
	CANADIAN	AUSTRALIAN	PUBLISHED	AVERAGE	CANADIAN	AUSTRALIAN	PUBLISHED	AVERAGE
1. Successful Sample:								
Proportion (fraction) of significant correlations	.35 (13/37)	.38 (14/37)	.56 (5/9)	.43	.34 (40/116)	.33 (38/116)	.56 (15/27)	.41
2. Unsuccessful Sample:								
Proportion (fraction) of significant correlations	.30 (11/37)	.24 (9/37)	.44 (4/9)	.33	.17 (20/116)	.22 (26/116)	.30 (8/27)	.23
3. Ratio of Proportions								
(Successful ÷ Unsuccessful)	1.17	1.58	1.27	1.30	2.0	1.50	1.87	1.78
4. p Value of Difference								
Between Successful and Unsuccessful Samples—Fisher Exact Test:	.40	.16	.50	.10	.002	.05	.05	.0001

from individual variables and assess the relationship between performance and *overall* across-category concerted change. To do this, we employed artificial variables whose intercorrelations could serve as a crude summary of across-category concerted change. The set of artificial variables was calculated by taking an arithmetic average of the variables within each category, so that there was one averaged variable in each of the four categories. High correlations among these variables would indicate that uncertainty-reduction, differentiation, and so forth tend to change together to the same degree.

Table 9-7 presents the results of the analysis. For every data base, the successful subsamples had higher average correlations than the unsuccessful subsamples, the average correlation coefficient being .55 in the first case and .35 in the second. Of the fifteen coefficients, those for the successful subsamples were greater than those for the unsuccessful subsamples eleven times, smaller two times, and the same twice. Given that we found eleven out of fifteen correlation coefficients to be superior in the successful samples, the null hypothesis that successful and unsuccessful populations contained an equal number of such superior coefficients could be rejected at the .01 level of significance using a binomial test of proportions. Crude as it is, our across-category analysis of overall concertedness seems to support our arguments for quantum change.

One of our unsuccessful Canadian firms had acquired a number of subsidiaries in related but distinct industries. Managers tried to respond by adapting the organization structure, moving from a functional to a divisional reporting framework. Profit centers and product divisions were set up to accomplish this. But little was done to establish controls that could adequately monitor the performance of the new divisions. As a result, problems in the newly acquired subsidiaries were concealed from top managers. These ultimately proved to be very costly. In effect, differentiation had increased without a matching increase in integration.

Dramatic vs. Incremental Change

Hypothesis 2a. *Successful groups of firms will have a larger proportion of extreme change scores along the variables than will unsuccessful groups.*

In Chapter 8, we predicted that major and decisive change would minimize the disruption and frequency of costly transition periods. The incrementalists argue that dramatic change is politically inexpedient, expensive, and risky. They might therefore make an opposite prediction.

To test Hypothesis 2a, we simply counted the scores along each variable for each of the six subsamples. Scores of 1 (maximum decrease) and 7 (maximum increase) were taken as *very extreme* changes, and those of 1, 2, 6, and 7 were considered *extreme* changes. Table 9-8 presents the results of

TABLE 9-7: Correlations among Categories for Averaged Variables

		CANADIAN SAMPLE				AUSTRALIAN SAMPLE				PUBLISHED SAMPLE		
		1	2	3	4	1	2	3	4	1	2	3
1. Uncertainty Reduction	S[a]	1.0	.41*	.88***	.66**	1.0	.56**	.74***	.40*	1.0	.44***	.70***
	U[a]	1.0	.48**	.21	.27	1.0	.50**	.60***	.66***	1.0	.44**	.57***
2. Differentiation	S		1.0	.44*	.60**		1.0	.51*	.40*		1.0	.05
	U		1.0	.44*	.13		1.0	.35*	.34*		1.0	-.04
3. Integration	S			1.0	.77***			1.0	.71***			1.0
	U			1.0	.08			1.0	.30			1.0
4. Dual	S				1.0				1.0			
	U				1.0				1.0			

[a]For each variable, the top row presents the correlation coefficients for the successful subsamples (S); the bottom row for the unsuccessful subsamples (U).

*, **, *** indicate that correlations are significant at the .05, .01, and .001 levels respectively. The sample sizes are given in Tables 9-2 through 9-4.

TABLE 9-8: Percentage of Extreme Change Scores

SCALES	CANADIAN SAMPLE — N = 17 SUCCESSFUL		N = 21 UNSUCCESSFUL		AUSTRALIAN SAMPLE — N = 23 SUCCESSFUL		N = 23 UNSUCCESSFUL	
1. Formal Rules, etc.: cap. Budgeting	66.7[a]	22.3[b]	57.1[a]	23.8[b]	26.0[a]	13.0[b]	13.0[a]	0[b]
2. Formal Rules, etc.: personnel Mgmt.	66.6	33.3	42.8	9.5	47.8	17.4	13.0	0
3. Constraints on Managerial Discretion	23.3	5.6	28.5	0	17.4	0	13.0	0
4. Group Decision Making	61.1	11.1	38.0	9.0	34.7	13.0	30.4	4.3
5. Scanning—formal—staff	27.8	11.1	33.4	9.6	39.1	4.3	26.0	0
6. Scanning—informal—managers	33.4	5.6	38.1	14.3	21.6	4.3	21.7	0
7. Briefings by Field Personnel	22.3	0	23.8	4.8	17.3	4.3	8.7	0
8. No. of Staff. Depts.	38.9	11.1	23.8	0	21.6	8.7	4.5	0
9. No. of Profit Centers	27.8	0	38.2	4.8	26.0	8.6	0	0
10. Delegation of Authority	27.8	11.1	23.8	4.8	26.0	4.3	26.0	4.3
11. Differentiation	27.8	0	33.3	9.5	21.7	0	21.7	4.3
12. Influence of Technocrats	55.6	0	28.6	0	43.4	4.3	17.4	0
13. Task Forces & Committees	55.6	16.7	52.4	9.5	30.3	13.0	26.0	13.0
14. Meetings & Communications	72.3	16.7	47.6	19.0	34.7	17.3	26.0	4.3
15. Formal Controls	50.1	27.8	65.2	14.3	43.4	17.4	30.4	17.4
16. Computerization	72.3	44.5	71.4	19.0	65.1	34.7	60.9	21.7
17. Long-Term Planning	50.1	16.7	27.6	14.3	26.1	8.7	30.3	4.3
18. Capital Budgeting	55.6	16.7	57.1	23.8	21.7	21.7	8.7	0
Mean % of Extremes for Subsamples	46.4*	13.9*	40.6	10.5	30.8**	10.8**	21.0	4.1

PUBLISHED SAMPLE

	N = 48 SUCCESSFUL		N = 41 UNSUCCESSFUL	
1. Delegation for Operating Decisions	27.9[a]	7.0[b]	7.5[a]	2.5[b]
2. Scanning	20.0	5.0	5.7	0
3. Analysis	20.5	6.8	5.3	0
4. Decentralization	10.9	0	17.1	4.9
5. Differentiation	4.2	2.1	2.4	0
6. Technocratization	0	0	0	0
7. Integration	14.9	2.1	15.0	0
8. Communication	20.6	5.9	16.1	0
9. Controls	23.8	4.8	20.0	2.9
Mean % of Extremes for Subsamples	15.9**	3.7**	9.9	1.1

[a,b] The *a* columns present the total proportion of change scores that are 1, 2, 6, and 7. The *b* columns present the proportion of scores that are 1 and 7.

* and ** respectively indicate that the mean percentages of extreme or very extreme scores is greater for the successful than for the unsuccessful samples at the .10 and .01 levels of significance using a test of proportions.

this analysis. For each subsample, the first column shows the percentage of scores that represents extreme changes, and the second column shows the percentage of scores that represents very extreme changes.

In each data base, the successful subsamples contain more extreme and very extreme change scores than do the unsuccessful subsamples. The mean percentage of extreme and very extreme scores is greater for the successful subsamples in every instance. When we look at individual variables, in 30 out of 45 cases, the percentage of extreme scores is greater for the successful subsamples than for the unsuccessful ones. The unsuccessful samples have a greater percentage of extreme scores in only 12 out of 45 cases. In the case of *very* extreme scores, the ratios are 29 out of 45 and 10 out of 45 respectively. Thus, there appears to be support for the predictions of Chapter 8. There is a pronounced tendency, particularly in the Australian and published data, for successful subsamples to change more dramatically, and perhaps more rapidly (since the period of change is fixed in the questionnaire data bases) than the unsuccessful subsamples.

One of our Canadian firms was run by a group of very conservative executives. Three times they had hired consultants who argued that greater responsiveness to the competition and customers would be needed to stem further losses. The consultants had outlined several plans for a structural overhaul that might help put the managers of the firm back in touch with its markets. The establishment of product divisions, the priming of information systems, and the creation of several coordinative committees were suggested. Three times the consultants presented their essentially identical proposals, and three times the managers responded with incremental half-hearted remedies. After the first report, accounts receivable were computerized and a product planning committee was established. After two years, continued losses, and a second report, the cost accounting system was improved. Eighteen months later, after the third report, a market research study was performed. Never were the changes sufficiently dramatic to address the problem at hand. Performance continued to decline.

Hypothesis 2b. *Groups of successful firms will have larger standard deviations along the variables than will groups of unsuccessful firms.*

Successful firms were expected to be in one of two states: those in which the variables do not change, and those in which they change a great deal. Firms pursuing such a strategy will therefore compose samples that show substantial standard deviations along the variables: Some firms will be changing a lot (scores of 1, 2, 6 and 7), and others may not change at all (scores of 4). In contrast, firms that adapt gradually will be stable or will undergo small changes (scores of 3, 4, or 5). Therefore the standard deviations will be lower along the variables for such samples. If we are correct in our assumption that revolutionary, dramatic change is most conducive to success, standard deviations will be higher in the successful than in the unsuccessful samples. If the proponents of gradual, incremental change are right, unsuccessful samples will probably have the highest standard deviations.

Table 9-9 presents the standard deviations for the successful and unsuccessful subsamples for the Canadian and Australian data. In the 36 comparisons, an *F*-test revealed that in fifteen cases, the variances for the scales were greater in the successful subsamples than in the unsuccessful subsamples at the .05 level of significance or better. At the .10 level of significance, this number increases to 21. Never were the variances in the unsuccessful sample significantly greater than those in the successful sample at or beyond the .10 level. Because the published data used ordinal rather than interval scales, the concept of variance and therefore the *F*-statistic become inapplicable. However, just to serve as a rough guide, we did calculate the standard deviations for the nine variables of the published sample. In seven cases, the successful sample's variances were greater than those of the unsuccessful sample.

When we look at the results of testing both hypotheses 2a and 2b, we see that there appears to be some support for the benefits of dramatic and rapid change in all three data bases. Some may want to argue that these results are due to extraneous factors. Variances might be greater for successful samples if their mean change scores were significantly higher (or lower) than those of the unsuccessful samples. A mean score of 6 or 2 would allow a possible deviation of five points, whereas a mean score of about 4 would allow a maximum deviation of three points on the 7-point scales. Also, the number of extreme scores might have been higher in successful samples because these face much more dynamic or uncertain environments. We tried to guard against such systematic differences. First, our data showed that there are almost no differences among the means of the variables for the different subsamples. In fact, a look at the means would have led us to conclude that successful and unsuccessful samples of firms pursue very much the same strategies of structural change, an observation that our findings have shown to be exceedingly inaccurate. Thus the first ad hoc explanation of the results seems to have no basis. Second, there were no apparent differences among successful and unsuccessful subsamples in terms of industry representation or size. Although this is a rather crude method of controlling for environmental differences, the internal diversity of the samples and the fact that there were three of them causes us to reject the notion that subsample differences in extreme scores are the result of a sampling anomaly. All this is not to say, however, that more research into the strategic and environmental influences upon structural change would not serve to considerably extend and qualify these findings.

TABLE 9-9: Standard Deviations of Successful vs. Unsuccessful Subsamples

	CANADIAN SAMPLE		AUSTRALIAN SAMPLE	
	N = 17 SUCCESSFUL	N = 21 UNSUCCESSFUL	N = 23 SUCCESSFUL	N = 23 UNSUCCESSFUL
Uncertainty Reduction				
1. Formal rules and policies: capital budgets	1.58**	0.85	1.15**	0.76
2. Formal rules and policies: personnel management	1.56**	0.75	1.31**	0.78
3. Constraints on managerial discretion	1.22	1.02	1.04	1.03
4. Group decision making	1.39**	0.91	1.09*	0.83
5. Scanning of markets: formal, by staff	1.06	1.24	0.95	0.94
6. Scanning of markets: informal, by managers	1.09	1.03	1.15**	0.79
7. Briefings by field personnel	1.05*	0.77	1.16**	0.79
Differentiation				
8. Number of staff departments	1.40**	0.81	1.31**	0.80
9. Number of profit centers	0.93	1.06	1.33**	0.81
10. Delegation of authority for strategic decisions	1.42	1.12	1.10	1.27
11. Organizational differentiation	1.30	1.21	1.11	1.01
12. Influence of technocrats	0.95	0.84	1.11*	0.86
Integration				
13. Formal task forces and committees	1.46	1.26	1.31*	1.00
14. Meetings and communications	1.42*	1.03	1.31	1.04
15. Formal controls	1.42**	0.91	1.24	1.01
Dual				
16. Computerization of information processing	1.47*	1.09	1.65**	1.02
17. Long-term planning systems	1.62**	1.04	1.22	1.11
18. Capital budgeting	1.64**	0.96	1.15**	0.79

*Variances are significantly greater for the successful than the unsuccessful subsample at the .1 level using an F test with $N_1 - 1$, $N_2 - 1$ degrees of freedom.

**Variances are significantly greater for the successful than the unsuccessful subsample at the .05 level.

CONCLUSION

For each of our four hypotheses, partial support was found for the benefits of quantum and dramatic change. In contrast, the conjectures that were liberally derived from the proponents of piecemeal and incremental change were usually cast into doubt. The major findings of the chapter can now be summarized. First, regarding the quantum-versus-piecemeal-change controversy:

1. Samples of successful firms show a higher percentage of significant correlations among *changes* in uncertainty-reduction, differentiation, integration, and dual-function variables than samples of unsuccessful firms.
2. But this does not imply that *all* variables must change in concert. Although it seemed important for correlations across classes of variables to be high, correlations among changes within classes were often highest for the unsuccessful subsamples.
3. In successful samples, our *overall* indices of structural change for each category of variables were more highly correlated than in unsuccessful samples.

Points 1 to 3 support the view that it may be useful for many structural variables to increase or decrease together. Concerted quantum change, at least *across* categories of variables, seems to be more highly associated with success than is piecemeal change.

In exploring the dramatic-versus-incremental-change positions, we found that:

4. Samples of successful firms generally have a higher percentage of extreme structural changes than do samples of unsuccessful firms. Dramatic change seems to be more closely associated with success than does incremental change.
5. Samples of successful firms also have higher standard deviations along structural variables than do samples of unsuccessful firms. Successful firms seem more likely than unsuccessful firms to alternate between great changes in structure, and stability.

Points 4 and 5 suggest that it may be useful for structural variables to increase or decrease dramatically and quickly. Incremental structural change was less likely to be undertaken by high-performing firms.[4]

[4]Some readers have objected that because we have measured change over substantial periods of time, our finding "concerted" and "dramatic" change among successful firms was simply an artifact of our method. Indeed, multifaceted and extensive changes are *bound* to occur if they are gauged by comparing the end points of a long enough interval. However, major differences were found in the concertedness and extent of change between our successful and unsuccessful subsamples, even though the time intervals over which change was measured were the same for both. This supports the functional nature of certain types of change, and therefore, perhaps, that of a certain set of configurations. Functionalists, of course, would argue that the tendency of a configuration to promote success would lead to its prevalence. Our findings revealed not simply multifaceted change, but that which was concerted, comple-

We can now speculate about the significance of the results. The findings appear to be quite consistent with the notion of structural configurations. Firms may be required to design their structures in a manner that ensures internal harmony among many of their elements. It may be as improper to have, say, a high level of uncertainty reduction with a low level of integration as it is to have a very bureaucratic structure with an uncertain environment. Thus, configurations may make change expensive and disruptive because many variables must change in concert to ensure harmony among structural elements. Since change will be costly, it is best to undertake it only when it is very necessary, and to perform the change as quickly and decisively as possible. This may require extreme changes in a brief period of time. If this view seems sensible, the hazards of piecemeal and incremental change can be readily seen. The former may destroy internal complementarities among the structural elements comprising an old configuration without having the scope to create a new one. The latter may protract the costly and disruptive period of dismantling the old configuration and building one that is more commensurate with new contingencies.

The findings are consistent with elemental *and* relational configurations. One could say that there exist a number of elemental configurations among our major classes of elements, each characterized by uniformly high, medium, or low scores across *all* classes. Alternatively, we might postulate only one relational configuration characterized by a positive alignment (relationship) among all the classes. This configuration may describe a large fraction of the successful subsample of firms.

The reader might object that since the variables are so neatly aligned, it makes no sense to distinguish among different configurations. If one configuration explains so much, the traditional samplewide contingency analysis would suffice. We can therefore forget about taxonomies and the approach of synthesis. But this is not true. This chapter has not attempted to discover the most predictive configurations, but rather to make some general discoveries about structural change. The chapters of Parts II and III that addressed this topic directly have established that there are often major differences in the relationships among structural variables across the various configurations. All we have found in this chapter is that there is a

---

mentary, and thematic. The former will almost always result if the period of analysis is long. But not the latter. And it is, of course, the second finding that best supports the case for configuration. It is also interesting that though our periods of analysis averaged five years, our published histories indicated that most of the changes took place over a 2-year period. But we could not use such a brief interval in our analysis. For many firms in our randomly selected questionnaire data bases, nothing would have happened during the *latest* 2-year period, the only practical one for which managers could be polled.

rough alignment among very *gross categories* of variables that pertains to a *fraction* of a successful subsample of firms. When we look at all firms in all samples, and at the individual variables rather than the rough categories, we are quite likely to find a variety of configurations—elemental and relational alike. There was in fact a good deal of variability in the alignment among variables within each of our samples, as can be seen from the low-order correlations.

Clearly, this chapter raises as many questions as it answers. But in an area of research that has been almost entirely ignored, that may not be such a bad thing.

10

Momentum, Reversal
and Configuration

INTRODUCTION

The two preceding chapters were concerned with structural change, contrasting the approaches of successful and unsuccessful firms. We turn now to examine changes in strategy making as well as structure, and to discover tendencies that are common to all firms, irrespective of their performance. Although the research on structural change reported in Chapters 8 and 9 supports the existence of elemental structural configurations, it does not say much about the processes of strategy making described in Chapter 4. We therefore wished to broaden our study of change to take it beyond the focus on structure. We also wanted to find more support for relational as opposed to elemental configurations. Recall from the introduction to Part I that a relational configuration is preserved when the relationships among its variables remain the same. But an elemental configuration can only be preserved when raw variable scores do not change much.

The kind of change that supports the existence of common elemental configurations is that in which periods of stability are infrequently punctu-

We are grateful to the Canada Council for Grants #S76-0378 and 410-77-0019 and to the Government of Quebec for FCAC Grant #EQ1162.

ated by periods of concerted change. In contrast, the type of change that would point to the prevalence of common relational configurations is that in which variables tend to continue to change together in concert in the same direction, and then, periodically, to show many flips in the direction of change as a new configuration is erected. This chapter will present evidence for the second type of change and the second kind of configuration.

We mentioned in Chapter 8 that the literature often portrays organizations as being very slow and reluctant to adapt to their environments. Change is said to be resisted because of conservatism, cognitive limitations, dysfunctional ideologies, inappropriate information systems, and the inability to deviate from bureaucratic programs and procedures. Clearly, any study of the adaptive process would be expected to reflect this natural resistance to change.

The literature seems to emphasize this resistance almost exclusively and to point out the advantages, in certain environments, of organizations that are loosely structured, organic, and oriented toward product-market innovation, open communications, expert-based power, and so on (Burns and Stalker, 1961; Thompson, 1967; Galbraith, 1973; Lawrence and Lorsch, 1967). More timely and presumably effective responses are expected to take place given such orientations.

Yet there seems to be a bias in this point of view. Histories by Filgas (1967), Wilson (1954, 1968), Hower (1943, 1949), Moore (1945), and others seemed to show, for example, that although it was true that increasingly "mechanistic" (from Burns and Stalker, 1961) firms tended to become still more mechanistic over time, it was also true that firms moving in an "organic" direction would become still more organic later. Initial increases in centralization would lead to still more centralization; but the same was true of the movement toward decentralization. A sort of momentum seemed to prevail that applied also to the rate of product-market innovation, the extent of organizational intelligence, the level of technocratization, the style of decision making, and many other features of strategy and structure. In other words, any emerging organizational tendency, whatever its direction, seemed to have momentum associated with it. The momentum could be functional or dysfunctional and appeared to be a central feature of organizational adaptation. So instead of just studying resistance to change, we thought it useful to begin to pay attention to resistance to flips (reversals) in the *direction* of change. Many organizations are often changing. But they appear to be biased in their direction of development so that they generally extrapolate past trends. These thoughts gave rise to a tentative model of organizational adaptation that this chapter begins to test.

A MODEL OF ORGANIZATIONAL ADAPTATION

The model has three related tenets, which are based on previous theoretical and empirical works in the literature on organizations.

1. **Momentum is expected to be a dominant factor in organizational evolution; that is, flips in the direction of change in variables of strategy and structure are expected to be relatively rare.**

The literature points to four important causes of momentum. First, Clark (1972) and Mitroff and Kilmann (1976) have shown that myths, ideologies, and goals are enduring factors directing an organization's evolution. Argyris and Schon (1977) and Wildavsky (1972) have shown that these ideologies often inculcate rather narrow, self-affirming views that reinforce past behavior and cause it to be amplified in the future. Second, Miller and Mintzberg (1974) and Hedberg, Nystrom, and Starbuck (1976) have pointed to the primacy of procedures and strategies that have enjoyed past success, and their consequent tendency to be extrapolated past their point of usefulness. Third, political coalitions in organizations often have vested interests in evolving particular strategies (Pettigrew, 1973, 1974). Reversing these is resisted, since it entails an admission of past failure and therefore erodes the political base and self-esteem of powerful individuals. Finally, an elaborate set of programs, goals, and expectations grow up around an organization (March and Simon, 1958; Cyert and March, 1963; Thompson, 1967). These represent the outcome of a rather complex bargaining and reconciliation process and reflect the developmental wishes of key members of the organizational coalition. Thus, continuity in the direction of development is more likely to be in line with operative goals, power structures, programs, and expectations and will be readily assimilated; for reversals, the opposite will be true.

2. **Momentum will probably coexist among a great many variables of strategy and structure at the same time; that is, momentum will be pervasive.**

Most of the organizational studies during the last several decades have shown that there are integral relationships among organizational variables. So momentum in one variable will lead to momentum in others. The findings of earlier chapters have shown the close interdependencies among variables of strategy, structure, and environment that characterize common configurations. In order to preserve the intricate complementarities within relational configurations, many variables will change in concert— that is, exhibit momentum simultaneously during the same time interval. As, say, dynamism and innovation continue to evolve as before, so will many variables of differentiation, delegation, and information processing.

Here quantum change might occur to cope with the new levels of dynamism and innovation.

   3.   Organizational adaptation is also apt to be characterized by periods of extensive reversal[1] in which there are flips in the direction of change across a significantly large number of variables of strategy and structure.

There are two reasons that underlie this assertion. The first relies on the configuration rationale conveyed in the last paragraph. When a major decision or event occurs (such as a new strategy, a new leader, or a dramatically altered market), it may destroy a configuration and result in a period of "unlearning yesterday" and "inventing tomorrow" (Hedberg, Nystrom, and Starbuck, 1976). As the organization tries to realign itself to the new realities, flips in the direction of evolution occur among *many* variables (Starbuck, Greve, and Hedberg, 1978; Miller and Mintzberg, 1974; Normann, 1971; Starbuck and Dutton, 1973; Hall, 1976; 1983). This effects a major new reconciliation among attributes of strategy, structure, and environment as a new configuration is sought. The second reason for expecting reversals is that sometimes, pervasive momentum has resulted in *many* excesses, all of which must be reversed to redress the balance between an organization's orientations and the demands of its environment (Miller, 1976). Again, quantum change will occur.

   The goal of the research was to operationalize and test this model of organizational adaptation.

METHOD

The variables and data selected for study were those of Chapter 5. Appendix 4-2 presents the definitions of the 24 variables used in the research. These characterize the environment of the firm, its structure, and its strategy-making methods. Two distinct data bases were used—detailed published histories of corporations, and questionnaires sent to the executives of these corporations to validate some of the information contained in the histories. The histories were split into discrete intervals of transition using the scoring heuristic of Chapter 5. An average of five transitions were studied in each of 26 firms, and periods averaged six years in duration, the shortest being 18 months, the longest 20 years. Usually, most changes took place during the first two years of the period.

---

   [1]In our previous discussion of these results ("Momentum and Revolution in Organizational Adaptation," *Academy of Management Journal*, 23, 1980b, 591–614), we referred to these reversals as revolutions. This would be inappropriate here, since the concept of revolution has been defined quite differently in Chapters 8 and 9.

As reported, the reliability and validity of the data were very acceptable. The scoring procedures, scales, and data were described in the appendices to Chapter 5. The earlier study encompassed 135 transition periods, but only 102 of these could be used for this research. This is because we are now interested in continuations or reversals in the direction of change, concepts that take on meaning only when we look at *two* temporally adjacent transitions. For 33 of the transitions used in Chapter 5, there were no adjacent transitions. Recall that transition periods were defined by 24 change scores for each of the variables. A score of 7 indicates a great increase in a variable during the period of transition, 1 indicates a great decrease, and 4 means that there was no change.

A variable will be said to change *continuously* over two consecutive transition periods if its transition score is either greater than or equal to 4 for both periods, or else less than or equal to 4 for both periods. Otherwise, the variable will be said to have *flipped* (from an increase to a decrease, or vice versa) from the first period to the second.

HYPOTHESES

The focus of the data analysis will be on whether nonenvironmental variables changed continuously or flipped over consecutive pairs of transition periods. Specifically, the data will be analyzed to test three hypotheses.

> *Hypothesis 1:* Flips in the direction of change in a variable from one transition period to its temporally adjacent period are expected to be much rarer than continuous changes—that is, changes that are not opposite in direction.
>
> *Hypothesis 2:* Because of the interdependencies among variables of organization and strategy making, continuous changes in some variables will cause continuous changes in others. Thus, there will be significantly many *simultaneous* continuous changes or "simultaneous continuity" among the variables. By simultaneous change, we mean that variables change in the same direction during the period of analysis. They need not, of course, change at exactly the same time to qualify as concerted quantum change.
>
> *Hypothesis 3:* For the same reasons, there will be significantly many *simultaneous* flips among the variables. For example, a firm that was becoming more decentralized but reverses itself in the next period to move toward centralization will tend to exhibit reversals in the evolution of many other structural and strategy-making characteristics.

Essentially, then, our hypotheses outline a model of organizational adaptation that predicts that organizations will have a significant tendency to keep evolving in the same direction, and that this will be pervasive across a significantly large number of variables of strategy and structure. This dominant mode of evolution is expected to be interrupted by periods of widespread reversal.

FINDINGS

Each hypothesis was tested and the results were interpreted using the details contained in the published historical accounts.

Hypothesis 1: The Tendency toward Momentum

The first hypothesis is very easy to test. If momentum is a basic adaptive tendency, we should *expect to find a preponderance of continuous links across adjacent periods.* A computer program was written to count the number of times each nonenvironmental variable changed continuously and the number of times it flipped. A test of proportions was used for each variable to see if the proportion of its flips was significantly smaller than the proportion of its continuous changes. For each variable, it was, with a significance level better than 0.001, so the first hypothesis was not rejected. The number of pairs of consecutive periods counted for each variable was between 54 and 89 inclusive. A pair of periods was not counted for a variable if one of its scores was missing. On average, continuous changes happened 75 percent of the time and flips 25 percent of the time, out of a total count of 1,764 changes for all nonenvironmental variables. So momentum is the dominant tendency for all variables, given the preponderance of continuous links.

Some theorists might be tempted to conclude that resistance to flips in the direction of evolution is bad. Hedberg, Nystrom & Starbuck (1976) and Miller & Mintzberg, (1974) have highlighted the dangers of organizational momentum. It tends to lead to excesses in structural and decision-making variables: Decentralization results in atomistic fragmentation, centralization may lead to autocracy, innovation can develop into the gratuitous depletion of resources and initial attempts at formalization and routinization can yield a programmed, unresponsive bureaucracy.

And yet, one remains reluctant to criticize organizations that wait for important, unmistakable problems to arise before they are persuaded to move against the momentum. Continuing to change in a consistent direction or to stick with a given orientation is easiest and probably, in the short run, is very economical. It entails the fewest interpersonal conflicts, role uncertainties, and costly changes in structural orientations. This is true whether the firm has been designed to pursue a simple, programmed, and stable course, or whether it has been designed to pursue a dynamic and innovative strategy. Although from a certain perspective, one firm is "changeful" and the other "stable," or perhaps in Burns and Stalker's

(1961) terms, one is "mechanistic" and the other "organic," a major change of orientation may be equally disruptive to both. The programming of an organic firm may be just as painful, costly, and necessary as the loosening of a mechanistic one. In both cases, the modus operandi changes, and confusion, dissatisfaction, conflict, and inefficiency may result. In contrast, for the mechanistic firm to add another standard operating procedure or for the organic firm to delegate more authority to one of its boundary spanning units is very much in accord with the prevalent organizational ethos and will not cause nearly as much confusion or dissatisfaction. Momentum, though sometimes taken to excess, will often very effectively extend or conserve the firm's most promising strategies and methods. Thus, it is difficult to criticize the tendency toward momentum.

An interesting parallel is to be found in the philosophy of science literature. Kuhn (1970, p. 76), in discussing resistance to paradigm shifts in the face of anomalous results, claims:

> So long as the tools a paradigm supplies continue to prove capable of solving the problems *it defines*, science moves fastest and penetrates most deeply. The reason is clear. As in manufacture, so in science—retooling is an extravagance to be reserved for the occasion that demands it.

The remainder of the chapter will show that a significantly large number of organizations tend toward *momentum* in all or almost all variables at once, and then, to correct the very many excesses that were caused or to create a brand new configuration among the elements of strategy and structure, they must change across the board via a major *reversal*.

Hypothesis 2: Simultaneous Continuity among Many Variables

We hypothesize that a very significant proportion of transition sequences will demonstrate continuity of change for all nonenvironmental variables simultaneously.[2] That is, many variables will evolve together in consistent directions and exhibit momentum across the board. The null hypothesis we used was that each variable changed continuously 75 percent of the time, as suggested in the test of the first hypothesis, and that it did so independently of the other variables. To reject this hypothesis is to affirm that the transition scores of different variables tend to exhibit continuity *together* during a given interval. Under our null hypothesis, the probability that a number r of the 21 nonenvironmental variables change continuously is given by a binomial distribution with parameters $p = 0.75$ and $n = 21$. If $r = 21$, the probability is $(0.75)^{21} = 0.005$. Our computer program counted

---

[2]Simultaneous continuity is not an artifact of the period definition heuristic, which merely ensured that multiple changes occurred, irrespective of their direction.

46 pairs of consecutive transition periods for which there were no missing values[3] and found four pairs for which the 21 variables all changed continuously. Now, the probability that the computer program counted u such pairs where all 21 variables changed continuously also follows a binomial distribution that, according to our null hypothesis, has parameters $P = 0.005$ and $N = 46$. From a binomial table, we can see that the probability that u is 4 or larger is less than 0.0001, so we reject the null hypothesis. Thus, the number of pairs of transition periods with all variables changing continuously is surprisingly large.

Two elaborations of this test were conducted to establish the robustness of the finding. For the 21 variables, we tested to see if the number of times the proportion of continuous variables was greater than or equal to ($\geq$) 18/21, 19/21, and 20/21 were also greater than what we could expect by chance. In every case, the results were significant (see Table 10-1, section 1). To effectively increase the sample of observations, the variables that had the highest percentage of missing values were deleted. This allowed a larger number of periods to be counted as complete. When the internal-communications variable was deleted, the number of complete transitions increased from 46 to 59. When proportions greater than or equal to 17/20, 18/20, 19/20, and 20/20 were tested using the same procedures as above, all were found to occur with statistically significant frequency (see Table 10-1, section 2). Finally, to increase the sample of observations still further, the scanning and controls variables were deleted because of their number of missing values. The number of complete transitions rose to 72, and again the high proportions greater than or equal to 16/18, 17/18, and 18/18 occurred with significantly higher-than-expected frequency (Table 10-1, section 3).

We were concerned that the statistical significance of our demonstration of simultaneous continuity might have been due to a very high-order correlation among only a few pairs of similar variables. To remove this possibility, we decided to find the *least* intercorrelated set of variables to discover if simultaneous continuity still occurred in the reduced set of more distinct variables.

To test whether this was true, we performed an orthogonal R-type factor analysis (Nie et al., 1975, option PA 2), employing a varimax rotated factor matrix. We took the five nonenvironmental variables with the highest loading on each factor and calculated whether the number of times *all* five of the variables exhibited continuous links was greater than could be expected by chance, given the average probability of a continuous link for the five variables (.78). The expected number of continuous links was $(.78)^5 \times 72$, or 20.8. The actual number was 28, and this is greater than 20.8 at the .05 level of significance. Thus, it does seem that simultaneous con-

---

[3]If data were missing on any one variable, the pair of transitions had to be deleted from consideration for hypothesis testing.

TABLE 10-1: Tests of Simultaneous Continuity

1. *21 variables; 46 transitions; p = .75*

PROPORTION	BINOMIAL PROBABILITY	× N =	EXPECTED NUMBER	ACTUAL NUMBER	P-VALUE
≥18/21*	.228	46	10.5	21	.01**
≥19/21	.103	46	4.7	15	.0001
≥20/21	.032	46	1.5	12	.00001
21/21	.005	46	.23	4	.0001

2. *20 variables; 59 transitions; p = .76 (p has changed slightly owing to deletion of variable)*

PROPORTION	BINOMIAL PROBABILITY	× N =	EXPECTED NUMBER	ACTUAL NUMBER	P-VALUE
≥17/20	.225	59	13.0	30	.0000**
≥18/20	.091	59	5.4	22	.0000
≥19/20	.024	59	1.5	18	.0000
20/20	.003	59	.2	7	.0000

3. *18 variables; 72 transitions; p = .75*

PROPORTION	BINOMIAL PROBABILITY	× N =	EXPECTED NUMBER	ACTUAL NUMBER	P-VALUE
≥16/18	.135	72	9.7	26	.0000**
≥17/18	.040	72	2.9	20	.0000
18/18	.006	72	.4	9	.0000

*Of course, only proportions greater than .75 need to be tested, since that is the probability of a continuous link under the H_0 of independence.

**Normal approximation used instead of the Poisson because of the high expected number.

tinuity is due to more than high-order correlations among only a few variables.

Simultaneous continuity is a powerful form of organizational momentum—a desire, or at least a tendency, to very broadly extend a previous orientation. Three reasons for pervasive momentum have been intuited from our published histories. First, there is a reluctance to depart from a trend in the development of strategy or structure that has been highly successful. Second, the cognitive limitations of managers induce many of them to resist uncharacteristic changes. Third, and most in line with the theme of the book, there is a reluctance to destroy relational configurations among variables of strategy, structure, and environment.

The Formula of Success: Ideology and Power.   Managers are faced with a complex concept-attainment task. They must try to discover which of their actions and orientations contribute to success and which contribute to failure. Given the multiplicity of elements that must be manipulated and the assorted feedback delays that conceal their interdependency, it is often impossible for managers to know just which of their behaviors were the most useful (Bruner, Goodnow, and Austin, 1956). Thus, if a firm is doing reasonably well, there will be a strong incentive to avoid tampering with any element of a "tried-and-true" formula (Watson, 1969). Unilever Ltd., during the early part of this century, and Litton Industries, much later, centralized power at the top, actively increased product-market innovation and acquisitions, and emphasized formal information systems. The firms continued to move further in these "successful" directions. The information systems *seemed* useful and were extended by gathering more of the same type of information. The leader had built up his reputation because of his past victories and was accorded more power, either formally, or by having other executives or board members reluctant to negate his proposals. Thus, de facto centralization kept on increasing. The same was true for the other variables. Since risk taking had been rewarding in the past, it tended to intensify. In this way, past success bred pervasive continuity and turned an orientation into an ideology (Clark, 1972; Mitroff and Kilmann, 1976). Since success accords more power to the initial advocates of the successful strategy, vested interests and their power base become inextricably intertwined with that strategy, and the political obstacles to strategic reorientation grow (Pettigrew, 1973, 1974).

Cognitive Limitations and Models of Reality. Because of the complexity of adaptive behavior, only some of the firm's practices are apt to be consciously viewed as causes of success (Watson, 1969; Argyris and Schon, 1977). The balance will be ignored. In fact, the *conscious* elements of the old strategy and structure are those most likely to be viewed as the causes of success and will be extended (Watson, 1969). The less explicit elements are not included in the manager's model of reality and are therefore not tracked—even though they may be flagging a crucial need for reorientation. For example, in the case of the Singer Company from 1969 to 1974, product diversification increased because it was erroneously believed to be useful, and because it was an explicit aspect of strategy. However, although the diversification was too uncontrolled, rapid, and costly, and capital resources began to dwindle, this was not noticed. Resources did not constitute an element that was tracked carefully. Also, even when the new product lines were poorly received by markets and new acquisitions lost money, the troubles were dismissed as anomalies or fleeting conditions. The confidence in past orientations garnered from the protracted period of success could not be easily eroded. Thus the events that could throw doubt upon the appropriateness of the firm's structure, strategy, or modus operandi either were not tracked carefully or were rationalized away in the light of past successes. So almost *nothing* happened that went against the momentum.

Momentum and Configuration in Strategy and Structure. We have already argued that a firm's adaptive orientation represents a tightly integrated package of situational, structural, and strategy-making elements. Any flip in a variable can throw off the configuration and so is likely to be resisted. Also, changes in one element are bound to be constrained by the influence of many other elements. Thus, there will be a tendency to maintain a relational configuration by keeping the rates of change and the direction of change of the different elements in line. For example, the Ford Motor Company before the Second World War was for many years a stagnant bureaucracy: It was in a stable environment, used formal rules and programs to coordinate and carry out tasks, and had highly routinized operating procedures and centralized power. It sold a narrow line of mass-produced cars that did not change much from year to year. A trend toward bureaucratization progressed while the rate of innovation declined. It was difficult to reverse the direction of change in even *one* of the variables simply because of their tight interdependencies. An increase in the variety or novelty of products was unlikely. It flew in the face of Henry Ford's philosophy of producing cheap and functional cars. The simplicity of the strategy and the machinelike nature of the firm, coupled with Ford's financial control, made it possible for him to centralize power very tightly. This power allowed him to protract his strategies without challenge well past the point where they became enormously dysfunctional. The poor information systems hid the hazards of these strategies, thus extending their life span. Finally, any change in strategy would have been extremely costly and therefore that much harder to implement. Broader product lines and frequent model changes would have required a good deal of retooling and rearrangement of the highly integrated and automated production apparatus. It seems, then, that everything fit together to rule against reversals. Such configurations cause many forces to converge in enforcing continuity of change or stability across many variables. Usually, things either change together according to a preestablished evolutionary plan, or they do not change at all.

Hypothesis 3: The Development of Reversals

The pervasiveness of momentum often results in excesses or problems in *many* conditions. These cannot usually be undone by piecemeal changes in orientation. Indeed, even if the firm remains viable it may be thought desirable to seize new opportunities or to restructure. This may frequently require the creation of a new configuration. In either event, a substantial reversal is needed. Sequences of change are called reversals if there are significantly many simultaneous flips in the variables. *We hypothesize that a significant number of sequences will have many variables simultaneously reversing their direction of change.*

To test whether such pervasive changes were significantly common, we employed the same hypothesis testing procedure that was used in the last section. Table 10-2 presents the results, employing the identical format as Table 10-1. Again, the same sets of 18, 20, and 21 nonenvironmental variables were used so that we might be assured of the robustness of the findings. When the expected number of links was less than .005, testing was halted because of the impossibility of gauging significance. In all cases, the significance levels of the odd-numbered proportions that are *not* shown on the table were between the significance levels of the adjacent even-numbered proportions. The results are once again highly significant.

To check whether there was any tendency for reversals among the most unrelated variables we again used the variables that had the highest loadings on the five orthogonal varimax rotated factors. On average these five variables flip 22 percent of the time. We thus expect the number of times that three or more variables flip simultaneously to be (from the binomial distribution) .0744 × 72 = 5.36. The actual number was 9. Although this number is almost twice as large, it is significant only at the .098

TABLE 10-2:   Tests of Simultaneous Flips

1. *21 variables; 46 transitions;* $p = .25$

PROPORTION	BINOMIAL PROBABILITY	× N =	EXPECTED NUMBER	ACTUAL NUMBER	P-VALUE
≥10/21	.0183	46	.95	6	.0003
≥12/21	.0014	46	.0644	5	.0000
≥14/21	.0005	46	.0230	2	.0000
≥15/21	∅	46	∅*	1	N/A

2. *20 variables; 59 transitions;* $p = .24$

PROPORTION	BINOMIAL PROBABILITY	× N =	EXPECTED NUMBER	ACTUAL NUMBER	P-VALUE
≥10/20	.0238	59	1.4	7	.0006
≥12/20	.0019	59	.12	5	.0000
≥14/20	.0001	59	.0059	2	.0001

3. *18 variables; 72 transitions;* $p = .25$

PROPORTION	BINOMIAL PROBABILITY	× N =	EXPECTED NUMBER	ACTUAL NUMBER	P-VALUE
≥ 8/18	.0847	72	6.12	11	.05
≥10/18	.0110	72	.792	6	.0002
≥12/18	.0005	72	.03	4	.0001

*When the expected number of links was less than .005 testing was halted because of the impossibility of gauging significance.

level. Still there seems to be a tendency toward simultaneous flips even in the set of least correlated variables, but this finding must remain tentative.

Our views on the causes of reversal are rather tentative and derive from eleven historical descriptions contained in our data base. Momentum tends to culminate in a reversal only under two rather significant types of pressure. The first is a shift in power that allows the emergence of a new organizational ideology and strategy; the second is a significant performance deterioration that provokes encompassing remediality. Each entails rather widespread and significant departures from previous directions of evolution and involves the creation of a new configuration among variables of strategy, structure, and environment. Whereas the first force is opportunistic and positive, the second is reactive and remedial.

A New Leader and a New Configuration.   Profound organizational reorientations may occur when there is a major shift in power between management groups of differing ideologies and perspectives. Effective leadership might, for example, pass from a conservative team of executives with production backgrounds to a bold cadre of managers who are marketing and financial specialists. There are a number of ways in which a radically different leadership group can ascend to power. Occasionally, former leaders depart without having groomed successors, so that no executives remain who have been amply steeped in the traditional ideology. Alternatively, there might be a departmental management team with a brilliant track record. Even though its members have a different approach, their record almost dictates their rise to power. A dearth of successors might even necessitate the recruitment of a key executive from another firm who begins to bring in other outside men. Finally, extensive changes in management may occur during mergers and acquisitions.

New leaders often bring with them a dramatically different concept of the business—a radically new perspective of the nature of the firm, its goals, strategies, and evolutionary directions. Kuhn (1970), in analyzing the major revolutions in science, provides an apt analogy for what happens in an organizational reversal when the new leaders begin by:

> . . . handling the same bundle of data as before, but placing them in a new system of relations with one another by giving them a different framework [p. 85]. Almost always the men who achieve these fundamental [reconceptualizations] . . . have been either very young or very new to the field [read 'from outside the organization'] [p.90].

Occasionally, a new leader enters a firm with a new strategy that causes broad reversals in the direction of evolution of structure and strategy. For example, when Kurt Lotz took over from Heinrich Nordhoff at Volkswagenwerk, he undertook to renew the product-market strategy by producing new types of cars and entering different market segments. This was accomplished through the creation and acquisition of new divisions and subsidiaries. A whole set of structural parameters began to evolve in a different direction to become consistent with the new strategy (Chandler, 1962; Channon, 1973; and Rumelt, 1974 have described this process). In essence, a new configuration was established among the variables of strategy and structure. Volkswagenwerk (1966–1973) went from a one-product, unified, functionally structured, increasingly conservative, and centralized firm operating in relatively stable markets to a multiproduct, diversified, divisionalized, risk-embracing organization operating in several more dynamic market segments. In spite of its broad scope this particular revolution failed because it was incomplete: The top man reserved too much power for himself, protracting a trend that had been established long ago, and the decline in the efficacy of scanning and control systems was not reversed. Both problems were aggravated by the accelerating complexity of the administrative task that was occasioned by the new strategy.

An almost identical reversal took place at General Motors in 1915, when William Durant took over from the conservative banker-trustees. The latter were trying to consolidate the organization and bring about better coordination and central control. Durant expanded product lines wildly while purchasing new companies. He neglected to control and monitor his subsidiaries. Comparing the trustees' and the Durant years, we see that reversals occurred in the direction of evolution in the willingness to innovate and take risks; the efficacy of scanning, control, and communication systems; and the degree to which decision making was analytical, multiplex, and integrated. Again a change occurred in the configuration which shifted from a conservative-bureaucratic to a bold-intuitive orientation.

After any major reversal in orientation, in order for a new configuration to emerge, rebuilding must often take place on many fronts, and this entails a reversal in orientation in *many* areas. In other words, quantum change normally occurs so that all the elements needed for the new configuration can fall into place. It is unusual, for example, to enter more turbulent markets with an intelligence system that gathers only internal data on costs and ignores environmental trends. It is just as incongruous to attempt this maneuver without giving more authority to boundary-spanning units or increasing the proportion of technocrats. The importance of configurations in triggering reversals may be considerable.

Encompassing Remedies. Between 1969 and 1974, the Singer Company expanded rapidly and recklessly. It acquired a complex set of businesses, many of which began to turn sour. The firm had undergone a period of escalating expansion and accelerating innovation. Also, power had become more centralized under an entrepreneurial chief executive. Intelligence efforts deteriorated as internal communications problems mounted and controls diminished. Subunits were becoming alienated from each other and from the busy man at the top. Again, there was a need to dramatically reorient *many* facets of the organization. This was done from 1975 to 1978. First, the Board got rid of the powerful chief executive whose ideology and actions originally got the organization into trouble. The old leader's departure made a significant change in orientation possible. New executives were recruited who recognized the need to decentralize power somewhat to cope with the size and diversity of the organization. Also, because organizational resources had been badly depleted by ill-conceived ventures and problem-ridden divisions, better intelligence systems, administrative rationalization, and a more conservative product-market strategy were implemented. Again, many past trends were reversed as the firm tried to consolidate.

It seems that because continuity had been so pervasive, it caused excesses in many realms. Remedies were therefore required in the power structure, methods of decision making, attitudes toward risk, information systems, and innovative practices. Thus, even where the concern is not with erecting a new configuration but merely with restoring an old one and solving a few problems, the roots of problems often run very deep and have widespread influences that have to be overcome (Hall, 1983).

Both the creation of new configurations and encompassing remedies seem to account for the frequency with which widespread reversals happen in our sample. In the first case, a major change, perhaps in strategy or leadership, causes many subsequent realignments in decision making and structure. In the second, organizational momentum that derives from economic, emotional, power, and cognitive forces results in many excesses. These are countered by quantum changes that reverse former orientations in a highly multifaceted way.

Notice that periods of pervasive momentum and reversal do entail quantum change, in that many strategic and structural variables are being changed together. But this does not mean that change is incremental, nor does it confirm dramatic change. In fact, our organizational histories demonstrated both types of change during intervals of momentum and reversal. In some cases, firms bunched dramatic changes into very brief intervals. These were surrounded by placid periods. In other instances, changes were more gradual and incremental. Periods of pervasive momentum and reversal do support the notions of quantum change and relational configurations. They do not require, however, that changes be revolutionary.

CONCLUSION

We shall summarize the three major findings of the chapter. Although these findings are tentative, they do suggest possible questions for subsequent investigators.

A topic more relevant than resistance to change in the study of organizational adaptation may be the tendency toward momentum. A very significant bias was found in favor of the proportion of continuous links. Flips in the direction of evolution were relatively rare for *all* nonenvironmental variables. Thus, entrepreneurial firms may become excessively entrepreneurial once they begin to move in that direction, just as mechanical bureaucratic firms can become excessively risk averse and rigid. Instead of our studying only stagnation, momentum may serve as an interesting focus.

Momentum is a pervasive phenomenon. Continuous links seem to breed more continuous links; that is, the presence of a continuous link for one variable is significantly associated with continuity in many other variables. An examination of corporate histories revealed that this could be explained by the reluctance to tamper with established views and ideologies; the narrow models of reality of executives; and the integrity of configurations among environmental, organizational, and strategy-making variables.

Reversals that display flips for a high proportion of variables also occur with very significantly high frequency. These major reorientations seem to take place because *many* excesses or deficiencies have developed during periods of pervasive momentum, or because a new strategy requires a realignment among many variables. Thus, there follows a myriad of structural and strategic reversals to erect a new configuration.

Organizations seem to evolve in a manner that is quite similar to the development of scientific knowledge. Kuhn (1970, p. 208) portrays progress in science as:

> . . . a succession of tradition-bound periods punctuated by non-cumulative breaks.

Scientific inquiry is both constrained and made more penetrating and cohesive by paradigms that delineate operative assumptions and orientations. A paradigm is not dispensed with just because some anomalous findings run counter to its predictions. Abandonment is prompted only by serious crises coupled with the emergence of more powerful paradigms—a situation Kuhn calls a "scientific revolution." Unfortunately, reversal may occur only many years after initial anomalies are recognized, and inquiry tends to be biased in scope, theme, and direction. But science is integrated and channeled by paradigms in a manner that makes for a more efficient, rapid, and complementary growth of knowledge. Indeed, if scientific theories were extremely amenable to change, altering with every surprising result, disorder and chaotic fragmentation would thwart the emergence of a sufficiently encompassing level of theoretical abstraction to focus and systematize research.

In the same way, organizations evolve consistently in accordance with a perspective, strategy, ideology, and mission of their own—concepts that are manifested by an integral alignment or configuration among environmental, organizational, and strategic variables. To reverse the trend of evolution and abandon this orientation in the face of every problem would be exceedingly costly and would result in many discrepancies and imbalances. Major stimuli are required to prompt a reversal. Managers demand a large potential benefit before they are willing to destroy the order and complementarity of elements inherent in the old configuration and begin to construct a new one. The price paid for this is sluggish responsiveness to the need to reverse evolutionary trends, and occasional revolutionary periods with all their turmoil, expense, and confusion. It is instructive to note, however, that a major difference between scientific revolutions and organizational ones is that the former are said to occur *only* in response to a crisis, whereas the latter can be proactive as well.

At this stage, it is important to interject a note of caution. Our focus has been on significant general tendencies, not conditions that hold for *all* historical sequences. Together, sequences of quantum reversals and momentum account for only a part of the sample; obviously, then, there are also piecemeal sequences of organizational transition. Our only contention is that the findings represent significant tendencies in our sample, not that they exhaust all the possibilities.

We hope that these results will encourage other researchers to look more closely at corporate histories to gain further insights into the dynamics of adjustment. Broader samples, more concrete variables, and a concentration on shorter time periods or more refined time-series data might all add significantly to the findings. By studying the process of adaptation as it evolves over time we can come to understand much more about the pitfalls and challenges facing strategists and designers of organizations.

POSTSCRIPT: LOOSE COUPLING
AND CONFIGURATION

In this chapter and the last, we have argued for the prevalence of quantum change, claiming that configurations require many structural and strategy-making variables to change together. This was largely borne out by our data. But it does seem to fly in the face of some of the important recent literature on organizations. Glassman (1973), Weick (1976) and Aldrich (1979) have argued that many elements of organizations can be changed independently; that perhaps organizations can adapt in piecemeal fashion. We too believe that this may often be the case. It all depends on the variables or elements that one selects for study.

Our finding predictive configurations and quantum change certainly relied on the types of variables and elements we chose to look at. Indeed, the relationships among the variables gave rise to the viability of the quantum view. Had we chosen variables that were unrelated—that could be *loosely coupled*—we would have found no useful configurations nor much evidence of quantum change.

Unfortunately, at this early stage of the research, it is difficult to know *a priori* which kinds of variables are apt to be loosely coupled and which tightly interdependent. It may not even be a very simple matter to decide this empirically, since low correlations across a wide sample of data may not be indicative of loose coupling. It may simply mean that two or more opposite relationships occur among the variables in different subsamples, and that these cancel each other when combined—that is, when samplewide analysis is used.

Our first thoughts are that loose coupling is likely to occur among very specific variables that describe the detailed activities of individual departments. It is less likely to occur between general variables describing overall organizational processes. The use of market surveys and customer polling would be an example of the first kind of variable, and environmental scanning or uncertainty reduction may exemplify the second. The more specific the activity, the more likely it is that it can be replaced by another that accomplishes the same end. Polling may be a substitute for demographic market analysis and can therefore be loosely coupled with the work of other departments. It is probable that the marketing group is able to change its market-analysis procedures without requiring changes in other areas of the firm.

But the case of general variables is quite different. These often gauge indispensible functions. A certain amount of environmental scanning is necessary for organizational survival. It is, as we have seen, tied to the level of innovation and environmental dynamism. It is part of a constellation of elements that tend to shift together. This is not to say that scanning and innovation always relate in the same way. Chapter 6 has shown how much this relation can vary. But once the context or the configuration is specified, many of the more general variables are tightly coupled. It is, of course, possible that variables that are closely related in one set of configurations are loosely coupled in another. In short, the range of applicability of the quantum view—that is, its appropriateness for different levels of organizational analysis—remains an open question. It represents a whole new area of study that has not even begun to be explored.

Epilogue

Our tone throughout the book has been bold. This is due more to our enthusiasm about the thesis than to any ignorance about its tentative and speculative nature. To forestall any misplaced confidence or primary misapprehensions, this epilogue discusses some of the major uncertainties that continue to surround the quantum view.

There are three central tenets to the quantum view. The first is that there are integral interdependencies among many variables of structure, strategy making, and environment. These produce common configurations that richly describe and collectively encompass a large fraction of organizations. Configurations will therefore be predictively useful. We believe that carefully constructed taxonomies and typologies will help to identify the most parsimonious and revealing sets of configurations.

The second tenet of the book is that different configurations often exhibit different relationships among their constituent variables. As a result, their identification as a first step in prediction will lead to more accuracy and fewer conflicts in organizational research. The dangers inherent in the common practice of subjecting large and diverse samples of organizations to linear statistical analyses should now be apparent.

The third tenet is a composite one. First, quantum and dramatic structural changes seem to be more closely associated with high performance than piecemeal and incremental structural changes. Also, organizations tend to preserve a configurational alignment among variables of structure and strategy during common periods of momentum, and erect new configurations during the much rarer intervals of reversal. The first tendency argues for the functional nature and therefore the prevalence of particular configurations. The second encourages the belief in configuration maintenance and construction as common forms of organizational activity.

Each of these tenets requires qualification and points to significant areas of ignorance. The concept of configuration has purposely been left flexible. Configurations represent any conceptually or empirically defined set of interdependencies among variables that make predictively useful distinctions in classifying organizations. A configuration can be constructed out of static attributes or indices of change; it can be defined by relationships among variables or by their raw scores; it can encompass performance, structural, strategic, and environmental features. Given such flexibility, it is obvious that our first tenet will not always be true. Useful configurations will not always be found. The predictiveness of configurations will depend upon the selection of variables, the grouping criteria and methods used, and the nature of the samples. Some variables will be loosely coupled or independent. Small samples that are either very uniform or very diverse will not yield useful taxonomies. And not all clustering methods will find predictive configurations even when they exist. Clearly, the identification of conceptually important configurations and the generation of useful taxonomies require the use of related variables, broad and sizable samples, and flexibility and ingenuity in statistical analysis and testing. The field is too young for us to make prescriptions beyond those of Chapter 2 that will guarantee results from the approach of synthesis. All we can say is that the early results seem promising.

Our second tenet was that there would often be different relationships among strategic, structural, and environmental variables in different configurations. Certainly, this will not always be as true as it was in the studies of innovation and entrepreneurship presented in Part III. No doubt there are many relationships that will remain the same in very different configurations. Our central point was that this is not universally the case and that it is hazardous to assume it is. Indeed, it is extremely likely that there will be a large number of nonlinear relationships among organizational variables. These account for the snake-like data surface that often describes our samples of organizations. The segments of this surface correspond to our configurations, which frequently contain very different relationships among the same variables. It would be most worthwhile, therefore, for researchers to compare relationships among variables in different configurations.

Our findings concerning organizational change do not prove that there are configurations—they are merely consistent with the notion that there might be. The significant clustering found in our taxonomies and our findings on change are complementary aspects of the same phenomenon. Our geometrical representation of configurations shows them to be parts of a curved surface of much smaller dimension than the number of variables by which they are characterized. The smaller the dimension of the surface relative to the space, the tighter the configurations and the greater the need for variables to change in unison. Such multifaceted change is required to allow the firm to remain on the surface that exhausts all possible states. But our configurations imply only multifaceted change. They do not require changes to be dramatic or revolutionary. Dramatic change, because it is often the most economical, may be common only in successful firms, whereas quantum change will result whenever there are configurations—functional or otherwise.

We would like to close by encouraging other researchers to seek out configurations and to construct taxonomies and typologies in the spirit of the approach of synthesis. By selecting a wide range of variables, by simultaneously using quantitative and anecdotal data bases, and by being persistent and resourceful in discovering and establishing the predictiveness and stability of configurations and taxonomies, we can advance our knowledge of organizations considerably. But we must harbor no illusions about the difficulties that lie ahead. It is much easier to use common linear statistical analyses to establish samplewide multivariate relationships than it is to discover unanticipated regularities by groping in a complex data base. The exploration of new multivariate grouping and hypothesis testing techniques may be somewhat unpalatable to those used to the softer research approaches. Also, the theory-free search for patterns might alienate organizational sociologists who are primarily concerned with elaborating encompassing functionalist, systems theory, resource-dependence, or population ecology perspectives. Finally, the reliance upon anecdotal evidence to discover more about individual configurations may disturb researchers who are reluctant to deviate from the scientific method. But we believe that there is room for all of these researchers within the approach of synthesis. Researchers with a qualitative bent may focus more on typologies than taxonomies and pay most of their attention to fleshing out and investigating individual configurations with anecdotal data. Theorists may wish to use their frameworks to guide the selection of variables and types. Methodologists may devise better methods of finding predictive configurations in empirical data bases—undertaking the crucial task of discovering better ways of finding complex nonlinear data surfaces. For the approach of synthesis to have its greatest impact it will be necessary for researchers with these and other orientations to work together, either directly or by building upon each others' results. Only then will we improve our chances of resolving many of the mysteries surrounding organizations.

Appendices

Chapters 4,5,7, and 9

APPENDIX 4-1: DISCOVERING AND TESTING THE ARCHETYPES

The Variables Studied. Appendix 4-2 contains a listing of the 31 variables and definitions that served as the focus for the research. Variables were chosen to describe the process by which an organization adapts to its environment. It was necessary to include elements of the environment, the structural/organizational attributes of the firm, the strategy-making repertoire used, and the resultant success or failure of the organization. We favored variables that were shown by previous researchers to influence the adaptive process, and that could be scored reliably for our data base.

The Data Base. Eighty-one undisguised series of cases on business organizations, which were published in *Fortune* magazine, the *Harvard Case Clearing House* series, and several policy textbooks have served as the data base for the research. Cases were believed to be of particular value, since they provide a vivid and detailed account of strategy-making activity. They are also longitudinal and provide insights into the time order in which variables change. Cases often supply published data on the firm's industry instead of simply subjective impressions of an executive of the company. It is more difficult to hide the real situation from a case writer who studies a firm in detail than from a remote researcher who asks a busy executive to rate a number of quantified scales. Finally, cases usually distinguish between facts and the opinions of company members.

Naturally, there are some disadvantages associated with case data. Different cases supply different types of information. In any given research sample, information on certain variables will be available for some cases and not for others. Also, there tends to be a relative paucity of case information on structural organization variables such as differentiation, integration, and bureaucratization. There are two levels of abstraction involved in the use of case data—the case writer must interpret the situation, then the researcher must interpret the written cases. Each step may cause distortion of data. Finally, case raters and writers might have narrowly preconceived mental models. These may influence the research data but fail to reflect the richness or complexity of the actual situation. This is a very real danger in the research, since the data base may be oversimplified.

Data Gathering and Scoring.   To offset some of the disadvantages that accrue from the use of case data, a number of precautions were necessary. Cases had to be selected that addressed most of our research variables. Once it became apparent that a large number of cases skirted some of the variables of initial interest, these had to be deleted from the study.

In order to use cases as a data base, it was necessary to employ a somewhat unusual scoring procedure. Since the information on any given variable is presented differently across cases, it is impractical to have a large number of refined scales to measure each variable. Information is either insufficiently detailed or too variable to enable raters to respond to very specific scale items for the majority of firms in the sample. For example, in order to measure environmental dynamism, it was impossible in many instances to obtain information on the exact nature of price, technological, consumer-taste, and source-of-supply dynamism. Most cases contained information on certain of these attributes, but not on others. Thus it was necessary to have only one rather general 7-point scale for each of the 31 variables. It was the task of experienced case raters to translate the specific facts of the case into numerical scores along these scales. Variables were operationalized for scoring via definitions and examples of the types of facts reported in the case that would influence variable scores.

A score of 1 represented a "very low" score on the variable, such that most firms in the rater's experience scored higher. A score of 7 represented the opposite, and a score of 4 implied that the firm was "about average" along the variable when compared to other companies. A sample scale is contained in Appendix 4-2, along with the individual variable definitions. We should point out that the case scorers (the authors, Dr. Kets de Vries of McGill, and a final-year management policy undergraduate) had each read dozens, if not hundreds, of case studies and were intimately familiar with the case method of analysis and instruction A number of different firms have to be analyzed and scored before ratings achieve maximum reliability, since it is hard to come up with relative scores without having internalized a somewhat broad basis for comparison.

Cases that lacked sufficient data for reliable scoring were rejected. In the event that only a few variables for a case could not be scored, neutral ratings (4) were given on the problematic scales. Because our scoring procedures placed so much reliance upon rater inferences, interrater reliability had to be verified. About 30 percent of the cases were rated by at least two independent scorers. Rating was performed in double-blind fashion. Less than 10 percent of the total number of ratings differed among raters by two or more points on the scales. The interrater reliability coefficient of .82 was judged to be extremely good.

It was somewhat more difficult to verify the validity of case data. Only the cases that had been written quite recently could be checked. These accounted for about 10 percent of the total sample (eight responses were received). For each case, five quotations that seemed important to the description of the firm were selected. These were often of an inferential and pejorative nature and were sent to top executives of the firms.

The executives were asked to comment upon the accuracy of the quotations selected and to pass judgment about the general validity of the case. Only one firm failed to respond to our inquiries. All respondents agreed with the vast majority of quotations. The less than 10 percent of all statements that met with disagreement were usually subject to qualification because of a minor technicality rather than a fundamental judgmental error on the part of the case writer. No respondent claimed that a case was basically inaccurate or misleading. These included managers whose firms were generally unsuccessful and had received unfavorable case writeups.

It is notable that 43 of the 52 firms used in the Canadian *field study* of Chapters 6 and 7 corresponded to one of the archetypes of Chapter 4 (Kets de Vries and Miller, 1980). The validity of published historical data bases is further established in Chapter 5. It is there shown that the archetypes derived from such data bases were borne out in a subsequent field study involving top executive respondents from still another distinct group of 50 firms.

Hypothesis Generation.   The hypothesis that is to be refined and tested is that the cases in the working population can be grouped into a few specific types. The first step in making our hypothesis precise is to consider the scores of a given case on the 31 variables along a 7-point scale. The sequence of 31 scores as measured from their average will be called the pattern of scores of the case. When the pattern of scores of one case is compared with that of another, it may be that the scores are correlated, in that they fluctuate above and below their respective averages on the same variables (see Figure A4-1).

We hypothesize that there are relatively few *basic* patterns of scores on the 31 variables, and that the pattern of each case is like one of these basic patterns. Inverse factor analysis (or *Q*-type factor analysis) can help identify such patterns (see Chapter 2). If a case is highly correlated with a factor, it

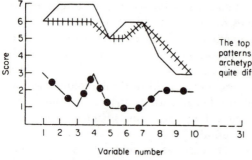

The top firms have similar score patterns and may belong to the same archetype while the bottom firm is quite different.

Variable number

FIGURE A4-1   Score Patterns. From Danny Miller and Peter Friesen, "Strategy Making in Context: Ten Empirical Archetypes," *Journal of Management Studies* 14 (October 1977).

will have a high loading on that factor. It follows that two cases loading highly on the same factor will have similar score patterns. Factor analysis is strictly valid only for interval scales, whereas the scales used in this study are all ordinal. Therefore, none of the numerical results of the analysis will be used. The archetypes will be tested separately and justified by the homogeneity among the firms within each type.

The inverse factor analysis was performed upon 52 cases. These were divided into successful and unsuccessful groups, and separate analyses were run for each. A varimax rotation of the factors was performed. Where a number of firms loaded highly (greater than 0.55) on a factor, it was used as a tentative basis for an archetype.

When three or more firms loaded most highly on a particular factor, that factor was used individually, and sometimes in conjunction with another factor, as the basis for a tentative archetype. A firm was included in a tentative archetype if it loaded highest on the corresponding factor(s). Ten mutually exclusive lists of companies, each forming a tentative archetype, were derived.

The scores on the 31 variables were inspected again for each firm in a tentative archetype. We noted the range of possible scores for each member firm on *each* variable. Ranges were expanded whenever, in our judgment, it was only accidental that the scores in the tentative archetype were not larger. This collection of 31 score ranges, one for each variable, for an archetype was called the region of scores corresponding to the archetype (see Figure A4-2). Ten regions were defined that corresponded to each hypothesized archetype (see Appendix 4-4). The range expansion was done from a knowledge of all the cases in a tentative archetype. The nature of an archetype becomes quite obvious when the cases in it are re-read as a group.

Let us define a sequence of scores on the 31 variables to be a site. A site is included in the region corresponding to an archetype whenever each

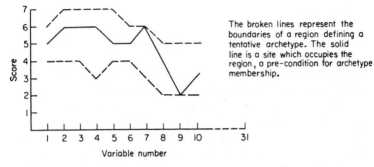

FIGURE A4-2 **Archetype Regions and Sites.** From Miller and Friesen, "Strategy Making in Context."

of the 31 scores of the site falls within the corresponding 31 ranges of the region. The region corresponding to an archetype specifies a certain collection of sites that fall within it. Any company that is in a tentative archetype will occupy a site that is located within the archetype.

It should be noted that the regions defined to correspond to the archetypes are different from each other only in their interiors. Some of the regions merge into each other, since their boundaries touch. A company on a site near the boundary between two regions would exhibit properties of both archetypes. As we cross from one archetypal region to another, one mode of organizational success or failure fades away and another becomes increasingly dominant.

As a matter of interest, the ten hypothesized archetypal regions together included only one ten-thousandth of the sites that could in principle be occupied.

Hypothesis Testing. The hypothesized archetypal regions may have resulted from the first 52 cases only by chance. That is, they might not recur in a larger sample. To test this possibility, a computer program was written to sort another 29 cases into the already-defined archetypal regions. If a case did not occupy a site in any of the regions, the program noted that fact. Then the program used the number of cases that fell into each region as a proportion of the total 29 to give a 95 percent confidence interval estimate of the proportion of companies that fell into the region. The sample proportion estimate (column 3 of Appendix 4–5) was compared to the occupation probability of the region given its size (column 5). The latter was simply the number of sites in the region (the product of all its score ranges) divided by the number of sites in the total Cartesian product space (the product of all the scale ranges). For every region, the lowest end of the confidence interval for the sample proportion was 100 to 1 million times higher than the occupation probability of each region. This means that the ten archetypes occur more commonly than could be assumed by chance, with a confidence level of better than 95 percent. We can reject the hypothesis that the archetypes occurred by chance (see Appendix 4-5 for the exact calculations).

Nothing inherent in Q-type factor analysis would allow us to test the significance of our factors in terms of the population densities of each of the archetype regions. In this study, we have been fortunate in that the orientations of the factors and the scatter of scores in an archetype have given us relatively small regions. Had we not been so fortunate, we would have had to subdivide the groups further on the basis of variable means and standard deviations. The modal scores of the 31 variables for all ten archetypes are presented in Appendix 4-3.

The Geometry of the Archetypes.   Our 31-dimensional space can be expressed as a surface of much smaller dimension. This is caused by complex nonlinear relationships among the variables and is the source of the predictiveness of the archetypes. Because the surface is complex and curved, the relationships among the variables vary from one part of the surface (that is, from one archetype) to another. The whole purpose of the research was to obtain as accurate a picture of the data surface as possible.

Our archetypes are dense regions in a 31-dimensional space of 31 variables. These occurred because our variables were strongly interdependent, although not necessarily discontinuous. The most natural way of representing the type of clustering that occurred is as an involuted surface of small dimension curving through the 31-dimensional space. An extreme, purely illustrative example of this phenomenon is a curve—a one-dimensional surface—forming an involuted arc in a space of many dimensions (that of Figure 2-1, for example). Because the variables are interdependent, some of their values are permitted by the interdependency and others are not. That is, some of the sites are permitted and others are not. The former fall on or near the arc. The rest of the space is empty, since it corresponds to values that are inconsistent with the nature of the interdependency. The curve traced out by the points (that is, the permitted sites often occupied by firms) fills a very small proportion of the space. It is in this sense that the points are clustered. We might, using the terminology of our introduction to Part I, call these points "quantum states," since they are permitted by the interdependency, just like the states of the atom.

For the sake of parsimony and simplicity, we wished to describe the surface of points by enclosing it in a series of small, overlapping, boxlike regions. The points within any small region may be said collectively to describe an almost linear relation among the variables. These regions define our archetypes, many of which might be connected to one another. The number and size of the regions are determined by how similar we wish the points (member firms) in each to be. The smaller and more numerous the regions, the more similar the member firms.

We found that the surface of our data had a very small dimension relative to the number of variables (5 or 6 versus 31). The number of archetypes was small simply as a consequence of the geometry of the surface. Linear multivariate methods such as multidimensional scaling or R-factor analysis of the total data sample could not have reduced the number of dimensions in the space nearly as much as our Q-analysis. This, as we explained in Chapter 2, is due to the curvilinear pattern of the data. The Q-analysis allows us to discover different parts of the dense regions in the data space. These collectively describe the curved surface, but individually, they are regions of very small dimension. In essence, we have tried to uncover some of the important features of the complex curvilinear data space by using a piecewise linear technique to locate some of its most revealing parts.

In our research, the number of regions (archetypes) was chosen to equal the number of significant Q-factors. Orthogonality ensured that the regions would each define different relationships among the variables. To illustrate the geometry of this, consider observations on four variables that have been standardized so that each observation has a zero mean. The standardization leaves only three degrees of freedom, so the points can be plotted in three dimensions, as in Figure A4-3. Assume also that the data fall on straight line ab on a plane through the origin. Then Q-type factor analysis will standardize the points so that they form the segment AB of a great circle on a sphere, as shown. Q-type factor analysis will represent these data with two orthogonal factors, and varimax rotation will place these factors at points 1 and 2 as shown. As a result, we would divide the data into two groups, enclosing each half of the line in a boxlike region. In this example, the linear relations among variables in the two groups would

FIGURE A4-3   Data in Three-Space.

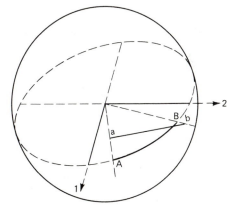

be identical. In practice, the data fall on a curved surface, so that variables show different linear relations in different regions.

If our regions are overlapping parts of a curved, densely populated surface, the binomial test of proportions of the last section will be significant. Regions between two archetypes would probably also be densely populated.

APPENDIX 4-2: DEFINITIONS OF THE VARIABLES

Although Chapter 4 uses all 31 of the following variables, the findings of Chapters 5 and 10 are based upon only 24 of these. The variables deleted are V1, V3, V5, V12, V14, V18, and V31.

Environment

Dynamism in the environment is manifested by the amount and unpredictability of change in customer tastes, production or service technologies, and the modes of competition in the firm's principal industries.

V1. *Past dynamism* (refers to dynamism which existed five years before case date).

Much less than   1 2 3 4 5 6 7   Much greater than
other firms   Same   other firms*

V2. *Current dynamism* (dynamism at the same time case was written).

Heterogeneity in the environment concerns the differences in competitive tactics, customer tastes, product lines, channels of distribution, and so on, across the firm's respective markets. These differences are significant only to the extent that they require very different marketing, production, and administrative practices.

V3. *Past heterogeneity* (five years before case date).
V4. *Current heterogeneity* (at time of case study).

Hostility in the environment is evidenced by price, product, technological, and distribution competition, severe regulatory restrictions, shortages of labor or raw materials, and unfavorable demographic trends (such as the drying up of markets).

V5. *Past hostility* (five years before case date).
V6. *Current hostility* (at time of case study).

Organization

V7. *Scanning* involves the search for problems and opportunities in the external environment of the firm. Firms are to be scored in terms of the amount of tracking performed of consumer tastes, competition, technological and administrative developments, and the like. Scanning may be done by staff departments, executives, the sales force, or others. The greater the number of factors tracked and the more widespread the participation in scanning activity, the higher the rating (score).

*Scales are identical for all variables except V11.

V8. *Delegation of operating authority* concerns the amount of authority transferred to lower and middle levels of management (any parties below VP) for administration of the day-to-day operation of the business. Operating decisions involve equipment replacement, production planning, adjustment of prices of goods, inventory purchases, hiring of lower-level personnel, and so on.

V9. *Centralization of strategy-making power* involves the distribution of power for making strategic decisions regarding acquisitions, diversification, major new-product introductions, long-term goals, and so forth. Centralization is high if the top executives alone make most of the decisions with a minimum of consultation; low if middle managers determine strategies by the default or intent of top executives (general manager and up).

V10. *Resource availability* concerns the state of the firm's material and human resources. Evidence of resource shortages are labor scarcity, poor raw-material supply, inadequate sources of capital, poor production facilities, and so on. If resources are abundant, score this scale high.

V11. *Management tenure* measures the length of time the most important (top) strategist or executive of the firm has been at the helm. If it is more than five years, score 2; if less, score 1.

V12. *Conflict* gauges the amount of dissent, overt or covert dissatisfaction, and hostility among members of the firm at and above the vice-presidential level. Conflict may concern organizational goals and means. It may be indicated if it takes very long to arrive at a consensus on courses of action, if management turnover is high, if there is much politicking, and so forth.

V13. *Controls* monitor the internal trends and incidents relevant to organizational performance. MIS, employee performance appraisals, quality controls, cost and profit centers, budgeting, and cost accounting are types of control devices. Score high if there is much emphasis on such controls.

V14. *Team spirit* involves the desire on the part of managers (one level below VP and up) to work unusually diligently to achieve organizational objectives and to do so in concert with others, so that team goals take precedence over individual needs.

V15. *Internal communication system* concerns the openness and fidelity of information channels in the organization. A high score is given when information reaches decision makers quickly, when it is relevant and undistorted, and when communication flows readily in top-down, bottom-up, and lateral directions.

V16. *Organizational differentiation* measures the degree of difference among organizational divisions in terms of their overall goals, marketing and production methods, and decision-making styles. The more disparate the divisions, the higher the score. Even functionally organized firms with only one division may have high levels of differentiation if there exist many different styles of behavior, management, and the like across respective departments owing to the nature of products and markets.

V17. *Technocratization.* Do there appear to be a great many staff specialists and professionally qualified people (accountants, engineers, scientists, doctors) as a percentage of the number of employees? If yes, score high.

V18. *Initial success of company strategies.* The initial strategy is either that formulated by the founder of the firm, or the basic product-market orientation that existed at least five years ago. Was this strategy quite intelligent and sound (score high), or did it seem destined to failure from the start?

Strategy-making

V19. *Product-market innovation.* Does the firm seem particularly innovative in terms of the number and novelty of new products and services that are introduced and the new markets that are entered?

V20. *Adaptiveness of decisions* concerns the responsiveness and appropriateness of decisions to *external* environmental conditions. For example, an adaptive pricing decision would take into account competitive strategies, customer buying habits, government regulations, and so on. Unadaptive decisions (score low) would consistently neglect an important set of external factors.

V21. *Integration of decisions.* Are actions in one area of the firm complementary or supportive of those in other areas (divisions, functions), or are they conflicting and mutually inhibiting? High integration would result in (or from) a concerted and well-coordinated strategy, whereas low integration might be manifested by fragmented or clashing tactics (for instance, acquiring new companies when there is inadequate ability to finance or run them; selling products that compete against each other).

V22. *Analysis of major decisions.* Do decision makers devote much reflective thought and deliberation to a problem and the array of proposed responses? The time spent on interrelating symptoms to get at the root cause of problems, and the effort spent to generate solutions (good or bad), are examples of the analytical process. A low score would be given when there is a very rapid intuitive response to an issue (this response could be ideal or the worst possible). Evidence of analysis comprises time delays, frequent meetings and discussions, the use of staff specialists, the writing of lengthy reports, and the like.

V23. *Multiplexity of decisions.* Do top managers address a *broad* range of factors in making strategic decisions, or merely a narrow set of factors (low score)? For example, in deciding whether to acquire a company, a multiplex strategist would consider marketing, financial, production, demographic, administrative, and other complementarities and problems, whereas low multiplexity would be evidenced by a focus on, say, marketing factors alone.

V24. *Futurity of decisions* concerns how far ahead the firm looks into the future in planning its strategies and operations. A relatively long time horizon (five years) warrants a high score. A focus on crisis decision making and staving off disasters warrants a low score.

V25. *Proactiveness of decisions.* Does the firm react to trends in the environment, or does it shape the environment by introducing new products, technologies, or administrative techniques? A reactive firm (low proactiveness) follows the leader; a proactive firm is the first to act.

V26. *Industry expertise of top managers.* Are top managers (VPs and up) very familiar with their products and markets? That is, are they in a position to make the most routine decisions because of their excellent knowledge of internal operations and the outside environment, or are managers removed from the field of action and cognizant only of the very gross aspects of the big picture (score low)?

V27. *Risk taking.* Is there evidence that top managers are risk-averse (score low), or does the firm frequently make large and risky resource commitments—those that have a reasonable chance of costly failure?

V28. *Consciousness of strategies* concerns the degree of top managers' conscious commitment to an explicit corporate strategy (that is, a set of objectives coupled with a number of stated favored means for attaining these). A low score is evidenced by unclear goals and the firm's muddling through.

V29. *Traditions.* Does the firm often rethink its strategies (objectives and means for their attainment), or are these tied largely to precedent (high score)?

Success

Success is measured in terms of growth in profits and sales, stability of profits, and returns on equity relative to other firms in the same industry.

V30. *Past success* (five years before case data).
V31. *Current success* (at time of case study).

APPENDIX 4-3: MODAL SCORES OF ARCHETYPES

	S_{1A} ADAPTIVE	S_{1B} ADAPTIVE	S_2 DOMINANT	S_3 GIANT	S_4 ENTREP.	S_5 INNOV.	F_1 IMPULS.	F_2 STAGNANT	F_3 HEADLESS	F_4 AFTERMATH
Environment										
1. Environmental dynamism—past	4	5	2	4	4	5	4	2	3	3
2. Environmental dynamism—current	5	6	3	6	5	6	6	5	5	5
3. Environmental heterogeneity—past	2	4	2	6	4	3	3	2	3	2
4. Environmental heterogeneity—current	4	4	3	6	6	4	6	2	5	3
5. Environmental hostility—past	5	X4	2	3	4	5	3	2	3	X4
6. Environmental hostility—current	6	6	3	7	4	X5	7	6	6	6
Organization										
7. Scanning of environment	5	6	5	6	6	4	3	2	3	3
8. Delegation of operating authority	6	6	4	7	6	5	X4	X3	6	4
9. Centralization of strategy-making power	6	5	6	4	7	7	7	5	1	6
10. Resource availability	5	7	6	6	X6	5	X4	X4	X5	1
11. Management tenure	2	2	2	2	2	2	2	2	2	2
12. Conflict	2	2	X3	3	2	X4	5	7	4	4
13. Internal controls	6	7	5	6	6	3	1	2	2	2
14. Team spirit	5	6	4	4	4	X5	3	1	X4	4
15. Internal communication system	5	6	4	6	6	4	2	1	2	3
16. Organizational differentiation	5	5	4	6	6	X6	6	2	X5	3
17. Technocratization	3	6	X7	6	X4	X6	3	3	X4	3
18. Initial success of company strategies	6	6	6	5	5	6	X4	1	4	2

continued

APPENDIX 4-3: (Continued)

	S_{1A} ADAPTIVE	S_{1B} ADAPTIVE	S_2 DOMINANT	S_3 GIANT	S_4 ENTREP.	S_5 INNOV.	F_1 IMPULS.	F_2 STAGNANT	F_3 HEADLESS	F_4 AFTERMATH
Strategy Making										
19. Product-market innovation	5	7	6	5	5	7	X4	2	2	5
20. Adaptiveness of decisions	6	6	6	5	5	4	2	1	2	3
21. Integration of decisions	5	6	6	5	5	5	2	3	1	2
22. Analysis of decisions	5	6	X4	6	6	3	2	2	4	X3
23. Multiplexity of decisions	5	6	X4	5	4	3	2	2	2	3
24. Futurity of decisions	5	6	X4	5	5	6	4	3	3	3
25. Proactiveness of decisions	6	7	5	4	6	7	6	1	2	X5
26. Industry expertise of top managers	6	6	7	6	X6	6	3	X5	3	X4
27. Risk taking	6	X5	4	5	6	6	7	2	2	5
28. Consciousness of strategies	6	6	6	6	6	6	X3	3	3	4
29. Traditions	X4	1	5	5	2	4	X4	6	6	X3
Success										
30. Past success of firm	X7	X7	7	7	7	7	X6	X4	5	X3
31. Current success of firm	7	7	7	6	7	6	1	1	3	1

Note: Scores are those most representative of firms within archetypes. They are modes (or an average of modes where there is more than one). An X indicates the score is unreliable, since the range on the variable for the archetype is greater than 3.

Appendix 4-4: Archetype Score Ranges

Archetype		ENVIRONMENT 1 PAST DYNAMISM	2 CURRENT DYNAMISM	3 PAST HETEROG.	4 CURRENT HETEROG.	5 PAST HOSTILITY	6 CURRENT HOSTILITY
S_{1A} Adaptive	U*	4	5	5	5	6	7
	L	1	1	1	1	3	4
S_{1B} Adaptive	U	5	5	5	5	4	5
	L	1	1	1	1	1	1
S_2 Dominant	U	7	7	5	5	7	7
	L	4	5	1	1	1	4
S_3 Giant	U	7	7	7	7	7	7
	L	3	4	3	5	3	5
S_4 Entrepreneurial	U	6	7	6	7	6	6
	L	2	3	2	5	2	3
S_5 Innovator	U	6	7	5	5	6	7
	L	3	4	1	1	1	1
F_1 Impulsive	U	5	7	5	7	4	7
	L	1	4	1	3	1	4
F_2 Stagnant	U	4	7	4	5	5	7
	L	1	1	1	1	1	3
F_3 Headless	U	4	7	7	7	4	7
	L	1	1	1	4	1	4
F_4 Aftermath	U	5	5	5	6	7	7
	L	1	1	1	2	1	4

Archetype		ORGANIZATION 7 SCANNING	8 DELEGATION	9 CENTRALIZATION	10 RESOURCES	11 TENURE	12 CONFLICT	13 CONTROLS	14 TEAM SPIRIT	15 COMMUNICATIONS	16 DIFFERENTIATION	17 TECHNOCRATIZ'N	18 PAST STRATEGIES
S_{1A} Adaptive	U*	7	7	7	7	2	4	7	7	7	5	7	7
	L	5	3	4	5	1	1	4	4	4	1	1	3
S_{1B} Adaptive	U	7	6	7	7	2	5	7	7	6	5	7	7
	L	4	3	4	4	1	1	4	4	4	1	1	1
S_2 Dominant	U	7	7	6	7	2	4	7	7	7	5	7	7
	L	5	5	3	4	1	1	4	4	4	1	4	1
S_3 Giant	U	7	7	5	7	2	5	7	6	7	7	7	7
	L	4	5	2	5	1	1	4	3	4	4	3	1
S_4 Entrepreneurial	U	7	7	7	7	2	4	7	6	7	7	7	7
	L	4	4	5	3	1	1	4	3	4	4	1	1
S_5 Innovator	U	5	7	7	7	2	7	5	7	5	5	7	7
	L	3	4	6	4	1	1	2	1	2	1	1	1
F_1 Impulsive	U	4	7	7	7	2	7	4	4	4	7	7	7
	L	1	1	4	1	1	4	1	1	1	3	1	1
F_2 Stagnant	U	4	4	7	7	2	7	4	4	4	5	7	7
	L	1	1	4	1	1	1	1	1	1	1	1	1
F_3 Headless	U	4	7	5	7	2	7	4	4	4	7	7	7
	L	1	4	1	1	1	4	1	1	1	3	1	1
F_4 Aftermath	U	5	7	7	4	2	7	4	7	5	5	7	7
	L	2	1	4	1	1	1	1	1	1	1	1	1

Archetype		STRATEGY MAKING 19 P-M INNOVATION	20 ADAPTIVENESS	21 INTEGRATION	22 ANALYSIS	23 MULTIPLEXITY	24 FUTURITY	25 PROACTIVENESS	26 IND. EXPERT.	27 RISK TAKING	28 CONSC. OF STRAT.	29 TRADITIONS
S_{1A} Adaptive	U*	7	7	7	7	7	6	7	7	7	7	7
	L	1	5	4	3	1	4	4	5	4	5	1
S_{1B} Adaptive	U	7	7	7	7	7	7	7	7	7	7	6
	L	4	4	2	2	1	1	3	5	1	5	3
S_2 Dominant	U	7	7	7	7	7	7	7	7	7	7	5
	L	5	5	5	4	4	4	5	4	3	4	1
S_3 Giant	U	7	7	7	7	7	7	6	7	5	7	6
	L	3	4	4	4	3	4	4	3	3	4	3
S_4 Entrepreneurial	U	7	7	7	7	6	7	7	7	7	7	5
	L	3	4	3	4	3	4	4	3	5	5	1
S_5 Innovator	U	7	5	5	5	5	7	7	7	7	7	7
	L	5	2	2	2	2	4	5	5	5	5	1
F_1 Impulsive	U	7	4	3	4	4	5	7	4	7	7	7
	L	1	1	1	1	1	2	4	1	5	1	1
F_2 Stagnant	U	4	3	7	4	4	4	3	5	4	7	7
	L	1	1	1	1	1	1	1	1	1	1	4
F_3 Headless	U	5	3	4	4	4	4	4	4	4	5	7
	L	1	1	1	1	1	1	1	1	1	1	4
F_4 Aftermath	U	7	5	5	5	4	5	7	6	7	6	7
	L	3	1	1	1	1	1	1	1	4	3	1

Archetype		SUCCESS 30 PAST SUCCESS	31 CURRENT SUCCESS
S_{1A} Adaptive	U*	7	7
	L	1	5
S_{1B} Adaptive	U	7	7
	L	1	5
S_2 Dominant	U	7	7
	L	1	5
S_3 Giant	U	7	7
	L	1	5
S_4 Entrepreneurial	U	7	7
	L	1	5
S_5 Innovator	U	7	7
	L	1	4
F_1 Impulsive	U	7	4
	L	1	1
F_2 Stagnant	U	7	4
	L	1	1
F_3 Headless	U	7	4
	L	1	1
F_4 Aftermath	U	7	4
	L	1	1

*U indicates that the figure represents the upper bound of the score range for the archetype along the 7-point scales; L indicates the lower bound of the range.

APPENDIX 4-5: STATISTICAL SIGNIFICANCE OF ARCHETYPES

	(1) ARCHETYPE	(2) SAMPLE PROPORTION	(3) LOWER BOUND OF 95% INTERVAL	(4) ARCHETYPE REGION SIZE	(5) COLUMN (4) DIVIDED BY NO. OF SITES IN CARTESIAN PRODUCT SPACE*
S_{1A}	Adaptive	5/29	5.8449E − 2†	2.4089E + 19	1.843E − 8
S_{1B}	Adaptive	3/29	2.1858E − 2	3.7756E + 18	2.889E − 9
S_2	Dominant	1/29	8.7357E − 4	2.8104E + 20	2.150E − 7
S_3	Giant	1/29	8.7357E − 4	5.6184E + 18	4.299E − 9
S_4	Entrepreneurial	1/29	8.7357E − 4	2.1849E + 19	1.672E − 8
S_5	Innovator	1/29	8.7357E − 4	3.0217E + 19	2.312E − 8
F_1	Impulsive	3/29	2.1858E − 2	2.7855E + 20	2.131E − 7
F_2	Stagnant	3/29	2.1858E − 2	3.4818E + 20	2.664E − 7
F_3	Headless	3/29	2.1858E − 2	1.2127E + 20	9.279E − 6
F_4	Aftermath	2/29	8.4610E − 3	6.1983E + 21	4.742E − 6
	OUTLIERS	2/29			
	MISCLASSIFIED	4/29			

*No. of sites = 1.307E + 27 = 2 × 7^{30} (or thirty 7-point scales, one 2-point scale).

†This is the notation for 5.8449 × 10^{-2}, or 0.058449.

As we can see, the proportions in Column 3 are always at least 1,000 times greater than those in Column 5, and so we can easily reject the null hypothesis for each archetype.

APPENDIX 5-1: CHECKING THE PUBLISHED DATA

It was important to establish the validity of the published data. Even if scoring reliability is high, the published accounts may be inaccurate or contain systematic distortion. Also, raters might bias findings through the manner in which they define periods. It was necessary to employ another data base ("data base 2") to check these possibilities.

Twelve of the 36 firms in the published sample still had top executives (presidents, chief executive officers, chairmen, or chief operating officers) who were vice-presidents or of higher rank during the entire final transition period recorded by the data. These executives were asked to complete a questionnaire designed to gauge the changes that took place during the final transition period of the firm. Changes were measured directly in the questionnaire sample rather than through the conversion of static scores, as was the case with the published data. In all, ten (83 percent) executives responded. The correspondence of the scores between executives and raters was good. We could not use the Spearman coefficient as an index of reliability, since it would have been insufficiently demanding; a very high correlation would still have been possible if raters and executives had disagreed on the direction of change for many variables. Given that the focus of the research is on the direction of change, this type of discrepancy would have been very serious, and so a closer examination of rating correspondence was necessary.

There are several different types of scoring discrepancies to consider. The first and least serious involves score changes in the same direction but differing in magnitude. For example, a transition score of 5, indicating an increase in the variable, may be accorded by the top executive, but a score of 6 may be given by the case rater. Because executives do not have in their experience a large sample of organizations for comparing the magnitude of change, it is unreasonable to insist on identical scores. It is sufficient for the types of conclusions we shall draw for changes to be in the same direction and within one rating point. Thus, score combinations of 1 and 2, 2 and 3, 5 and 6, and 6 and 7 were counted as matches. In 67 percent of the 177 cases, this form of agreement existed between executives and raters.

A more serious disagreement occurs when one scorer reports a one-point increase or decrease (5 or 3), and the other reports no change (4). This form of disagreement occurred in 19 percent of the cases. This is not too daunting, since such discrepancies did not change findings as established in the section of Appendix 5-2 on hypothesis testing. Discrepancies that would distort findings are thus limited to two varieties. The first occurs when one rating reports no change (4) and another shows an extreme increase (6 or 7) or decrease (1 or 2) in a variable. This occurred 13 percent of the time. The last and most severe discrepancy happened when ratings reported changes in opposite directions (such as 3 versus 5; 2 versus 6).

Fortunately, this occurred in only 2 percent of the cases. The test of the validity of the scores and their adequacy for the types of conclusions we shall draw is demonstrated in the hypothesis-generation and hypothesis-testing sections.

Hypothesis Generation

The objectives of the research were to identify common configurations or patterns of transition. Patterns are defined by the 24 transition scores (one for each variable) for each transition period. It is a relatively simple matter to group patterns according to their fluctuations along several variables.

Grouping the Patterns. To discover the natural groupings among the score patterns, an inverse or *Q*-type factor analysis procedure was used. A random half of the transition periods (63) from the published sample were iteratively factored using the orthogonal, varimax rotation options of SPSS (Nie, Bent, and Hull, 1970, PA2). Patterns that loaded more than .5 on a given factor were tentatively combined into a group. Nine groups were found with memberships ranging from three to eight patterns. By coincidence, the means and standard deviations of patterns within a group did not vary much.[1] We did not intend the factor analysis to serve as anything other than a vehicle to help us perceive similarity. Since factor analysis is usually bound to come up with some groupings, the output of such a procedure is of very little interest in and of itself, and was not used to verify the stability and parsimony of the categorization scheme. The rationale for using factor analysis as an exploratory technique upon ordinal data as well as a more elaborate justification of our methodology was provided in Chapter 2 and Appendix 4-1. The means and standard deviations of the variables are given in Appendix 5-4.

Defining the Groups. To be precise about the outcome of the tentative categorization scheme, we operationalized our concept of a group to take it beyond the vague definition given to it by a loading on an abstract factor. The members of each group were all plotted on a graph (one graph per group) so that their score ranges on each of the 24 variables collectively defined the boundaries of a *region*. This procedure is the same as that explained in Appendix 4-1. The actual boundaries for the nine regions are given in Appendix 5-3A. Should any of these regions or groups of possible patterns prove to be statistically significant, they will be called *transition archetypes*.

---

[1]Since inverse factor analysis groups patterns only according to their correlational similarities across the 24 variables, it is possible for patterns in a group to differ significantly in their means and standard deviations. But this did not happen. Should there have been too much variance here, it would have been a simple matter to further subdivide groups into subgroups with homogeneous means and standard deviations.

Only if the groups satisfy the following three sets of requirements can we consider them as archetypes that collectively contribute to a predictive taxonomy. First, groups must be potentially predictive. By this we mean that, given a transition pattern and a set of groups, it is possible by using only few variables to identify the group of which the pattern is a member. Then we can predict the remaining variable scores solely by making reference to group characteristics. Thus, the proportion of space occupied by a region must be small compared to the proportion of the sample it encompasses.

Second, groups must be stable within and across different data bases. That is, the same groups must occur in different data bases. Only if this is true can findings be considered generalizable.

Third, groups must be able to be found easily by replicators of the research. Our conditional scoring heuristic device must be shown to be robust in identifying transitions. Small variations in the way transition periods are defined should not completely obscure findings.

It is to the verification of each of these three sets of requirements that the hypothesis-testing section devotes itself.

Hypothesis Testing

A computer program was written to sort the remaining half of the published history profiles (data base 1) and a new questionnaire sample of 50 firms (this is data base 3, described in Appendix 5-5) into the nine regions. After determining the number of members in each of the regions, we tested whether regions were more densely occupied than could be expected by chance, given their size. If so, because we are using a new sample of firms to test the groups, their stability is confirmed. Also, since the transition period in the questionnaire sample is standardized at five years,[2] the significance of groups attests to their robustness under a different period definition.

Under chance, we would expect that the proportion of patterns that fall into a region would be roughly the same as the proportion of space occupied by the region—that is, the proportion of all sites occupied by the region. The total number of sites—that is, the number of possible score patterns along 24 seven-point ordinal scales—is 7^{24}. The number of sites that fall into the region can be expressed as:

$$(1) \quad (V_{1,2} - V_{1,1} + 1)(V_{2,2} - V_{2,1} + 1) \ldots (V_{24,2} - V_{24,1} + 1)$$

where $V_{i,2}$ is the upper bound of the ith variable for the region, and $V_{i,1}$ is

---

[2]A 5-year interval was chosen because it is the modal length of periods of analysis in the published data sample.

the lower bound. The expected proportion of patterns to fall into the regions is therefore found by dividing equation 1 by 7^{24}.

Were it equally likely to have any score on any variable, our test would be complete. However, because transition scores are involved and raters are biased against or have good empirical reasons to avoid extreme scores (for instance, 1 or 7), some scores (3, 4, and 5) are far more common than others. Obviously, then, if one were to construct regions comprising scores 3 to 5 inclusive across all variables, we would, *a priori*, expect such regions to be more densely populated than regions comprising scores of 1 to 3 or 5 to 7 across all variables.[3] We must then take into account the probability of a variable's having a particular score. To do this, we modify equation 1 to account for the frequency of scores of each variable and adjust the probabilities for the percentage of missing data on each variable, to obtain:

(2) $(pV_1)(pV_2) \ldots (pV_{24})$

Here, pV_i is the probability under the null hypothesis that the ith transition score will be in the ith range defining the region.

A program was written to calculate the expected proportion of companies falling into each of the nine regions. The proportion is given by equation 2. To determine whether the actual proportion of firms (excluding, of course, those used for hypothesis generation) falling into a region was significantly greater than this expected proportion, a simple Poisson test of proportions was used. The test calculates the Poisson probability of the actual proportion or more given the expected proportion. The probability of finding k members in the region can be expressed as $P(k) = u^k e^{-u}/k!$, where u is the expected number of patterns. All regions were given transition numbers T_1 to T_9. They are quantitatively defined and their statistical significance levels are given in Appendix 5-3. When the 50 questionnaires of data base 3 alone were used,[4] only regions T_2, T_3, T_4, and T_7 were significant at the .05 level, and T_5 and T_8 at the .10 level. When only the published data of data base 1 were used, all regions were significant at the .03 level or better. This indicates that, at least for regions T_2, T_3, T_4, T_5, T_7, and T_8, the transitions characterized periods of corporate history not only in the sample of published data, but in a very different sample of questionnaire responses. Such regions and the archetypes defined by them are thus generalizable, stable, and very common. The remaining regions are also stable and common, but they are not borne out by the questionnaire data, and so their generality is more limited. In all, 86 per-

---

[3]This was not true in the analysis of static archetypes of Chapter 4 where all scores occurred with about equal frequency.

[4]Two variables, consciousness of strategies and tenure, were not measured by the questionnaires, and equation 2 was adjusted accordingly.

cent of the transition score patterns from the published data and 54 percent of the questionnaire patterns fit into archetype regions that collectively had a chance of less than 4 percent of occurring, according to the null hypothesis. Finally, it is encouraging that all patterns from data base 2 fit the same archetypes as those of the corresponding rater-scored patterns.

		1 Dyn.	2 Host.	3 Heter.	4 Scan.	5 Cont.	6 Comm'n.	7 Cent'n.	8 Deleg'n.	9 Techn.	10 Resour.	11 Proact.	12 Risk	13 P.M. Inn.	14 Anal.	15 Multip.	16 Integ.	17 Futur.	18 Cons. St.	19 Tenure.	20 Diff'n.	21 Adapt.	22 Ind. Exp.	23 Success	24 Trads.
T_1 Fragmentation	U*	5	6	5	4	5	3	3	5	4	4	5	5	5	4	4	4	4	4	3	4	4	3	3	5
	L*	4	4	4	3	3	3	2	4	4	3	3	3	3	3	3	3	3	3	3	4	3	3	2	3
	M*	4	5	5	3	4	3	3	5	4	3	4	4	4	3	3	3	3	3	3	4	3	3	3	5
T_2 Revitalization	U	7	7	7	7	7	7	6	7	7	6	7	7	7	7	7	7	7	7	7	7	7	7	7	5
	L	4	1	4	4	4	4	1	3	4	1	4	3	4	4	4	3	1	3	1	4	4	3	3	1
	M	5	5	5	6	5	5	5	6	5	4	5	5	6	5	6	5	5	5	3	5	6	5	5	3
T_3 Consolidation	U	6	6	5	5	7	5	4	7	6	7	3	4	5	5	5	7	4	4	7	5	5	5	6	7
	L	3	4	3	3	4	3	1	1	4	1	1	1	1	4	3	4	1	1	1	4	3	3	3	4
	M	4	4	3	4	6	4	2	5	5	5	3	2	3	5	4	6	3	3	2	4	4	4	4	5
T_4 Stagnation	U	5	7	5	4	4	5	4	5	5	6	4	4	4	4	4	5	5	5	7	5	4	4	5	7
	L	2	3	2	1	1	1	1	1	1	1	1	1	1	1	1	1	1	1	1	3	1	1	1	4
	M	4	5	4	2	2	3	3	5	4	4	3	3	2	3	2	3	2	3	5	4	2	2	3	6
T_5 Centralization, boldness	U	5	7	6	5	4	5	7	5	6	6	6	7	6	4	7	4	7	7	7	6	4	5	5	4
	L	3	3	4	2	2	2	4	1	3	1	4	4	3	1	1	1	1	1	1	4	1	1	1	1
	M	5	4	5	4	2	3	6	3	5	3	5	6	5	3	3	2	4	5	5	5	2	4	4	2
T_6 Initiation by fire	U	5	7	6	5	5	5	4	6	6	4	6	6	6	5	4	5	7	5	4	6	5	5	3	4
	L	3	4	4	4	3	3	2	2	4	1	4	4	4	4	2	2	4	1	1	4	3	1	1	1
	M	5	6	5	5	4	4	3	5	5	3	5	5	5	4	4	3	5	3	3	5	4	3	2	3
T_7 Maturation	U	6	6	6	7	7	7	5	6	6	7	3	4	5	7	7	7	7	7	7	6	7	7	7	6
	L	2	1	4	4	4	4	2	3	4	1	1	1	2	4	4	4	1	3	1	3	4	3	3	3
	M	4	4	5	5	6	5	3	5	5	5	3	2	4	5	5	6	4	5	4	5	5	5	4	4
T_8 Troubleshooting	U	5	6	5	6	7	7	6	4	5	7	4	4	4	7	7	7	7	4	6	5	7	7	7	5
	L	3	3	3	4	4	4	4	1	3	3	1	1	1	4	4	4	1	1	3	3	4	4	1	3
	M	4	5	4	5	6	5	6	3	4	4	3	3	3	5	5	5	4	3	5	4	5	5	5	4
T_9 Formalization	U	5	5	5	5	5	5	4	6	5	6	5	4	5	4	5	4	4	5	7	5	5	5	7	7
	L	3	2	4	3	3	4	3	4	4	4	3	2	3	3	3	4	3	4	4	4	3	4	4	5
	M	4	4	4	4	4	4	4	5	4	5	4	3	4	4	4	4	4	4	5	5	4	4	5	6

*U and L are upper and lower region boundaries; M is the modal score pattern.

APPENDIX 5-3B: SIGNIFICANCE LEVELS OF TRANSITION ARCHETYPES

	T_1	T_2	T_3	T_4	T_5	T_6	T_7	T_8	T_9
					REGION				
S_1**	.0001	.03	.0008	.0009	.0098	.0002	.0064	.0021	.0001
S_2**	NS	.0001	.04	.04	.09	NS	.004	.10	NS

Figures indicate that regions are significant at or beyond the indicated level.

$N =$	3	40	8	20	17	8	12	8	10

Number of transitions in archetype.

**S_1 tests significance for data base 1; S_2 tests for data base 3.

APPENDIX 5-4: MEANS AND STANDARD DEVIATIONS FOR THE 24 VARIABLES ON THE 7-POINT ORDINAL SCALE

VARIABLE	MEAN	STANDARD DEVIATION
1. Dynamism	4.2	0.7
2. Hostility	4.3	1.2
3. Heterogeneity	4.3	0.5
4. Scanning	4.2	0.9
5. Controls	4.3	1.1
6. Communication	4.2	1.1
7. Centralization	3.9	1.0
8. Delegation	4.3	1.0
9. Technocratization	4.2	0.6
10. Resources	4.1	1.0
11. Proactiveness	4.0	1.1
12. Risk taking	4.0	1.1
13. Product-market innovation	4.1	1.1
14. Analysis	4.2	1.0
15. Multiplexity	4.2	1.1
16. Integration	4.1	1.0
17. Futurity	4.1	1.0
18. Consciousness of strategy	4.1	1.1
19. Tenure	4.0	1.6
20. Differentiation	4.3	0.6
21. Adaptiveness	4.1	1.2
22. Industry expertise	4.0	1.0
23. Success	4.0	1.5
24. Traditions	4.0	1.2

APPENDIX 5-5: DATA BASE 3:
THE QUESTIONNAIRE DATA

Firms in this sample were randomly selected from the Canadian Financial Post Survey of Industrials, subject to three constraints: Sales had to be greater than $20 million, and the number of employees had to be greater than 250, so that small and simple enterprises not reflected in the published sample would be excluded; also, highly diversified firms were avoided because of potential measurement problems. The firms chosen show much variation in sales growth, market concentration, size, and industry type. Responses were received from transportation, banking, trust, finance, steel, chemical, paper, retailing, electrical equipment, public utility, hotel, food, meat packing, mining, and brewing industries. No industry accounted for more than 8 percent of the sample. The variation in size was great; 18 percent of the firms had sales of less than $30 million, and 21 percent had sales of more than $500 million (the average was $290 million). Our sample thus seems quite representative of medium-to-large nondiversified firms. Respondents were the CEOs of the firms. These people were expected to have the greatest possible knowledge of companywide structure and strategies. For ten of the firms, the general managers also responded. The response rate was 52 percent, and a total of 50 companies replied.

Pradip Khandwalla helped us to design the questionnaire, which is available from the senior author. Except for variables 18 and 19, which questionnaires deleted, the same variables were measured in all data bases. All questions examined the changes in environment, structure, and strategy-making practices that had taken place over the preceding five years. Scoring reliability between raters of a given firm averaged .79 (product moment correlation). Coefficients ranged from .74 to .89 across the variables and were significant beyond the .001 level with one exception. For one firm, the correlation coefficient of .60 indicated an unacceptable level of agreement among executives, and the firm was dropped from the sample. Responses were averaged when there was more than one rating-point disagreement among the executives of a firm. In all other cases, only the scores of the CEO were used. The validity of responses could be ascertained only by examining the similarity between published and questionnaire data. Our discussion in the text and the hypothesis tests show that this was great.

APPENDIX 7-1: PRODUCT MOMENT CORRELATIONS OF VARIABLES WITH ENTREPRENEURSHIP FOR THREE TYPES OF FIRMS

	SIMPLE FIRMS				PLANNING FIRMS				ORGANIC FIRMS				ALL TYPES			
	ENT.††	I.††	P.††	R.††	ENT.	I.	P.	R.	ENT.	I.	P.	R.	ENT.	I.	P.	R.
Locus of Control of Leader	−.66**	−.44*	−.44*	−.61**	−.43*	−.08	−.42*	−.45*	−.16	−.01	−.29	−.20	−.64**	−.45**	−.70**	−.62**
Environment																
1. Dynamism	.09	.09	.05	.05	−.06	.24	−.06	−.33†	.52*	.48*	.38†	.47*	.35**	.36**	.20†	.16
2. Heterogeneity	.18	.26	.18	−.13	.22	.46*	.24	−.27	.44†	.38*	.60*	.17	.41**	.49**	.35**	.15
3. Hostility	.24	.46*	−.03	.10	.12	.44*	0	−.25	.50*	.60*	.29	.33	.26*	.43**	.02	.04
Organization/Structure																
4. Scanning	.41*	.03	.44*	.45*	.21	.18	.32†	−.04	−.01	.03	.21	−.27	.26*	.08	.36**	.18
5. Controls	.12	.04	.16	.04	.13	.18	.14	−.06	−.11	−.08	.06	−.26	.11	.07	.19	.05
6. Communication	−.09	−.29	−.16	.40*	.27	.02	−.01	.54**	−.38†	−.29	.01	−.65†	.08	.01	−.03	.39**
7. Resources	−.10	−.19	−.11	.13	−.11	.03	−.01	−.27	−.18	−.11	.01	−.38†	−.07	−.05	−.07	−.01
8. Centralization	.40*	.31†	.24	.35†	−.06	−.28	.14	.06	−.60†	−.44†	−.44†	−.69**	−.01	−.03	−.16	−.13
9. Technocratization	.51*	.45*	.33†	.34†	.36†	.47*	.19	.04	.53†	.54*	.24	.46†	.46**	.44**	.34**	.27*
10. Differentiation	.19	.29	−.02	.17	.34†	.55**	.07	.03	.10	.08	.14	.03	.46**	.48**	.24*	.29*
11. Integration	.31†	.06	.09	.69**	−.11	−.42*	−.28	.48	.00	−.06	−.15	.23	.10	−.03	−.04	.36
Decision Making/Strategy																
12. Analysis	−.10	−.28	.03	.07	.20	.24	.13	.04	.42†	.50†	.42†	.11	.19†	.10	.20†	.18†
13. Futurity	.15	.18	−.10	.33†	.10	.13	−.06	.10	.37†	.40†	.48*	.06	.25†	.21†	.15	.26†
14. Explicitness of Product-Market Strategy	.24	.15	.22	.18	.69**	.51*	.54**	.46*	.43†	.60*	.44†	−.01	.39**	.35**	.30†	.27†
15. Strategic Integration	.02	−.03	.08	−.02	.33†	.10	.34†	.29	−.31	−.14	−.22	−.47	−.09	−.11	−.01	−.10
Entrepreneurship																
16. Innovation	.74**				.70**				.91**				.82**			
17. Proactiveness	.74**				.68**				.86**				.76**			
18. Risk Taking	.72**				.72**				.79**				.80**			

The symbols †, *, and ** indicate that the correlations are significant at the .10, .05, and .01 levels respectively.

††The abbreviations ENT., I., P. and R. refer to the variables of entrepreneurship, innovation, proactiveness, and risk taking respectively.

Appendix 9-1: Detailed Correlational
Analysis of Structural Changes

This appendix examines each of the ten cells of the correlation matrices presented in Tables 9-2 through 9-4, comparing the percentages of significant correlations between successful and unsuccessful subsamples. It presents an analysis that is more detailed and more qualitative than that contained in the discussion of Hypothesis 1a.

Table A9-1 summarizes the results of the ten cells of the correlation matrices for all three samples. It gives the number of correlations that are significant at the .05 level for each of the successful and unsuccessful subsamples. The overlap, or number of correlations common to both subsamples, is also reported, to show how similar the individual correlations are between successful and unsuccessful groups. The column headings *A*, *C*, and *P* refer to the Australian, Canadian, and published samples respectively, and the fourth column of each cell provides the average percentage (AV.%) of significant correlations for the three samples, according equal weight to each sample. The "Ratio" figure gives the quotient of the average percentages of significant correlations for all three successful and unsuccessful subsamples. For example, the ratio of 5.55 in cell 9 indicates that there are 5.55 times more significant correlations between dual and integration variables in successful than in unsuccessful subsamples (61% ÷ 11% = 5.55).

The first thing to notice from Table A9-1 is that although in most cells successful subsamples have many more correlations than unsuccessful subsamples, in some cells this simply does not occur. For example, we see from cell 8 that there is a tendency for integration devices to be highly correlated in both successful and unsuccessful samples. A similar condition holds in the dual-variable cell (10), where there are a modest number of significant correlations for both subsamples. In cell 5, only the Canadian successful sample shows a significantly large number of correlations; but the three samples combined do *not* support the contention that changes in the differentiation variables are more highly correlated in successful firms. Thus, except in the case of uncertainty reduction, it seems that correlations among the variables *within* a given class of variables are not quite as strongly associated with success as are correlations across classes. Perhaps, then, in many cases, the various differentiation and dual devices can serve as substitutes for one another. For example, sophisticated capital-budgeting programs might serve in place of planning systems. We hesitate, however, to apply this substitutability rationale to the integration cell (8), because all firms appear to increase or decrease their use of integration devices simultaneously. For example, as the tendency to use task forces and committees increases, so does the frequency of internal communications and interdepartmental committees, and the use of formal controls. Perhaps the joint

TABLE A9-1: COMPARISON OF NUMBER OF SIGNIFICANT CORRELATIONS BY TYPE BETWEEN SUCCESSFUL AND UNSUCCESSFUL SAMPLES

CELL 1: UNCERTAINTY REDUCTION

	A*	C*	P*	AV.%
Significant r's in Successful Sample	5	8	2	43
Significant r's in Unsuccessful Sample	3	7	0	16
Overlap	1	3	0	6
Out of a possible	21	21	3	100

Ratio = 2.69

CELL 2: UNCERTAINTY REDUCTION WITH DIFFERENTIATION

	A	C	P	AV.%
Significant r's in Successful Sample	11	4	5	32
Significant r's in Unsuccessful Sample	4	3	3	18
Overlap	2	0	2	9
Out of a possible	35	35	9	100

Ratio = 1.78

CELL 3: UNCERTAINTY REDUCTION WITH INTEGRATION

	A	C	P	AV.%
Significant r's in Successful Sample	9	12	7	59
Significant r's in Unsuccessful Sample	5	4	5	32
Overlap	3	3	5	28
Out of a possible	21	21	9	100

Ratio = 1.84

CELL 4: UNCERTAINTY REDUCTION WITH DUAL

	A	C	P	AV.%
Significant r's in Successful Sample	4	11	N/A**	36
Significant r's in Unsuccessful Sample	7	3	N/A	24
Overlap	3	1	N/A	10
Out of a possible	21	21		100

Ratio = 1.50

CELL 5: DIFFERENTIATION

	A	C	P	AV.%
Significant r's in Successful Sample	5	1	0	20
Significant r's in Unsuccessful Sample	1	1	1	18
Overlap	1	1	0	7
Out of a possible	10	10	3	100

Ratio = 1.11

CELL 6: DIFFERENTIATION WITH INTEGRATION

	A	C	P	AV.%
Significant r's in Successful Sample	5	3	3	29
Significant r's in Unsuccessful Sample	3	6	0	20
Overlap	2	0	0	4
Out of a possible	15	15	9	100

Ratio = 1.45

CELL 7: DIFFERENTIATION WITH DUAL

	A	C	P	AV.%
Significant r's in Successful Sample	4	4	N/A**	27
Significant r's in Unsuccessful Sample	5	4	N/A	30
Overlap	0	0	N/A	0
Out of a possible	15	15		100

Ratio = 0.90

CELL 8: INTEGRATION

	A	C	P	AV.%
Significant r's in Successful Sample	3	3	3	100
Significant r's in Unsuccessful Sample	3	2	3	89
Overlap	3	2	3	89
Out of a possible	3	3	3	100

Ratio = 1.12

CELL 9: INTEGRATION WITH DUAL

	A	C	P	AV.%
Significant r's in Successful Sample	5	6	N/A**	61
Significant r's in Unsuccessful Sample	2	0	N/A	11
Overlap	2	0	N/A	11
Out of a possible	9	9		100

Ratio = 5.55

CELL 10: DUAL

	A	C	P	AV.%
Significant r's in Successful Sample	1	1	N/A**	33
Significant r's in Unsuccessful Sample	1	1	N/A	33
Overlap	1	0	N/A	17
Out of a possible	3	3		100

Ratio = 1.0

*A, C, and P refer to the Australian, Canadian, and published data samples.
**The published sample does not contain any dual-function variables.

employment of these devices has become a practice that is favored by successful and unsuccessful firms alike.

The major differences between the successful and unsuccessful sub-samples are to be found in the cells showing correlations *across* classes of variables. Cells 2 and 3 show that changes in uncertainty reduction are most highly correlated with changes in differentiation and integration in the successful samples. This is in line with the predictions of Khandwalla (1972; 1973) and Galbraith (1973). As the environment becomes more uncertain or heterogeneous, or as the firm diversifies or tries to innovate more often, it must begin to more thoroughly and regularly scan and analyze its surroundings. In order to accomplish this, the structure will have to free managers for these tougher administrative tasks by delegating operating authority to lower levels and by routinizing and formalizing those aspects of operations that are susceptible to it. These devices of uncertainty reduction may best be accompanied by increased differentiation (see cell 2). This may take the form of departments that specialize in a particular area or aspect of the environment, technocrats who are sophisticated scanners and innovators, and managers who are specialists in areas of uncertainty that cannot be handled routinely by first line managers. In other words, uncertainty reduction and differentiation may have to increase together. Where this does not happen, the increase in uncertainty reduction activity may result in overburdened managers, an organization that is too monolithic to deal with the new contingencies it faces, or a misguided adherence to rules and procedures. The very many correlations between uncertainty reduction and integration variables in the successful subsamples may also be particularly useful (see cell 3). Given an increase in programs, rules, and delegation, there is a greater need to ensure that the organization does not become an agglomeration of uncooperative fiefdoms. Effective decision making not only depends on gathering the right types of information and performing sophisticated analyses, but also upon the collaboration of those from diverse areas of expertise. Note, for example, that correlations between variables 1 and 13, 1 and 14, 1 and 15, 2 and 13, 2 and 14, 4 and 13 are significant in the successful Canadian and Australian subsamples but not in the unsuccessful ones.

Let us now look at the opposite direction of change. When the firm enters a more placid, stable, and homogeneous environment, it can economize by substantially reducing its use of uncertainty-reduction devices (except, perhaps, rules and programs) *and* by reducing differentiation and integration. Cutting the emphasis on only one class of variables may provide insufficient scope for economies. It may also create conflict and divisiveness as, say, the level of delegation becomes too confining for the technocrats, or the number and diversity of departments too great for the primitive information systems.

Given these arguments, we would have expected the relationships between changes in differentiation and integration to have been more numerous than those shown in cell 6. However, perhaps the summary column is misleading here, since the Canadian sample is the only one that causes this result. If we count the number of times the cell's correlations are higher for the successful than for the unsuccessful subsample, these numbers are 11 out of 15 for the Australian sample, and 7 out of 9 times for the published sample. It is possible that the anomalous findings in the Canadian data were due to the initial but rapid diversification and acquisition efforts that were taking place in some of our Canadian firms and the early takeover profits they were making because of this. Such firms might have seemed successful in spite of their initial neglect of integration activities. The test of the soundness of conglomerators' strategies typically comes in the period *after* the acquisitions are made. Perhaps a follow-up study would better distinguish between the performance of firms that boosted integration efforts to manage differentiation and those that did not.

Comparing cells 6 and 7, we can see that the relationships between changes in differentiation and integration better distinguish between successful and unsuccessful firms than do the relationships between changes in differentiation and dual-function devices. This may be because most of the integrative devices bring people together to work and to discuss disagreements. They can therefore effectively integrate the efforts of managers and departments and reduce conflicts caused by increased differentiation. The dual-function devices, however, can be quite ineffective, since they may fail to enhance communication or to broach conflicts directly. One can computerize, plan, and budget without effecting better communication, coordination, or cooperation, or without even becoming aware of any problems of organizational integration. In contrast, task forces and meetings promote a more direct interface among different parties. For example, the links between changes in the use of technocrats and the use of integrative devices seem much stronger in all the successful subsamples than in the unsuccessful ones (compare the subsample correlations between scales 12 and 14, and 12 and 15, in the questionnaire data, and between variables 6 and 7, 6 and 8, and 6 and 9 in the published data). This suggests that for firms to operate properly, close cooperation is necessary between technocrats with a theoretical knowledge of science, technology, and systems, and managers with a practical knowledge of markets, production processes, and decision-making information needs. Where technocrats are not properly integrated into the firm or exposed to the key business realities, their contributions may miss the mark.

Cell 9 shows that integration and dual function devices might work well together, perhaps because the use of interpersonal integrative devices becomes more fruitful when there is better information to help effect coordination and to resolve conflicts. The increased use of information systems, long-term planning, and capital budgeting might make meetings, committees, and task forces more effective by ensuring that agendas include the most relevant information and address the most critical issues. Note, for example, that correlations between variables 12 and 16, 13 and 16, 14 and 16, and 15 and 16 are significant for the successful subsamples but not for the unsuccessful ones.

Of the remaining cells, number 4 is too ambiguous to warrant comment while number 1 shows that successful firms are more likely than unsuccessful ones to change uncertainty-reduction variables in concert. It is interesting that there is very little overlap between the subsamples in cell 1. The successful firms are more likely to balance increases in rules and programs with the use of scanning devices. Scanning can reveal whether the rules and programs are catering properly to the demands of the environment and the strategy.

We conclude this Appendix by stressing some general trends. First, there are significant differences among the cells of the matrices in their ability to distinguish between successful and unsuccessful subsamples. Second, except in the case of cell 1, the cells correlating variables *within* a given class did not distinguish successful and unsuccessful firms as well as did the cells that portrayed *across*-class correlations. This might be explained by the substitutability of some of the variables within classes, and the truth of the theses of Khandwalla (1972, 1973), Galbraith (1973), and Lawrence and Lorsch (1967) that predict that uncertainty-reduction, differentiation, and integration variables should covary positively. If this is the case, then the changes in these variables must covary positively as well. But these conclusions must remain tentative. The differences among our three data bases highlight the need for cautious interpretation.

Bibliography

AAKER, D. *Multivariate Analysis in Marketing.* Belmont, Calif.: Wadsworth, 1971.

ACKOFF, R. L. *A Concept of Corporate Planning.* New York: Wiley Interscience, 1970.

ADIZES, I. "Organizational Passages: Diagnosing and Treating Life Cycle Problems in Organizations," *Organizational Dynamics,* Summer 1979, pp. 3–24.

AGUILAR, F. *Scanning the Business Environment.* New York: Macmillan, 1967.

AHMAVAARA, Y. "The Mathematical Theory of Factorial Invariance Under Selection," *Psychometrika,* 19 (1954), 27–38.

ALDRICH, H. E. "Reaction to Donaldson's Note," *Administrative Science Quarterly,* 20 (1975), 457–59.

——— *Organizations and Environments.* Englewood Cliffs, N.J.: Prentice-Hall, 1979.

ANDERBERG, M. R. *Cluster Analysis for Applications.* New York: Academic Press, 1973.

ANDERSON, T. R., and S. WARKOV "Organizational Size and Functional Complexity: A Study of Administration in Hospitals," *American Sociological Review,* 26 (1961), 23–28.

ANDREWS, K. *The Concept of Corporate Strategy.* Homewood, Ill.: Irwin, 1980.

ANSOFF, H. I. *Corporate Strategy.* New York: McGraw-Hill, 1965.

ARGYRIS, C., and D. SCHON *Organizational Learning: A Theory of Action Perspective.* Reading, Mass.: Addison-Wesley, 1977.

BAKER, N., J. SIEGMANN, and A. RUBENSTEIN "Effects of Perceived Needs on the Generation of Ideas in R&D Labs," *IEEE Transactions on Engineering Management,* 14 (1967), 156–63.

BASS, B. "Iterative Inverse Factor Analysis: A Rapid Method for Clustering Persons," *Psychometrika,* 22 (1957), 105–7.

BECKHARD, R., and R. HARRIS *Organizational Transitions.* Reading, Mass: Addison-Wesley, 1977.

BENSON, J. K.   "Organizations: A Dialectical View," *Administrative Science Quarterly,* 22 (1977), 1–21.
BLAU, P., and P. A. SCHOENHERR   *The Structure of Organizations.* New York: Basic Books, 1971.
BLAU, P., and W. R. SCOTT   *Formal Organizations.* San Francisco: Chandler, 1962.
BOEKE, J.   "On Quantitative Statistical Methods in Taxonomy," *Blumea,* 5 (1942), 47–65.
BRAYBROOKE, D., and C. LINDBLOM   *A Strategy of Decision.* New York: Free Press, 1963.
BRUNER, J., J. GOODNOW, and G. AUSTIN   *A Study of Thinking.* New York: Wiley, 1956.
BURNS, T.   "The Comparative Study of Organizations," in V. Vroom, ed., *Methods of Organizational Research.* Pittsburgh: University of Pittsburgh Press, 1967.
————, and G. STALKER   *The Management of Innovation.* London: Tavistock 1961.
BURT, C.   *The Factors of Mind.* London: University of London Press, 1940.
CARPER, W., and W. SNIZEK   "The Nature and Types of Organizational Taxonomies: An Overview," *Academy of Management Review,* 5 (1980), 65–75.
CARTER, C., and B. WILLIAMS   *Industry and Technical Progress: Factors Governing the Speed of Application of Science.* London: Oxford University Press, 1957.
CARTER, E.   "The Behavioral Theory of the Firm and Top-Level Corporate Decisions," *Administrative Science Quarterly,* 16 (1971), 413–28.
CARTWRIGHT, T.   "Problems, Solutions, and Strategies: A Contribution to the Theory and Practice of Planning," *Journal of the American Institute of Planners,* 39 (1973), 179–87.
CATTELL, R.   "r_p and Other Coefficients of Pattern Similarity," *Psychometrika,* 14 (1949), 279–98.
————   "Three Basic Factor Analytic Research Designs," *Psychological Bulletin,* 49 (1952), 499–520.
CHANDLER, A.   *Strategy and Structure.* Cambridge, Mass.: M.I.T. Press, 1962.
CHANDLER, M. K., and L. B. SAYLES   *Managing Large Systems.* New York: Harper & Row, 1971.
CHANNON, D.   *Strategy and Structure in British Enterprise.* Boston: Harvard University Press, 1973.
————   "Corporate Evolution in the Service Industries: 1950–1974," in L. Hannah, ed., *Corporate Strategy and Management Organization.* London: Macmillan, 1976.
CHENHALL, R.   "Diversification within Australian Manufacturing Enterprise," *Journal of Management Studies,* 20 (1983), in press.
CHILD, J.   "Organizational Structure, Environment and Performance: The Role of Strategic Choice," *Sociology,* 6 (1972), 2–22.
————   "Parkinson's Progress: Accounting for the Number of Specialists in Organizations," *Administrative Science Quarterly,* 18 (1973), 328–49.
————   "Comments on Donaldson's Note," *Administrative Science Quarterly,* 20 (1975), 456.
CLARK, B.   "The Organizational Saga in Higher Education," *Administrative Science Quarterly,* 17 (1972), 178–84.
COLE, A. H.   "An Approach to the Study of Entrepreneurship," *Journal of Economic History,* Supplement VI (1946), 1–15.
COLLINS, O., and D. G. MOORE   *The Organization Makers.* New York: Appleton-Century-Crofts, 1970.
————, and D. UNWALLA   *The Enterprising Man.* East Lansing: Bureau of Busi-

ness and Economic Research, Graduate School of Business, Michigan University, 1967.

COOPER, A. C.   "Technical Entrepreneurship: What Do We Know?" *Research and Development Management*, 3 (1973), 59–64.

CRONBACH, L., and G. GLESER   "Assessing Similarity between Profiles," *Psychological Bulletin*, 50 (1953), 456–73.

CROZIER, M.   *The Bureaucratic Phenomenon*. Chicago: University of Chicago Press, 1964.

CYERT, R., and J. MARCH   *A Behavioral Theory of the Firm*. Englewood Cliffs, N.J.: Prentice-Hall, 1963.

DARWIN, C.   *The Origin of Species*. Middlesex, England: Penguin Books, 1968. Original edition published in 1859.

DAY, R., and E. TINNEY   "How to Cooperate in Business without Really Trying: A Learning Model of Decentralized Decision Making," *Journal of Political Economy*, 76 (1968), 583–600.

DIESING, P.   *Patterns of Discovery in the Social Sciences*. New York: McGraw-Hill, 1971.

DONALDSON, L.   "Organizational Status and the Measurement of Centralization," *Administrative Science Quarterly*, 20 (1975), 453–56.

DOWNS, A   *Inside Bureaucracy*. Boston: Little, Brown, 1966.

DOWNS, G. W., and L. B. MOHR   "Conceptual Issues in the Study of Innovation," *Administrative Science Quarterly*, 21 (1976), 700–14.

DU MAS, F.   "On the Interpretation of Personality Profiles," *Journal of Clinical Psychology*, 3 (1947), 57–65.

DUNCAN, R. B.   "Multiple Decision-Making Structures in Adapting to Environmental Uncertainty: The Impact on Organizational Effectiveness," *Human Relations*, 26 (1973), 273–91.

ETZIONI, A.   *A Comparative Analysis of Complex Organizations*. New York: Free Press, 1961.

FILGAS, J.   *Yellow in Motion*. Bloomington: Indiana University Press, 1967.

FILLEY, A., and R. HOUSE   *Managerial Process and Organizational Behavior*. Glenview, Ill.: Scott, Foresman, 1969.

FISHER, W.   "On Grouping for Maximum Homogeneity," *Journal of the American Statistical Association*, 53 (1958), 789–98.

FOURAKER, L. E., and J. M. STOPFORD   "Organizational Structure and the Multinational Strategy," *Administrative Science Quarterly*, 13 (1968), 47–64.

FRANK, R., and P. GREEN   "Numerical Taxonomy in Marketing Analysis: A Review Article," *Journal of Marketing Research*, 5 (1968), 83–98.

FRIESEN, P. H., and D. MILLER   "A Mathematical Model of Organizational Adaptation." Working paper, Faculty of Management, McGill University, 1981.

GALBRAITH, C., and D. SCHENDEL   "An Empirical Analysis of Strategy Types." Working paper, Purdue University, March 1982.

GALBRAITH, J.   *Designing Complex Organizations*. Reading, Mass.: Addison-Wesley, 1973.

————   *Organizational Design*. Reading, Mass.: Addison-Wesley, 1977.

GARTNER, W.   "An Empirical Model of the Business Startup, and Eight Entrepreneurial Archetypes." Doctoral dissertation, University of Washington, 1982.

————, K. VESPER, and T. MITCHELL   "Eight Archetypes of Entrepreneurship." Conference paper, Academy of Management meetings, New York, August 1982.

GLASSMAN, R. "Persistence and Loose Coupling," *Behavioral Science*, 18 (1973), 83–98.

GORONZY, F. "A Numerical Taxonomy of Business Enterprise," in A. Cole, ed., *Numerical Taxonomy*. New York: Academic Press, 1969.

GREEN, P., R. FRANK, and P. ROBINSON "Cluster Analysis in Test Market Selection," *Management Science*, 13 (1967), 387–400.

GREENWOOD, R., and C. R. HININGS "A Research Note: Centralization Revisited," *Administrative Science Quarterly*, 21 (1976), 151–55.

GREINER, L. "Evolution and Revolution as Organizations Grow," *Harvard Business Review*, July–August 1972, 37–46.

HAAS, J. E., R. H. HALL, and N. J. JOHNSON "Toward an Empirically Derived Taxonomy of Organizations," in R. V. Bowers, ed., *Studies on Behavior in Organizations: A Research Symposium*, pp. 157–80. Athens: University of Georgia Press, 1966.

HAGE, J., and M. AIKEN *Social Change in Complex Organizations*. New York: Random House, 1970.

HAGE, J., and R. DEWAR "Elite Values versus Organizational Structure in Predicting Innovation," *Administrative Science Quarterly*, 18 (1973), 279–90.

HALL, R. H. *Organizations: Structure and Process*. Englewood Cliffs: Prentice-Hall, 1972.

HALL, R. H., J. E. HAAS, and N. J. JOHNSON "An Examination of the Blau-Scott and Etzioni Typologies," *Administrative Science Quarterly*, 12 (1967), 118–39.

HALL, R. I. "A System Pathology of an Organization: The Rise and Fall of the Old *Saturday Evening Post*," *Administrative Science Quarterly*, 21 (1976), 185–211.

HALL, R. I. "The Natural Logic of Management Policy Making," Working Paper, Faculty of Administrative Studies, University of Manitoba, 1982.

HAMBRICK, D. "Some Tests of the Effectiveness and Functional Attributes of Miles and Snow's Strategic Types," *Academy of Management Journal*, 26 (1983a), in press.

HAMBRICK, D. "An Empirical Typology of Mature Industrial-Product Environments," *Academy of Management Journal*, 26 (1983b), in press.

_____, I. MACMILLAN, and D. DAY, "Strategic Attributes and Performance in the Four Cells of the BCG Matrix," *Academy of Management Journal*, 25 (1982), 510–31.

HAMBRICK, D. and S. SCHECTER "Turnaround Strategies for Mature Industrial-Product Business Units," *Academy of Management Journal*, 26 (1983), in press.

HANNAN, M., and J. FREEMAN "The Population Ecology of Organizations," *American Journal of Sociology*, 83 (1977), 929–64.

HARMAN, H. *Modern Factor Analysis*. Chicago: University of Chicago, 1960.

HARTMAN, H. "Managers and Entrepreneurs: A Useful Distinction," *Administrative Science Quarterly*, 3 (1959), 429–51.

HARVEY, E. "Technology and the Structure of Organizations," *American Sociological Review*, 33 (1968), 247–59.

_____, and R. MILLS "Patterns of Organizational Adaptation: A Political Perspective," in M. Zald, ed., *Power in Organizations*. Nashville, Tenn.: Vanderbilt University Press, 1970.

HATTEN, K., D. SCHENDEL, and A. COOPER "A Strategic Model of the U.S. Brewing Industry: 1952–1971," *Academy of Management Journal*, 21 (1978), 592–610.

HEDBERG, B., P. NYSTROM, and W. STARBUCK "Camping on Seesaws: Pre-scriptions for a Self-Designing Organization," *Administrative Science Quarterly,* 21 (1976), 41–65.

HELMSTADTER, G. "An Empirical Comparison of Methods for Estimating Pro-file Similarity," *Educational & Psychological Measurement,* 17 (1957), 71–82.

HICKSON, D., D. PUGH, and D. PHEYSEY "Operations Technology and Orga-nization Structure: An Empirical Reappraisal," *Administrative Science Quarterly,* 14 (1969), 378–97.

HOFER, C., and D. SCHENDEL *Strategy Formulation: Analytical Concepts.* St. Paul, Minn.: West, 1978.

HOFFMAN, L. R., and N. R. F. MAIER "Quality and Acceptance of Problem Solutions by Members of Homogeneous and Heterogeneous Groups," *Jour-nal of Abnormal and Social Psychology,* 62 (1961), 401–7.

HOLDAWAY, E. A., J. F. NEWBERRY, D. J. HICKSON, and R. P. HER-ON "Dimensions of Organizations in Complex Societies: The Educational Sector," *Administrative Science Quarterly,* 20 (1975), 37–58.

HOWER, R. *History of Macy's of New York, 1858–1919.* Cambridge, Mass.: Harvard University Press, 1943.

——— *The History of an Advertising Agency: N. W. Ayer.* Cambridge, Mass.: Harvard University Press, 1949.

HUNT, R. G. "Technology and Organization," *Academy of Management Journal,* 13 (1970), 235–50.

INKSON, J. H. K., D. S. PUGH, and D. J. HICKSON "Organization, Context and Structure: An Abbreviated Replication," *Administrative Science Quarterly,* 15 (1970), 318–29.

JENNERGREN, L. P. *Decentralization in Organizations.* Working paper, Interna-tional Institute of Management, West Berlin, 1974.

JOHNSON, S. "Hierarchical Clustering Schemes," *Psychometrika,* 32 (1967), 241–55.

KAMEN, J. "Quick Clustering," *Journal of Marketing Research,* 7 (1970), 199–204.

KATZ, D., and R. KAHN *The Social Psychology of Organizations.* New York: Wiley, 1966.

KELLER, R., and W. HOLLAND "Boundary Spanning Roles in an R&D Organi-zation," *Academy of Management Journal,* 18 (1975), 388–93.

KENDALL, M. *Rank Correlation Methods.* London: Griffin, 1948.

——— *A Course in Multivariate Analysis.* London: Griffin, 1957.

KETS DE VRIES, M. F. R. "The Entrepreneurial Personality: A Person at the Crossroads," *Journal of Management Studies,* 14 (1977), 34–57.

KETS DE VRIES, M. F. R. and D. MILLER "A Study of the Determinants of Innovation," Working Paper, Faculty of Management, McGill University.

KHANDWALLA, P. "Environment and Its Impact on the Organization," *Interna-tional Studies of Management and Organization,* 2 (1972), 297–313.

——— "Viable and Effective Organizational Designs of Firms," *Academy of Man-agement Journal,* 16 (1973), 481–95.

——— *The Design of Organizations.* New York: Harcourt Brace Jovanovich, 1977.

KIMBERLY, J. "Issues in the Creation of Organizations: Initiation, Innovation, and Institutionalization," *Academy of Management Journal,* 22 (1979), 437–57.

———, and R. H. MILES *The Organizational Life Cycle.* San Francisco: Jossey-Bass, 1980.

KLATT, L. *Small Business Management: Essentials of Entrepreneurship.* Belmont, Cal-if.: Wadsworth, 1973.

KLATZKY, S. P. "Relationship of Organizational Size to Complexity and Coordi-nation," *Administrative Science Quarterly,* 15 (1970), 428–38.

KRUSKAL, J.   "Multidimensional Scaling by Optimizing Goodness of Fit to a Nonmetric Hypothesis," *Psychometrika,* 29 (1964a), 1–28.
_____   "Nonmetric Multidimensional Scaling: A Numerical Scaling Method," *Psychometrika,* 29 (1964b), 115–30.
KUHN, T.   *The Structure of Scientific Revolutions,* 2nd ed. Chicago: University of Chicago Press, 1970.
LAVOIE, D., and S. A. CULBERT   "Stages in Organization and Development," *Human Relations,* 31 (1978), 417–38.
LAWRENCE, P. R., and J. W. LORSCH   *Organization and Environment.* Boston: Harvard University Press, 1967.
LEVINS, R.   *Evolution in Changing Environments.* Princeton, N.J.: Princeton University Press, 1968.
LEWIN, K.   *A Dynamic Theory of Personality.* New York: McGraw-Hill, 1935.
LIKERT, R.   *New Patterns of Management.* New York: McGraw-Hill, 1961.
LILES, P. R.   *New Business Ventures and the Entrepreneur.* Homewood, Ill.: Irwin, 1974.
LINDBLOM, C.   "The Science of Muddling Through," *Public Administration Review,* 19 (1959), 79–88.
_____   *The Policy Making Process.* Englewood Cliffs, N.J.: Prentice-Hall, 1968.
LITWAK, E.   "Models of Bureaucracy Which Permit Conflict," *American Journal of Sociology,* 67 (1961), 177–84.
MCGUIRE, J.   *Factors Affecting the Growth of Manufacturing Firms.* Seattle: University of Washington Bureau of Business Research, 1963.
MCKELVEY, B.   "Guidelines for the Empirical Classification of Organizations," *Administrative Science Quarterly,* 20 (1975), 509–25.
_____   "Organizational Systematics: Taxonomic Lessons from Biology," *Management Science,* 24 (1978), 1428–40.
MACMILLAN, I., D. HAMBRICK, and D. DAY   "The Association between Strategic Attributes and Profitability in the Four Cells of the BCG Matrix," *Academy of Management Journal,* 25 (1982), 733–55.
MCQUITTY, L.   "Hierarchical Syndrome Analysis," *Educational & Psychological Measurement,* 20 (1960), 293–304.
MAHALANOBIS, P.   "On the Generalized Distance in Statistics." *Proceedings National Institute of Science,* India, 12 (1936), 49–58.
MANIHA, J., and C. PERROW   "The Reluctant Organization and the Aggressive Environment," *Administrative Science Quarterly,* 10 (1965), 238–57.
MANNS, C.   "Review of 'Formalization and Centralization: The Case of Polish Industry,'" by Lena Kolarska, in A. M. Jaeger, ed., *Seminars in Organizations,* pp. 64–66. Stanford, Calif.: Stanford University Press, Winter and Spring 1976.
MARCH, J., and H. SIMON, *Organizations.* New York: Wiley, 1958.
MEYER, M. W., and ASSOCIATES   *Environments and Organizations.* San Francisco: Jossey-Bass, 1978.
MILES, R., and C. SNOW   *Organizational Strategy, Structure and Process.* New York: McGraw-Hill, 1978.
MILES, R. H.   "Findings and Implications of Organizational Life Cycles Research: A Commencement," In J. R. Kimberly and R. H. Miles, eds., *The Organizational Life Cycle.* San Francisco: Jossey-Bass, 1980.
MILLER, D.   "Strategy Making in Context: Ten Empirical Archetypes," Ph.D. dissertation, McGill University, 1976.
_____   "The Role of Multivariate 'Q-Techniques' in the Study of Organizations," *Academy of Management Review,* 3 (1978), 515–31.

———— "Strategy, Structure and Environment: Context Influences on Bivariate Associations," *Journal of Management Studies*, 16 (1979), 294–316.

———— "Towards a New Contingency Approach: The Search for Organizational Gestalts," *Journal of Management Studies*, 18 (1981), 1–26.

———— "Evolution and Revolution: A Quantum View of Structural Change in Organizations," *Journal of Management Studies*, 19 (1982), 131–51.

MILLER, D., and P. H. FRIESEN   "Strategy Making in Context: Ten Empirical Archetypes," *Journal of Management Studies*, 14 (1977), 259–80.

———— "Archetypes of Strategy Formulation," *Management Science*, 24 (1978), 921–33.

———— "Archetypes of Organizational Transition," *Administrative Science Quarterly*, 25 (1980a), 268–99.

———— "Momentum and Revolution in Organizational Adaptation," *Academy of Management Journal*, 23 (1980b), 591–614.

———— "Structural Change and Performance: Quantum vs. Piecemeal-Incremental Approaches," *Academy of Management Journal*, 25 (1982a), 867–92.

———— "The Longitudinal Analysis of Organizations: A Methodological Perspective," *Management Science*, 28 (1982b), 1013–34.

———— "Successful and Unsuccessful Phases of the Corporate Life Cycle," *Organization Studies*, 4 (1983a), 339–56.

———— "A Longitudinal Study of the Corporate Life Cycle," *Management Science*, 1983b, in press.

———— "Strategy Making and Environment: The Third Link," *Strategic Management Journal*, 5 (1983c), 221–235.

MILLER, D., M. F. R. KETS DE VRIES, and J.-M. TOULOUSE   "Locus of Control and Its Relationship to Strategy, Environment and Structure," *Academy of Management Journal*, 25 (1982), 237–53.

MILLER, D., and H. MINTZBERG   "Strategy Formulation in Context: Some Tentative Models." Working paper, McGill University, 1974.

MILLER, R. E.   *Innovation, Organization and Environment*. Sherbrooke, Quebec: Institut de Recherche et de Perfectionnement en Administration, Université de Sherbrooke, 1971.

MINTZBERG, H.   "Strategy Making in Three Modes," *California Management Review*, 16 (1973), 44–58.

———— *The Structuring of Organizations*. Englewood Cliffs, N.J.: Prentice-Hall, 1979.

MITROFF, I., and R. KILMANN   "On Organizational Stories," In R. Kilman et al., eds., *The Management of Organization Design: Volume 1, Strategies and Implementation*, pp. 189–208. New York: American Elsevier, 1976.

MOHR, L. B.   "Determinants of Innovation in Organizations," *American Political Science Review*, 63 (1969), 111–26.

MOORE, C.   *Timing a Century: The History of the Waltham Watch Company*. Cambridge, Mass.: Harvard University Press, 1945.

MORRISON, D.   "Measurement Problems in Cluster Analysis," *Management Science*, 13 (1967a), B775–80.

———— *Multivariate Statistical Methods*. New York: McGraw-Hill, 1967.

MORSE, J.   "Organizational Characteristics and Individual Motivation," in J. Lorsch and P. Lawrence, eds., *Studies in Organization Design*, pp. 84–100. Homewood, Ill.: Irwin-Dorsey, 1970.

MUELLER, W. F.   "The Origins of the Basic Inventions Underlying DuPont's Major Product and Process Innovations, 1920–1950," in R. R. Nelson, ed., *The Rate and Direction of Inventive Activity*, pp. 323–60. Princeton, N.J.: Princeton University, 1962.

MYERS, J., and F. NICOSIA "On the Study of Consumer Typologies," *Journal of Marketing Research*, 5 (1968), 182–93.

MYERS, J., SUMMER, C. and D. G. MARQUIS *Successful Industrial Innovation.* Washington D.C.: National Science Foundation, 1969.

NIE, N., D. BENT, and C. HULL *Statistical Package for the Social Sciences.* New York: McGraw-Hill, 1970.

NIE, N., ET AL. *Statistical Package for the Social Sciences*, 2nd. ed. New York: McGraw-Hill, 1975.

NORMANN, R. "Organizational Innovativeness: Product Variation and Reorientation," *Administrative Science Quarterly*, 16 (1971), 203–15.

NUNNALLY, J. "The Analysis of Profile Data," *Psychological Bulletin*, 59 (1962), 311–19.

OVERALL, J. "Note on Multivariate Methods of Profile Analysis," *Psychological Bulletin*, 61 (1964), 195–98.

PAINE, F., and C. ANDERSON "Contingencies Affecting Strategy Formulation and Effectiveness," *Journal of Management Studies*, 14 (1977), 147–58.

PARKINSON, C. N. *Parkinson's Law.* London: John Murray, Limited; and Boston: Houghton Mifflin, 1957.

PARSONS, T. "Suggestions for a Sociological Approach to the Theory of Organizations," *Administrative Science Quarterly*, 1 (1956), 68–85, 225–39.

——— *Structure and Process in Modern Societies.* New York: Free Press, 1960.

PENNINGS, J. M. "The Relevance of the Structural-Contingency Model for Organizational Effectiveness," *Administrative Science Quarterly*, 20, 1975, 393–410.

PERROW, C. *Organizational Analysis: A Sociological View.* Belmont, Calif.: Wadsworth, 1970.

——— *Complex Organizations: A Critical Essay.* Glenview, Ill.: Scott, Foresman, 1972.

——— "Is Business Really Changing?" *Organizational Dynamics*, Summer 1974, 31–44.

PETERS, D. H. "Commercial Innovation from University Faculty: A Study of the Invention and Exploitation of Ideas." Sloan School of Management working paper, No. 406-69, M.I.T., 1969.

PETERSON, R., and D. BERGER "Entrepreneurship in Organizations," *Administrative Science Quarterly*, 16 (1971), 97–106.

PETTIGREW, A. *The Politics of Organizational Decision Making.* London: Tavistock, 1973.

——— "Internal Politics and the Emergence and Decline of Departmental Groups." Working paper, London Graduate School of Business, 1974.

PFEFFER, J. *Organizational Design.* Arlington Heights, Ill.: AHM Publishing, 1978.

PINDER, C., and L. MOORE "The Resurrection of Taxonomy to Aid in the Development of Middle Range Theories of Organizational Behavior," *Administrative Science Quarterly*, 24 (1979), 99–118.

PINTO, P., and C. PINDER "A Cluster-Analytic Approach to the Study of Organizations," *Organizational Behavior and Human Performance*, 8 (1972), 408–22.

PONDY, L. R. "Effects of Size, Complexity, and Ownership on Administrative Intensity," *Administrative Science Quarterly*, 14 (1969), 47–60.

PUGH, D. S., D. J. HICKSON, and C. R. HININGS "An Empirical Taxonomy of Structures of Work Organizations," *Administrative Science Quarterly*, 14 (1969), 115–26.

———, and C. TURNER   "Dimensions of Organization Structure," *Administrative Science Quarterly*, 13 (1968), 65–105.

QUINN, R., and K. CAMERON   "Organizational Life Cycles and Shifting Criteria of Effectiveness: Some Preliminary Evidence." Working paper, Graduate School of Public Affairs, SUNY at Albany, New York, 1981.

QUINN, J. B.   *Strategies for Change: Logical Incrementalism*. Homewood, Ill.: Irwin, 1980.

READ, W.   "Upward Communication in Industrial Hierarchies," *Human Relations*, 15 (1962), 3–15.

REDLICH, R.   "The Origin of the Concepts of Entrepreneur and Creative Entrepreneur," *Explorations in Entrepreneurial History*, 1 (1949), 145–66.

REEVES, T. K., and J. WOODWARD   "The Study of Managerial Control," in J. Woodward, ed., *Industrial Organization: Behavior and Control*. London: Oxford University Press, 1970.

ROBINSON, W.   "A Method for Chronologically Ordering Archaeological Deposits," *American Antiquity*, 16 (1951), 293–301.

RODGERS, W.   *Think: A Biography of the Watsons and IBM*. New York: Stein and Day, 1969.

ROGERS, D., and T. TANIMOTO   "A Computer Program for Classifying Plants," *Science*, 132 (1960), 1115–18.

ROGERS, E. M., and F. SHOEMAKER   *Communication of Innovations: A Cross-Cultural Approach*. New York: Free Press, 1971.

ROSNER, M. M.   "Administrative Controls and Innovation," *Behavioral Science*, 13 (1968), 36–43.

ROTTER, J. B.   "Generalized Expectancies for Internal versus External Control of Reinforcement," *Psychological Monographs*, 80 (1966), 1, Whole No. 609.

RUMELT, R. P.   *Strategy, Structure, and Economic Performance*. Cambridge, Mass.: Division of Research, Graduate School of Business Administration, Harvard University, 1974.

RUSHING, W. A.   "The Effects of Industry Size and Division of Labor on Administration," *Administrative Science Quarterly*, 12 (1967–68), 273–95.

SAMPSON, A.   *The Sovereign State of ITT*. New York: Stein and Day, 1973.

SAMUEL, Y., and B. MANNHEIM   "A Multi-Dimensional Approach toward a Typology of Bureaucracy," *Administrative Science Quarterly*, 15 (1970), 216–28.

SAPOLSKY, H.   "Organizational Structure and Innovation," *Journal of Business*, 40 (1967), 497–510.

SAWREY, W., L. KELLER, and J. CONGER   "An Objective Method of Grouping Profiles by Distance Functions and Its Relation to Factor Analysis," *Educational and Psychological Measurement*, 20 (1960), 651–73.

SCHENDEL, D., R. PATTON, and J. RIGGS   "Corporate Turnaround Strategies." Working paper, Purdue University, 1975.

SCHLAIFER, R.   *A Q D Manual for Statistical Programs*. Boston: Harvard University Press, 1977.

SCHON, D.   *Beyond the Stable State*. New York: Norton, 1971.

SCHUCHMAN, A.   "Letter to the Editor: Free For All," *Management Science*, 13 (1967), B688–91.

SCHUMPETER, J.   *The Theory of Economic Development*. Cambridge, England: Cambridge University Press, 1934.

SCOTT, B. R.   *Stages of Corporate Development*, Case #9-371-294. Boston: Intercollegiate Case Clearing House, Harvard Business School, 1971.

SEGAL, M.   "Organization and Environment: A Typology of Adaptability and Structure," *Public Administrative Review*, 34 (1974), 212–20.

SHAPERO, A. "The Displaced, Uncomfortable Entrepreneur," *Psychology Today*, 11, 7 (November 1975), 83–89.

SHEPARD, R. "The Analysis of Proximities: Multidimensional Scaling with an Unknown Distance Function: I and II," *Psychometrika*, 27 (1962), 125–40, 219–46.

SILVESTRI, L., M. TURRI, L. HILL, and E. GILARDI "A Quantitative Approach to the Systematics of Actinomycetes Based on Overall Similarity," in G. Ainsworth and P. Sneath, eds., *Microbial Classification*, 12th Symposium of the Society for General Microbiology, pp. 333–60. Cambridge, England: Cambridge University Press, 1972.

SIMON, H. A. *Administrative Behavior*. New York: Free Press, 1957.

_____ *The Sciences of the Artificial*. Cambridge, Mass.: M.I.T. Press, 1969.

SLOAN, A. *My Years with General Motors*. New York: MacFadden, 1964.

SNEATH, P. "The Application of Computers to Taxonomy," *Journal of General Microbiology*, 17 (1957), 201–26.

SOKAL, R., and C. MICHENER "A Statistical Method for Evaluating Systematic Relationships," *University of Kansas Science Bulletin*, 38 (1958), 1409–38.

SOKAL, R., and P. SNEATH *Principles of Numerical Taxonomy*. San Francisco: Freeman, 1963.

STARBUCK, W. "Organizational Growth and Development," in J. G. March, ed., *Handbook of Organizations*, Chapter 11. Chicago: Rand McNally, 1965.

_____, and J. DUTTON "Designing Adaptive Organizations," *Journal of Business Policy*, 3 (1973), 21–28.

STARBUCK, W., A. GREVE, and B. HEDBERG "Responding to Crises," *Journal of Business Administration*, 9 (1978), 111–37.

STEINER, G. *Top Management Planning*. New York: Macmillan, 1969.

STEPHENSON, W. "The Inverted Factor Technique," *British Journal of Psychology*, 26 (1936), 344–61.

_____ "Methodological Consideration of Jung's Typology," *Journal of Mental Science*, 85 (1939), 185–205.

_____ "Some Observations on Q-Technique," *Psychological Bulletin*, 49 (1952), 483–98.

_____ *The Study of Behavior*. Chicago: University of Chicago Press, 1953.

STINCHCOMBE, A. L. "Bureaucratic and Craft Administration of Production," *Administrative Science Quarterly*, 4 (1959), 168–87.

_____ "Social Structure and Organizations," in J. G. March, ed., *Handbook of Organizations*, Chap. 4. Chicago: Rand McNally, 1965.

STOPFORD, J. M., and L. T. WELLS, JR. *Managing the Multinational Enterprise: Organization of the Firm and Ownership of the Subsidiaries*. New York: Basic Books, 1972.

TERRIEN, F. W., and D. L. MILLS "The Effect of Changing Size upon the Internal Structure of Organizations," *American Sociological Review*, 20 (1955), 11–13.

THOMPSON, J. *Organizations in Action*. New York: McGraw-Hill, 1967.

THOMPSON, V. *Modern Organizations*. New York: Knopf, 1961.

_____ *Bureaucracy and Innovation*. University of Alabama: University of Alabama Press, 1969.

TORGERSON, W. *Theory and Methods of Scaling*. New York: Wiley, 1958.

TOULOUSE, J.-M. *L'Entrepreneurship au Québec*. Montreal: Les Presses H.E.C., 1980.

TRYON, R. "Cumulative Communality Cluster Analysis," *Educational & Psychological Measurement*, 18 (1958a), 3–35.

————   "General Dimensions of Individual Differences: Cluster Analysis vs. Factor Analysis," *Educational & Psychological Measurement*, 18 (1958b), 477–95.

————, and D. BAILEY   *Cluster Analysis*. New York: McGraw-Hill, 1970.

TURNER, B. A.   "The Organizational and Interorganizational Development of Disasters," *Administrative Science Quarterly*, 21 (1976), 378–97.

TUSHMAN, M. L.   "Special Boundary Roles in the Innovation Process," *Administrative Science Quarterly*, 22 (1977), 587–605.

UDY, S. H., JR.   "The Comparative Analysis of Organizations," in J. G. March, ed., *Handbook of Organizations*, Chap. 16. Chicago: Rand McNally, 1965.

URWICK, L. F.   "The Manager's Span of Control," *Harvard Business Review*, May–June 1956, pp. 39–47.

UTTERBACK, J. M.   "The Process of Technological Innovation within the Firm," *Academy of Management Journal*, 14 (1971), 75–88.

VAN DE GEER, J.   *Multivariate Analysis for the Social Sciences*. San Francisco: Freeman, 1971.

VAN DE VEN, A.   "A Framework for Organizational Assessment," *Academy of Management Review*, 1 (1976), 64–78.

————, and D. FERRY, *Measuring and Assessing Organizations*. New York: Wiley, 1980.

VICKERS, G.   "Is Adaptability Enough?" *Behavioral Science*, 4 (1959), 219–34.

WARD, J.   "Hierarchical Grouping to Optimize an Objective Function," *Journal of the American Statistical Association*, 58 (1963), 236–44.

————, and M. HOOK   "Application of an Hierarchical Grouping Procedure to a Problem of Grouping Profiles," *Educational & Psychological Measurement*, 23 (1963), 69–82.

WATSON, G.   "Resistance to Change," in W. Bennis et al., eds., *The Planning of Change*, pp. 488–98. New York: Holt, Rinehart & Winston, 1969.

WEBER, M.   *The Theory of Social and Economic Organization*. New York: Free Press, 1947.

WEICK, K.   *The Social Psychology of Organizing*. Reading, Mass.: Addison-Wesley, 1969.

————   "Educational Organizations as Loosely Coupled Systems," *Administrative Science Quarterly*, 21 (1976), 1–19.

WELLS, W., and J. SHETH   "Factor Analysis in Marketing Research," in R. Feber, ed., *Handbook of Market Research*. New York: McGraw-Hill, 1971.

WHITE, O.   "The Dialectical Organization: An Alternative to Bureaucracy," *Public Administration Review*, 29 (1969), 32–42.

WILDAVSKY, A.   "The Self-Evaluating Organization," *Public Administration Review*, 32 (1972), 509–20.

WILENSKY, H.   *Organizational Intelligence*. New York: Basic Books, 1967.

WILSON, C.   *The History of Unilever*, 3 Vols. London: Cassel, 1954, 1968.

WILSON, J. Q.   "Innovation in Organization: Notes toward a Theory," in J. D. Thompson, ed., *Approaches to Organizational Design*, pp. 193–218. Pittsburgh: University of Pittsburgh Press, 1966.

WOODWARD, J.   *Technology and Organization*. London: HMSO, 1958.

————   *Industrial Organization: Theory and Practice*. London: Oxford University Press, 1965.

WRIGLEY, L.   "Diversification and Divisional Autonomy." D.B.A. Thesis, Harvard Business School, 1970.

YOUNG, F., and W. TORGERSON   "TORSCA, A Fortran IV Program," *Behavioral Science*, 12 (1967), 498–99.

ZALTMAN, G., R. DUNCAN, and J. HOLBEK   *Innovations and Organizations*. New York: Wiley, 1973.

Index